William Boyd Dawkins and the Victorian Science of Cave Hunting

For my daughters, Megan, Kirsten and Mathilde

*   *   *

Frontis: Sir William Boyd Dawkins, in the 1920s
(Reproduced courtesy Derbyshire County Council – Buxton Museum).

William Boyd Dawkins and the Victorian Science of Cave Hunting

Three Men in a Cavern

Mark J. White

PEN & SWORD
ARCHAEOLOGY

First published in Great Britain in 2017 by
PEN AND SWORD HISTORY
an imprint of
Pen and Sword Books Ltd
47 Church Street
Barnsley
South Yorkshire S70 2AS

ISBN 978 1 47382 335 8

Printed and bound in England
by CPI Group (UK) Ltd, Croydon, CR0 4YY

Typeset in Times New Roman by
CHIC GRAPHICS

Pen & Sword Books Ltd incorporates the imprints of Pen & Sword
Archaeology, Atlas, Aviation, Battleground, Discovery,
Family History, History, Maritime, Military, Naval, Politics, Railways,
Select, Social History, Transport, True Crime, Claymore Press,
Frontline Books, Leo Cooper, Praetorian Press, Remember When,
Seaforth Publishing and Wharncliffe.

For a complete list of Pen and Sword titles please contact
Pen and Sword Books Limited
47 Church Street, Barnsley, South Yorkshire, S70 2AS, England
E-mail: enquiries@pen-and-sword.co.uk
Website: www.pen-and-sword.co.uk

Contents

CONTENTS

Acknowledgements

A number of people have given me assistance in writing this book. First and foremost I'd like to thank Ros Westwood at Buxton Museum, and David Gelsthorpe at Manchester Museum without whose help and patience I don't think the book could have been written. I hope what you read here was worth the effort.

In no particular order, I'd like to thank the following people for supplying information, images or papers: Ian Wall (formally Creswell Heritage Museum and Visitor Centre); Kelly Allen (Newberry Library, Chicago); Pam Brimstow (Brampton, Derbyshire); Caroline Lam (Geological Society of London); Adrian James (Society of Antiquaries); Andrew Morrison & Elizabeth McAuliffe (BGS); Nick Ashton (British Museum); Keith Moore and the library staff at the Royal Society; Annette Reuhlmann (Institute of Civil Engineers); Duncan McCormick (Salford Local History Museum); the late Chris Jeens and Owen McKnight (Jesus College, Oxford); Mike Bishop; Tom Lord; Donald McFarlane; Jeff Veitch; Martin Dodge; Dan Adler; as well as the helpful staff at Derbyshire Local Studies Library, Wells Museum, Warwick Country Records Office and the National Portrait Gallery.

Finally, thanks to Paul Pettitt, Beth Upex and the Third Duke of Warmington for reading drafts and providing useful feedback, and to Julian Stasiuk for free accommodation in the heart of Dawkins country and nearly 40 years of laughter.

Preface

My relationship with William Boyd Dawkins began as a postgraduate student at Cambridge, where I studied for a PhD on the British Palaeolithic under Professor (now Sir) Paul Mellars. Dawkins' name was one that would frequently crop up in the literature, not just the Victorian sources I mined for information on some of the older sites and early digs, but in modern writings too. In most cases, these references were rather unflattering.

As my attention moved from the Lower to the Middle and Upper Palaeolithic, Dawkins became an even more prominent figure, as the excavator of some of the most important sites of that age in the country and author of some of the key papers on sites long since dug-out. Like many before me, I was not overly impressed by some of Dawkins' work, particularly in the field. On gaining a post at the University of Durham in 1999, I found myself passing this rather negative impression onto students.

And that is probably where it would have stayed if not for a visit to Durham by Eloise Hanson in 2011. Eloise came to Durham to talk about prospective books that people might be thinking of writing. I told her I was amazed that nobody had ever written a book on Dawkins, and that it would be great if she could find somebody willing to do it. A year later she phoned me up to ask whether I'd thought any more about writing 'that book on William Boyd Dawkins'. The result is the current volume. Have my opinions changed? Yes, in many and various ways.

Mark White
Durham, September 2015

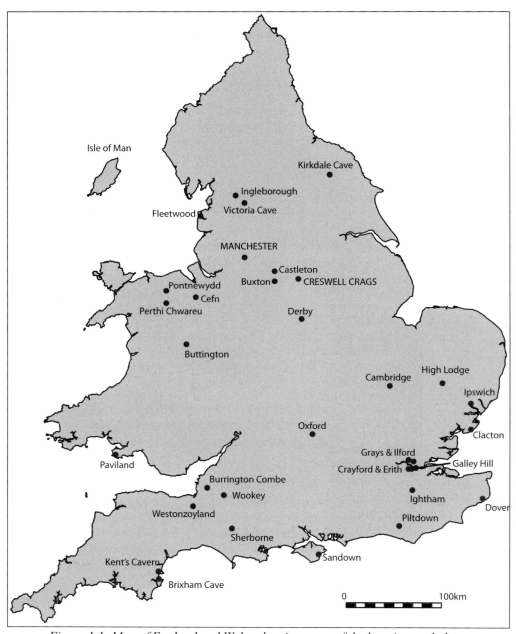

Figure 1.1: Map of England and Wales showing some of the key sites and places mentioned in the text.

Chapter 1

Cave Hunting

Protagonist
William Boyd Dawkins (1837-1929) was one of the second wave of 'cave hunters', those geologists, archaeologists and natural scientists who used the fossils and artefacts discovered within cave sediments to reconstruct the history of the earth and its inhabitants. He was one of first, however, to work within a scientific framework that recognised a deep antiquity and long evolutionary context for humans and other animals. It was a field he would practically make his own. This is his story.

Caverns Measureless to Man
Humans have always had a strange, intimate relationship with caves. Since the Palaeolithic period they have been used as residential bases and temporary camps, and occasionally as burial grounds. During the Neolithic and Bronze Age, caves were extensively used as sepulchres, natural mausoleums in which to inter the dead. For the ancient Greeks and Romans caves were places to be feared, inhabited by legendary monsters such as the Minotaur, Gorgon and Cyclops. Similar folklore lasted well into the historical period, when caves were home to chimaeras, pixies, fairies, witches and boggarts as well as the more mundane, but no less scary, hags and hermits (as names such as Mother Shipton's Cave and Mother Grundy's Parlour reveal). Caves have been associated with smuggling in coastal areas and seen everywhere as refuges for outlaws. Sometimes, where they presented a lofty entrance, they were used as workshops, for example in Castleton, Derbyshire where Peak Cavern (also known as the Devil's Arse because of the gurgling caused by a subterranean river) was used for the manufacture of rope, the workers carving themselves dwellings in the sediments and living troglodytic lives. During the late eighteenth and early nineteenth centuries some of the more spectacular caves became tourist attractions, while the Romantic poets were fascinated by these liminal places, natural cathedrals, which served as metaphor and motif in some of their famous works.[1]

1

Breaking the Time Barrier[2]

It was really only in the 1820s that caves became the subject of geological and archaeological enquiry when, because of the fossils and artefacts they were found to contain, they assumed particular importance in the quest to understand the real time-depth of human antiquity.[3] As early as 1821, Rev. William Buckland (1784-1856), Professor of Geology at Oxford University, explored Kirkdale Cave, Yorkshire, where through careful observation and comparison he was able to identify it as an ancient hyaena den, the animals, he supposed, occupying Britain before the Biblical Flood.[4] In 1823, he explored Goat Hole, Paviland, on the Gower Peninsula of Wales, where he discovered the remains of extinct animals, stone tools, ivory ornaments and a partial human skeleton human stained with red ochre. Although we now know this to be the skeleton of a Gravettian man some 33-34,000 years old,[5] Buckland disassociated it from the animals and interpreted it as the remains of a Romano-British witch, 'the Red Lady of Paviland'.[6]

During this period, new bone caves were discovered with enviable regularity. In 1824 Buckland and the writer/inventor Thomas Northmore (1766-1851) explored Pixies Hole, Chudleigh, and Kent's Cavern, Torquay, at the latter finding evidence of a hyaena den alongside flint implements. Shortly after, Rev. John MacEnery (1797-1841), Chaplain to the Cary Family at Tor Abbey, began his extensive explorations in Kent's Cavern, which continued intermittently from 1825 until 1829. MacEnery found incontrovertible evidence of the co-existence of extinct animals and humans, enough to challenge the prevailing notion that humans had only existed for some 6006 years.[7] Similar discoveries had been made in Europe, but the sceptics maintained that caves were unreliable sources of information. Even though finds were often sealed beneath unbroken stalagmites that had lain undisturbed for millennia, many still believed cave sediments to be stratigraphically insecure: animal activity, later human burials, hearths, ovens or other interference could easily have caused such an admixture, it was claimed. Largely in deference to Buckland's opinions, MacEnery never published his findings in his lifetime.[8] Buckland's pupil, R.A.C. Godwin-Austen (1808-1884) later made a strong case in favour of MacEnery's findings,[9] and another excavation in 1846 by the Torquay Natural History Society confirmed the presence of human artefacts and extinct animals beneath intact stalagmites. Neither managed to bring about a radical swell of scientific opinion.

Prevailing interpretation on the character of cave fauna created other, self-imposed, obstacles. The fossil contents of all the known caves were thought to be very similar, duplicates of one another even, and the presence/absence of certain species regarded as happenstance rather than chronologically or environmentally significant.[10] Therefore, more attention was paid to extracting exceptional specimens than to documenting their provenance and associations. Sequences could not be re-established, specimens from different sites were mixed together with no way of untangling them, and assemblages had been dispersed piecemeal – 'the evil is now beyond remedy', lamented the palaeontologist Hugh Falconer (1808-1865) in 1858. Having just completed a tour of caves in, or cave assemblages from, Bristol, Devonshire, the Mendips, South Wales, Cefn and Kirkdale, Falconer was at this juncture not only in a position to understand the problems attendant on this archive, but also uniquely placed to try to resolve them.

Indeed, when the 'orthodox' views were suddenly and dramatically overturned by a series of events between January 1858 and April 1859, it was Falconer who stood squarely at the vanguard. In response to the discovery of a new, undisturbed cave at Windmill Hill, Brixham, Devon in January 1858, Falconer instigated and chaired a Committee of the Geological Society to examine the site, principally to explore the succession of animals over time. Other than Falconer, the Committee comprised a number of influential scientists: the geologists Charles Lyell (1797-1875), Joseph Prestwich (1812-1896) and R.A.C. Godwin-Austen, and the palaeontologist Richard Owen (1804-1892), along with William Pengelly (1812-1894) of Torquay, who wanted a sample for the local museum. The site was carefully excavated using a system devised by Pengelly (see Chapter 3), resulting in incontrovertible evidence of human artefacts associated with extinct animals sealed beneath stalagmites.[11] On its own it was not enough to convince the scientific world: although a virgin cave, it was still a cave, and the usual uncertainties remained. It was enough, however, to prompt a re-examination of work being conducted on open-air fluvial sites in France, visited first by Falconer in October 1858, and later by Prestwich and Evans in April 1859.

Since 1837, a French customs official, Jacques Boucher de Perthes (1788-1868), had been amassing evidence for humanly modified flints and extinct animals in the gravels around Abbeville and Amiens in the Somme Valley. His claims were never taken particularly seriously, and despite independent verification in 1855, his work was never accepted in his own country.[12] Fresh from the Brixham excavations, Falconer was impressed by what he saw, and returned home enthusiastic about de Perthes' material. He encouraged others to take the time to visit. When Prestwich and Evans visited in April 1859, they too came home convinced that de Perthes was correct, not least because they had witnessed a stone tool – a hand-axe – removed from in situ gravel that also contained Pleistocene animals. Papers read before the Royal Society, the Society of Antiquaries, the Geological Society and others bombarded the British scientific community with the evidence, and by the end of the year the antiquity debate was all but won. It is simply coincidence that 1859 also saw the publication of Charles Darwin's *On the Origin of Species*.

Cave Hunters
With the conceptual obstacles removed, cave archaeology became a respectable business, alongside the sister pursuit of scouring quarries and brickpits for artefacts and bones. One, of course, had to be careful about disturbance and admixture, but the evidence of ancient human activity in caves was now much more readily accepted. In France, cave archaeology of this period is almost synonymous with French palaeontologist Édouard Lartet (1801-1871) and English banker and archaeologist Henry Christy (1810-1865), who together excavated an unparalleled series of iconic caves/rockshelters in the Perigord, including Le Moustier, Aurignac, La Madeleine, Crô-Magnon, Laugerie Haute, Laugerie Basse, Roc de Tayac and Grotte des Enfers[13].

In Britain, Victorian cave exploration is mostly associated with two men. The first is William Pengelly, excavator of Brixham Cave and, more famously, Kent's Cavern, where for 19 years from 1865-1884 he systematically excavated every chamber and passage down to a uniform depth of 4ft.

The other is, of course, William Boyd Dawkins. Unlike Pengelly, whose reputation remains immaculate, Dawkins is a more controversial figure whose field practices left much to be desired even in his own time. His career began in 1859 with excavations at Wookey Hole, just as the question of human antiquity was being settled. He later joined the Geological Survey of Great Britain before taking up the curatorship of a new museum at Owens College, Manchester, an institution where he would quickly rise to Professor. He directed excavations at Creswell Crags, Victoria Cave and numerous other famous British cave sites, and was involved in some of the most pressing geological and archaeological questions of the day (and also some of the most famous geological engineering projects, such as the Channel Tunnel attempt of 1881 and the Manchester Ship Canal). While national and international recognition came at an early age, Dawkins was nonetheless a provocative and pugnacious man who was equally revered and reviled during his own lifetime. Surprisingly then, he is today largely forgotten outside academic circles. Several of his contemporaries, friends and colleagues were honoured with a 'Life and Letters' that are still read today, but nobody ever compiled such a homage to Dawkins and nor has anybody ever produced a biography. That said, most visitors to Creswell Crags, Buxton Museum or Manchester Museum would have seen his visage displayed on large banners and poster boards and he often features as a minor player in histories of geology and archaeology.

This book aims to redress this situation, and provide a balanced account of William Boyd Dawkins' life and career as a geologist and archaeologist, examining his contemporary contribution to his science and beyond. The book is narrative in style and as linear in structure as the various themes and events permit, tracing Dawkins' life from boyhood to burial. At its core, though, lies a detailed account of one of Victorian archaeology's darkest hours – the fallout from the Creswell Crags excavations of 1875-1879 – in which nobody involved comes out completely untarnished.

A Note about Taxonomy
Dawkins was primarily a palaeontologist, who specialised in Pleistocene mammalian fauna. I have where possible used the common English names for most animals, extinct or extant. Occasionally, however, the use of the binomial Linnaean name is preferable or unavoidable. One problem here is that species names often change over time, and the name used by Dawkins and his contemporaries might be different from the modern one. In these cases I have taken the step of retaining the Victorian name, not only in quotations but throughout, inserting the modern name in parenthesis on the first time of usage.

A Note on Measurements
Dawkins and his contemporaries normally employed the imperial system of measurements. I have not, as is usual, inserted a metric equivalent in parenthesis as I felt that this broke up the text. A quick conversion is: 1 inch = 2.54 cm; 1 foot = 30.48 cm; 1 yard = 91.44 cm. There are 12 inches to 1 foot, and 3 feet to 1 yard.

A Note on the Spelling of Cres(s)well
The modern spelling of the town and adjacent Crags is Creswell, although Dawkins and colleagues variously spelled it Creswell or Cresswell. Where the latter spelling was used in quotes I have retained it without constantly then suffixing in with [sic].

Chapter 2

William Boyd Dawkins

Early Life

William Boyd Dawkins[1] was born on 26 December 1837 at Buttington Parsonage, Montgomeryshire, Wales, the only surviving child of the Reverend Richard Dawkins (1796-1861) and his wife Mary Anne (nee Youngman, 1811-1893). (A brother, Edward Richard, had died the previous February, aged just eight months).[2] His childhood was comfortable. Richard Dawkins' established living was endowed by royal bounty and parliamentary grant and included a tied parsonage, a large stone building adjacent to the church and graveyard (Plate 2). As perpetual curate he also received one-quarter of the great and small tithes of the parish,[3] leaving the family wealthy enough to employ two domestic servants; in 1841, when Dawkins was three years old, these were two local girls Sarah Roberts and Mary Turner.[4]

The social landscape of Dawkins' childhood was small and remote. The population of the entire parish was just 820, made up of the townships of Cletterwood, Trewern and Hope.[5] Richard Dawkins ministered to both Cletterwood (All Saints', Buttington) and Trewern (Trewern Chapel), while a Methodist Chapel served Hope; his Sunday morning services in 1851 attracted congregations of 190 (from a population of 250) and 89 (of 389) respectively. All Saints' also offered afternoon and evening prayers for 'scholars', while two small day schools and a Sunday school, funded by charitable donations and the Church,[6] took care of the parish's educational needs. It is unclear whether Boyd Dawkins attended these or was privately educated. In contrast to young Boyd's social world, the rural landscapes of Montgomeryshire were enormous. Buttington is situated on the road from Welshpool to Shrewsbury on the eastern bank of the River Severn, the parish in the 1850s comprising '4500 acres, of which 1200 are arable, 500 meadow, 2100 pasture, 400 plantation, and the remainder waste; the scenery is picturesque and beautiful, and the wood consists chiefly of oak'.[7] Looking from the Church, the horizon is formed by lush wooded slopes with the three peaks of the Breidden Hills – Craig Breiddin, Cefn Cestyll and Moel-y-Golfa

– dominating the northern skyline. From their summits, these hills afford stunning views of the Severn Valley, the rich cultivated plains of Shropshire, the Cheshire Hills and mountains of North Wales. So, within a few hundred yards of the lawns and gardens of the church and parsonage, Dawkins would have had access to a fertile playground containing rivers, water meadows, fields and woodlands as well as some fabulous Silurian geology. Offa's Dyke, the impressive Eighth Century earthwork between England and Wales, runs just 20m past the back of the parsonage and the hills are studded with the vestiges of several Anglo-Saxon encampments.[8]

It is little surprise that from an early age Boyd Dawkins developed a keen interest in geology and natural history,[9] according to the few surviving sources. Snippets of information are preserved in newspaper interviews written much later in his life or as oral traditions passed from Dawkins to his protégé J. Wilfred Jackson (1880-1978).[10] They tell of geological destiny rather than childhood naughtiness: as a small boy of five he had discovered carboniferous plants preserved the household coal stores; while at school in Lancashire he started a collection of fossils from the Fylde boulder clay. By the age of ten he claimed to have explored the limestone caves at Llanymynech Ogof, Montgomeryshire.[11]

When he turned twelve, Dawkins was sent to Rossall School in Fleetwood, Lancashire, an all-boys institution founded in 1844 as the 'Northern Church of England School'.[12] The school offered few home comforts and the hours were long: 7am-8.30am, 9.45am-12pm and 2pm-5pm with evening prep between 8.30pm-9.30pm. At its foundation, the school had been under the headmastership of Dr John Woolley (1816-1866), 'a man of the highest culture and sweetest temper, whose only fault was putting too much trust in the goodness of human nature'.[13] This trust combined with the use of the monitor system typical of Victorian public schools allowed the twin vices of fagging and bullying to become quickly established at Rossall, with Woolley often finding himself unable to control his prefects. Rev. William Osborne, a disciplinarian who introduced a number of reforms and improvements to the school and who managed to keep a much tighter rein on his charges and their parents, replaced Woolley the year before Dawkins' arrival. Still, the monitor system and its attendant problems remained. Dawkins' performance at Rossall appears to have been unremarkable, apparently winning no prizes or positions, but the school was clearly the crucible from which our central protagonist's character was cast. As the first School Captain, Rev. T.W. Sharpe, later recalled: '...in its early days the comfortless life was often trying to delicate boys. But to us who could beat the winds and brunt the storm, it gave a hardening strength which braced us for life'.[14] Dawkins' own recollection was similar and while he looked back on his schooldays with rosy affection he remembered them as ferocious, full of hardship, fagging, fighting and marauding.[15]

The same year, 1850, Dawkins' parents moved to Bettws Cedewain, a village twelve miles south-west of Buttington, where his father took up the benefice at St Beuno's Church. Four years later the family left Wales altogether, moving to the Parish of Westonzoyland, Somerset. For Dawkins this marked the beginning of a long association with the county, and he would later claim to be a 'Somerset man by adoption'.[16]

In 1857, Dawkins went up to Jesus College, Oxford, matriculating in March at the end of the Hilary Term.[17] His initial interests were in the Classics, but having secured a second in his Classic Mods, he turned his attention to the Natural Sciences. Dawkins' university years saw the scientific world he would soon join transformed. The antiquity of humanity debate was won, Darwin had finally published *Origins* and a new discipline – geological archaeology – was opening up. Under the tutelage of John Phillips,[18] Professor of Geology, and George Rollaston,[19] Linacre Professor of Anatomy and Physiology, Dawkins was able to study geology, anatomy and palaeontology. These three subjects defined his career, but as invaluable as his training in comparative anatomy would become, at the time it was Phillips' teaching that particularly inspired and shaped Dawkins. It was through the Professor's lectures in the Old Clarendon Buildings that Dawkins was introduced to the cavern researches of William Buckland (until his death in 1858 a friend and colleague of Phillips') and others; he would later state that without Buckland's *Reliquia Diluviana* and collections from the bone caves of Britain and Germany he might never have taken up cave hunting at all.[20]

The esteem between the Professor and his student was mutual. Jack Morrell holds Dawkins up as Phillips' favourite pupil and paints the Professor as something of an *eminence gris* in Dawkins' life, using his power and influence to engineer his student's success.[21] Phillips supported Dawkins' fellowship of the Geological Society in 1861, gave him introductions to the geological elite, secured him access to the library of the Royal Society and helped him to 'wriggle' into a job at the Geological Survey.[22] Phillips' extensive scientific networks would also have enabled Dawkins to keep abreast of the latest findings, such as those coming from Brixham Cave in 1858 and the news from Amiens in 1859. Phillips also actively persuaded the Palaeontological Society to invite Dawkins to prepare their mammalian monograph series. He also supported his candidature for the Royal Society Fellowship and spoke warmly of various grant applications, including monies to carry on excavations at Victoria Cave, Settle (for all of these, see below). This was indeed strong patronage but then academia has never been a stranger to favouritism and preferment. Given Dawkins' ambition, drive and talent for self-promotion he would probably have succeeded on his own merits, although of course the helping hand of Phillips did not hurt. He continued to seek his old mentor's advice and support until Phillips' tragic death in 1874.

Among Dawkins' friends at Oxford was the historian John Richard Green (1837-1883) (Plate 3). Green was sociable but sensitive, and until Dawkins' arrival had no friends at Jesus: a college full of clannish Welshmen.[23] The two became inseparable, to each a much needed confidant with whom to freely exchange views, but 'Dax' and Johnny also seem to have had that bad habit of taking out their frustrations on those closest to them. Dawkins was often able to laugh away Green's ill temper and Green able to criticise Dawkins without awakening the beast, but the two frequently fell out.[24] Their mutual friend E.A. Freeman (1823-1892; see below) was often left to pick up the pieces and serve as mediator.[25]

Green was amazed by Dawkins' energy: 'Look at that little fellow Dawkins, God bless him! Warmer heart and cooler head never balanced one on another than in him – but look at what he has done by sheer steady work, and blush!'[26] He also applauded Dawkins' realism – 'Dawkins-ism' as he called it – although the two did have lofty plans. While Dawkins was still an undergraduate they decided to write a history of Somerset from the earliest times, but although their early letters occasionally mention this 'opus' nothing ever came of it. They later made an even more ambitious pact: together they would write the whole history of England. Green taking the historical period from the Romans onwards; Dawkins the prehistoric past as revealed by archaeology and geology.[27] While such brash claims are not unusual from undergraduates, the two made good on their promise, Green going on to become a celebrated historian whose *Short History of the English People* (1874) and four-volume treatment *A History of the English People* (1878-1880), dovetailed neatly with Dawkins' two prehistoric tomes.

At Oxford they also began a college magazine, 'The Druid', the first issue of which appeared in Easter 1862. It was a reasonably professionally produced offering. At eighty pages between green softcover, it carried articles ranging from poetry, fiction, history, geology and anything else 'the college man and the Welshman...especially cared for'.[28] The College dons did not approve, and hinted to Dawkins that his energies would be better used learning rather than teaching, but he and Green took this as a challenge and produced a second edition. They were eventually persuaded to stop by the production costs – an unsustainable £15. Most of the work, and much of the writing, appears to have been done by Green. Dawkins produced two articles: the first a potted history of the antiquity of man, the second a piece about stone quarries. Green was not impressed with the latter, 'I asked for a paper on quarries: you sent me a quarry on paper'.[29]

Dawkins graduated in 1860 with a first in the Natural Sciences, and within a year had become the first Burdett-Coutts Geological Scholar. This was a new scholarship established by Angela Burdett-Coutts (1814-1906, later Baroness Burdett-Coutts) for the promotion of the 'study of Geology and of Natural Science as bearing on Geology'.[30] Each scholarship was tenable for two years, giving him a fantastic opportunity to hone his craft.

Cave Hunting at Hyaena Den, Wookey Hole Ravine

Away from Oxford, the family's new home in Westernzoyland placed Dawkins at the heart of a cave hunter's paradise. He was 18 miles – a few hours' ride on horseback – from the Somersetshire caverns of Cheddar Gorge, Burrington Combe, and Wookey Hole, while the Devonshire caves at Kent's Cavern, Chudleigh, Torbryan and Brixham were accessible by train from the neighbouring town of Bridgwater. Throughout 1859 he kept a notebook in which he jotted information and pasted newspaper cuttings relating to the Somerset caves[31] and later claimed to have 'explored' three caves that year.[32] One of these was a small cave at the head of Cheddar Gorge, which had already produced fossils of wolf, fox, wild boar, goat, cattle and horse, as well as a human skull. Another was a small cave in the Wookey Hole Ravine, which he excavated in December 1859 with Rev. J. Williamson, vicar to the hamlet of Theale (five miles west of Wookey).

Wookey Hole Ravine sits on the southern flank of the Mendip Hills, two miles north-west of Wells; it is one of many that dissect the Triassic Dolomitic Conglomerate of Somersetshire. In 1862 Dawkins described it as being open to the south and running near-horizontally until it meets a vertical cliff some 200 ft high, 'ivy covered and affording a dwelling place for innumerable jackdaws'.[33] At the base of this cliff sits the Great Cave of Wookey Hole, the lower end of a cave system that drains much of the Mendip Plateau and from which emerges the River Axe. The cave known as Hyaena Den lies on the east side of the ravine about 100 m from the Wookey Hole resurgence (Plate 2). Dawkins surmised that it was probably once a side branch of the main cave system before the roof collapsed to form the gorge. It was first discovered in 1852 during the cutting of a mill leat for the local paper mill, at which time some 12 ft of deposit was removed from its front and stacked up to make an embankment.[34] The remainder of the cave had been disturbed only by badgers and rabbits, and was still full to the roof.

During the dig, Dawkins lodged with Williamson at the parsonage, where Johnny Green and others joined him. Green was at a loose end while he awaited ordination, and spent the holidays getting a taste for geology and coaching Dawkins for his upcoming examinations.[35] Their first excavation took place on 21-22 December 1859, with a workforce made up of local labourers.[36] The depth of sediment forced them to 'cut' their way into the cave, but their efforts were quickly rewarded. Close to the entrance, and about 5 ft from the roof, they encountered three black layers that sloped upwards towards the southern end of the cave, where they merged into one.[37] Within and between these layers lay a profusion of bones, including the remains of woolly rhinoceros, mammoth, bear, wolf, horse and hyaena. Virtually all of the hollow long bones were splintered and gnawed, only the solid bones with no medullar cavity remaining intact. The patterns were identical to those Buckland had observed at Kirkdale Cave, which he had shown by comparison with animal refuse in zoological gardens to be characteristic of hyaena gnawing. Examining the wear on the hyaena teeth, Dawkins was able to show that the cave had been occupied by animals of all ages; the cave was clearly a hyaena den, and so he named it. The excavation ceased about 12 ft from the entrance.

Dawkins and Williamson resumed their work at Wookey in April 1860. The excavation of the previous December had yielded a single flint flake, not a rich haul but enough to demonstrate the presence of prehistoric people in the cave. Starting again 12 ft from the entrance they were immediately rewarded by more finds: a hand-axe (Figure 2.1), a blade-point, some crude chert implements and waste flakes. Dawkins also described two triangular arrowheads made of bone, never illustrated and never to be seen again when the photographer entrusted to make plates of them managed to lose them.[38] By the end of the 1860 season, the trench had been extended to a length of 24 ft. They returned again in April 1861, pressing inwards into the cave, which now narrowed and bifurcated. Here the cave was choked with gnawed antlers and a pasty deposit consisting largely of phosphate of lime, which Dawkins identified as decayed *album graecum* – hyaena dung. They finished their explorations 34 ft from the entrance, where large stones contained in a vertical passage made it too hazardous to continue.

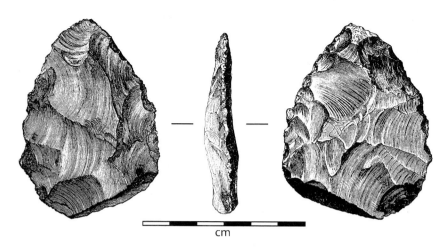

Figure 2.1: A hand-axe from Hyaena Den (after Dawkins 1874a).

Dawkins could hardly have hoped for better results, and the work certainly got him noticed in the right scientific societies. This did not stop him trying to inflate its importance further still. In concluding his first paper on Wookey Hole, he asked whether the makers of the implements could have been contemporary with the extinct fauna, which would make them much older than the scripturally-derived age of the Earth, or whether they appeared later, after the animals had gone.[39] Following a short debate with himself, he unsurprisingly settled on the former. The question was, of course, entirely rhetorical. Dawkins' excavations started months after the presence of Pleistocene humans had been accepted at sites in England and France and his paper was read two years after that. Yet, as Sir Arthur Keith (1866-1955) noted fifty years later, Dawkins' work started early enough to have helped clinch the matter[40], at least in caves.

Like many sites of this vintage, Wookey Hole was discovered too early for its full potential to be achieved, and Dawkins' personal triumph carried a heavy price for future archaeologists. His notes on the first season consist of little over a page: an outline of the fossils found, a basic record of the geology and extent of the excavations, but no drawings. The records for later seasons are fuller, but Dawkins never developed a completely satisfactory system of on-site recording and his excavation methods were crude, although by no means unusual for this period. The hired labourers performed the manual work inside the cave, with Williamson beside them, candle in hand, watching them dig. Dawkins stood outside the cave, examining 'every shovelful of debris as it was thrown out'.[41] To gain ingress they first cut a passage through the cave earth from floor to roof, and then removed the earth on either side in blocks until the chamber and its passages were cleared of all contents. The distance covered was measured every evening and marked on a ground plan with the date, and each bone or object was labelled with its find date, so it could be associated with the plan.[42] Vertical sections were recorded from time to time. Of the artefacts, Williamson found only the hand-axe in situ, leaving Dawkins to recover the rest from the spoil thrown out from the 'same place'. This was hardly an elaborate three-dimensional system that left 'no doubt as to their [the artefact's and fauna's] exact position' and rendered 'error of observation... very improbable', as Dawkins blithely stated at the time.[43] Even if 'supplemented by constant supervision of the workmen', it was far from being 'sufficiently accurate to satisfy the demands of scientific research', as Dawkins claimed 15 years later.[44] This overconfidence in such imprecise methods is a characteristic of all Dawkins' field investigations, and would be to his lasting cost.

Adding to the uncertainties, the workmen gave him little but trouble. One man, named Swell (or Shell), decided he had no interest in the work and spent his time 'contemplating the scene from a gallery – shivering with cold'. Another Swell 'amused himself by throwing red ochre at his friends and by facetious remarks'. Their favourite sport was Dawkins baiting, whose youth and inexperience probably lent him little gravitas. One labourer proclaimed that 'the Bishop' [presumably of Bath and Wells] had insisted Noah's Flood had introduced all the bones to the cave, and that one in the British Museum was shaped like a [?] bird.[45]

Bereavement and Change
On 20 May 1861, a few weeks after the end of the third season at Wookey Hole, Richard Dawkins died aged 64.[46] This left a profound hole in the lives of William Boyd Dawkins and his mother, both of whom had relied on Richard spiritually, financially and for the family home. To support them, Boyd Dawkins now had to secure a permanent and regular position. Although only 23, he was rapidly making his name in the world of geology. In 1861 he was elected a Fellow of the Geological Society. To become a Fellow, a candidate had to be first proposed and recommended by at least three existing members, one of whom had to have personal knowledge of the applicant.

The proposal took the form of an admission certificate, normally completed by the main sponsor, which was displayed in one of the public rooms at Burlington House. Voting would then take place at the specified Ordinary Meeting of the Society, and if a candidate won the approval of at least two-thirds of those present he would be accepted into the Society. Admission forms of unsuccessful applicants were destroyed.[47] Dawkins was proposed on 8 May 1861, and elected on 5 June 1861.[48] His main sponsor was his Oxford mentor John Phillips, the other signatories being Sir Roderick Impey Murchison (1792-1871; director of the British Geological Survey), Thomas H Huxley (1825-1895; who at this time was Professor of Natural History at the Royal School of Mines and naturalist at the Geological Survey) and John Morris (1810-1886; Professor of Geology at University College, London). Dawkins was amassing powerful advocates. He had also by late 1861 met and made friends with the publisher Alexander MacMillan. Johnny Green congratulated him on making such a hit and asked for an introduction to the 'pet publisher'.[49]

On becoming FGS, Dawkins put himself forward for the salaried role of Assistant Secretary, Librarian and Curator within the Society, a position that had become vacant when the former post-holder, T. Rupert Jones (1819-1911), was appointed Professor of Geology at Sandhurst Royal Military College. H.M. Jenkins, who had served as Jones' assistant since February 1859, ultimately beat Dawkins for the position.[50] The eminent palaeontologist Hugh Falconer wrote to express his condolences, telling Dawkins that even though his claims and rating were the highest. The fact that Jenkins had been trained up within the Society tipped the balance in his favour.[51] Dawkins also put himself up for a position in Southampton, possibly at the newly established Hartley Institution (now Southampton University), but again was unsuccessful.[52] Despite these disappointments, as a Fellow of the Geological Society, Dawkins found himself rubbing shoulders with the elite of the geological world – the year he was admitted, the council included such luminaries as botanist Joseph Hooker (1817-1911), arch-Darwinist Thomas Huxley, archaeologist John Lubbock (1835-1913) and geologists Sir Charles Lyell, Sir Roderick Murchison and Joseph Prestwich. Dawkins wasted no time in getting noticed, presenting his first paper (on Hyaena Den) to the society on 22 January 1862, with Murchison in the Chair.[53] Shortly after, in May 1862, Dawkins secured a position at the Geological Survey, which outside the preciously rare university jobs represented one of the few openings for professional geologists at the time.[54]

14

Working out the Hyaena Den
Before taking up his prestigious new post, Dawkins set about completing the work at Wookey,[55] returning between 29 April and 8 May 1862 in the company of James Parker[56] of Oxford (1833-1912) and Henry Catt[57] of Brighton (1823-1905). The team had one aim – to completely clear the cave of its contents to establish the relationship between the human artefacts and the animal remains. They began by clearing out the left of the entrance to Chamber A (which Dawkins had named The Antrum) where they found more fossil mammals, some in association with two concentrations of artefacts and bone-ash (b and c on the Figure 2.2 & 2.3). One bone of rhinoceros had been

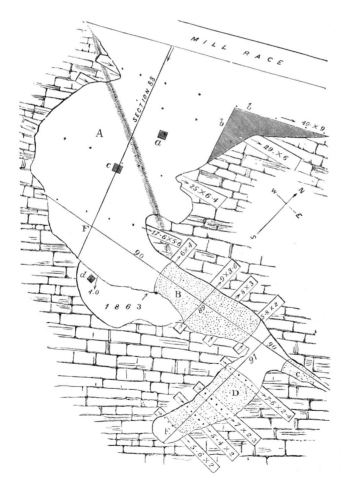

Figure 2.2: Plan of the Hyaena Den at Wookey Hole (after Dawkins 1874a). Key: Line = Sections. Dotted Areas = bone-beds. Shaded areas a-d = ashes and implements. Capital letters = Dawkins' alphabetical designation for the different chambers.

calcined in a manner that suggested it was still juicy when roasted, demonstrating what Dawkins had believed all along – that the stone age humans and extinct animals were contemporary. They next worked out the rear of The Antrum, up to Fissure F, before moving into the more constricted Passage B. In this passage a stalagmite crust capped the geological sequence; calcium carbonate had also percolated through and cemented the subjacent deposits. In places the cemented breccia was so strong was that it had to be broken up with gunpowder,[58] the resulting blocks being taken outside to be smashed with hammers, to much excitement and anticipation. Where the stalagmites ended a bone-bed began – a twisted mass of innumerable bones, teeth and coprolites in all states of decay. Some 547 bones were preserved, a mere fraction of what was present, although many had decayed to powder or paste.

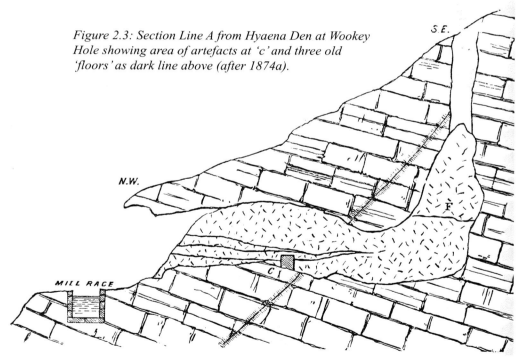

Figure 2.3: Section Line A from Hyaena Den at Wookey Hole showing area of artefacts at 'c' and three old 'floors' as dark line above (after 1874a).

After exhausting the bone-bed in Passage B (on 1st May), they moved onto Passage C, in the process discovering a new passage (D) splitting off to the right. Both were emptied, as far as was physically possible, between 2nd

16

May and 8 May 1862. The sequences in A, B, C and D were all similar, although at the end of Passage D the familiar bone bed and cave earth ran out, giving way to sand and grey clay from floor to roof. They ended their endeavours at a vertical fissure, termed Passage E. Dawkins returned for one last season in 1863, this time with William Ayshford Sanford (1818-1902), a palaeontologist who John Green once described as the 'frankest and most openhearted of men'.[59] Their most notable discovery was another stone tool on a ledge at the very rear of The Antrum, where only human hands could have put it (d on the plan).

During this short season, two strangers arrived on site and introduced themselves as Edward A Freeman of Somerleaze and 'Flos Juventutis' (actually the lawyer, historian and, later, politician James Bryce, 1838-1922). Freeman was a historian (later Regius Professor of History at Oxford), who has been described as 'repulsive in most respects' but with 'a great gift of friendship'.[60] He and Dawkins became close friends and colleagues, Freeman particularly enjoying having a tame 'man of bones' and geologist to call upon. He must sometimes have received more than he bargained for. After requesting information on the eleventh century geography of the exiled Harold Godwinson's landing site, Freeman wrote again the following week to urge Dawkins: 'pray don't write to me "all you know" about alluvia &c &c, which would simply be overwhelming, but do tell me, in your character of geologist to *Norman Conquest*, enough to enable me to draw a picture of Porlock as it stood in 1052. *Where* did Harold Land?'.[61] Closer still to Freeman was Johnny Green. Dawkins had introduced the two men at an archaeological meeting at Wellington and they forged a life-long affiliation.

Questionable excavation methods aside, the final Wookey explorations provide a snapshot of Dawkins' growing competence and confidence, although it is doubtful he ever wanted for the latter. The notebooks for this season[62] provided a brief account of the days' work and a note of significant finds. The progress through the cave is clear, but the alphabetical designations given to passages and chambers in the publication are absent, and must have been a post-excavation expedient for ease of description. Detailed measurements are few and only one section is recorded, although Dawkins later mentions that Parker took the measurements for the published plan,[63] which presumably explains the measurements in Figure 2.2 (see also footnote 58). Augmenting the daily records was a long catalogue containing summary descriptions of the teeth, using the system described in the first Wookey paper.

In 1863, the study of cave fauna was only forty years old, and still in a state of infancy. Dawkins was following the pioneers, but also driving his own agendas. His two Wookey Hole papers demonstrated a mastery over the evidence, his anatomical descriptions were precise and he made use of comparative material studied in the Oxford Museum and the British Museum. He also introduced his own cataloguing and recording methods. A major concern was taxonomy, whether the extant animals found in the caverns were representatives of modern species or something different. The second Wookey paper showcased two of Dawkins' earliest judgements.[64] One concerned the reindeer. At least three species of reindeer were believed to have occupied Pleistocene Britain, *Cervus tarandus* (=*Rangifer tarandus*), *Cervus guettardi* and *Cervus bucklandii*, the latter first described by William Buckland at Kirkdale Cave.[65] Dawkins argued that these three species were not satisfactorily separated, the distinction being based only on antler beam size and the position of the antler on the brow, which varied even within the same individual – a skull in Taunton Museum bearing antlers of both *C. tarandus* and *C. guettardi* was proof enough of that. For Dawkins *C. guettardi* was founded on a young antler, and *C. bucklandii* on an old antler – all could be subsumed within the living species, *tarandus*. The other example was the curiously named *Strongyloceros spelaeus*, the cave deer, first described by the indomitable English palaeontologist Richard Owen based on specimens from Kent's Cavern, which Dawkins reclassified as nothing more than a large red deer.[66]

The work at Hyaena Den also provided Dawkins with a better understanding of the complex depositional histories of cave, and the factors that affected the distribution of sediments and the objects contained within them. He realised that while many of the bones, teeth and coprolites seemed to occur in positions in which they might have originally been gnawed and abandoned, others were in cramped spots too small to accommodate a hyaena, for example those towards the rear that touched the roof. He reasoned that if water had flowed from the rear of the cave, then the bones should all have been moved forwards towards the entrance, but this was not the case. This led him to suggest that the River Axe had periodically flooded the cave, the floodwaters gently seeping in, floating bones lying near the surface and depositing them in nooks and crannies when the flood receded; all achieved without disturbing any sediments or stones. There were historical precedents for this – a few years earlier the outlet of the stream flowing through the Great Cave at Wookey Hole was blocked, causing water to rise to a height of 16 ft; when it receded it left behind it a red earth similar to that found in the caves.[67]

Equally, Dawkins was an early practitioner of palaeoecology and palaeogeography, using the range and inferred tolerances of the animals to help understand the environments and landscapes of the past. By comparing the known distribution of Pleistocene animals from different parts of the country, the fact that horse seemed more common on the ancient plains of Somerset, while bison dominated the landscapes around Yorkshire,[68] he began to develop a basic biogeography of Pleistocene fauna. There was a vegetation story unfolding too. Horse and bison were used as evidence of extensive plains, while deer were testament to woodland on the flanks of the Mendips. The absence of hippopotamus, beaver, otter, and water vole was argued to show that the site was some distance from a major river. The latter is revealing in two ways: first it shows that Dawkins had not at this stage in his career begun to differentiate between cold- and warm-adapted animals; and second that he had not yet begun to develop any ideas about the succession of animals through the Pleistocene (biostratigraphy) or what this might mean. Certainly, artefacts and hearths showed that humans used the cave, but logic dictated that this would have been during periods when hyaenas were not physically present there; perhaps humans had driven them out or had made only a brief sojourn at the site.[69] Elsewhere Dawkins was rather disparaging of the 'Wookey savages', regarding their workmanship to be inferior to those who made the hand-axes found at St Acheul in the Somme Valley or Hoxne in Suffolk, and speculated that this might reflect a greater antiquity.[70]

From the beginning, Dawkins was keen to bring his story to the masses, and was a lifelong exponent of education for the working classes. He was already a superb orator, and in his more popular writings was capable of poetic joy, painting vivid pictures with words to capture his audience's imagination:

'...[W]e are, to a certain degree, at home, the trees and even the mosses, and, probably, also, the wild flowers are the same; even the main features of the landscape are identical. The Quantocks, and the Mendips, and the Blackdowns are still overlooking the plain at their feet. Thus far, but no farther. In the forests lurk the lion and the bear, ready to spring on the rhinoceros, and the deer, and the gigantic ox as they pass to their watering-places, wolves hunt down the reindeer, the hyaenas, issuing at the approach of night from their dens, drag back again mammoth or rhinoceros from the woodlands, or red deer, Irish elk and reindeer, but more frequently horses, from the plain, and hesitate not to attack lion or bear, even in their prime...In the foreground stands man, fire-using...but far worse armed with his puny weapons of flint, and chert, and bone than his contemporaries with their sharp claws and strong teeth'.[71]

The Geological Survey Years, 1862-1869

Dawkins joined the British Geological Survey as an assistant geologist on 30 June 1862[72] (Plate 3). After several reshuffles in the 1840s and 1850s, the Survey was now under the auspices of the Department of Arts and Science[73] and as a government employee Dawkins had to sit a civil service exam. At receiving this news, he penned a short satirical essay entitled *'The Experiences of a Geological Surveyor'*.[74] In it he described a fictional debate with his Oxford chums about whether antediluvian man had continuously growing teeth like the rabbit, bemoaned the fact that he was to be examined *the very next week* in history, Latin, geography (of which he claimed total ignorance) and maths (of which he declared himself a hater) and expressed trepidation on 'leaving [his] cosy room at Oxford, its seclusion, and its delightful society for a plunge in the cold world'. His imaginary friend, who was more interested in snagging himself a hearty breakfast and pewters of pale ale, could do little more than alarm our 'Dear Dax' with third-hand tales of the sheer awfulness of the civil service exam, tempered by a feeble attempt to reassure him how splendid he would look in his blue uniform and cap, which would surely cause simple country folk to mistake him for a small policeman or superintendent of the post office.

However unprepared he felt, on 19 July Dawkins received notification that he had passed the exam, with an honorary addition for 'creditable proficiency in translating from Greek'.[75] He was assigned to an established team tasked with mapping the Weald and Kent, but would also spend part of the year at the Survey's headquarters and museum at Jermyn Street, London. Johnny Green romantically described Dawkins' life at this point as '...reading, geologising, slanging Browne, writing papers, organising a Natural History Society, sketching curates, finding a bone cave in the sermon, off to the British Association'.[76] Dawkins' assignment saw him working alongside some of the Survey's most respected geologists, including William T. Aveline (1822-1903), Frederic C. Bishopp (?-1863), Henry W. Bristow (1817-1889), Frederick Drew (1836-1891), Clement Le Neve Foster (1841-1904), Charles Gould (?-1895), Thomas Polwhele (1831-1917) and William Topley (1841-1894).[77] The team worked wonders with rudimentary resources. The geology was mapped onto 1-inch/mile topographical maps with hachuring rather than contours; the 6-inch/mile series would not become available until the 1880s.[78]

Each field surveyor was expected to cover between 200-300 square miles during the field season[79]. Dawkins' first duty was assisting his colleagues in mapping the complicated Hastings Beds, and contributing a short stretch of the horizontal section through the eastern-central Weald. After the solid geology was complete, the team turned their attention to the superficial deposits, mainly the gravels. Topley mapped the rivers Darent and Medway, the others were left to Dawkins. Topley later noted that part of the area had to be resurveyed to divide the gravel from the brickearth,[80] perhaps an indication that Dawkins had not been particularly diligent in his work.

This was not the only occasion on which Dawkins' true commitment to the survey could have been questioned. A.H. Green (1832-1896), who during his thirteen-year tenure at the Survey (1861-1874) authored ten geological memoirs, commented that 'many men look upon the Survey now only as a step to something better, Dawkins for instance...they come for their own convenience to get a practical knowledge of geology and a position, but with a fair determination from the first not to stop'.[81] Others were equally scathing of his skills as a field geologist. Searles V. Wood Jr (1830-1884), who had mapped the Wealden deposits independently of the Survey, disclosed to geologist Thomas McKenny Hughes (1832-1917) that Dawkins had selectively borrowed from his privately produced sheets and simply made up the rest.[82]

Dawkins also found himself in hot water with the Director-General, Roderick Murchison, over his 1864 paper on the Rhaetic Beds of Somerset.[83] Murchison, and his predecessor de la Beche, imposed pernicious restrictions on publishing BGS work outside official vehicles and chastised staff who dared to break the rules.[84] While Dawkins' fieldwork in Somerset had preceded his joining the Survey, the organisation had spent decades mapping south-west England.[85] Worse still, in the early 1860s Murchison had become interested in how far the Rhaetic Beds could be represented by a different colour on the maps, and after visiting key localities he decided it was desirable to adopt a new name based on a British type-locality, proposing the term 'Penarth Beds' for this purpose.[86] It was bad enough that Dawkins was publishing outside his own patch, but for Murchison the bigger sin was the failure to use the newly implemented Survey terminology.[87] Murchison tempered the admonishment by assuring Dawkins of his value as a colleague and a geologist, the sort of reassurance that today would have almost certainly been followed forty-eight hours later by a resignation. In all, Dawkins' incumbency at the Survey was rather a tarnished affair and he left with a reputation as a poor fieldworker, a feeling summed up by Searles V. Woods:

'I was not surprised to find that his work was all put aside at Jermyn Street & fresh Geologists put on to do it all over again'.[88]

Dawkins may have been a substandard field geologist by his colleagues' measures, but the same cannot be said for his work as a vertebrate palaeontologist, endeavours that probably contributed to the neglect of his main duties at the Survey. From 1863, Dawkins kept notebooks of fossil mammals, seven volumes of which survive in Buxton Museum alongside painted sketches and tracings compiled from his many visits to museums and private collections up and down the country.[89] Between 1863 and 1864 he examined collections housed in the British Museum and Royal College of Surgeons, and in Bath, Brighton, Bristol, Chichester, Leeds, Oxford, Taunton, and York Museums. He also looked in private collections belonging to Dr. Spurrell of Crayford and Rev. F. Warre of Weston-super-Mare, amongst others, and still managed to find time to conduct 'elicit' field visits to Somerset (Uphill Cavern and Burrington Combe), West Sussex (Hardham Romano-British Cemetery) and the Lower Thames (Grays Thurrock, Erith and Crayford).

The Belvedere Set
Survey life required Dawkins to spend part of his time in the field and part in the London office. He therefore took a house, with his widowed mother, on Bexley Road, Belvedere, a leafy hamlet in the Parish of Erith (now part of the London Borough of Bexley but then subsumed within the vast estate of Baron Sir Culling Eardley). Erith in 1862 was a small parish about three miles across in either direction, of which about half consisted of Thames marshland. Belvedere lay west of Erith village, the ground rising steeply towards its woody heights, culminating in a summit dominated by an eighteenth century Italianate mansion, Belvedere House.[90] It was an ideal location: gentrified, conveniently situated on the northern edge of the Weald, linked by the extensive Victorian rail network to both work loci, and close to the Thames sites around Crayford being studied by his friend and fellow Belvedere resident Dr. Flaxman Spurrell.

While surveying the Weald and moonlighting at museums or sites nationwide, Dawkins somehow found time to court Miss Frances Evans (1839-1921), daughter of Robert Speke Evans (1811-1874) and Elizabeth Selina Evans (1820-1880). Robert Evans was a Clerk to the Admiralty, a career he had pursued from the age of sixteen, and in which, by 1847, he had risen through the ranks to become one of only six First Class Clerks. His position commanded a handsome starting salary of £600 per annum plus £25 annual increments.[91] Frances' upbringing had thus been comfortable, her childhood spent in fine surroundings in Kensington, before the family moved to Ealing in the 1850s, and then to Temple Mount, Belvedere shortly after 1861.[92] She had been educated at home, alongside her younger brother Robert Henry (b. 1844), the family of four being well looked after by a governess, a cook, a parlour-maid, a nurse, and a housekeeper (Mrs Evans' widowed sister-in-law Mary Blow). Both the Admiralty man and the geologist worked for the Government, and it must surely have been among Belvedere's polite upper-middle class society, the circle of Eardley's tenants in which Boyd and Frances undoubtedly moved, that the two were introduced.

The populace of Belvedere certainly had much to talk about on the morning of 1 October 1864 (Plate 4). In the early hours two barges had left the powder mills of Hall & Sons, Dartford laden with gunpowder destined for the magazines at Erith. They arrived at Erith with the sun rising on the horizon, when at 6.40am one of the barges exploded, followed instantly by the second boat and shortly after by the entire magazine; the initial spark was blamed on someone smoking. It was estimated at the time that the magazine stored 750 barrels of gunpowder, the barges another 200, each barrel containing around 100lbs of explosive.[93] Boyd Dawkins was an eyewitness to the devastation wrought by the explosion, and wrote to the papers graphically describing the scene:

'On Saturday morning while reading in my bed I was startled by a tremendous concussion that made the walls of my room crackle, and brought down portions of the ceiling. Under the impression that an earthquake was destroying my house, I sprang up and made for the doorway. The instant I got there a loud explosion shivered my window to atoms, and covered my bed with pieces of glass and mortar. At the same time my drawing-room bay window was dashed in, and in another room two windows, with frames and brickwork, were blown in without the glass being broken. I dressed as quickly as possible, under the impression that half the place, at least, was in ruins. On going out I witnessed the most extraordinary sight. The fronts of the houses and the shops on either side of Bexley Road had lost their glass, and very generally even their window frames. Doors were blown in, and strong shutters smashed. The confusion, the screaming, the rushing about in night dresses, and the anxiety of the mothers for the safety of their children surpass all powers of description. The very dogs yelped with fear. By this time the dark column of smoke, after ascending to a considerable height, spread like a gigantic mushroom at the top, proved that the mischief was done by the explosion of gunpowder...the breakage of glass extends on this side of the Thames along a radius at least five miles from the scene, including Bexley and Woolwich'.

'The force of the explosion may be inferred by...small charred fragments of powder kegs found...at a distance of 2.5 miles in a straight line. On going to the place that commanded a view of the marshes I found the site that had been occupied by one of the magazines, a smoking crater, one side of which had been blown away into the Thames, making a breach of 50 yards at least in the embankment. I looked in vain for a row of neat cottages that formerly stood there. It was fortunately, low water, or an inundation would have added to the mischief. The number of killed...is not yet known, because all those in the immediate neighbourhood of the magazines were blown to atoms. One human head was picked up at least a mile from the spot; a leg here, and a breast there... human flesh was fished out of the river.

'...Everything within a radius of half a mile – trees, houses, barns – have been utterly destroyed, and the debris jumbled in a most extraordinary manner...Erith Church, about a mile from the magazines, has had its ceiling blown in, and partially the roof also...' [94]

After the initial shock, the biggest threat to public safety was the incoming tide, a fact recognised by two local engineers Mr. Moore, who had been involved in work on the Thames Embankment, and Mr. Houghton, one of the staff on Joseph Bazelgette's London Sewer Scheme. They quickly enlisted 400 men engaged in the construction of the Southern Outfall Sewer at Crossness, who rushed to the site armed with all the tools they could carry. Moore's experience proved vital. He supervised the construction of a makeshift wooden breakwater, and had the presence of mind to request reinforcements from the army; later the same day 1500 soldiers from Woolwich Barracks arrived with thousands of sandbags that they filled with local clay and rammed against the rampart. The following day navvies sent by the Dartford Commissioners finished the job.[95] Owing to the total obliteration at ground zero, the total number of casualties was never properly established, but five were known to have perished on the barges and five more were known to be 'missing'. Dawkins and Frances survived unscathed by the blast, at least physically.

Whatever the secrets behind their romance, Dawkins finally succeeded in wooing Frances on 17 December 1865, when he wrote in his diary: 'The day when I won Fanny'.[96] The couple married at Erith Parish Church – which had presumably had its roof repaired – on 26 July 1866. Reverend Johnny Green conducted the ceremony. (Plate 4) Shortly after, the newlyweds moved to a large house in Upminster (annual rent £13 16/- 0d): a small Essex village 15 km east of the City of London (now part of the London Borough of Havering) that had gained popularity with successful London merchants in the late 1600s and 1700s and had consequently seen investment and the erection of several grand houses.[97] It was certainly well stocked with inns and public houses, although it was a strange choice of location for Dawkins. His life during this period was peripatetic, involving daily travel to different towns, but the nearest train station was at Romford, three and a half miles north-west of Upminster. Dawkins' mother, Mary, remained in the house in Bexley Road, Belvedere, which Dawkins often used as a base. His diaries show that 'Mamma' was quite a financial burden, requiring an allowance, rent and frequent loans.

Extracurricular Activities
Dawkins' published output during his BGS tenure was prodigious. Virtually none of it was related to his 'official' work, although in this he was not unusual among Survey staff. Several members of the Survey held university or other posts concurrent with their Survey employment, as the pay for both was fairly dismal. The British Geological Survey now holds very little archive on Dawkins [98] and it is impossible to know how far Huxley or other senior colleagues endorsed his extracurricular activities, or whether Dawkins carried on the work as a private sideline. Whatever the case, he spent these years developing his knowledge of the British Pleistocene fauna. By the time Dawkins left the Survey he had amassed details of the mammals from 148 assemblages. Dawkins had personally examined most of these faunal collections and would take on trust the identifications of only four colleagues: George Busk (1807-1888, see Chapter 4), Falconer, Sanford and Owen. This database put him in an unparalleled position to examine the taxonomy and distribution of Pleistocene species, as its sheer size and scope shielded him from the usual problems attendant on such endeavours, particularly the question of normal variation within a species and geographical lacunae caused by rarity or ecological variation. It is ironic, then, that Dawkins felt that by keeping him away from books, societies and collections, his job rather retarded his progress in the field to which he had devoted his life –

palaeontology. He was keen to move on, and on learning that that a lecturing post might soon become vacant at the Survey, wrote to Andrew Crombie Ramsey (1814-1891), the Survey's Local Director for England, declaring his intention to compete for it and expressing hope that Ramsey would not be at all hurt by the news.[99]

Following his success with the reindeer, Dawkins next turned his attention to the taxonomy of the rhinoceroses, which in 1863 was in some disarray. The prevailing classification was largely based on the skull morphology and the architecture of the nasal bones, which were easily broken and easy to misread from drawings [100], but Dawkins concentrated on the teeth, which he thought the most reliable elements for identifying and differentiating species. He adopted the method of anatomical landmarks and the alphabetical code devised by the Prussian palaeontologist Johann Brandt (1802-1879), which made it possible to establish subtle similarities and differences between taxa. The four papers on the woolly rhinoceros (in 1863 called *Rhinoceros tichorhinus* = *Coelodonta antiquitatis* in current nomenclature), the steppe rhinoceros (*R. megarhinus* = *Stephanorhinus kirchbergensis*), the narrow-nosed rhinoceros *(R. leptorhinus* = *S. hemitoechus*) and the Etruscan rhinoceros (*R. etruscus* = *S. etruscus*) were highly accomplished, authoritative and tediously technical.[101] Each dealt with the history, distribution, conspecifics, definition and anatomy of a single species, accompanied by tables of measurements.[102] Dawkins was equally concerned with correcting the many anatomical errors that had become established as fact. For example, the mistaken belief of Owen, the great French palaeontologist George Cuvier (1769-1832) and his equally distinguished countryman Henri De Blainville (1777-1850) that the adult woolly rhino possessed a first premolar, which it did not. By 1868, Dawkins had succeeded in organising the rhinoceroses into a series of well-defined species that are, nomenclature notwithstanding, for the most part still accepted today; when Falconer's memoirs were published in January 1868, Dawkins was justly proud that (again aside from differences in the names) his arrangement agreed with that reached independently by the late great palaeontologist.

The *Rhinoceros leptorhinus* paper had initially been submitted to the Royal Society for inclusion in their *Philosophical Transactions*, where George Busk and William Henry Flower (1831-1899: conservator to the Hunterian Museum and later director of the Natural History Museum) had reviewed it.[103] Both reviewers recognised its merits, but could not recommended it for publication because it dealt mainly with the 'minute peculiarities' of rhinoceros teeth, spent too much time dealing with generalities (a criticism that Freeman had also laid at Dawkins' door), and the key message had already been published in *The Natural History Review* (for which Busk was editor). Busk's report was the more detailed but in the main the objections were very similar, so much so that one might suspect that the two men, who were both based at the Royal College of Surgeons, may have discussed the paper prior to sending their reports. It was published as an abstract in the Society's *'Proceedings'*.[104]

The successes achieved at Wookey Hole were not repeated in Dawkins' second cave hunting episode. Accompanied by William Ayshford Sanford (1818-1902), 1864 saw Dawkins explore the caves of Burrington Combe, a ravine 3 miles north-east of Cheddar Gorge cutting through the North Mendips of Somerset. Four caves were explored – Aveline's Hole (named after his Survey colleague and friend W.T. Aveline), Plumley's Den, Whitcombe Hole and Great Goatchurch Cavern. Despite extensive excavations, including a 38 ft deep shaft at the rear of Aveline's Hole, the caves produced only Neolithic and later material. This was not what Dawkins wanted, and the site was cursorily published in 1864, mentioned in the introduction to the first Palaeontological Memoir (below) and then largely forgotten.[105] Ten years later it received a short mention in Dawkins' first book, *Cave Hunting,* not for its palaeontology but in relation to the processes that had formed the Goatchurch Cavern, and the ubiquitous 'legend of the dog'.[106]

In 1865, Dawkins tackled the hyaenids, which were also plagued by a proliferation of species based on tiny study samples, sometimes a single tooth. Three species were supposed to have occupied Pleistocene Britain – *Hyaena spelaea, Hyaena perrieri* and *Hyaena intermedia* – all of which were considered distinct from one another and from extant African species. Richard Owen and Henri De Blainville both believed that the modern hyaena and cave hyaena could be distinguished from each other by the root and crown of the upper molar. Dawkins realised that variation within species was greater than previously acknowledged and to properly answer any question of taxonomy a large sample was required. He used 200 jaws and 500 teeth from Wookey Hole, which had the double advantage of being an enormous sample belonging to the same fossil population. The Wookey material showed high levels of variation, subsuming a number of species, leading Dawkins to the logical conclusion that a single, highly variable species was present. He also determined that the cave hyaena was identical to the living spotted hyaena *Crocuta crocuta* – he retained the name *Hyaena spelaea* to designate the Pleistocene beast as a chronospecies only[107].

Other papers resolved the status of the musk-ox and British fossil oxen,[108] the latter pursuit mildly offending the irascible Richard Owen who sent excuses for any inadequacies in his old identifications.[109] The musk-ox paper again received a poor reception from Royal Society reviewers, despite having been read before the society by Thomas Huxley. The referees' comments were similar to his previous submission to the *Philosophical Transactions*: there was too much general background on musk-ox (Rollaston), there was little novelty (Busk) and he had over-played his hand regarding the age of the Crayford deposits (Ramsey).[110] Busk suggested that a detailed report on the skull, the stratigraphy, and associated remains would be a useful addition, but Dawkins demurred. Only an abstract appeared in the *Proceedings*, the full details published later as part of the Palaeontological Society's monograph series,[111] but only after Dawkins had engaged in a yearlong battle with the Royal Society for the return of the manuscript. The Society was happy for him to copy it, but requested that he do it in its own library. Dawkins complained that he was too busy to come to London, that his work was at a standstill as a result of not having the manuscript, and that he could not afford to hire a copyist. Even a day of his holiday spent at Carlton House would prevent him from taking his planned holiday to Germany, he moaned.[112] It is easy to understand Dawkins' frustration, and it actually beggars belief that the Royal Society rejected his paper and then refused to return the handwritten manuscript, tables, quarto plate and woodcuts, although this was apparently standard practice.

Following the 1865 publication of Lubbock's *Pre-Historic Times*,[113] Dawkins finally woke up to the centrality of the human story. Emulating his friend, he penned a speculative essay on the conditions of life in Palaeolithic times, in which he divided them into flint folk (older) and reindeer folk (younger) and pontificated on everything from stone tools, hunting, clothing and architecture to art, animism and spirituality.[114] Despite this and other writings, humans remained something of an epiphenomenon in Dawkins' World, shadows cast over his main protagonists – mammals. By 1866, Dawkins' growing reputation (with perhaps a little encouragement from John Phillips, see above) led the Palaeontological Society to invite him to author a series of monographs on British Pleistocene fauna. The series aimed to bring palaeontological science up to date and incorporate advances that had taken place in knowledge, understanding and number of fossils in the 20 years since Richard Owen had published *A History of British Fossil Mammals, and Birds* (1846). Working with Ayshford Sanford, Dawkins proposed to take each of the known species in turn, and publish them as a part work, the different parts of each volume appearing at irregular intervals.[115] It was a daunting task that Dawkins knew he would never finish – completing the job would be left up to future generations. He and Sanford would merely provide the blueprint for those that came after. As it transpired, Dawkins lived for another sixty-three years and could quite easily have finished it himself had he felt so inclined.

The first monograph was on Pleistocene cats – the *felidae* – and opened with a series of desiderata and a plea for information. This was followed by an introduction to the series, giving a brief conspectus of the evidence from cave and fluvial sites alongside a list of species that went extinct, those that survived to the present, and those introduced in prehistoric or historical times. Their control over the subject is magisterial. In just a few pages they provided a summary of all major orders, outlined the key species, problems surrounding classification, and chronological and geographical range. Not satisfied with simple cataloguing, they also explored the tolerances and seasonal movements of modern animals, which were used as a barometer for understanding past climatic regimes and the range of seasonal fluctuations. This led Dawkins to adopt an idea often attributed to Lyell, which explained the seemingly paradoxical co-occurrence of 'arctic' and 'southern' animals in the same strata as the result of long-range seasonal migrations.[116] This would later bring him into acrimonious conflict with several co-workers.

The volume is nonetheless one of pure erudition, referencing modern scholars, classical writers and medieval chroniclers. The bulk of the monograph provides anatomical element-by-element descriptions of cave lion (*Felis spelaeus*), lynx, leopard and the lesser scimitar-toothed tiger (*Machairodus latidens* = *Homotherium latidens*). The last of these would similarly assume an unpleasant and unwarranted importance in Dawkins' later career, which in archaeological circles has come to define his legacy (see Chapters 5-7). The series was also useful in setting out Dawkins' theoretical position. He was critical of other palaeontologists who treated each geological period in isolation, arguing that this generated nothing but confusion and caused past members of living species to be classed as something else. It is significant in this regard that the monograph concluded that *Felis spelaea*, the cave lion, was nothing more than a large form of modern lion, *Felis leo* (=*Panthera leo*). That said, Dawkins emphasised that just because two animals could not be differentiated skeletally, this did not mean that they would have had exactly the same coat colouring or texture, although he was quick to point out that where the pelage was vastly different from modern species, such as in the woolly mammoth and woolly rhinoceros, then skeletal differences tended to follow.

Ultimately, Dawkins would write only Volume 1, Volume 3.5 and Part A of the Treatise. The series then lapsed for three decades before Sidney Reynolds, Professor of Geology at Bristol University, took up the mantle between 1902-1939. The final series comprised[117]:

Volume 1: *The Felidae*
Volume 2: *The Hyaenidae, Ursidae, Canidae and Mustelidae*
Volume 3.1: *Hippopotamus*
Volume 3.3: *Giant Deer*
Volume 3.4: *Cervidae*
Volume 3.5: *Ovidae*
Volume 3.6: *Bovidae*
Treatise Part A

Volume 3.2 was never completed. There are several major gaps in coverage, not least the rhinoceroses, the elephants, the equids, and most orders of small mammals including rodents, lagomorphs and insectivores. Nonetheless, in 1867, just as the second part of Volume 1 appeared, Dawkins was honoured with one of the greatest accolades in British science – Fellowship of the Royal Society – aged twenty-nine. Just five years after leaving Oxford, Dawkins had truly taken his place among the Victorian scientific elite. Huxley, Phillips, Rollaston, Lyell, Lubbock, Ramsey, and several others signed his certificate. The same year saw his appointment to the staff of *The Saturday Review of Politics, Literature, Science, and Art,* a popular forum for 'educated opinion' that provided a wide platform from which to air his views;[118] although Freeman warned him to take it slowly and establish himself before taking on the heavyweights.[119] He was also busy carving out an international reputation. He presented papers at the 2nd International Congress of Prehistoric Archaeology in Paris, written and delivered in French, and while there took the opportunity to network with key figures including Albert Gaudry (1827-1908), who in 1872 became Professor of Palaeontology at the Jardin des Plantes, Paris.

Dawkins thanked God's blessing for his prosperity, but found the work rate punishing. Having accepted an invitation to speak in Brighton, he wrote to his old friend Willett asking to be let off, his excuses being deadlines on three papers (two in French), the second volume of the faunal monograph, survey work and essays for magazines.[120] He was genuinely distressed to have to disappoint such a close friend, but was nearing exhaustion. In a rare confession of weakness he confided to Willett that 'all my old cock-combing [has been] knocked out of me', a measure both of how deflated Dawkins felt and an acknowledgement of the pomposity others found so infuriating. The letter contained further bad news for Willett – Frances could not visit Brighton either. Fanny had to forgo such pleasures because she was too busy writing for him, a rare insight into the Dawkins' marital arrangements.

Dawkins must have quickly regained his spirit, for 1868 was another bumper year that saw the publication of over a dozen new papers. He resolved the classification of *Rhinoceros etruscus* (see above), authored a highly opinionated thirty-four-page book-review on Darwin's *The Variation of Animals and Plants under Domestication*, and penned popular accounts on the former range of the reindeer and mammoth in Europe.[121] The latter two were the denouement of a decade's research, and used examples from cave and fluvial sites to examine distribution, climate and ideas regarding when Britain was isolated from Europe. Dawkins was certain that animals were useful tools for the reconstruction of past climates, in contrast to Cuvier who had emphasised that the lion, tiger, fox and wolf had wide tolerances, and were thus not reliable indicators of environment. Dawkins appealed to a different biogeographical principle: carnivores depended on meat, available in many packages from many environments; their distribution is controlled more by the distribution of herbivores than by climate. Herbivores, though, depended on vegetation, which is more-or-less climate dependant, and they therefore do provide a tolerably reliable indicator of past conditions. Ever the polymath, ever the entertainer, Dawkins regaled his readership with romantic accounts of Germanic tribes encountering and naming the reindeer (apparently from *rennen*, to run), their possible survival in Caithness, Scotland into the historical period and wondrous tales of the frozen mammoth corpses of Siberia. A separate paper dealt with age of the mammoth. Prevailing ideas on the divisions of the Pleistocene recognised only three phases: a warm pre-glacial period, a cold glacial period, and a cool post-glacial period, each with a characteristic found (see Chapter 3). Dawkin's emerging ideas on the occurance of different species within each of these periods forced him to disagree with the famous French cave hunter and palaeontologist Édouard Lartet, and with his hero and friend the late Hugh Falconer, both of whom had postulated the existence of mammoth in the pre-glacial forest-bed deposits of Norfolk. If this were true, then the mammoth would lose all biostratigraphical significance as a member of the emerging 'post-glacial' faunal suite, which for Dawkins was now unthinkable. By careful examination of putative cases from the Cromer Coast, Dawkins was able to show that none had a secure provenance and that, in all probability, they had fallen onto the beach from younger gravel deposits above. These papers were intended for non-specialist audiences, but were full of detail and served to get Dawkins' views in the public domain.

August 1868 brought the 3rd International Congress of Prehistoric Archaeology to England, running concurrently with the 38th meeting of the British Association for the Advancement of Science (BAAS), that year held in Norwich. Dawkins was a member of the special committee of the Congress, and had secured himself a place on the organising committee alongside influential men in the spheres of archaeology, ethnography, anthropology, geology and the biological sciences.[122] Dawkins characteristically took every opportunity to showcase his broad archaeological talents to the assembled international audience, and presented three papers in three different sessions, more than any other delegate. His topics were admirably diverse, with two short offerings on early antiquities in Portugal and the antiquity of iron mines in the Weald, followed by a long treatise on the prehistoric mammals of Great Britain.[123] His grand designs were somewhat marred by George Busk, whose comments on two of Dawkins' talks were less than complementary. Most embarrassingly, Busk pointed out that he and Evans had already presented a paper on the same Portuguese antiquities to the Ethnological Society (Francisco Pereira da Costa of Lisbon Polytechnic had earlier sent casts to Charles Lyell, who must have passed them to Busk). Busk had other issues with Dawkins' use of the term 'prehistory', not because Dawkins used it to describe the post-Pleistocene/pre-Roman period, but because Busk saw two phases within it- one with humans and wild animals, one with humans and domesticated animals. Dawkins deflected the questions, preferring to fight his battles on his own terms.

The year was topped off with the naming of two new species of deer in back to back papers in the same issue of the *Quarterly Journal of the Geological Society.*[124] The first, which he named *Cervus brownii* (Dawkins), was based on 41 antlers collected by Mr John Brown of Stanway from the Freshwater Beds at Clacton-on-Sea. It had previously been recognised by Falconer, who recorded it in his unpublished notebooks as *Cervus clactonianus* but had not formally defined it. As such, Dawkins dispensed with the normal rules of precedence when naming species, and opted to call it after its discoverer and give himself authority for doing so; this act of hubris has since been revoked, for it is now recognised as an extinct species of fallow deer, and has been renamed *Dama clactoniana* (Falconer). The second species was from the Norwich Crag and was again based on fossils first noted by Falconer. Dawkins named it *Cervus falconeri.*

Kent's Cavern is an iconic site that has been excavated on and off since 1824, the most significant work being that conducted by William Pengelly under the auspices of the BAAS from 1865-1884.[125] In his fifth report on behalf of the Kent's Cavern Committee, Pengelly recorded that following the 1868 BAAS meeting in Norwich, Dawkins had expressed a desire to visit Torquay to examine the fauna from the site.[126] This was not the first time Dawkins had tried to gain access to the Kent's Cavern material. He had originally approached Pengelly after the 1866 Nottingham meeting of the BAAS, but his timing on that occasion was poor.[127] George Busk had only just been added to the Committee as site palaeontologist and Pengelly intended to send the identifiable bones to Busk without delay, with the hope that the next report could contain a list of species. Busk evidently never even started the task, and when Dawkins asked again Pengelly was delighted to accept, not least because in the four years since excavations had recommenced thousands of bones had been placed into storage. Dawkins was co-opted onto the Committee, Pengelly noting that the task was of Herculean dimensions – indeed it was, and Dawkins never finished it.[128]

Dawkins wrote to Pengelly asking when he could start: 'I wish to finish them as soon as I can; for delay with me is a synonym for laziness. If possible I should like to get the task done before the year's end ...'[129] Dawkins visited on 10 November 1868, accompanied by Sanford.[130] Prior to the visit, Pengelly busied himself numbering the bones[131] while Dawkins meticulously planned a strategy to maximise productivity: 'The best plan of attack is, I fancy, to open the boxes according to their numbers ... In this way the work will progress swiftly, and we can do some thousand per diem. I know all the species at sight, except Grizzly and Brown Bear, and these I am getting up...Don't trouble about lists or a catalogue; I have it all sketched out, and all the names of the beasts are down—all that we shall find ...'. [132] For the 1869 BAAS meeting in Exeter,[133] Dawkins produced the preliminary catalogue of species Pengelly had long hoped for, with a relative estimate of abundance (in fact Sanford did the majority of the work, as Dawkins graciously admitted in print). Over 400 specimens were processed in the first year, about ten per cent of the total collection and far fewer than the anticipated thousand *per diem*.

Arguably, Dawkins' greatest achievement of the decade, the culmination of ten years' intensive work on British fossil mammals, came in February 1869, with a paper on the distribution of post-glacial mammals. This presented his tabulated data on every museum and private collection available in the whole of Great Britain, including the few known from Scotland and

Ireland. Dawkins used his vast knowledge and understanding of variation within species to lump several species together, as he had done for the red deer and reindeer, in doing so highlighting the fact that taxonomy and nomenclature was still in a mess. Dawkins' series of papers notwithstanding, the example of the rhinoceroses demonstrated the confusion that still reigned at this time, where new species had been named by different authorities without consulting adequate comparative materials. Dawkins' explication is a paragon of perplexing simplicity: '*Rhinoceros leptorhinus* Owen. This term is used as the exact equivalent of *R. hemitoechus* of Dr. Falconer and of the *R. merckii* of M. Lartet. If the validity of the species *R. leptorhinus* of Cuvier be proved by subsequent investigation, *R. leptorhinus* of Owen must be exchanged for *R. hemitoechus* of Falconer, and Cuvier's species must be taken to represent the *R. megarhinus* of Christol.'[134] Dawkins' extensive compass and knowledge of the fossils were exemplary, as a palaeontologist he was at the top of his field. Even today the paper remains a useful resource, and Dawkins would continue to draw from its depths for many years to come. The theoretical frameworks he maintained in interpreting the chronological and spatial patterning were less well received, however, another contention that would see him embroiled in what Wilfred Jackson euphemistically called 'acrimonious discussions'.[135]

Versus Searles Valentine Wood Jr

As Dawkins entered his thirties he began to display a confrontational side that hitherto, publicly at least, had remained hidden from view. He could never have been considered a shrinking violet, and his earliest work demonstrates that even as a scholar at Oxford he was full of pomp and self-importance. After his elevation to FRS in 1867, his willingness to compromise, admit mistakes or demure to critics seems to have suffered a fatal breakdown. Harsh words, acrimony and heated tempers were no doubt commonplace in the chambers of learned societies, which led the Geological Society of London, and probably others, to forbid detailed recording or reporting of their discussions.[136] The first published instance of Dawkins' volatility was a brief spat with Searles Valentine Wood Jr (1830-1884) over the geology of the Lower Thames.

Living in Belvedere, Dawkins had spent many hours exploring the Lower Thames brickearths of Kent and Essex (the latter a short hop away on the Gravesend-Tilbury river ferry) and in 1866 had, to his delight, pulled the skull of a musk-ox out of the brickearth at Stoneham's Pit, Crayford. In compiling materials for the planned monograph series, he came to the realisation that the geology and fauna from the famous Thames sites south of the river at Crayford and Erith and north of the river at Ilford and Grays Thurrock differed from those found in more low-lying terrace deposits[137]. All four sites had the same sedimentary sequence – three successive units of fluvial sands and gravels overlain by 'trail', a contorted bed of silt, sand and gravel that Dawkins considered evidence for glaciation and ice-wash, equivalent in time to the boulder clay. The mammalian assemblages were 'intermediate' between the warm-climate fauna of the Norfolk and Suffolk forest-beds and the classic cool fauna of the caves. Dawkins concluded that the whole series was older than the low-level gravels and all the same age: the combination of 'trail', warmth-loving Pliocene relics and a group of 'post-glacial' animals (from which the reindeer was notably absent), leading him to assign them to a period before the glacial, but after the forest beds. On the final page of the essay, in an almost throwaway remark, he noted that whether or not true boulder clay was deposited in the Thames Valley proper, it could be found in the confluent systems of the Roding and Blackwater.

Few shared his views on the Thames Valley and the reading of the paper before the Geological Society in January 1867 resulted in 'a great fight'[138] although one would never guess this from the published version, which censored the discussion. Among the audience, however, were Searles Wood Jr, who had spent years privately researching the Thames gravels, and William Whitaker, who would later author the Geological Survey memoir on the Thames Valley.[139] Both found Dawkins' conclusions completely unacceptable, Whitaker being heard to remark that 'if the palaeontologists cannot make their palaeontology square with the Geology so much the worse for the former!'[140] Wood was apparently a begrudging admirer of Dawkins' palaeontological work, but privately thought him an incompetent field geologist who, like many Survey men, did not understand the full context of the geology they were sent to work on, only their small part of it.[141] Some of Wood's scorn possibly stemmed from the fact that Dawkins was encroaching on his patch, but in an ostensibly collegiate spirit wrote a private letter pointing out an unfortunate error of fact in Dawkins work that should be corrected in future versions of the theory. In return, Wood received not a polite 'thank you', but an indignant refusal to admit any error along with a challenge to set out his case in print, which Wood duly did.[142] On 19 June 1867, Dawkins wrote in his diary 'to London OHMS to fight Searles Wood'.[143]

Wood disagreed with Dawkins on two fundamental points. First, Dawkins saw no difference in the age of the Crayford and Grays brickearth, despite the fact that they sat at different heights above the river and were presumably laid down at different times. This presented no obstacles for Dawkins who argued that the East Anglian forest beds were at or below sea level yet were the oldest, and that during glacial submergence one might reasonably expect different localities to have been subject to different rates of depression and elevation. But Wood also felt the faunal composition of Grays and Crayford were incompatible, one testifying to warm forested conditions, the other cold steppic environments, with Grays Thurrock being younger than the other sites. For Wood, the 'trail' that Dawkins depended on to support his case was not a valid formation. Its occurrence above all four sites was a total irrelevance and its use as a *terminus ante quem*[144] for the brickearth a fallacy. Wood had personally mapped the gravel of the low-lying terrace passing *under* the brickearth at Grays, which would make it younger than the low-lying gravel and among the youngest in the valley. Time would show that Wood was correct on the first count (the 'trail' could potentially have been formed during any period of intense cold), but wrong on the second (Grays is actually older than the other three sites). Dawkins was wrong on both, his errors stemming from his belief in the occurrence of a single period of glaciation (see below), rather than multiple cold events, leaving him no option but to squeeze everything inside a remarkably compressed timeframe, although he was correct in placing it all before the last glacial period.

The second matter of contention was the occurrence of boulder clay in the Thames Valley.[145] Dawkins had stated that boulder clay could be found in the valleys of the Roding and Blackwater; Wood argued that this was simply not true. In his 'indignant' letter, Dawkins provided his evidence, stating that boulder clay could be found at Navestock in the Roding and at Ingatestone, Buttbury and Mountnessing in the Blackwater. The former, according to Wood was an illusion created by localised depressions, the latter totally irrelevant as none of the places cited were to be found within ten miles of the Blackwater – they were in the River Wid.[146] Dawkins' published response barely concealed his irritation[147], how dare Wood question the field expertise of a Survey man! Dawkins had personally examined the sections involved, and nothing in Wood's mapping could make him alter his beliefs. In fact, Dawkins was quite correct on this point – boulder clay can be found in the River Roding at Navestock, the whole town sits on it, and patches can be found in the River Blackwater at Witham, Maldon and elsewhere – but that is hardly the issue. Instead of making a reasoned case, Dawkins resorted to what would become a favourite tactic – chicanery. He chastised Wood for citing a 'hurried note' that he had little dreamt would be quoted in print, and insisted that if Wood had shown the decency to refer to Dawkins' notebooks, he would have seen that Dawkins had meant to say Witham Station. In his haste he had run his finger up an affluent of the Blackwater rather than the main stream. We can safely ignore the arcane niceties of Victorian geology contained in Wood's retort, as both men were right and wrong in almost equal measure, but we cannot pass on Dawkins' continued subterfuge. Wood claimed that his motive for sending the original letter was to help quietly correct a silly mistake. Dawkins' angry response was unexpected, and had contained no indication of the unfortunate 'slip of the finger' he now relied upon. Far from exonerating him, Dawkins' published excuse only made matters worse. As Wood pointed out, he could not possibly, in haste or otherwise, have inadvertently traced his finger up the Wid to Ingatestone and Mountnessing instead of up the Blackwater to Witham, because the former were fifteen miles distant and on another Ordnance Sheet![148] It would have been better to have gratefully accepted the correction, than to lie and have that lie publicly exposed.

Chapter 3

Manchester, England

The Origins of the Manchester Museum

The Manchester Natural History Society (MNHS) was formed by a group of gentlemen-scholars and collectors in 1821, primarily to preserve the collection of insects and birds in the 'cabinet' of the late John Leigh Phillips (1761-1814), a well-known Manchester manufacturer.[1] The Society (and its ever-expanding collection) was originally based in rooms in St Ann's Place, later moving to larger premises in King Street and eventually, in 1835, into a purpose-built museum on Peter Street. This building was extended in 1850, when the collections of the Manchester Geological Society (MGS: founded 1838) were added to the displays. The collections were originally for the private viewing of members and their guests only, but this rule was rescinded in 1838, when the MNHS decided to open the museum to the public for an entrance fee of one shilling. For two decades the Society prospered, but by the early 1860s it had begun to fall on hard times – members' subscriptions were down, and visitor numbers dropped by 75% in ten years – a situation precipitated by the establishment of free municipal museums such as that at Peel Park, Salford.[2] Matters continued to deteriorate until in 1864 the MNHS offered the museum and its contents to the Corporation of Manchester, but no agreement could be reached. The Salford Corporation then made a bid to acquire selected parts of the collections, as did Owens College of Manchester, but again mutually acceptable solutions could not be found and both proposals foundered. By 1866 the MNHS was in serious debt and the decision was made to close the museum.

A reprieve came in March 1867 when Owens College, which had just committed to a major phase of expansion, approached the MNHS with a new proposal.[3] Over a period of two months an arrangement was reached. The MNHS agreed to transfer the entirety of its properties and collections to Owens College, and in return the College would maintain the collections and provide an appropriate museum and library: adequately staffed, publicly accessible and free to living members of the Society. In addition, they would provide courses on natural history and public lectures on popular science. The existing museum would be mortgaged for £5000, some of the monies raised going to the College's new buildings fund, the rest invested to pay the salary of a curator, maintain the library and enhance the collections. By 1869, the MGS had also agreed to transfer its collection to Owens College. These two sets formed the germ from which the later Manchester Museum would grow, but right now Owens College found itself in urgent need of a curator who could deal with both natural history and geology.[4]

A Plum Job

In July 1868, Dawkins received a letter from one of Owens College's trustees, the Manchester lawyer Robert Dunkinfield Darbishire (1826-1908), who wrote at the suggestion of Thomas Huxley and on behalf of the College Commissioners to ask him to consider the curatorship.[5] Darbishire explained that it would be at least 4-5 years before the new buildings would be finished, but the right man was needed to put the collections in order and take charge when the new museum finally opened to the public and students. The salary would be £300-£400, the curator would be given assistance in the work and the right to call upon the Professor or Department of Natural History. Periods away from Manchester during museum time might also be negotiated. Not a wealth of promises, he admitted, but all in all a fine opening for any gentlemen wishing to pursue a career in this line. Dawkins obviously agreed that this was a fine opportunity, for by the middle of the following week he was dining with Darbishire in Manchester.[6]

The negotiations took a further six weeks, but on 6 September 1868 Dawkins wrote conditionally accepting the offer,[7] on the understanding that:

1   The starting salary would be £400 per annum;
2   Lecturing would not be a contractual duty of the Head Curator, only something he would do if he wished. Dawkins felt that given the poor state of the collections the museum work would demand his full attention, and that even after full amalgamation with Owens College all lecture series would still more properly fall into the province of the professors;
3   Two years at least must elapse before practical classes in zoology and physiology could be considered;
4   The Head Curator would have the same vacation entitlement as the professors in Owens College;
5   Having got the museum up to first rate, the Head Curator would have assurances that they would not be 'turned out'; he was, after all, leaving

a permanent position at the Survey for a post that might only last four years;

6   He would need an assistant or assistants to clean, prepare and articulate specimens, and as much money as possible for new acquisitions and maintenance.

Throughout the discussion, Dawkins emphasised that his key concern was the educational value of the collections, and that his experiences at Oxford, Cambridge and London had shown that good teaching stemmed naturally from good collections, which meant greatly improving them. He was happy to teach and demonstrate, but on his own terms.

He started at Manchester on 25 March 1869 (Plate 1). He and Fanny set up home at Birch View, 11 Norman Street, Rusholme. Today it is a suburb of Manchester, back then it was a leafy rural area of Lancashire dominated by the Platt and Birch Estates: a retreat for the burgeoning middle classes eager to escape the mills and factories of the city two miles north. The family would remain there until 1882.

From Curator to Professor

Dawkins' concerns about leaving a full-time post at the Survey for a potentially insecure curatorship could not have been more apposite. The Colleges' plans were not as advanced or certain as Darbishire had implied in his letter and a final resolution was several years away. In 1868, the year Dawkins was offered the curatorship, Owens College had twice been turned down for a Government grant to expand its properties: first by Disraeli in March, and then by Gladstone following the Liberal's election victory in November.[8] This was disappointing, but what rankled most among Manchester's promoters was that they felt the city had been badly used by Westminster. The University of Glasgow – in a city that had contributed far less to the economy and growth of the Empire than the great manufacturing centres of north-west England, or so they argued – had been granted £120,000 by the Conservatives. Manchester was given nothing by either party, and private and corporate donations for the cost of the building work were short of what was needed.[9] More worryingly, although called the 'Owens College Extension' the proposal actually involved the incorporation of a new educational body, which would then amalgamate Owens College, requiring changes to the College's constitution and Parliamentary approval. The plans had many influential supporters but other interested parties, such as Leeds College and the late John Owens' solicitors, put up strong opposition.[10] The

Owens College Extension Bill had three readings in Westminster, eventually receiving royal assent on 4 July 1870, almost two years after Dawkins' appointment.[11] The amalgamation act joining the original college and the extension college under the name 'The Owens College' passed through Parliament on 24 July 1871. It officially took effect on 1 September 1871, a year after the Duke of Devonshire had laid the foundation stone to much fanfare, pomp and ceremony.[12]

Despite the uncertainties created by the College executive's grand designs, Dawkins threw himself into the work. The collections, once first rate, were in a wretched state. The natural history collection was quite moribund and much had to be destroyed, particularly the birds and insects, and although the geological specimens were in better condition the displays were dreadful.[13] One of Dawkins' first tasks was to move the collections from the old MNHS museum in Peter Street to Owens Colleges' premises on Quay Street, where lack of space meant that the stuffed animals that survived destruction had to be mothballed in the attic. The geological collections were arranged in the basement, which though cramped at least meant the public and students could view the specimens.

As the museum took shape the College contemplated the future of its geological teaching and in 1872 decided to appoint a Lecturer in Geology. Dawkins was the unanimous choice, and for two years fulfilled the joint role of curator and lecturer that he had been so keen to avoid on appointment (although the two lectures per week he was engaged to give cannot be considered arduous). This advancement meant that Dawkins was financially, on paper at least, £60 a year worse off. His museum stipend was reduced to £200 per annum, supplemented by £140 a year for his lecturing post plus a share of the student fees.[14] A little consultancy was taken on the side to fill the void.

Dawkins spent nearly four years sorting and expanding the collections before the new buildings on Oxford Road were opened on 7 October 1873, when the whole ensemble had to be moved once more.[15] By August 1874 the museum was nearly complete, and would be ready for students to use by the beginning of the new term. Darbishire was delighted, and proposed to the college council that they should hold a soirée to commemorate the opening, which they approved. Thus, on 2 October 1874 an exhibition was staged on the geology of the district, alongside prehistoric artefacts and the fossil remains of extinct animals. The whole college was 'thrown open' and lighted (except the attics), guests were permitted to bring ladies, and the exhibition was left open for public viewing the following day – 1400 guests attended on the opening night alone.[16]

Exactly two weeks after the triumphant opening of the new displays, on 16 October 1874, Dawkins was promoted to Professor of Geology and Palaeontology.[17] The Council obviously felt that they could not lose their star curator, especially as he had just published a major work on caves and had twice in the past two years made very public attempts to secure positions elsewhere (see below for both of these). He retained his position as Head Curator, and the appointment letter explicitly stated that his duties as Professor should not be allowed to interfere with his museum work. Geology was still a minority subject at Owens College, and although it was periodically earmarked for major investment these initiatives usually came to little. A few small adjustments were made, such as Dawkins' internal advancements, but generally the cyclical flimflam of urgency followed by the quagmires of committee and review prevailed, a modern wasting disease obviously inherited from our Victorian forefathers. By the time Thompson wrote his history of Owens College in 1886, the situation was unchanged. During the 1870s the college also developed designs to teach mining, a rather obvious departure given the proximity of the coalfields of North Wales, Staffordshire and Yorkshire, the lead mines of Derbyshire and the copper mines of Lancashire and Cumbria.[18] The committee established to promote this initiative imagined Manchester as a centre of instruction to rival the mining schools of Paris and Freiberg. They envisaged evening classes in geological science attended by working men actively engaged in mining, counterpoised by practical classes for students taught in working mines, a fusion of theory and practice designed to provide a superior education. A public appeal for funds was made, and a curriculum developed, but the response was poor and only seven people from the whole mining district around Manchester contributed to the special fund. Dawkins delivered the relevant lectures, but they were not numerous nor well attended, and the provision attracted criticism from the College Senate who described it as 'reduced to the smallest dimensions consistent with efficient teaching'.[19] Dawkins begged for more support and more money, and urged that geological science be put on an equal footing with other sciences, but it would take many years for his vision to be fulfilled, by which time Owens College had metamorphosed into the Victoria University of Manchester and the Museum had relocated to a purpose built home on Oxford Road.

Manchester's Man of Science
Dawkins' activities beyond the museum provide insights into his public image and personal beliefs (or at least those that he chose to air in public)

that are otherwise difficult to gauge. As we have seen, he arrived in Manchester just as the Owens Extension College Act was being scrutinised by Parliament and external assessors, one particular cause célèbre being the clause that would allow women to study for a degree. Writing anonymously in the *Pall Mall Gazette* (this would become a favourite ploy), Dawkins raged that there was no reason why women should not have the same opportunity of education as men, and that the admission of women at Harvard University had been a success. Owens College should keep its nerve, he insisted, as the proposals put it at the front of the education movement in England.[20] Later, in 1876, he was again among a small number of professors who supported the admission of women to the college. This did not immediately come to pass. A separate women's college was set up in Brunswick Street in October 1877, not directly affiliated with Owens College but reliant on it for much of its teaching and governance. The two eventually merged in June 1883, with women then eligible to qualify, at the discretion of Council, for a Victoria University degree, although teaching was still predominantly conducted at Brunswick Street, which became the Department for Women.[21]

Local and national societies were the life-blood of Victorian geology and archaeology, populated by men whose calling may have been in the natural sciences but whose livelihood was usually made elsewhere. Dawkins was one of the few people lucky enough to be paid to do his hobby, but he was equally an enthusiastic member of many societies. He was elected to the Geological Society of London in 1861 and the Society of Antiquaries in 1873, joined the Somerset Archaeological and Natural History Society in 1862 (President 1912), and quickly on arrival in Manchester had joined the city's Geological Society (President 1874-75) and Literary and Philosophical Society (Vice-President 1874-75; President 1876-77). In 1884 he also helped found the Manchester Geographical Society.

It is worth particular note that coincident with his appointment at Manchester, Dawkins assumed a more dominant role in the BAAS. He had been an elected member since 1864 but had not particularly engaged with its activities other than a paper on Wookey Hole delivered at Cambridge in 1862 and another on Somersetshire bone caves given at Bath in 1864 (where he had also served as secretary to the Geology Section). This was a very limited presence compared to that staged by his peers, at an event labelled Britain's 'Parliament of Science'.[22] In 1868 he joined his first BAAS Committee, the Kent's Cavern Exploration Committee (Chapter 2) and served as secretary to Section C (Geology) for 1869 and 1870. By 1871 he was a member of three committees, by 1874 four committees, and there was not a single year from 1868 to his death sixty-one years later that Dawkins was not a member of a BAAS committee. He sat on Council as regulations allowed: he was president of two different sections (Section D, Biology, for 1882 and Section C, Geology, for 1888), and served as vice-president for Section C, Section E (Geography) and Section H (Anthropology) a combined total of 12 times. The first in 1878, the last in 1919 in his 82nd year.

Like other members of the Victorian middle classes, Dawkins had a clear sense of responsibility (and superiority) to the working classes. He had a reputation as a skilled populariser of science, and a style that was informal but informing according to his friend Bonney.[23] He published accessible accounts of Pleistocene reindeer, bears, wolves and lions in the *Popular Science Review*, a 'Quarterly Miscellany of Entertaining and Instructive Articles on Scientific Subjects'.[24] Rich in information these offerings were 'popular' only in the sense that they excluded anatomical tedium. He also undertook reviews for the prestigious liberal magazine *The Edinburgh Review* including highly opinionated, critical and long assessments of books by Darwin and Lubbock and lectures by Huxley.[25]

Intriguingly, for a man whose working life was spent in the distant past, tracing the ebb and flow of living and extinct species, Dawkins had little time for Darwinian evolution. In his anonymous and scathing review of the *Descent of Man*,[26] Dawkins described natural selection as a 'hopelessly inadequate' and self-contradictory hypothesis that failed to explain the human body, brain, ear, eye, larynx, language, intellect, or much else. He was particularly vexed by the notion that natural selection had the power to originate new species, but conceded that it might act on pre-existing features to improve them. His opinion of Darwin's other key mechanism, sexual selection, whereby certain features arise to make mates more attractive to one another, was equally dismissive and he berated Mr Darwin for failing to produce a 'shadow of proof that sexual selection is capable of producing the changes…he attributes to it'.[27] Furthermore, where Darwin had provided case studies to illustrate his theory (I hesitate to say 'the proof'), Dawkins pedantically and myopically gainsaid them all, seeming incapable of absorbing the power of the whole and contenting himself instead with nitpicking at the minutiae. 'Never, perhaps in the history of philosophy, have such wide generalisations been derived from such a small basis of facts… this test of the truth of natural selection…has broken down at every point,' he concluded.[28] In sum, Dawkins rejected natural and sexual selection as speculative flights of fancy that would compete with the novel in the parlours and drawing rooms of Victorian England.

Bravely spoken from behind the cloak of anonymity, Dawkins' real motives for this scientific hubris are not difficult to find. He was horrified by Darwin's relegation of man to 'merely a superior sort of brute, the great Ruler of the world a mere shadow of ourselves projected by our own imagination' insisting that Darwin 'has not advanced any proof that we worship a God which is merely an expression of our own high mental activity, and not the cause of it'.[29] His antipathy towards Darwinism reflected the religious beliefs he received from his upbringing in Wales, and not his scientific training; ironically the Reverend Johnny Green thought it wonderful.[30] Green had actually been present at the infamous 1860 debate in Oxford between 'Darwin's bulldog' Thomas Huxley and the Bishop of Oxford 'soapy' Sam Wilberforce, and had written enthusiastically to Dawkins describing it.[31] In the end Dawkins sided with Alfred Russell Wallace, co-originator of the theory, believing humans to be outside of the scope of natural selection.

Another of Dawkins' convictions was the important role that museums could play in education, and he was an active advocate of public education, lecturing to audiences at Manchester Museum, local societies and public venues.[32] He wasted no time on arriving in Manchester. In 1870 he gave a '*Science Lectures for the People*' talk 'on coal' at Hulme Town Hall, and in 1872 a whole series on physiography at Altrincham School; a decade later he was still going strong. Dawkins' public lectures were much admired and very well attended and he was noted for his breezy accessible style; to his audience he projected an 'impression of warm humanity, of remarkable all-aliveness, and of fine courtesy', 'the happy frankness of the man [giving] cheer to many whose contacts with him were no more than casual'.[33] The archive in Buxton also contains numerous newspaper cuttings describing various geological 'ramblings' Dawkins led for students and interested others (including women) to explore local geological highlights, as well as syllabuses for evening classes from the 1880s and 1890s. These short courses usually comprised six to eight weekly or fortnightly lectures on Ancient Britain or the ancient history of the Earth, with associated practical demonstrations and field trips. These were delivered across the region, a select sample detailing courses at the Friend's Institute, Manchester, Stockport Grammar School, the Court Rooms at Worsley, the Withington Association and Leigh Technical School. Tickets were sold through local post-offices or co-operative stores. In the early days and in public assembly rooms, Dawkins would illustrate his lectures with large diagrams pinned over boards but by the 1890s he was proudly declaring the use of oxyhydrogen lantern slides in his University based presentations.[34] From the few surviving images from Dawkins' lectures, it appears that he may have initially drawn directly onto the 3-inch square transparencies (Figure 3.1).

Outside of education and academia, Dawkins campaigned to improve the working conditions of miners. After an explosion in a Wigan Colliery in 1869 killed twenty-seven men, Dawkins wrote to the *Pall Mall Gazette* lamenting

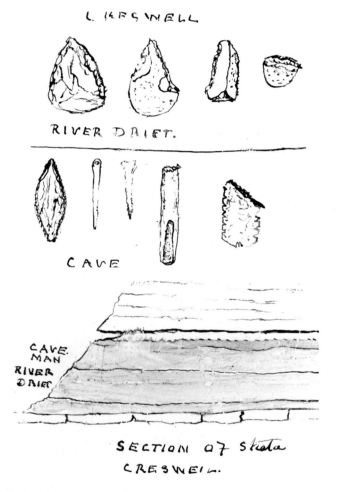

Figure 3.1: Dawkins' Lecture Illustrations, showing artefacts and sections from Creswell (British Museum Jacobi Archive, Courtesy of the Trustees of the British Museum).

the fact that explosions were such a regular occurrence that it was almost possible to predict the number of annual fatalities.[35] Most of these, he believed, were caused by poor conditions and poor training, especially in the misuse of the safety lamp, which actually ignited 'fire-damp' if opened or allowed to burn red hot. The best solution, he advised, would be improved ventilation in the mines.

Dawkins would become a true citizen of Manchester: a champion of the city, its university, its people and its industries. Yet he was often absent in the pursuit of other agendas,[36] sought advancement elsewhere at least twice, and while he may have exuded warmth and friendship when he chose, those who crossed him found a very different persona lurking just beneath the surface.

The Oxford and Cambridge Club

Dawkins' elevation to Professor of Geology at Owens College placed him among the elite ranks of British geology, and secured his future commitment to Manchester. His was one of a handful of Chairs, alongside key positions at Cambridge, Oxford, King's College London, University College London, Edinburgh, Sandhurst and the Royal School of Mines. In 1874 these were held by Thomas McKenny Hughes, John Phillips (1800-74), John Morris (1810-86), Peter Martin Duncan (1824-1891), Archibald Geikie (1835-1924), T. Rupert Jones (1819-1911) and Andrew Crombie Ramsey (1814-91), respectively, all of whom we have heard of or will hear of in coming chapters. Previous to his promotion, though, Dawkins had unsuccessfully applied for the Chairs at both Cambridge and Oxford.

When Adam Sedgwick (1785-1873) died on 27 January 1873, aged 87, the Woodwardian Chair of Geology at Cambridge became vacant for the first time in 55 years. By Statute of the University, a new appointment had to be made within one month,[37] so the following day the University announced that the election of his successor would take place at one o'clock in the afternoon of 20 February, giving candidates twenty-five days to promote their suitability.[38] Members of the University urged potential applicants to begin their campaigns early, stressing that the field was open and that votes were there for the taking. A panel of electors comprising Heads of House, Professors, University Examiners, and resident members of Senate would make the final decision.[39] It was also important to gain favour among the Colleges, particularly the larger and more powerful ones, in order to secure as far as possible the 'block vote', although fellows could be temperamental and difficult if they felt they were being coerced.[40] The game, then, was to gain favour with as many members of the electoral panel as possible, via any means possible, sometimes involving a direct approach by influential advocates, but more usually through testimonials. This left some in a difficult position, especially when asked to provide a testimonial by more than one candidate, which in many cases led to awkward refusals. To modern eyes the whole affair is squalid and unseemly, making the candidates and their supporters behave more like canvassing politicians than men of science, with all the whispering campaigns, diversionary tactics, back-stabbing and defamation of character we have come to expect of modern parliamentarians.

Other than Dawkins, eight geologists came forward to compete for the Woodwardian Chair, in alphabetical order these were:

1   Rev. Thomas George Bonney (1833-1923), Fellow and Tutor at St John's College, Cambridge where he lectured on geology. He was best known for his work on glacial and Alpine geology. In 1877 elected Professor of Geology at UCL.[41]

2   Rev. Peter Bellinger Brodie, formerly of Emmanuel College Cambridge and an authority on fossil insects. In 1873 Brodie was working as a cleric.[42]

3   Peter Martin Duncan, Professor of Geology at University College London and Lecturer at the Indian College of Civil Engineering at Cooper's Hill, best known for his work on fossil corals.[43]

4   Rev. Osmond Fisher (1817-1914), former Fellow and Tutor of Jesus College, Cambridge, who worked principally on mathematical models of the Earth's crust.[44]

5   Alexander Henry Green (1832-1896), Survey geologist and Lecturer in Geology at the School of Military Engineering at Chatham.[45]

6   Thomas McKenny Hughes of the Geological Survey, and alumnus of Trinity College Cambridge. Hughes had surveyed the Medway, parts of the Thames Valley, the Lake District, and at the time of the election was engaged in surveying north-west England.[46]

7   William King (1809-1886), Professor of Mineralogy and Geology at Queens College, Galway, expert on Permian palaeontology and the scientist who formally named the Neanderthals in 1864.

8   John Morris, Professor of Geology at King's College London, a renowned authority on Eocene and Jurassic rocks and author of *A Catalogue of British Fossils* (1843). He had acted as Deputy Woodwardian chair for two years prior to Sedgwick's death.[47]

Dawkins declared his candidature within the first week, and was one of three names listed in the *Pall Mall Gazette* on 3 February, alongside Bonney and Fisher.[48] By 7 February, Duncan, Green and Hughes had joined the race, with Morris (11 February) and King (15 February) entering late.[49] Most of the candidates withdrew before the polling began, another pulled out during the vote. Those interested in the fate of all the candidates are referred to Anne O'Connor's article, *The Competition for the Woodwardian Chair in Geology, Cambridge, 1873*;[50] here I am concerned only with the fortunes of William Boyd Dawkins.

In support of his candidature, Dawkins obtained testimonials from Charles Darwin, John Evans, William H. Flower, Edward A Freeman, Rev. Charles Kingsley (1819-1875, retired Professor of Modern History at Cambridge), John Lubbock, Joseph Prestwich, John Phillips, George Rolleston and J. G. Greenwood (1821-1894; Principal of Owens College).[51] Lyell, who favoured Hughes, refused Dawkins or anyone else a reference. Dawkins' colleagues and superiors at the Survey are notable by their absence. The list of names is impressive, but their testimonials are decidedly lacking in sparkle. While Darwin was certainly the mightiest name among them, his endorsement only ran as far as stating that Dawkins was 'very well fitted' to the Chair and that the study of the more recent periods was very difficult. He signed off by wishing Dawkins the best of success. Evans' testimonial also stated that Dawkins would be 'well fitted' to teaching geology, but specifically praised his knowledge of mammalian palaeontology and its relationship to humans, which he felt had gained Dawkins a European reputation. Phillips and Prestwich emphasised Dawkins' geological training, either at Oxford or with the Survey, but they too drew special attention to his palaeontological skills. The remaining testimonials said even less. Flower, Freeman, Rolleston, Greenwood and Lubbock all demurred or neglected to comment on Dawkins' geological savoir-faire, choosing instead to heap praise on his masterful command of mammalian palaeontology and/or museum curatorship. All undoubtedly had the best of intentions, but one cannot help feeling that they would have been more appropriate had the vacant Chair been in zoology or comparative anatomy, and as such did little to help his cause. As for Charles Kingsley, his reference could hardly have been more insipid: 'I have the highest opinion of your teaching powers. Your geological knowledge – especially of the latest epochs – is so much greater than mine that it would be an impertinence in me to praise it'. He may just have well acquiesced to Mary Lyell and supported Hughes instead.

Dawkins' poor reputation during his time at the Survey proved another detriment to his chances, which his detractors were keen to capitalise upon. Collectively the Survey, which favoured Hughes, had a powerful voice in the geological world and opinions from its members reached Cambridge through testimonials and private networks. Much of it was intended for the attention of Rev. Henry Luard (1825-1891), Registrary to the University of Cambridge, and little of it was complementary. One letter from the metaphysicist and Shakespeare scholar, Dr. Clement Mansfield Ingleby (1823-1886), citing Survey intelligence passed on by William Whitaker (1836-1925), began 'As this letter's rather slanderous you'd do well to burn it'.[52] It goes on to describe, as we have heard before, that Dawkins' time at the Survey was largely spent seeking preferment: 'So he got made F.R.S., & a good lectureship at Manchester. He's an impudent brute, & has been known to boast that he shall certainly succeed Sedgwick. That's W. Boyd Dawkins FRS & I hope & thank there's no fear of yr. having him.'[53] The fact that Dawkins was known to dabble as a consultant in industrial geology, an ignoble profession to some, was also frowned upon. He withdrew his candidature on 15 February, when it became clear that Hughes and Bonney were gaining an unassailable lead. It was probably no consolation at the time, but six weeks later, on 27 March, Dawkins was elected a Fellow of the Society of Antiquaries of London. In the end, Hughes won the chair. He had always been Sedgwick's preference to succeed him, and from the outset been championed by Charles Lyell and his energetic wife Mary. (Hughes would hold the Chair until his death in 1917, a total of forty-four years).

The following year saw another opportunity, although at a high personal cost. After dinner at All Souls College Oxford on the evening of 23 April 1874, John Phillips, Professor of Geology of 18 years, tripped over a mat at the top of a flight of fifteen stone steps and fell headfirst and backwards to the bottom.[54] He never regained consciousness and died of his injuries the following day. He was buried in York on 29 April, next to his beloved sister, Anne. Dawkins had lost his geological father, adding to the family's grief in a year that had already seen Frances Dawkins lose her biological father Robert Speke Evans, at the age of just sixty-three.

As in Cambridge, the vacancy sparked a competition to find a replacement. Dawkins, Phillips 'favourite' pupil, naturally declared his candidacy. Succeeding his mentor and champion, and taking up his 'rightful' place at Oxford, his alma mater, would have crowned Dawkins' career. He had strong support at home and abroad, the famed Swiss palaeontologist and zooarchaeologist Ludwig Rütimeyer (1825-1895) expressing hope that the importance of 'the history of life' would be recognised,[55] but both he and

Dawkins were to be disappointed. After all the candidates had declared their interest, after all the testimonials had been written, and with the hubbub of canvassing in full swing, the Vice-Chancellor of the University, Rev. Henry George Liddell (1811-1896), ignored them all and instead offered the Chair to Joseph Prestwich. Prestwich had never been a candidate for the post, and the offer came as a great surprise – he had even provided testimonials for two of the applicants.[56] His first thought was whether his health could stand the strain, but after taking advice from his doctor, Prestwich accepted the job on 23 June 1874. Dawkins' future lay in Manchester where (as we have seen) four months latter he was given his heart's desire – a professorship.

The Caverns of Wales
In Manchester, Dawkins found himself within striking distance of the limestone country of northern England and Wales, with its many caverns. For the first time since joining the Survey he was in the right place and with sufficient time to resume his cave hunting activities, the last major episode of which had been the disappointing work at Burrington Combe in 1864. Within weeks of his arrival he was elected a fellow of the Manchester Geological Society, and by December had been installed as an Honorary Secretary. Dawkins already had some friends among the fellowship and he would gain many more, but so too would come enemies, John Plant (1819-1892), curator of Peel Park Museum at Salford since 1849, being the most vocal and mettlesome amongst them. When or why this animosity arose is unclear, but as early as October 1870 Darbishire was looking forward to Dawkins' return from one of his trips so that the pair could go to Salford and 'dig up Plant'.[57]

The summer and autumn of 1869 saw Dawkins in Wales, exploring his old childhood haunt Offa's Dyke (with General Augustus Lane-Fox – later Pitt-Rivers) and the caves at Perthi Chwareu and Cefn in Denbighshire. The presence of fossiliferous caves on the northern limestone ridge at Perthi Chwareu, a farm house situated about ten miles east of Corwen and a mile to the west of the village of Llandegla, had been brought to Dawkins' attention by a box of bones sent by Charles Darwin, an association he no doubt delighted in revealing to his audience.[58] In fact, the two men were fairly frequent correspondents, exchanging books, ideas and views on a range of palaeontological topics from aurochs to rhinos,[59] and while Dawkins did not subscribe to natural selection it is obvious from his letters that the great naturalist awed him. It was to Darwin that Dawkins expressed his disdain for using captive animals as a comparative sample, as he had seen how captivity could cause skeletal changes. In the hyaena, for example, the prehensile character of the jaw was lost, the skull changed shape and the jaw became shortened – 'for purposes of comparison I find the bones of animals from menageries absolutely useless', he opined.[60]

The bones sent by Darwin were largely domesticated species, including dog, but Dawkins was excited by the prospect of a new bone cave and made a special detour to visit the area. Dawkins' account tells that after making enquiries he was given permission to excavate and the use of a free workforce by the landowner, Edward Lloyd.[61] Judging from Lucas' detailed reconstruction of events, however, the whole venture was more likely instigated and organised by Mrs. Lloyd, who then asked Dawkins to visit.[62] The excavation was rather unrewarding, yielding more bones but no artefacts to constrain their age. Undeterred, Dawkins decided that they were the remains of a 'refuse heap' left by prehistoric people.

The crew then turned their attention to another cave lower down the rock face but this too gave up nothing of note. Probably disheartened and no doubt a little bored, Dawkins left the men to their work and walked across the valley to the southern limestone ridge, where he found a small rock shelter overlooking the valley that seemed a likely prospect to have been inhabited by prehistoric people.[63] Dawkins set the team to work, immediately finding mammalian remains similar to those sent by Darwin. As they continued to dig they began to find human remains between and underneath a mass of rocks and on removing this obstruction they discovered a low, narrow cave filled to the brim with red silt and sand. At this point Dawkins was 'compelled to go away', but the work was carried on by Mrs Lloyd, superintended by a Mr Reid. The cave was excavated to a distance of 28 ft from the entrance in the space of six days, producing more human remains, bones of domesticated animals, and a broken flint flake; near the entrance they also found recent glazed pottery and coal which had probably been introduced by burrowing animals. The human remains belonged to at least sixteen individuals of all ages and both sexes, with heavily worn teeth and platycnemic tibia that gave them 'bandy-legs'.[64] Dawkins concluded that the cave had been used as a tomb over a long period of time and although he was unable to date it based on the finds, by comparison with other burials he attributed it to the Neolithic. While these explorations were taking place, news reached Dawkins that human remains had been accidentally discovered in a cairn at Tyddyn Bleiddyn, near Cefn, which he excavated later that same year with Mrs Williams Wynn, Rev. D.R. Thomas (vicar of Cefn) and Rev. H.H. Winwood.

North Wales held a strong attraction for Dawkins and between 1869-1872 he spent four successive seasons exploring its caves. It was most definitely not all work: 'I am off for Easter to Wales, where I fish in the Elwy for salmon & trout, and in caves ... for more bones,' he told John Phillips in March 1871.[65] At Perthi Chwareu the team ultimately discovered five 'sepulchral' caves within a few hundred yards of the original 'refuse heap', all containing crouched burials.[66] Dawkins named them Cave No. 1, Cave No. 2, Cave Rhosdigre No. 1, Cave Rhosdigre No. 2 and Cave Rhosdigre No. 3, but sadly failed to provide an adequate plan of the valley. As local place names have changed the individual caves cannot now be re-identified with certainty,[67] but Cave Rhosdigre No 1 did produce a beautiful Neolithic polished-stone greenstone axe, confirming Dawkins' suspicions of a prehistoric age for the burials (Figure 3.2). In 1871 a second chamber was discovered at Tyddyn Bleiddyn, excavated by the team of Dawkins, Thomas and Winwood. Similarities between the skeletons of the cairns and the caves suggested to Dawkins that the same people had buried their dead in both.[68]

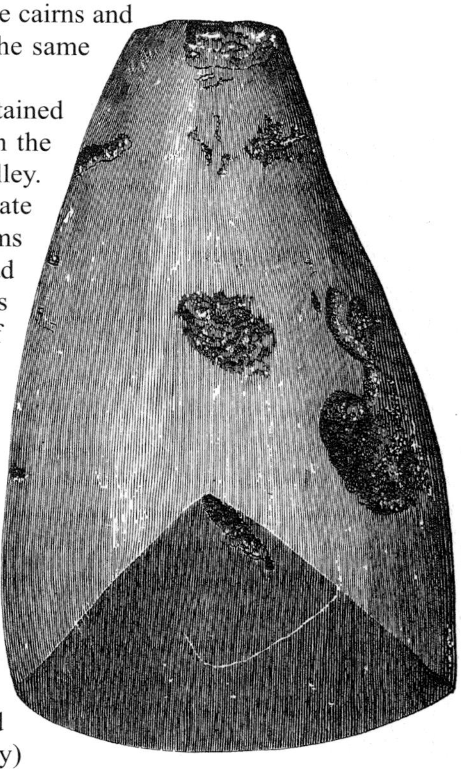

The Williams Wynn estate also contained the famous Cefn Caves, located within the Carboniferous limestone of the Elwy Valley. Originally part of Edward Lloyd's estate (passing to his heiress Mrs Anna Williams Wynn, nee Lloyd, d.1926),[69] the caves had been included in an early 1800s landscaping project in the grounds of Cefn Hall, which had created steps and paths, modified rock outcrops to create scenic walks, and opened up their entrances. This had exposed fossiliferous deposits, which were used for fertiliser before they attracted the attention of collectors. Charles Darwin and Adam Sedgwick had visited whilst on a geological tour in 1831, the latter finding a rhinoceros tooth, and in 1832 the Reverend Edward Stanley (1779-1849; later Bishop of Norwich and President of the Linnaean Society) collected bones from the fields and excavated inside the cave, sending his finds

Figure 3.2: Greenstone Axe from Wales (after Dawkins 1874a).

to William Buckland at Oxford. Lloyd eventually amassed a large collection, which Lord Enniskillen had urged Dawkins to examine in 1865 (Falconer had already seen it, in 1859).[70] Dawkins finally did this during his 1869 trip, after which he became a regular visitor to the Williams Wynn's home; his diaries record nine visits between 1870-1877, some of which lasted ten days.[71] Precisely what Dawkins did in the Cefn Caves is unknown, beyond a single reference in *Cave Hunting* to a deposit of comminuted (crushed) bone he had examined in 1872. What we do know is that Dawkins was confused about which finds came from which cave. His version contradicted the original accounts of Stanley and is in error, but is still the most often cited.[72]

Half a mile upstream of the Cefn caverns sits Pontnewydd Cave[73]. First noted by Stanley in 1832, who remarked that that it had never been opened,[74] it remained untouched for decades. The first excavation on record involved Dawkins, although his report in *Cave Hunting* could hardly have been more superficial: 'The same group of animals [as at Cefn] has been obtained by Mrs Williams Wynn, the Rev. D.R. Thomas and myself out of a horizontal cave at the head of a defile leading down from Cefn to Pont Newydd, in which the remains are embedded in a stiff clay, consisting of rearranged boulder clay, and are in the condition of waterworn boulders. From it I have identified the brown, grizzly and cave-bear'.[75] These seventy words tell us almost nothing. It does not even say when Dawkins was at the cave, although it must have been prior to 1874, because Hughes had started excavations by then.

When McKenny Hughes and Rev. Thomas began their work at Pontnewydd in 1874, they noted that 25 yards of sediment had already been removed from the cave.[76] This has often been assumed to have been largely Dawkins' doing.[77] That Hughes and Thomas found felstone artefacts and a human tooth in the spoil thrown out by earlier workers is certainly consistent with the supposition that Dawkins was involved. As one critic would later remark '…Boyd Dawkins… Same old tale! Pick axe and Shovel! Nothing smaller than a horse. It was always the same. He never [worked?] material as it should have been, so that he never got any small things. I have sent my friends and students behind him in the Caves and they have recovered lots of the small vertebrates, and from one of the most important Caves one of my friends brought me out of material rejected by B.D. human toe bones!'[78]

Yet there are good reasons to believe that Dawkins has been unfairly accused of despoiling the entrance to Pontnewydd. In the opening sentence of their first report, Hughes and Thomas stated in perfectly plain terms and with no room for misunderstanding that it was the landowner Mr Williams Wynn who had partly excavated the cave 'some years ago'. This refers to

Herbert Watkin Williams Wynn (1822-1862), husband of Anna, which dates the work to sometime before his death in 1862. They did not mention Dawkins once in relation to earlier clearances. Thomas would surely have known the full extent of Dawkins' involvement, having dug with him on the one occasion we can be certain Dawkins was present – the episode described in *Cave Hunting*. Given the association of Thomas and Mrs Williams Wynn with the region and its archaeology, we might justifiably assume that Dawkins was not the principal investigator but had briefly joined the other two in an exploration they had been conducting for some years.[79] It was therefore not his right nor responsibility to publish the details. Judging by his phenomenal output, he would certainly have published a full account had he been in charge, and if he had been the first to explore the cave, he would not have been shy in saying so. It also seems unlikely he would have relinquished this promising prospect to Hughes, or if politically obliged to do so had not insisted on forming a BAAS Committee to retain an influence. I suspect that the level of Dawkins' involvement at Pontnewydd has been exaggerated, probably because he had undeniably been involved and his widely known slapdash fieldwork made him an obvious target for criticism.

Hughes, originally from Aberystwyth, maintained a strong presence in North Wales from 1870 onwards, excavating at least two other caves at Galtfaenan and Plas Heaton, for which Dawkins identified the fauna. These caves yielded a fairly typical suite of Pleistocene animals that included wolf, bison, reindeer, horse, hyaena and cave-bear but Plas Heaton also yielded a jaw bone of wolverine: a very rare animal that had previously only been found as isolated canines in three British caves at Banwell, Bleadon and Gower.[80] Dawkins was delighted with the find. The new discovery removed any doubts concerning his earlier identifications or the beast's Pleistocene credentials, and he used it to bolster his seasonal migration hypothesis. It was also Hughes who instigated formal excavations at Victoria Cave, Settle, a pursuit destined to bring Dawkins into conflict with one of his old Survey friends.

To the Caverns of Northern England
Victoria Cave, near Settle, North Yorkshire, sits at the base of a 250 ft high cliff in the Carboniferous limestone of Ribblesdale, in a 'lonely' ravine known as King's Scar.[81] It is a horizontal solution fissure that in the mid-1800s comprised three ill-defined chambers filled almost to the roof with sediment (Figure 3.3). In front of the entrances, facing south-west, the ground sloped steeply away towards a glacially modified dry valley beneath, the

Figure 3.3: Victoria Cave (C), elevation and section (after Dawkins 1874a, 82.A & B are Albert Cave).

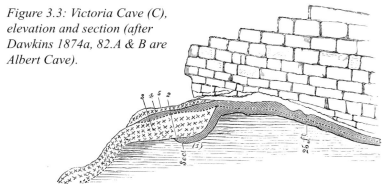

slope being covered by a coarse talus created by weathering of the cliff.[82] The cave was first discovered on 28 June 1838 – Queen Victoria's Coronation Day – by a local plumber and glazier named Joseph Jackson (1816-1886), who patriotically named the cave in honour of the new monarch. Or so the story goes. Typically, the story is apocryphal. The outer chamber of the cave was actually discovered in the spring of 1837 by Michael Horner, a tinsmith and mechanic employed by Jackson.[83] Horner showed Jackson artefacts he had collected from the cave, and took him there a few weeks later;[84] Jackson then discovered the inner chamber in June 1837, the month of Victoria's ascension.

Jackson began excavating the cave in the autumn of 1837 and continued on-and-off until the 1860s, in the process finding a wealth of Roman and 'Celtic' artefacts, the remains of food animals and the occasional bone or tooth of Pleistocene hyaena. In 1840 Jackson enlisted the help of the antiquarian Charles Roach Smith (1807-1890), and together they published the results of the work in *Collectanea Antiqua*,[85] a subscription journal dedicated to historical archaeology that just happened to be compiled and largely written by Smith himself. During this long period of activity the cave naturally attracted attention from local geologists, the wealthy landowner James Farrar and banker John Birkbeck amongst them, and national figures such as William Buckland (who identified the hyaena remains). By 1869, the scientific reputation of Victoria Cave and neighbouring caverns was such that Hughes proposed forming a committee to oversee formal investigations.[86] A prospectus was drawn up, which stated that 'it had long been known, that in the district of Craven there are many bone caves, and it has been thought desirable to organise a thorough and systematic exploration of them. From the report of those who have visited the Caves, there is reason to hope that discoveries of great scientific interest may be made'.[87] The Committee comprised twenty-three men, among them nationally renowned scientists and politicians: Sir James P. Kay Shuttleworth (Chairman), Sir Charles Lyell, Sir John Lubbock, Rev. Prof. Adam Sedgwick, Prof. John Phillips, A.H. Lane-Fox, William Boyd Dawkins and U.J.K. Shuttleworth (son of J.P. and MP for Hastings). The remaining 16 members were all local geologists and natural historians, and included James Farrar, John Birkbeck, Rev. G. Style (Headmaster of Giggleswick Grammar School) and the landowner Thomas Stackhouse.

As Dawkins was the only member of the committee with any experience in cave exploration, he was the obvious choice to oversee the excavations, although the day-to-day running of the work was left to Jackson and team of paid labourers. It is worth noting that despite Dawkins' involvement, Kay Shuttleworth wrote to William Pengelly asking for advice concerning excavation methods[88] and in March 1870 Joseph Jackson visited Kent's Cavern to familiarise himself with Pengelly's mode of operation. Pengelly's system involved laying a datum across each chamber, from front to back,

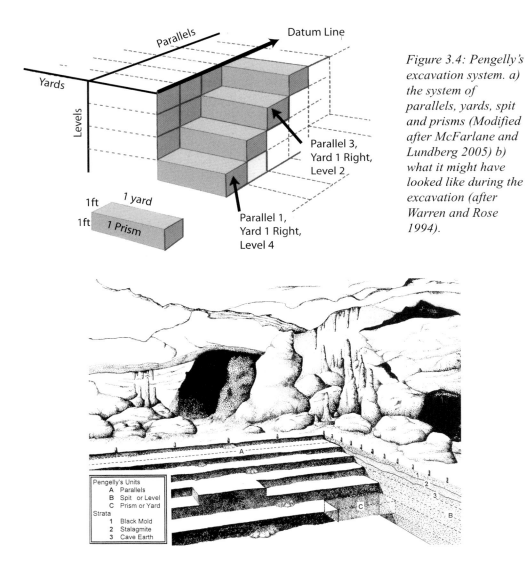

Figure 3.4: Pengelly's excavation system. a) the system of parallels, yards, spit and prisms (Modified after McFarlane and Lundberg 2005) b) what it might have looked like during the excavation (after Warren and Rose 1994).

forming a baseline from which to divide the area of the cave into a number of standard units (see Figure 3.4). From the datum, lines 1 ft apart were extended at right angles, forming a series of 'parallels'. Each parallel was divided along its length into stretches 3 ft long, termed 'yards', the resulting 3 ft x 1 ft area being excavated down in a series of discrete 1 ft 'levels'. In this fashion, the excavation removed a series of 3ft x 1ft x 1ft blocks, which Pengelly labelled 'prisms'. The finds from each prism were given individual numbers and stored together in wooden boxes, with the location recorded according to its parallel, yard and level. As crude as it might seem today, this was highly advanced for its time, and was justly celebrated.[89]

A variation on this method was certainly used at Victoria Cave during Richard Hill Tiddeman's (1842-1917) tenure as director, another Survey man whose study area included Yorkshire. Tiddeman's team used 2 ft parallels and marked each bone with the year, find number, parallel number, distance from the datum left or right, and depth.[90] Photography was also used for the first time to record a cave excavation, with copious images being taken by Anthony Horner, showing the work as it progressed.

The inaugural season's excavations (1870) began in the mouth of Chamber A, cutting a trench and removing the talus into the black layer that had previously produced Romano-British and Celtic objects (Plate 6). This provided headroom and allowed daylight to flood into Chamber A where work began along a series of 2 ft parallels across the width of the chamber.[91] The first season's excavations ran from mid-March to the end of December, during which time Dawkins visited on only a handful of occasions.[92] When he did deign to visit, he decided that things were not moving fast enough and, deviating from the agreed method, sunk a deep shaft instead.

Reporting the results of the excavations, Dawkins described a 'strange' mix of luxury objects – elaborately carved bone utensils and Roman samian ware – alongside hearth debris, domestic refuse, animal bones and 'rough implements of daily use'.[93] Late fourth century coins were also found, leading Dawkins to conclude (as Jackson and Roach had done earlier) that the site was a refuge for a wealthy family who fled their villa to escape the 'barbarian hordes' streaming into Britain from the north and east at that time. Beneath the black layer was another scree, at the base of which occurred flint flakes, bear bones and a biserial bone harpoon, all of which Dawkins assigned to the Neolithic.[94] This layer was in fact a Late Glacial bone deposit formed largely by wolf denning, and the biserial bone harpoon late Upper Palaeolithic in age, but it had been disturbed during the Neolithic and Bronze Age when domestic and other extant animals had become mixed into it. Had Dawkins correctly identified the presence of reindeer in the same layer,[95] he would have surely been alerted to the true age of the deposit or at least the possibility of mixing, but he mentioned only red deer and roe deer. The omission is perplexing, but it would not be the first time Dawkins had misidentified specimens. I doubt it was deliberate – it did not threaten his seasonality model (see below), he had no vested interest in the material being Neolithic, and he was always willing to acknowledge admixture when it suited him. I suspect he was thrown by the abundance of domestic animals, working through the material at such a pace that he saw what he expected to see, not what was there. Dawkins made other mistakes, confusing the provenance of a Romano-British bead from Chamber B and attributing it instead to his Neolithic deposit at the cave entrance. When he subsequently illustrated this find as coming from the Neolithic layer, everybody became confused. Jackson, who kept very good records (although the 1870-1873 records are mysteriously missing) must have known that Dawkins' report was wrong, but he did not speak up, possibly out of deference, possibly because he feared losing his position.[96]

Inside the cave the beds below the Roman and 'Neolithic' layers consisted of an upper cave earth and a lower cave-earth, separated by up to 12 ft of laminated clay. Ever the master of the quick result, Dawkins could not wait to reach the bottom of the clay, and sunk a 25 ft shaft through it into the Lower Cave Earth. He found no trace of human or animal activity and failed to reach the bottom, but on resuming proper excavations in 1872, the team were rewarded with a Pleistocene fauna including hyaena, red deer, and cave bear, 16 ft into the Lower Cave Earth and close to the cave's entrance.[97] Moving to the mouth of the cave the team discovered boulder clay resting on the edges of this hyaena bed, the stratification of the two beds showing that the bone bed was deposited first – in other words, it appeared to be pre-glacial.[98] Tiddeman later deduced that the clays had been formed by a moraine or ice sheet blocking the cave entrance, allowing water to trickle in from melting ice, the fine laminations representing the quotidian rhythms of daily thaws and nightly freezes.[99] On a purely theoretical level, Dawkins could not agree, regardless of what the evidence in front of him said.

For the first three years, the excavation had no official source of income but depended on private finances drawn from subscription; hence the prospectus. Large sums came from John Birkbeck, who wanted the finds to go the Giggleswick School Museum.[100] This changed in 1873, when the explorations were awarded a grant from the BAAS, a development no doubt linked to the discovery of a curious tibia in the same bed as the Pleistocene mammals, which after long deliberation Busk declared on 7 October was 'no doubt human'.[101] This was a total game changer – human fossils associated with extinct fauna that might just be pre-glacial – and raised the possibility that more human fossils might be brought out of Victoria Cave, perhaps even skulls. The money came at a price, for the original Settle Cave Exploration Committee found themselves overrun by a new panel appointed by the BAAS. There was no room on this body for Kay Shuttleworth or other local gentlemen, only the scientific elite – Lubbock, Phillips, Hughes, Dawkins and Miall, with Tiddeman as secretary. The award for 1873 and 1874 was £50 per year, raised to £100 for each of the years 1875-1877, which put Victoria Cave on an equal footing with Kent's Cavern in terms of official finances, with additional monies continuing to come from subscriptions.

The May 1873 season concentrated on the bone bed, but met with poor results,[102] after which Dawkins resigned as superintendent citing pressures of work. Unable to give it up entirely he retained his position on the exploration committee. Richard Tiddeman took over the running of the excavations, remaining in charge until 1878 when the BAAS cut the funding. The site was abandoned, the sections crumbled where Tiddeman had left them, lost to science for the best part of a century.[103] However, Victoria Cave was to play one more significant part in Dawkins' story, as one of the chief battlegrounds upon which the wars of the glacial succession were played out. We will return to this at the end of the chapter.

While much of Dawkins' cave hunting has the appearance of a sedate gentleman's pursuit, idling away the hours at the front of a cavern while workmen toiled by candlelight inside, some of his exploits bordered on the reckless. In 1871 he explored the caverns around Ingleborough in Yoredale, which included a nightmarish descent into Helnpot:

'I must tell you that into Helnpot a stream of water pours from the surface … and also that a stream of water flows through an accessory cave, until it arrives also at the pot-hole and descends in the form of a stream … We arranged our descent by having two large logs of timber stretched across [the] chasm. Then we had a platform placed upon them. Then we had a windlass and a cage with a kind of shelter over the top to deaden the weight and force of the water which would fall upon those going down. Very unfortunately the place where we were obliged to go down from the form of the fissure was where we had the water pouring on our heads most of the way down. There were thirteen of us who ventured down, including three ladies, who were rather braver than the generality of their sex … When we came to the bottom … we found ourselves in the bed of a torrent which leapt downwards, forming a series of cascades, until at last we came to a place where the fall was very considerable, something like 18-20 feet. At this fall we found our ladders were too short to reach from the top to the bottom. We were therefore obliged to let the ladder down, and the five of us who ventured further were let over by a rope till we got footing on the uppermost round of the ladder … the secretary of the Alpine Club was with us, and he was brave enough to be the first to venture down into [the] lower part, where unfortunately he met with an accident. We gave him rather too much rope, and when we let him down a few feet he found we had let him into a deep pool of water, in which his torch was put out'.[104] (Figure 3.5).

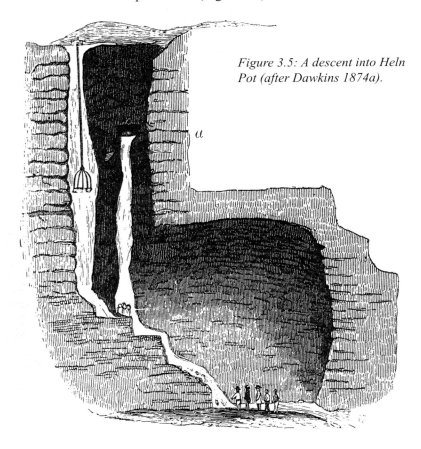

Figure 3.5: A descent into Heln Pot (after Dawkins 1874a).

The current from the falling streams was so great that when the rest of the party descended their torches were similarly extinguished. All this for a six-page article that explained how the caves had formed by a combination of underground rivers and chemical solution, and some speculations on the rate of stalagmite formation.[105] If nothing else Dawkins was dedicated to his science.

Windy Knoll is a 'wild and cheerless place' situated on a ' dreary upland' near the top of the Winnats Pass, immediately south-west of Mam Tor and just outside the Peak District village of Castleton, Derbyshire.[106] Although Dawkins was not the chief protagonist, he did excavate there in 1876, and it remains a useful case study into the machinations of the local scientific communities of Victorian England. Two people claimed to have discovered the site – Dawkins' friend Rooke Pennington (1844-1887) and his old adversary John Plant. Dawkins initially took no side and congratulated both men for a most wonderful discovery, until one of the claimants made the fundamental error of criticising the great Professor, with predictable results.

John Plant was the first to describe the site, at the 28 April 1874 meeting of the MGS.[107] Plant told how two young men, Henry Hindshaw and Ethelbert Ramsbottom, were hunting the hills around Castleton for fossils and plants when they exposed part of a long fissure, some 3-4 ft wide, with bones sticking out from among clay and limestone. They cleared away some loose earth and recovered a number of large bones from a cemented breccia, including a frontal bone of a bovid complete with horn cores. The pair took the bones to Plant at Salford Museum, who sent some drawings to Dawkins for identification. They visited the site again on the 18 April, and on 25 April Plant accompanied them to the quarry, where he collected bones and made sketches and sections of the geology. Plant made no claim to priority, but noted that bones had often been found there in the past and that the quarrymen, assuming them to be modern, had sent them to a bone mill. The Chairman, Joseph Dickinson, supported this, saying that he had personally found bones at the locality many years earlier. On Plant's request Dawkins stood up and expounded on the fossils, the sheer volume of which, he said, had taken him by surprise. Bison dominated, with smaller numbers of reindeer and roe deer. Dawkins drew particular attention to the high frequency of vertebrae, which suggested to him that the hyaena had not been present to destroy them. In closing Dawkins expressed his personal gratitude to the 'gentlemen who were enterprising enough to discover this place, and who took the trouble to carry these bones all the way from Castleton to Chapel-en-le-Frith,'[108] but not before shamelessly plugging his own discovery of mammoth and woolly rhinoceros in another freshly discovered cave at Gelly (or Hartle) Dale, which he had explored with Rooke Pennington and John Tym (1829-1901).

The latter two are recurring characters, so it is worth introducing them. Rooke Pennington was born in Leeds on 2 October 1844. He studied law at Wesley College, Sheffield, where he graduated in 1866 with a degree conferred by the University of London; in 1868 he was called to the bar.[109] He first practiced law in Manchester, but moved in 1870 to Bolton where he became a partner in the solicitor's firm of Ramwell, Pennington and Hindle.[110] An ardent Conservative, Pennington was no stranger to controversy, his alleged (and denied) comment that if the President of the Board of Trade, Joe Chamberlain, was stabbed in the park it would be his just desserts, was even discussed in the Commons.[111]

During the 1870s Pennington acquired a number of properties in Castleton, and in 1876 established a private museum there run by John Tym, a local fossil and mineral dealer. Tym had been born in Castleton in 1829 and had previously been the lessee of Speedwell Cavern.[112] To gain entrance to the museum, one had to pass through Tym's spa and marble shop, which highlights just how long museums have been using that particular enticement. Pennington was elected as a member of the Geological Society of London in 1875, and of the Manchester Geological Society in 1877, no doubt sponsored on both occasions by his friend Dawkins, whom he had known since at least 1870. The two were obviously close: Pennington dedicated his 1877 book *Notes on the Barrows and Bone-Caves of Derbyshire* to Dawkins, and when Dawkins embarked on a round-the-world tour in 1875, it was to Pennington that he entrusted his will.[113]

Pennington put the contents of the museum up for sale in 1883, and began to disperse his own collection, auctioning off his china, books, engravings, curios, minerals and shells through Hayhurst and Taylor of Bolton, presumably because the costs of housing and maintaining it had become burdensome.[114] The contents of the museum remained unsold until after his death in 1887, however, eventually being put up as a single lot in 1888 when it was bought by Bolton Museum. Tym left Castleton to take up the curatorship of Stockport Museum in 1885. Pennington died on 5 July 1887; probate records shows a personal fortune of £6,873 5s 3d left to his widow Clara Grace and their daughter. To this was added the proceeds of the many properties Pennington owned in Castleton, sold in seven lots at auction on 12 June 1888, raising a total of £729 12s 6d.

Pennington's account of the Windy Knoll discovery is the same story viewed from a different angle. He described how, in October 1870, he was in the Windy Knoll Quarry when he noticed a large tibia projecting through some debris.[115] He extracted the bone and took it to Dawkins, who identified it as aurochs (wild cattle; although on being presented with a larger sample, he revised this to bison). At that time, it had been impossible for Pennington to explore the site further because the position of the fissure meant that it could not be worked without removing the rock that supported it, which would have interfered with the quarrying operations.[116] (Figure 3.6) As a compromise, Pennington struck up an understanding with workmen and obtained the consent of the proprietor to collect fossils, which he did from time to time. Four years went by until 2 April 1874, the day before Good Friday, when the workmen saved a number of bones from an earth fall and placed them in a basket. Unfortunately, they forgot to deliver them to Castleton, and the following day 'some men from Manchester' (i.e. Hindshaw and Ramsbottom) carried them off; they returned on at least two occasions and according to Pennington caused considerable damage by pulling soil away.[117]

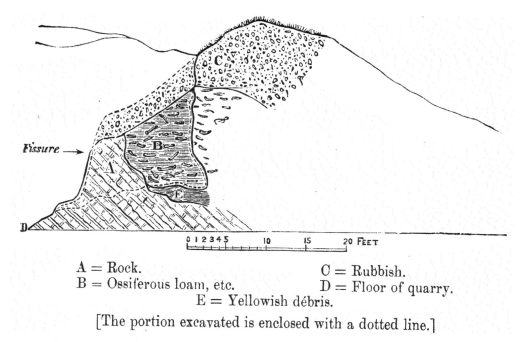

A = Rock.
B = Ossiferous loam, etc.
C = Rubbish.
D = Floor of quarry.
E = Yellowish débris.

[The portion excavated is enclosed with a dotted line.]

Figure 3.6: Geological Section at Windy Knoll (after Pennington, 1875, 243).

Later the same month, Pennington began work on the fissure, and in May 1874 spent two weeks at the site with John Tym and four labourers who were kept 'constantly' at work. There is no record of Dawkins' participating in the excavations, the competition for the Oxford Chair, the last push on his book *Cave Hunting*, and the death of his father-in-law, Robert Speke Evans, probably kept him occupied elsewhere. Pennington and Tym first removed surface material and debris from behind the retaining rock wall, the wall itself was then removed by blasting to expose the sediments. The surface material produced nothing, but in the fissure fill, 4 ft below the surface, they found an astonishing quantity of bones – bison, reindeer, bear, wolves – all mingled together in an unstructured mass. The uppermost part of the fill was a wet sticky loam containing rotten bones that were difficult to extract, but lower down this changed to a limestone breccia resting on angular limestone gravel, where the bones were in almost perfect condition. As they worked on, the fissure expanded to form a basin filled with clay, bones and rock fragments, which Pennington surmised was an older water swallow. The work was not pleasant: 'it seemed impossible to go within a quarter of a mile of the place without being bespattered. Not white mud, not the quick-drying limestone, but good sturdy not-to-be-brushed-off yellow clay, converted by half-an-hour's rain into a miry slough, and not to be persuaded into friableness by any amount of sunshine'.[118]

Pennington and Tym returned to the site in the spring of 1876, this time accompanied by Dawkins and a team of experienced miners.[119] Under the direction of Tym the workforce took six weeks to dig out the basin, their wages and other sundries funded by Pennington and the Manchester Museum. Bones were recovered in anatomical articulation, the animals having fallen to their death when the fissure was open. Some of the bones were smashed, presumably by rock falls. Dawkins concluded that the clay had formed an impervious layer that caused ponding, animals crowding round the resultant watering hole, some drowning in its depth, others becoming mired. He conjectured that the site was located on a major Pleistocene migration route at the head of Winnats Pass, which afforded free passage from the Derwent Valley to the plains of Lancashire and Cheshire, and used the age profile of young animals to suggest that different species passed through at different times – bison in the summer-autumn, reindeer in the winter-spring.[120] At the base of the sequence was yellow limestone debris, beneath which a vertical fissure extended into the void. Dawkins speculated that further work would reveal a cave, although Pennington never believed that such a cavern existed.[121]

Ultimately Dawkins identified several thousand bones from Windy Knoll, 3500 from Pennington's collection plus those provided by Plant. He made one (known) mistake, erroneously identifying a bear sacrum as that of a young bison. As we have seen above, Dawkins was by his own admission perhaps not entirely comfortably with the *Ursidae*, but when Plant rather gleefully challenged him on it, Dawkins refused to admit any error. He took the bone back for re-examination, and before returning it defiantly wrote on it 'Bison, W.B.D'. He also publicly reaffirmed his original opinion before the Manchester Literary and Philosophical Society in October 1874,[122] where he accused Plant of making use of a 'fancied resemblance' to the sacrum of a bear in conjunction with two analytically useless tooth stumps. Not to be deterred, Plant pressed on with his belief that the sacrum was bear, and specifically cave bear. He sought a wide range of opinions, including William Davies of the Zoological Department of the British Museum. All came back with the same answer – bear, perhaps cave bear. In February he showed it to the godfather of British palaeontology – Sir Richard Owen – who also declared it a bear. If that pill were not bitter enough, Owen is quoted as saying: 'no palaeontologist who had ever made this comparison could risk the mistaking of a bear's sacrum for one of a bovine quadruped'.[123] Dawkins was finally forced to concede the issue, but did so with ill grace.[124] He insisted that the matter had no scientific interest, and that the real question was whether it was cave bear as Plant believed, or brown bear as the freshly converted Dawkins insisted. Sneaking around in the background, Dawkins contacted Busk and Davies, and got them to admit that it was not possible to identify a bear to species based on the sacrum alone; Davies vowing that had he known that the diagnostic jaws and dentition from the site were probably brown bear, he would never have dreamed of suggesting that the sacrum was cave bear. Once again, Dawkins claimed a dubious triumph.

Describing the competing claims for the discovery of Windy Knoll five years later, Thomas Heath (1838-1886), of whom we will hear much more in the following chapters, remarked:

'With the rival claims for the priority of this important discovery I have nothing to do. It is alleged that it was made by Mr. Rooke Pennington in 1870. If so, it is a great misfortune for science that he was unable to work it out before 1874, since considerable depredations were committed by farmers and quarrymen—by the former, who are stated to have carted the bones away for manure, and by the latter, some of whom informed me they had been in the habit for years of carrying them home for the "owd 'oman to sell ta'te ragman for a pint o' beer"…The first intimation the public received of this find was in a paper read on April 28th, 1874, before that remarkably intelligent and impartial Society,[125] locally known as the Manchester Geological Society, by my friend Mr John Plant, F.G.S., curator of the Royal Museum, Salford, to whom several students from Owen's College had taken a number of bones for identification. Messrs Pennington and Dawkins' first paper was read before the Geological Society, at Burlington House, May, 1875. Who first recognised the real scientific value of this important and fertile fissure is mere hypothesis, but to Mr Plant and the students, undoubtedly, belong whatever honour there may be in being the first to make it known to the scientific world; an honour that is enhanced by their perfect ignorance of Mr. Pennington's alleged previous discovery in 1870'.[126]

The final chapter in the Victorian explorations of Windy Knoll is farcical. In 1879 the *Manchester City News* published letters from a mysterious correspondent who identified himself only as 'T.E.' T.E. disputed the age of the Windy Knoll fossils, arguing that the bison were just modern oxen, the supposed wolves nothing more than domestic dogs, and the reindeer part of a modern herd roaming the High Peak. As for the bear bones, these were the tragic remains of animals who had been used for baiting in the recent past, their carcasses dragged up to Windy Knoll and thrown down a swallow hole. T.E. added to the insult by expressing his high regard for Messrs Plant and Heath, who by this time were *personae non gratae* within Dawkins' inner circle (see Chapters 4-7). Pennington responded to these ludicrous claims in the only manner possible, tongue-in-cheek.[127] He thanked T.E. for shattering the reputations of half the geologists in the country, a confederacy of dunces which the British public were fool enough to credit with some authority, and for revealing himself, undoubtedly the worlds greatest palaeontologist, to the populace. 'Unveil yourself to an admiring universe,' Pennington entreated. He also thanked T.E. for alerting him to the phantom reindeer of the High Peak, which would undoubtedly delight hunters who would no longer have to trek to Norway for their sport but could simply step off the Midland Railway. He did, however, point out basic errors in the length of time taken for the fissure to fill, and the fact that the animals were most definitely not the usual kind found in the district, even if it were true that cows and other beasts occasionally fell down holes and over precipices in hilly regions. He also noted that some of T.E's lucubrations echoed opinions voiced by Plant many years earlier. It is clear from the tone that Pennington could not take T.E. seriously, but through the jokes felt compelled to rebut his nonsense lest some member of the public thought it held any merit. The initials T.E. are curious and probably subterfuge. The whole affair reeks of artifice, and I would not be at all surprised if John Plant were not behind it, chuckling maliciously to himself from Salford.

Cave Hunting

In October 1874 Dawkins' first book was published – *Cave Hunting: Researches on the Evidence of Caves Respecting the Early Inhabitants of Europe* – the culmination of fifteen years study into the caves and cave deposits of Europe. Dawkins dedicated the volume to Baroness Angela Burdett-Coutts, who had endowed his geology scholarship at Oxford all those years earlier, a nice touch but for the tang of vainglory in his words: 'a slight acknowledgement from her first scholar'. A lovely octavo volume, bound in brown cloth with an impressed woodcut of stalactites and stalagmites from the Fairy Chamber on Caldey Island, Wales, on the front board and a bronze bracelet from Thor's Cave on the spine. *Cave Hunting* came in at a weighty 455 pages, 129 illustrations and twenty-six tables.

The book is divided into twelve chapters covering the prehistoric and Palaeolithic periods (with a brief excursion into Romano-Celtic material), and tackling key issues such as archaeology, palaeontology, palaeogeography and climate:

1   Introduction
2   Physical history of caves
3   Historic caves in Britain
4   Caves used in the ages of Iron and Bronze
5   Caves of the Neolithic Age
6   The range of Neolithic Dolicho-cephali and Brachy-cephali
7   Caves containing human remains of doubtful age
8   The Pleistocene caves of Germany and Great Britain
9   The inhabitants of the caves of north-western Europe, and the evidence of the fauna as to the Atlantic coast-line
10 The fauna of the caves of southern Europe, and the evidence as to the Mediterranean coast-line in the Pleistocene age
11 The European climate in the Pleistocene Age
12 Conclusion

In these chapters, Dawkins covered every *major* cave find then known, those he explored personally being given lengthy treatment (especially Victoria Cave), those derived from published sources often treated more cursorily but no less critically. Such is the sweep of the book that nobody has attempted a similar conspectus of cave archaeology since, and although much of the information it contained had been published elsewhere in a remarkably similar form[128] cave hunting provided a snapshot of Dawkins' Palaeolithic *weltanschauung* on the eve of Creswell. For our purposes, Chapters VII to XI are the most critical.

Dawkins began his survey of the Pleistocene by dismissing almost every claim for human remains from the Palaeolithic Period, quite the 'unbelieving Thomas' as a reviewer in the *Glasgow Herald* dubbed him. His conclusions were based on two principal lines of reasoning: 1) the stratigraphical association between the human remains and other items and 2) craniology, the practice of using skull shape to determine race. Two types of skull were recognised in Europe – dolichocephalic (long-headed) and brachycephalic (broad-headed) – both of which Dawkins associated with the Neolithic and Bronze Age, the former type representing non-Aryan ancestors of the Basque and Berber people, the latter type the forefathers of the Celt, Finn and Slav. The Palaeolithic races of Europe, he contended, were all extinct although they did have one living group of descendants – the Eskimo. Using these two criteria, the human remains from the famous Upper Palaeolithic site of Aurignac, discovered by accident in 1852 and quickly reburied in the local churchyard, were dismissed as coming from a Neolithic sepulchre. Although this is the type-site for the eponymous Early Upper Palaeolithic industry, the Aurignacian, Dawkins noted that the skeletons lay not within the Aurignacian layers but above them and, contrary to the great Édouard Lartet (whose excavations in the cave took place only after the locals had thoroughly ransacked it), could only conclude they were later in age. He similarly rejected the burials at Gailenruth, Germany, Trou du Frontal and Gendron, Belgium, and Lombrives, France, where Neolithic materials such as pottery, domesticated animals or polished axes had been found in association with the skeletal remains. Similar logic was used to exclude another set of sites – notably Paviland, Wales, Crô-Magnon and Bruniquel, France – where he suggested later prehistoric graves had been dug through much older layers beneath, resulting in the misleading association of human remains, Pleistocene animals and Palaeolithic artefacts. The crania from the French sites were in any case dolichocephalic, part of the Neolithic race that buried their dead in caves. History has shown that he was also overcautious in rejecting at least some of these sites. He was positively wrong in dismissing the Neanderthal fossils from Engis, Belgium and the Feldhofer Cave in the Neander Thal (Valley), Germany, which he did not because he denied they were strange but because he deemed the circumstances behind their discovery too opaque. He followed Huxley and others in believing that the morphology of the Neander Thal bones represented not a 'missing link' but an extreme or retrograde form of modern people, perhaps caused by a 'savage' lifestyle (despite the fact that the Neander Valley specimen had been designated as a separate species a decade earlier at the Newcastle-Upon-Tyne meeting of the BAAS,[129] this would not be fully accepted for several decades). Only two sites passed Dawkins' rigorous test – Trou de Naulette in Belgium, and Victoria Cave, Settle, although as we shall see, his faith in the latter did not last long.

Dawkins was equally iconoclastic on the divisions of Pleistocene time and the Palaeolithic period. Almost as soon as the excitement surrounding deep human antiquity had died down, the task of ordering the materials into some sort of chronological sequence had begun. By 1861, a growing dataset at his disposal, Evans noticed a pattern in the Somme gravels, observing that the pointed implements (hand-axes) were most frequent in the highest river deposits, while the flakes that had been carefully shaped prior to removal from their parent core (i.e. Levallois flakes) were more common in the lower level gravels.[130] The following year, the banker and ethnologist Henry Christy (1810-1865), who along with Édouard Lartet (1801-1871) had been actively exploring the caverns of the Dordogne, presented his ideas on stone tools to the Ethnological Society of London, distinguishing three divisions: 1) The Drift Period, associated with mammoth and rhinoceros; 2) The Cave Period, associated with reindeer; 3) The Surface Period, with ground stone axes;[131] a system very similar to that used by John Evans.[132] Lartet himself had by 1861 already produced what was to become a very influential scheme, particularly in France, in which Pleistocene time was divided on the basis of mammalian fauna. Lartet distinguished four epochs, from oldest to youngest: the Age of the Cave Bear, Age of the Mammoth, Age of the Reindeer and Age of the Aurochs.[133] Christy's version was an attempt to align the mammals and the stone tools in a unified evolutionary sequence.

The most influential classification was undoubtedly that of Louis Laurent Gabriel de Mortillet (1821-1898), curator at the Musée des Antiquités National, St-Germain-en-Laye, Paris. In 1867 de Mortillet was tasked with classifying the prehistoric exhibitions for the Universal Exposition in Paris. He chose to base his scheme on the human cultural achievements preserved in stone tools rather than faunal variation, which he believed showed little change through time and to be influenced by too many complicating factors.[134] The scheme went through several versions from 1867 onwards, introduced terms such as Acheulean, Mousterian, Aurignacian, Solutrean, and Magdalenian and to this day dominates the classification of the European Palaeolithic.

Dawkins accepted none of these as adequate. He felt that Lartet's system lacked substance. The mammoth, reindeer, cave bear and aurochs were contemporaries in Europe, found together in many bone cave assemblages, while in terms of first arrivals the cave bear came no earlier to Europe than the mammoth, so had no right to priority. The difference between animal frequencies in different caves was, for Dawkins, nothing to do with the age of the deposits, but rather determined by human prey selection and ease of capture. De Mortillet shared this view, but that did little to spare his own scheme from Dawkins' critical pen. Dawkins rejected the idea that the level of sophistication, or conversely the crudeness, of an industry was an indication of age, arguing that variation could merely reflect different tribes with different cultures. Indeed, the difference between implements from two caves was no greater than that observed in two tribes of modern Eskimos (his term). Lubbock and others had used the Eskimo as an analogy, but Dawkins held the belief that the similarities were too close to be the result of ecologically driven convergences in technology and actually revealed a direct blood-line from Palaeolithic Europe to modern Alaska.

Palaeogeography was also a major concern in *Cave Hunting*. Dawkins had been plotting the distribution of Pleistocene animals for years, using the results to understand the former range of animals and from this the configuration of the land. Here he used soundings taken in the Irish Sea, English Channel and North Sea (aka German Ocean) – to calculate the bathymetry of these basins and from this to estimate how far *the land would have to rise* to connect Britain to Europe. The resulting map (see Figure 3.7) is very similar to those produced by modern scholars. This also gave Dawkins a way of explaining variation in the Palaeolithic record. The Somme, Seine and Thames were part of a common hunting ground shared by the same race of people, whereas the cave sites of the west and south-west were used by a different tribe or race who favoured a different toolkit. Such patterns of territoriality and cultural distinctiveness were just common sense to Dawkins, and could be seen among contemporary American tribes.[135] A similar mechanism could explain the presence of terrestrial or freshwater mammals such as elephants and pygmy hippos on Mediterranean islands. Dramatic uplift of the earth's crust of some 4-500 fathoms (~905 m/3000 ft) had, according to Dawkins, split the Mediterranean Sea into two basins, with a closed Strait of Gibraltar and the islands of Sicily and Malta connected together and linked to Africa. He was not entirely wrong. Some of the connections demanded by the distribution of fauna had indeed taken place, more than once, but the cause was not only crustal uplift, but reduced sea-level during glacial periods when vast quantities of the Earth's water was locked up in terrestrial ice-sheets and the poles. It is worth noting, however, that none of his conclusions were without side but were inextricable linked to the heated defence of his seasonal migration theory (below); it is, in fact, quite clear that the theory actually drove the palaeogeographical reconstructions.

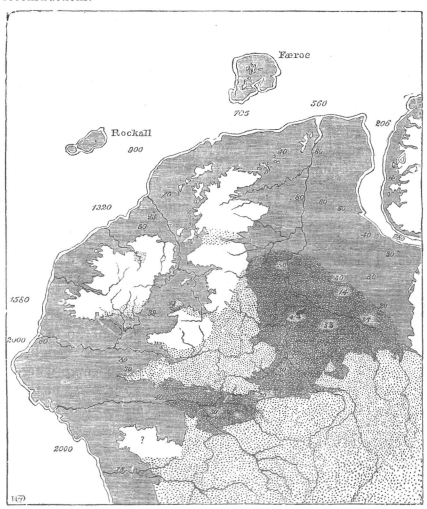

Figure 3.7: Dawkins' reconstruction of the palaeogeography of late Pleistocene Britain. Shaded area = land now submerged; dotted area = region occupied by animals; blank regions = area occupied by glaciers (after Dawkins 1874a, 363).

Cave Hunting was an instant triumph, and assumed a place alongside other pioneering tomes of the Victorian age – Lyell's *Antiquity of Man*, Lubbock's *Pre-historic Times*, and Evans' *Ancient Stone Implements of Britain*. It was also similar to these in its pedagogical philosophy – written to communicate not conceal, deliberately understandable to all educated men and women, yet containing a wealth of scientific information. It quickly entered the scientific and popular consciousness, making Dawkins, if not quite the household name, certainly the country's pre-eminent cave specialist. Contemporary reviews, which a proud Dawkins pasted into a scrapbook,[136] sung its praises:

'If Lord Chesterfield's advice is to be adopted – "hunt something, whether it be an elephant in the forest or a flea in the blanket" – not a bad thing to hunt is a cave, or if Fate keeps us from personally enjoying such a chase, then the next best thing is to hunt through Mr Dawkins' very interesting volume'[137]

'The style is at once simple and graphic, and those to whom the past is a book to be read not only in printed lines, but in all the evidences of previous life which the earth we tread affords, will penetrate the caves with Mr Dawkins in perfect confidence that they are in the hands of an experienced guide who can explain their wonders'[138]

'...an exhaustive work treating of caves and their contents, as well as of the information afforded by them about the sojourn of man in Europe, about the animals associated with him, and the vast but gradual changes in climate and geography which they illustrate...a fit supplement to Antiquity of Man and Prehistoric Times'[139]

Not everybody was unequivocally positive. A reviewer in the *Glasgow Herald* for 25 November 1874, (whose identity we may soon be able to guess) levelled criticism at Dawkins' ideas on the mingling of arctic and southern faunas seen in many Pleistocene deposits, which he described as inadequate. A reviewer in the *Spectator* for 12 November 1874, on the other hand, described this theory as the 'best piece of original work in the book,' uncharitably implying that the rest was rather derivative and showing ignorance to the fact that Dawkins had been thumping that particular tub for almost a decade. Much to Dawkins' annoyance, the final product contained an unfortunate number of errors and omissions. Twenty-seven spotted in the proof stage or afterwards were noted on pages xxiii and xxiv of the book itself, dozens more were privately recorded by Dawkins on various scraps of paper now held in Buxton Museum, and still others were pointed out by well-meaning members of his readership, which as the months went on must have become increasingly tiresome.[140] The archaeologist Daniel Wilson (1816-1892), who had coined the term prehistory in 1851,[141] innocently wrote asking Dawkins where he could find a copy of Lubbock's *Prehistoric Man* cited in the preface and text of *Cave Hunting*.[142] Wilson was anxious because *Prehistoric Man* was the title of his own work, which was just about to go into its third edition. Dawkins could not oblige, because it was a mistake; he had meant *Prehistoric Times*. It is hard to know whether these were mistakes by Dawkins or the typesetters, but each and every one must have made his heart sink. At least Charles Darwin merely thanked him for the free copy.[143]

Fame brought 'fan mail', mostly of the 'I have found something that may interest you' or the 'in my own experience your statement on page x is quite correct/absolute nonsense' variety. Dawkins replied in a kindly fashion at least to some, but this ran the risk of encouraging further correspondence. Other letters included invitations to visit new caves and fissures, among them the Chudleigh Caves, Devon and Brean Down, Somerset, which had produced important archaeological and/or faunal assemblages.[144] That neither are mentioned in future articles or books implies that these new leads were not followed up. Academics saw other opportunities. John Green sent his old chum hearty congratulations with rosy reminiscences of their days at Wookey, alongside an appeal that Dawkins write a 'primer' on prehistoric people suitable for young folk and the general reader.[145] He never did.

We leave this brief overview of Cave Hunting with two topics that have a major bearing on the next phase of Dawkins' life and on the next four chapters of this book. The first relates to his views on the chronological distribution of the lesser-scimitar cat *Machairodus latidens*. The material Dawkins studied during a visit to France in the autumn of 1873 had left him in no doubt that the sabre-toothed tiger, as it is often wrongly called, was a Pliocene species. Its presence at Kent's Cavern alongside the familiar 'post-glacial' Pleistocene fauna was a geological accident – the blocking of passages, the action of streams etc; indeed given the vast timescales involved, we should not be surprised that such accidents leave animals of widely different ages lying side-by-side, or even the older resting upon the younger, Dawkins confidently declared. He roundly rejected the views of Lyell and Pengelly – that because the condition of the cat teeth was identical to the other remains in the cave there was no reason to assume they were not the same age – because it suited him at this point to argue that condition was an unreliable guide and might be expected to vary even within different parts of the same cavern. What puzzled him, though, was the evidence of hyaena gnawing, leading him to the conclusion that the *Machairodus* had actually inhabited Devonshire during the *earliest* phase of the Pleistocene, although was not a regular visitor.

The second topic was field techniques, discussed by Dawkins in his first Appendix. Despite hardly ever following his own advice, Dawkins lectured his reader on the necessary equipment and techniques required for proper cave hunting. These were the instruments that James Parker, Ayshford Sanford and Dawkins found most valuable.

'Apart from the tools of the workmen' (i.e. pick, shovel, spade), upon the handles of which Dawkins would rarely have dirtied his hands, the prescribed kit was:

1   A hammer with an ash handle, about twenty inches long, inserted into a square head of best steel, ending in a chisel edge in the same place as the handle, weighing almost eight ounces, and seven inches in length.
2   A steel chisel ten inches long
3   A prismatic compass
4   A thermometer for taking the temperatures of the air and water
5   An aneroid (barometer)
6   A steel measuring tape
7   Abney's patent level, used for laying down the datum-line for plans, as well as for taking dips and angles
8   A stout rope not less than twenty feet long with a 'horse's girth' at the end for the exploration of vertical fissures, so the explorer may be let down without any great danger. Dawkins warned that no large unknown cave should be explored without a rope, *or by a party of less than three* (my emphasis)
9   For the exploration of water-caves, a raft
10 The most convenient lights for use in caves were common composite candle. Paraffin candles guttered, lanterns did not give sufficiently diffused lights and the smoke of paraffin torches or flambeaux dipped in turpentine or tar was intolerable. Magnesium wire revealed the beauties of the higher roofs.[146]

Rabbits, badgers and foxes were the most reliable discoverers of caves. Where their burrows, setts, and dens could be seen to extend into a vertical rock face, a cave was undoubtedly to be found. Location was also another guide, for the old cave dwellers had generally chosen the sunny side of ravines and valleys, in spots that afforded a wide view. Once a cave was discovered, there were several ways of proceeding. First, one could adopt the approach Dawkins had taken at Wookey Hole (see Chapter 2). When faced with a great depth of deposit, then one might sink shafts, as Dawkins had done at Victoria Cave. The most elaborate method of the era was that used by William Pengelly at Kent's Cavern, described above, but Dawkins rarely troubled himself too much with this fussy procedure.

Carving up the Ice Age
The emergence of glacial theory in Britain was a suitably slow process involving visionary leaps of faith met by reactionary intransigence. Dawkins had a foot in both camps. Since at least the 1820s geologists had detected signs – from arctic faunas, peculiar landforms, scratched rocks, contorted sediments, and other phenomena observed in modern glaciated landscapes – that northern temperate regions had experienced a major and recent glaciation. Other than catastrophe theories, the most widely accepted explanation was that proposed by Charles Lyell in the 1830s, which invoked a period of submergence by cold seas carrying great armadas of stone-laden icebergs. This sea-ice drifted across the oceans depositing sediments ('drift') over the drowned continent as it melted; when icebergs occasionally collided with land or became grounded they scratched rocks and contorting the superficial deposits beneath them.[147] The theory was flexible enough to accommodate new data, and offered a uniformitarian alternative to the notion that the superficial deposits that the 'diluvium' (as it was known in the early nineteenth century) had been produced by one or more massive (for some Biblical-style) deluge that surged across the land and reworked unconsolidated sediment.[148]

The development of land-ice theory in the late 1830s is associated with the young Swiss palaeontologist Louis Agassiz (1807-1873), although he readily acknowledged his debt to the earlier geologists and other observant locals in the Alpine regions.[149] Using existing evidence that the Alpine glaciers had once been far more extensive and his own field observations, Agassiz developed the 'extravagant' theory that the whole northern hemisphere was once covered by a vast mobile ice-sheet. Although shocking for some, the theory quickly attracted powerful supporters, among them William Buckland and Charles Lyell, who undertook a study tour with Agassiz to look for British evidence of a terrestrial glaciation.[150] Others were fiercely opposed to the idea, Murchison and de La Beche of the Survey, ichthyosaur and plesiosaur expert William Coneybeare (1787-1857), and Cambridge polymath William Whewell (1874-1866) chief amongst them. The debates were bitter. After only a few months as an advocate, marked by hostile criticism from his peers and some unpleasant clashes in the Geological Society (with Murchison in the presidential chair), Lyell renounced Agassiz's theory, taking refuge in his earlier submergence model. The controversy concerning the mechanisms would continue, but the concept of *The Ice Age* was firmly established.

The italics above are significant, denoting the fact that for most geologists of the Victorian era there was but one period of glaciation – The Great Ice Age. Immovable and unchangeable it provided a key stratigraphical marker, which in 1853 John Phillips had used to divide Pleistocene time into pre-glacial, glacial and post-glacial periods.[151] Another thing that Dawkins and almost everybody else agreed on at this time was that humans had arrived in Europe after the Great Glacial. At around the same time, however, Andrew Crombie Ramsey and others at the Geological Survey were noticing evidence for multiple glaciations and interglacials, both recent and ancient, although few were receptive to their claims.[152] The full acceptance of multiple (usually four) past glaciations would not come until the early twentieth century, and the modern framework of 100+ climatic cycles evident the Marine Isotope Record was over a century and a half away.[153] For most of the nineteenth century the monoglacialists had the upper hand, and Dawkins had a strong interest in maintaining this status quo.

As a palaeontologist, Dawkins was a firm believer in the primacy of fauna above all other forms of evidence, especially for sorting the geological record into the correct order. As mentioned in the previous chapter, his punishing research programme of identifying and cataloguing all available cave and river-drift faunas had by the end of the 1860s provided him with an unparalleled database of 148 sites from which to construct such schema. The resulting models – of which there were many variants – were not always well received, and in the discussions following his talks objections were raised from several quarters, usually involving conflicting interpretations of lithology rather than fauna. Dawkins' main problem in devising a coherent scheme – apart from the usual lack of consensus on practically everything – was his unswerving faith in his old tutor John Phillips' glacial chronology and the belief that after the Pliocene the earth had gradually become colder. He held onto these maxims long after they had outgrown any practical usefulness and long after his own work should have alerted him to the fact that they offered a highly compressed framework – comprising just two warm periods and one glacial[154] – that simply did not allow him enough time or flexibility to make all the animal suites fit. So he lumped them all together.

Dawkins' first attempt at dividing the British fauna in 1867 recognised three divisions, the closest he could manage to Phillips' scheme.[155]

1   The pre-glacial fauna (Pliocene);
2   The pre-glacial fauna of the Thames Valley; —Great Glacial—
3   The post-glacial fauna.

The earliest and latest groups were fairly straightforward. The pre-glacial fauna was composed almost exclusively of southern thermophiles and Pliocene relicts, some of which survived into later periods, some of which went extinct before or during the Great Glacial. It was evolutionarily the oldest group, and stratigraphically underneath the glacial beds. Most of the fauna from the caves and the river drift included a more 'modern' mix of warm- and cold-adapted animals that could be stratigraphically demonstrated, at least in places, to post-date the glacial. (This did not, as some recent authors suggest, have any necessary implications for Dawkins' belief that the two races of humans found with this fauna were of different ages – the river-drift folk being earlier than the reindeer people[156] – because the length of time represented by the post-glacial fauna was sufficient for different races of humans to have come and gone). The Lower Thames group, however, contained elements from both of the others and was therefore assigned to a transitional position.[157] The balance of key species (i.e. absence of reindeer, abundance of red deer) led Dawkins to look 'backwards rather than forwards in time' and situate the group before the glacial.[158]

This was quickly superseded in 1869 by a four-fold sequence, in which the Thames Valley material had been split into two groups:[159]

1   The pre-glacial (?Pliocene) fauna of the Norfolk forest beds
2   The transitional pre-glacial fauna of Clacton; —Great Glacial—
3   The transitional post-glacial fauna of the Thames Valley
4   The main post-glacial series

There were two reasons behind this rapid re-think – the site at Clacton-on-Sea, only latterly brought into his canon, and the discovery of musk-ox at Crayford, which he found just after the 1867 paper had gone to press. Like the other Lower Thames sites, the problem at Clacton was that many of the species were common to both the pre- and post-glacial, but the marker species that would normally help to determine precisely where a site belonged – an abundance of 'forest-bed' animals on the one hand; woolly mammoth, reindeer, woolly rhinoceros on the other – were absent. This ambiguity suggested that Clacton belonged to neither group but to a 'passage' or transitional time too cold for most forest-bed animals, but not cold enough for the reindeer and allied arctic species. Furthermore, the unique blend of species and absence of the 'North-Asiatic mammal' (an unnecessarily elliptical reference to musk-ox) at Clacton prevented it from simply joining the existing Lower Thames group. This left Dawkins only one option, Clacton belonged in a passage group of its own, the balance of species suggesting it belonged before the Great Glaciation but after the pre-glacial *sensu stricto*. By the same logic the Lower Thames group, which had previously occupied this time period, was now regarded as more characteristic of the post-glacial, although the absence of reindeer still rendered them distinctive. Dawkins therefore placed them in a later transitional period at the terminal glacial/early post-glacial boundary when the incoming cold fauna had not 'taken full possession of the district'. Shaping the data to fit the model, Dawkins' solution offered convoluted patterns of coastline evolution and yo-yoing temperatures to explain how species that were climatically incompatible, such as musk ox and the 'southern' rhino (*Rhinoceros megarhinus*), could co-exist, but at least it shows that Dawkins' opinions were not immutable and he was capable of publicly changing his mind – just as long as the discovery of any inadequacies in his earlier positions fell to him and not his critics.

By the time he came to write *Cave Hunting*, Dawkins' position had changed again.[160] He still adhered to Phillips' three-fold division, but a series of small awakenings – increasing awareness of the complexity within the mammals, a fuller European purview, and the realisation that climate change was not necessarily linear – led him to the epiphany that there was no one-to-one correlation between 'life-eras' and geological eras.[161] Dawkins instead split the Pleistocene mammals into three divisions, which he emphasised did not correspond to the pre-glacial, glacial or post-glacial:

1   The Late Pleistocene Division – the classic arctic and semi-arctic fauna of the British caves, including reindeer, hyaena, mammoth and woolly rhinoceros.

2   The Middle Pleistocene Division – as represented in Britain by the fauna from the Lower Thames brickearths, Clacton, Kent's Cavern breccia and Oreston Cave, Plymouth. A true association of species from the

Characteristic Pre-glacial Fauna	Characteristic Post-glacial Fauna
Etruscan bear (Ursus arvernensis)*	Palaeolithic humans
Cave Bear	Wolverine/Glutton
Shrew	Cave Bear?
Desman†	Grizzly Bear?
Mole	Cave Lion
Roe deer	Cave Hyaena
Red deer	Panther?
Cervus sedgwickii (extinct deer)†	Musk-Ox
Cervus ardeus (extinct deer)†	Woolly Rhino
Aurochs	Woolly Mammoth
Hippopotamus	Lemming
Horse	Cave Pika
Rhinoceros megarhinus	Pouched Marmot
Etruscan rhinoceros†	Ground squirrel/Marmot
Straight-tusked elephant	(Reindeer)
Mammoth meridionalis†	(Bison)
Beaver	(Hippopotamus)
Giant beaver †	

Table 3.1: List of Characteristic Pre-Glacial and Post-glacial Fauna, according to Dawkins 1869. Those marked † went extinct during or after the Great Glaciation. Those in brackets are not included in Dawkins' original list as they survived into the present, but are nonetheless important members of this fauna zone and are important to later discussion.

other two groups, with notable arrivals (humans) and many departures, mostly 'southern species' (e.g. all of the characteristic Pliocene deer; Etruscan rhino; the southern mammoth, *Mammuthus meridionalis*). 'Northern forms of life were present, but not in force'[162].

3   The Early Pleistocene Division – as represented by the Norfolk and Suffolk forest-beds, and presenting a 'peculiar' mixture of Pliocene and Pleistocene species, many of them thermophilous. No arctic animals had arrived.

Dawkins' revised model still failed to please all of his peers, and when presented at the Geological Society drew another wave of criticism from Prestwich, Flower and Evans, amongst others.[163] With hindsight, we can see that Dawkins had actually managed to capture the essence of the faunal chronozones recognised in Britain today, although his divisions are crude and minimalist by modern standards.

Once again, the middle group was the most confused, containing species with apparently conflicting chronological ranges, some looking to the Early Pleistocene/Pliocene, others to the Late Pleistocene. One might argue that this Middle Pleistocene Division was merely a dustbin for mixed sites or sites that just did not fit elsewhere, were it not for the fact that it had some stratigraphical basis and is a crude representation of what we would today regard as a group of Middle Pleistocene faunas from different interglacials (MIS11 at Clacton [ca. 400,000 years old], MIS9 at Grays [ca. 300,000 years old], and MIS7 at Crayford [ca.200,000 years old). The real problem then, was that it contained sites spanning a period of over 200,000 years with three warm phases and two glacials. Conveniently for Dawkins, it provided him with a large amount of wiggle-room. In *Cave Hunting*, he wilfully avoided drawing any definite conclusions about the precise age of sites, noting only that the Glacial Period did not separate one 'life-era' from another, but rather the Middle Pleistocene Division actually straddled it. He skirted around the options, ultimately settling on a non-committal 'intermediate age', leaving the reader (and his opponents) to make up their own minds as to exactly what he meant by this or where Middle Pleistocene sites fitted in relation to one another. It also allowed the canny Dawkins to elide the question of whether humans were pre- or post-glacial in Britain, an issue he would otherwise have had to tackle head on, given Rev. Osmond Fisher's discovery of flint artefacts in the Lower Brickearth at Crayford in April 1872, an occasion at which (perhaps fortunately for Fisher) Dawkins had been present.[164] Indeed, had these finds been made five years earlier Dawkins would have by his own logic been forced to accept a pre-glacial age for the Crayford humans.

Dawkins realised that to better understand the relationship of people and animals to the Glacial Period he needed to better understand the Glacial Period itself. Drawing on the work of 'eminent observers', he now envisaged the Great Glacial as a three-fold system that began with the advance of terrestrial ice sheets, precipitated by the land being far higher, and thus far cooler, than today.[165] This was followed by a period of depression of the land (required, as was ever the case, to explain the occurrence of high altitude marine shells) during which even the mountains of Wales were submerged beneath a wide sea awash with icebergs. These icebergs had released the 'middle drift', marking a period that Dawkins believed would have experienced a warmer climate, due to the moderating effect of the sea. Finally the land was re-elevated and a second, smaller ice-advance occurred, with isolated glaciers over Scotland, Northern England, Wales and Ireland. Dawkins had therefore finally accepted the possibility that a warm(ish) 'interglacial' had occurred during the Ice Age, although not in the way that James Geikie (see below) or modern scholars would use the term. In fact, so reluctant was Dawkins to accept multiple and temporally distinct glaciations that he failed to realise that the absence of Pleistocene mammals from the river gravels of Scotland, Northern England, Wales and Ireland was because all the relevant deposits had been destroyed by a more recent ice advance. Instead he postulated that these regions had still been covered in glaciers from the second wave of advance, which barred the contemporary post-glacial/Late Pleistocene mammals and humans in the south and east of England from entering. Again, Dawkins' reconstructions of Europe's palaeogeography was inextricably linked to his monoglacialism and seasonal migration theory, which necessitated major swings in temperature and the physical conditions to drive them.

Glacial Wrangling Part 1: Seasonal Migration
We arrive at the long-heralded seasonal migration theory. It brought Dawkins little but conflict and yet he stubbornly refused to abandon it or modify it, even in the face of irresistible evidence to the contrary. The post-glacial, or as it became the Late Pleistocene fauna, was that closest to Dawkins' heart – it was the fauna of the caverns, which he had worked so long and hard to make his own. He had long observed that it contained a marked and highly curious mixture of species – some like the reindeer adapted to arctic environments, others like the hippopotamus to tropical climes. His early statements make no judgements about how this might have come to pass, noting only that the co-occurrence of forest species like the narrow-nosed rhinoceros and steppe species like the mammoth and woolly rhinoceros bore the same geographical relationship as modern red deer and reindeer in northern latitudes (i.e. Scandinavia). From the comparative rarity of southern species he inferred that the climate was generally cold, and southern visitors quite rare, the rarity of young or juvenile hippos leading him to suspect that they rarely bred in this country. Ultimately, three climatically distinct groups were identified: a southern group, a temperate group, and a northern/arctic group.[166] (Table 3.2)

Dawkins' explanation for these faunal patterns relied on the occurrence of an extreme continental climate in Late Pleistocene Britain, with strong seasonal shifts in temperature. In his own words:

Southern Species	Northern Species	Temperate Species
Lion	Marmot	Beaver
Caffir Cat	Pouched Marmot	Hare
Spotted Hyaena	Lemming	Rabbit
Striped Hyaena	Alpine Hare	Wild Cat
Serval	Tailless Hare	Martin
Hippopotamus	Glutton	Stoat
African Elephant	Arctic Fox	Otter
Porcupine	Musk-Ox	Brown Bear
Rhinoceros megarhinus †	Reindeer	Grizzly Bear
Rhinoceros leptorhinus †	Ibex	Wolf
Straight-tusked elephant†	Chamois	Fox
Machairodus latidens †	Woolly Rhino†	Horse
Pigmy elephant†	Mammoth†	Aurochs
Dwarf hippopotamus†		Bison
		Saiga Antelope
		Wild Boar
		Red Deer
		Roe Deer
		Cave Bear†
		Irish Elk†

Table 3.2: Dawkins' (1874) Geo-climatic Groupings for the Pleistocene Mammalia. Those marked † are extinct. The mammoth is not considered a northern species by Dawkins, but is included in the list by Geikie (1874, 419).

'The hypothesis of a series of conditions in Europe, in Pleistocene times, similar to those of Northern Asia or of Northern America, would amply satisfy the difficulty of the case. In the Pleistocene winter the northern animals would pass southwards, and in the summer the southern forms would creep northwards; and to this swinging to and fro of the animals, according to the seasons, the peculiar intermixture of their remains, over what may be called the debatable ground of Central Europe, may be accounted for, the head quarters of the northern animals being to the south-east of a line drawn from Yorkshire and Königsberg, and the head quarters of the southern being the regions bordering the Mediterranean'.[167]

Hypothesising the land lay at a considerably greater height than today, with an extended continental shelf and much smaller inland seas (see above), he suggested:

'The land stretched continuously without any impassable barrier northwards and eastwards into Euro-Asia; while, on the other hand, it reached southwards over a considerable portion of what is now the Mediterranean, almost, if not quite, touching Africa. The winter cold and summer heat of so great a mass of land must necessarily have been more severe than now, when the Mediterranean occupies a far wider

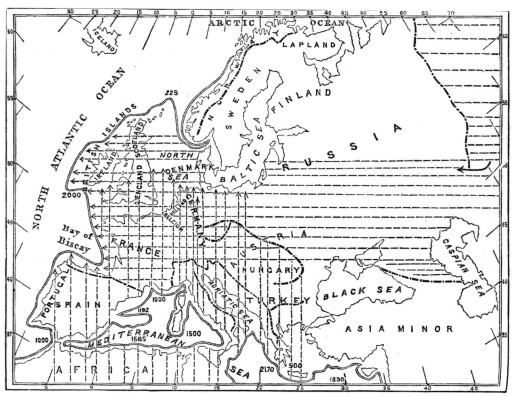

Figure 3.8: Dawkins' faunal provinces for Late Pleistocene Europe. The double line represents the probable outline of the Pleistocene land. The vertical broken line shows the range of the southern mammals, the horizontal ones that of the northern forms (after Dawkins 1874a).

area, and when the Atlantic and the Baltic and the North Sea have considerably diminished the area of the land. It is therefore by no means to be wondered at that a southern animal, such as the hippopotamus, should have wandered northwards and westwards as far as the latitude of Yorkshire, and it is worthy of note that this is the extreme northern limit of the range of that animal. On the other hand, during the severity of winter the reindeer and the musk sheep descended southwards, and occupied an area which they deserted at the approach of summer. Such, in my belief, is the explanation of the mixed character of the Pleistocene fauna'.[168] (Figure 3.8)

For Dawkins this was the only hypothesis that accounted for all the available facts. Sir Charles Lyell, with whom the idea originated, was still of a like mind, imagining a time when hippos 'may have swum in a few summer days from rivers in the south of Spain or France to the Somme, Thames, or Severn, making timely retreat to the south before the snow and ice set in'.[169] What were the alternatives? Prestwich suggested that Pleistocene hippos could survive because they were woolly, with warm seal-like coats, a proposal that 'mortified Falconer'[170] and was openly rejected by Lubbock, who pointed out that the aquatic hippopotamus could hardly survive in waters that froze every winter, even if protected by fur. The view favoured by Lubbock held that the contemporaneity was actually illusory, and that the Arctic and African animals had occupied Britain during different periods with different climates. But this would require the different groups to occur in discrete strata, a situation that just never occurred in Britain or the Continent where the bones were mixed together in the same condition, at least according to Dawkins.

Sitting in the audience as Dawkins gave a version of his scheme to the delegates of the 1871 BAAS in Edinburgh was James Geikie, listening to words he deplored while waiting for the discussion, his opportunity to speak out. James Geikie (1839-1915: Plate 5) was a Scottish geologist who had joined the Geological Survey in Scotland in 1861, becoming District Surveyor for the Geological Survey *of* Scotland in 1869 when the recently empowered body (it had been given its own identity in 1867) was under the directorship of his brother Archibald Geikie.[171] His main task at the Survey was mapping the glacial deposits of Scotland, an assignment that led him to the conclusion, just as it had done his predecessor Ramsey, that the accepted story of the Ice Age was wrong in Scotland and by extension also wrong in England. He left the Survey in 1882 to succeed his brother as Murchison

Chair of Geology at Edinburgh, a position Archibald had held concurrently with his survey duties and only resigned because he was appointed Director-General of the Geological Survey in London. James was never comfortable with the fact that he was gifted the job without interview or opposition.

Geikie had spent a decade mapping the superficial geology and coal measures of western Scotland before reaching the unorthodox conclusion that the Ice Age was not a single period of unrelenting cold but actually a period of considerable climatic instability, with separate glacials interrupted by warm interglacials. This revelation owed much to the mathematical modelling of his Scottish Survey colleague James Croll (1821-1890), who had used astronomical calculations and the physics of atmospheric and oceanic circulation and insolation to show that quite normal variations in the Earth's orbit (specifically orbital eccentricity and precession of the equinoxes) would periodically trigger ice ages, and that these would be separated by prolonged warm periods.[172] Geikie also rejected the idea that the fauna of the river drifts and the caves were 'post-glacial', a term he reserved for a totally different, and modern, usage. Descriptions of Geikie's emergent theory are preserved in letters to his colleague, Benjamin Neeve Peach (1842-1926), sent throughout the latter part of 1871.[173] These were followed by a series of seven papers published in the *Geological Magazine* between December 1871 and June 1872 under the same title: *On changes of climate during the Glacial Epoch*. These essays formed the nucleus for Geikie's 1874 volume *The Great Ice Age*, possibly the book he described to Peach as being written for 'the bloody public'.[174] The fifth and sixth papers, tackling the issue of Pleistocene fauna, set Geikie on an inevitable collision course with 'the Dawkins', a situation he predicted in letters to Peach and Hughes.[175]

Geikie's fifth paper of April 1872 dealt with the seasonal migration theory 'ably advocated by Mr Dawkins, who has brought a wide knowledge of the subject. His case is stated with great clearness, and he seems to have employed all the arguments that can be adduced in its favour. Yet I cannot see my way to accept his conclusions. Had these conclusions followed from a consideration of paleontological evidence alone, I should hardly have ventured to dispute the position maintained by one who had devoted so much time to this special study; the question, however, is one chiefly of climate and physical conditions'.[176] This diffident and almost apologetic preamble hid the fact that Geikie abhorred Dawkins' explanation and considered it 'full of the wildest absurdities'.[177] Having dispensed with the scholarly courtesies, Geikie was anything but timorous. While short, only five pages of text, the attack is precise, tearing into the seasonal migration theory on three major fronts: climate, animal behaviour and resources.

What kind of climate, Geikie asked, would we expect to find in Dawkins' so-called post-glacial Britain and Western Europe? Would it really be a highly continental regime like Siberia, with frigid winters in the north and baking summers in the south, a zone of debatable ground in the middle where faunas of the different provinces mixed?[178] Hardly. The climate of modern Siberia was controlled, Geikie asserted, by the winds. In winter they are bitterly cold irrespective of direction: westerlies are robbed of any warmth before they cross the Urals, northerlies bring arctic cold, and southerlies harbour biting temperatures from the Mongolian plateau. In summer the situation is reversed as dry, hot winds sweep in from the Mongolian desert and the endless arctic sun warms the northern plains. Such winter conditions could not pertain in post-glacial Western Europe as long as the Atlantic was there to exert a moderating influence. But Dawkins had another mechanism up his sleeve – the postulated presence of glaciers across Scotland, Wales and Northern England, presumably matched by others in Scandinavia and Switzerland and permanent snow-fields in the Vosges and Black Forest. These would certainly act to reduce winter temperatures, Geikie conceded, but by the same token their very existence would prevent summer temperatures reaching Siberian levels. Furthermore, a logical corollary of British glaciers is extensive arctic ice sheets, from which large numbers of icebergs would calve in summer, cooling the seas around Britain and depriving the south-westerly winds of their warmth. Any negative impact that this might have on the Gulfstream would only serve to reduce summer temperatures further.

Geikie's next major objection was rudimentary ethology – the hippopotamus is not a migratory animal, and could not realistically walk from the Mediterranean to northern England, and back, in a single season. None of the pachyderms, not the straight tusked-elephant or the two extinct species of southern rhinoceros, could feasibly make such 'wonderful migrations' in just a few weeks. Even putting disbelief aside and supposing they could, the resources available in the north would not have been able to support them, Geikie maintained. This was Geikie's other main point – that the logical consequence of Dawkins' arctic winters with glaciers, snowfields and frozen rivers was, obvious as it might seem, major spring-summer thaws. 'Burst[ing] their icy bonds, and, swollen with heavy rains and the torrents derived from the melting of the snowfields and glaciers, [our rivers] would overflow the low grounds, and carry devastation far and wide. Over broad areas…there could be little vegetation'.[179] What would the hippopotamus and other heavy weight grazers, each individual of which needs tens or hundreds of kilos of forage per day, find to eat? The conditions would only really be suitable for the musk-ox, reindeer, marmot, hare and lemming, used to eking out an existence from mosses, lichen and scraggy shrubs, and then probably not in numbers that would encourage prides of lion or vast cackles of hyaena to leave their temperate headquarters and explore the British landscape. The fact that the archaeological record left no room for doubt – hyaenas and therefore herbivores were present in large numbers – showed Dawkins' envisaged conditions were nonsense. The only plausible explanation was that the temperature fluctuations occurred over much longer periods, with distinct glacials and interglacials populated with animals adapted to the prevailing conditions. Dawkins could not see this because his framework was inadequate and his concept of a post-glacial was flawed. Picking this up in his sixth paper, Geikie explained that the term post-glacial should be reserved for the current warm period, after the last major European ice sheets had melted, quite different from Dawkins' post-glacial which included anytime after his singleton glaciation.[180] For Geikie, Dawkins' post-glacial and its related fauna actually belonged to an earlier cool-temperate period within a very complex glacial sequence. There was no evidence whatsoever that the reindeer-mammoth fauna was post-glacial in England – it was actually 'a physical impossibility'.[181] This may be one of the reasons why shortly after 1871 Dawkins adopted the term Late Pleistocene to describe the same group.

Geikie was more-or-less correct on every count, but Dawkins had peddled his theory for years, and was not about to give it up without a fight. In fact, he was not about to give it up full-stop. Dawkins responded two months later, dedicating two pages towards the end of a thirty-seven-page article on the classification of Pleistocene strata to Mr Geikie's 'very able article'.[182] Given such a swift turnaround, the relevant paragraphs may have added at the editing or proof stage of an already complete article. They contain little of substance. Dawkins largely contented himself with gainsaying each of Geikie's points, providing not a considered rebuttal but a reaffirmation of old positions augmented by a few glib comments. So, in the world according to Dawkins, the facts were: that the landmass of Europe was significantly larger in the past; the proximity of glaciers in the mountains was irrelevant in determining temperature on the plains – as those in the Alps and Himalayas testified; hippos reached Yorkshire so de facto had migrated; Siberia has significant floods that did not destroy the vegetation. There was only one point that Dawkins did amend, perhaps the most significant of all – the scale of seasonal migrations. The earlier papers seem fairly unambiguous –

Dawkins imagined the long north-south treks as taking place in a single year, animals returning in the winter to the grounds they had left in the summer. He now sought to clarify this idea, stating that the mixing of warm- and cold-adapted animals did *not* imply that each group walked from its 'headquarters' to the extremes of its range in a single year. By discussing this in the core argument and not the main reply to Geikie, he further gave the impression that he had decided upon it of his own volition, irrespective of his opponents previous comments. But the revision is opaque and it is difficult to fully comprehend how it fits into the Dawkins' overall thinking:

'In the secular lowering of the temperature, the northern animals would compete with the southern for their feeding-grounds, according to the season. And this competition, if the climatal conditions were stationary, might be carried on, over a very small area, for a very long time – the debatable ground being a narrow band between the invaders and the animals in possession. There were probably many such pauses. Nor does it imply that there were no reversions to a warm, or temperate state … the mixture of forms brought about by the southward advance of northern animals would be the same as that of their retreat'.[183]

This argument appears hurried and half-formed, but one must conclude that Dawkins now believed that seasonal migrations occurred on a smaller scale, overprinted by long-term temperature trends that altered the latitudinal limits of the northern and southern animal groups over many decades. When and where the limits of their ranges overlapped, elements from both groups would be found as seasonal visitors to the same locations.

It is only necessary to note that in his own reply Geikie once more rejected the idea of peripatetic hippos, refused to accept the analogy of glaciers in the Himalayas or the Alps because they occurred at totally different latitudes, and re-modelled the climate of Europe using Dawkins' parameters, although he was baffled by the logic of using the presence of pygmy hippopotamus on Mediterranean islands to suppose the region had been uplifted by an astonishing 3000 ft. 'Would not an earlier incursion or a series of small hops along now submerged islands not be more parsimonious?' he asked. Geikie concluded that as long as Europe retained a long Atlantic Coast, and had more-or-less the same physical features, then its climate would differ from that of Asia and North America, whether or not Britain was joined to continental Europe or the land around the Mediterranean greatly increased.[184]

We cannot escape the fact that both men were equally pertinacious, Dawkins totally incapable of retreat, Geikie primed to fight for his unorthodox views. The pair sat on opposite sides of a geological Parliament, but unlike Churchill, neither was about to cross the floor. In 1874 both Dawkins' *Cave Hunting* and Geikie's *Great Ice Age* rehearsed the same arguments using the same facts, both men unable to resist the temptation to have just one more swipe at their opponent. Dawkins' tome, interestingly, made no further reference to the hurriedly adopted revision to the seasonal migration theory and, ignoring every one of Geikie's objections, wrote a clear reaffirmation of his classic model, all scalar considerations apparently abandoned:

' ...[concerning] the present distribution of animals in northern Asia and North America. As the winter comes on the arctic species gradually retreat southwards, and occupy the summer feeding-grounds of the elk, red deer, and other creatures which are unable to endure the extreme severity of an arctic winter. In the spring the latter pass northwards, to enjoy the summer herbage of that area, which had been the winter-quarters of the arctic group of animals. Thus there is a continued swinging to and fro, over the same region...it will be seen that these conditions were amply satisfied in the Pleistocene. There were no physical barriers to migration, from the shores of the Mediterranean, as far north as Ireland. If the winter cold were severe, the reindeer and the musk-sheep might advance as far south as the Pyrenees, and if the summer heat were intense there would be nothing to forbid the hippopotamus and African carnivores advancing northward'.[185]

Glacial Wrangling Part 2: Victoria Cave
As the Geikie-Dawkins feud ran itself into an impasse, another skirmish broke out in North Yorkshire. In 1874 Richard Hill Tiddeman (Plate 5), a Geological Survey geologist whose main research area included Yorkshire, had taken over from Dawkins as director of the Victoria Cave excavations with a grant of £50 from the BAAS, a much needed cash boost. Dawkins' tenure as director had left the excavations with debts of £37, paid off in full by John Birkbeck senior so that the work could go forward free of all liabilities, but when the original Settle Committee met on 9 October they decided that the excavation would only recommence when the total funding pool exceeded £100. Local subscriptions eventually added £113 4s 3d to the BAAS award, but however much they raised it was never enough. The excavations of 1874-1878 continued on a year-round basis, but most years Tiddeman was forced to suspend work due to lack of funds, the men being laid off for up to two months while additional subscriptions were sought.[186]

The year of Dawkins' departure had been eventful. Busk had identified a fibula from the Lower Cave Earth as human, while Tiddeman published in full his conclusion that the context and contents were pre-glacial;[187] neither much impressed Dawkins. The excavation committee decided that the next year should be dedicated to examining new exposures of the lower beds inside and outside the cave to establish beyond doubt their stratigraphic relationships. By July 1874, Jackson had removed more of the external talus, to a point just above the boulder clay, working the sediment in horizontal layers according to the Pengelly method (apart from a single 4 ft hole excavated at the instigation of Joseph Prestwich in front of a large fallen block). To avoid any suspicion about the accuracy of his observations, Tiddeman invited all interested parties to see the evidence for themselves.[188] On the day only Miall, Tiddeman and John Birkbeck attended from the two Committees, but a number of other 'gentlemen' were present including two Survey men, William Aveline and John Dakyns, mappers of the country around the Lake District and West Yorkshire, respectively. The new geological sections confirmed Tiddeman's conclusions and the party was unanimous that the boulder clay could not, as Professor Hughes insisted, have fallen from the cliff above in postglacial times. The cliff top was free of boulder clay, as was the body of the talus, and the boulders lay so close to the base of the cliff that if all the weathered limestone contained in the talus was restored to its original position, the cliff would project beyond them. They simply could not have fallen into their current resting place, a glacier must have directly deposited them there. Prestwich and Bristow (another Survey man) agreed. Later, the boulder clay was found to be so extensive that any remaining suggestions that it was just an isolated fallen block vanished completely.

Inside the cave, the fauna from the Lower Cave Earth was enriched by the discovery of hippopotamus, straight-tusked elephant and narrow-nosed rhinoceros in Chamber D. By the end of the 1875, Tiddeman believed he had two distinct faunas, separated from each other by 12 ft of solid clay.[189] The upper assemblage was a cold-adapted fauna that contained reindeer, the lower one consisted exclusively of warm-adapted Pleistocene species, previous identifications of mammoth and woolly rhino in this fauna now seen to be in error.[190] (Table 3.3) Tiddeman was aware that this pattern supported Geikie's ideas of separate interglacials, and refuted Dawkins' seasonal migration hypothesis. Two chopped goat bones had also been found in association with the lower fauna, further evidence of contemporary humans according to Tiddeman, although others expressed serious and reasonable doubts about the Pleistocene credentials of goat. Knowing that goat had been found alongside Pleistocene fauna in Belgian Caves, Tiddeman solicited a testimonial from Eduard Dupont, a man considered in his own country as

	Human	Hyaena	Horse	Grizzly Bear	Brown Bear	Straight-tusked elephant	Narrow-nosed rhino	Hippopotamus	Red Deer	Reindeer	Aurochs
Upper Cave Earth	*		*	*					*	*	
Lower Cave Earth	*	*		*	*	*	*	*	*		*

Table 3.3: Fauna from Victoria Cave, showing differences between the Upper Cave Earth and Lower Cave Earth. (After Tiddeman 1875, omitting Holocene intrusions).

arrogant and authoritarian. Dupont obliged, but the age of the goat was still doubtful – in fact they are probably Roman in age and show hack marks consistent with military tools.[191]

One potential complication was a single record of reindeer marked with a depth of '8'.[192] If this denoted 8 ft, then reindeer occurred well below the upper fauna horizon, although Tiddeman believed it to be a clerical error that should have read .8, or 8 inches. Dawkins also wasted no time in reminding Tiddeman that reindeer had, in fact, been found in the lower bone bed at the mouth of the cave when he (Dawkins) was in charge, although with his far superior understanding of the cave Tiddeman was able to summarily dismiss this quibble. The lower bone bed at the spot mentioned by Dawkins was found 16 ft beneath the laminated clays, far below the point where the reindeer in question was recovered. That notwithstanding, hyaena and reindeer, common enough in the cave, were only found mixed together at the ends of the sections where the beds converged and were mutually exclusive where the two bone beds were isolated by the full thickness of deposits. In other words, they were only found together where the chances of cross-contamination were high and never where the integrity of the deposits was maintained.[193]

These conclusions were anathema to Dawkins, who simply could not and would not accept that the two faunas were chronologically distinct, for obvious reasons. Dawkins went on the offensive, taking the first opportunity – which happened to be a talk before the Geological Society about a completely different site (Creswell Crags, see Chapters 4-7) – to deliver a verdict on Victoria Cave.[194] He totally dismissed the claimed human fibula, identifying it as a large bear instead, and rejected the testimony of Tiddeman's pre-glacial fauna because the deposits above it could not be shown to Dawkins' satisfaction to be glacial. He disingenuously argued that the laminated clay contained no boulders and was simply derived from 'the wreck of boulder clay at a higher level', while the boulders outside the cave had fallen from above, repeating Hughes' idea which, though totally discredited by field observations, agreed with Dawkins' opinion and was therefore entitled to 'the greatest weight'.[195]

According to Dawkins, doubts about Victoria Cave had troubled him since he had been in charge of the excavations. Whether these were based on fact, prejudice or were conjured up after the event is hard to say, as Jackson's records from 1870-1873, the period of Dawkins' directorship, are missing. Tom Lord, the modern authority on Victoria Cave, suspects that Dawkins may have destroyed these notes to silence unwelcome evidence.[196] Dawkins himself was anything but silent, a fact exposed by Joseph Prestwich who asked him whether the 'impression that prevailed in some quarters that there had been a want of care in the excavation of the Victoria Cave was well founded,' a question Dawkins never directly answered, merely stating that '*at present*, the Victoria Cave is being carefully worked' [my emphasis].[197] We can guess from this that Dawkins did not restrict his criticisms to public fora, but was also conducting a whispering campaign behind the scenes,[198] one loud enough to reach the ears of Prestwich and no doubt most other members of the geological community. There could be only one purpose behind this – to undermine Tiddeman's credibility and cast doubts on his conclusions at Victoria Cave. Some loyally came out in defence of Tiddeman, John Dakyns writing to the *Geological Magazine* and stating in indignant tones that from his many visits to the cave he had been impressed by the great care taken in the work and scrupulous accuracy in recording.[199] But the seeds of doubt had been sown far and wide, and could not fail but to bear fruit.

On 22 May 1877, the Royal Anthropological Institute of Great Britain and Ireland (RAI) held a special event to debate the current state of the 'Antiquity of Man' question. There were three speakers on the programme – Dawkins, Hughes and Tiddeman – with John Evans, as the Society's President, in the Chair. Like Dawkins, Evans was a monoglacialist and a post-glacialist, who following his pioneering observations had settled into entrenched positions.[200] He opened the event by calling for a strong evidential basis, emphasising that many interconnecting types of information would be needed to resolve the problem but that each of these should be left up to those who knew them best.[201] Dawkins spoke next, tackling the evidence from the caves.[202] Posing the question of whether any of the evidence could be considered pre-glacial or interglacial, he went on to rehearse the usual litany of sites, naturally finding nothing that might support Geikie's model. He could barely conceal his disdain for the Geikie/Croll notion that faunas originally separated by intervals of 5-12,000 years (the speculative duration of glacial/interglacial cycles) could end up mixed in the same layer in the same condition, while Geikie's shortcomings in palaeontology were further exposed by his foolhardy declaration, in Dawkins' eyes, that the co-existence of reindeer and hyaena was an impossibility.[203] The sheer abundance of hyaena-gnawed reindeer bones in the record showed this to be nonsense. For Dawkins the only valid model was of course the seasonal migration theory. Victoria Cave added 'nothing to the evidence'. Dawkins repeated his conviction that the 'human' fibula was in fact a bear and that reindeer was a genuine part of the lower faunal suite: those were the facts and neither Tiddeman's refusal to accept them nor the curious disappearance of the reindeer specimen from the collection at Giggleswick Grammar School could change that. Hughes spoke next, giving a short talk on the evidence from the river gravels of East Anglia.[204] East Anglia was the survey area of Sidney Skertchley (1850-1926), who had only recently announced the discovery of stone tools in brickearth deposits at Brandon and Thetford that could be traced to positions both above and beneath boulder clay. Yet, until this was demonstrated to his satisfaction, Hughes found no reason to alter his previous opinion and maintained that there was no evidence for interglacial or pre-glacial man. Tiddeman had the unenviable, and undoubtedly engineered, task of speaking last,[205] his arguments on the fauna and age of Victoria Cave having been refuted by Dawkins before Tiddeman had even uttered a word. Tiddeman was at pains to stress that the testimony from the site did not depend entirely on the fibula, and explained that the absence of earlier traces of humans or animals from northern and eastern England was a result of a recent ice advance, which had laid waste to land surfaces and destroyed all traces of life in its wake. Dawkins had unwittingly provided some of the evidence for this himself, when he noted that geographical lacunae in fossil remains coincided with regions bearing the freshest glacial markings. But for Tiddeman this was not, as Dawkins believed, because glaciers had excluded animals from these areas but because glaciers had obliterated any evidence of their presence. The only places where evidence might be found were caverns, such as Victoria Cave.

The final talk was followed by a discussion, a version of which was published after the main papers. From the nature of the comments, one would be excused for wondering whether most of the audience had been asleep. At least Busk and Prestwich, both of whom sided with Tiddeman, had been listening, with Busk confirming his belief that the fibula was human and Prestwich giving an extempore lecture on the Thames terraces. How far the published version of the proceedings was censored will never really be known, but Geikie[206] wrote to *Nature* expressing his disappointment that nothing new had come from the conference, where the same faces proposed the same controverted stories and where new facts had been removed from consideration before they had even been published[207], on the dubious basis of due caution.

Dawkins also harassed Tiddeman personally. He was absent when the Victoria Cave report was read before the 1878 BAAS meeting at Dublin, but later extracted from Tiddeman a promise to revise the text of the Committee's report to his satisfaction and to give him final approval before publication.[208] Dawkins then resigned as secretary to the Committee. Tiddeman also received letters telling him that he had misrepresented the views of William Davies (British Museum) on the fibula, and demanding to know why reindeer had not been mentioned in recent accounts of the cave.[209] The tone of Dawkins' (lost) outward missives is unknown, but judging from those sent in response to other perceived slights one can guess that it was passive aggressive. Tiddeman's replies were polite and friendly. He was horrified to find that Davies did not believe the fibula was human, as he was of the impression that he had told him just the opposite. Reindeer had been omitted because it was both modern and ancient, like the wolf, bear and bison, and was therefore not much of a guide to age; if he had failed to answer adequately the first time he was asked (presumably at a Society meeting), it was because the questions had been unexpected and he floundered. '*Nemo mortelium omnibus boris sapit,*' he wrote – no man is wise at all times.

On 8 August 1878 Busk retracted his identification of the fibula, having decided on the basis of new comparative materials that it did, after all, belong to a large bear. Dawkins was vindicated on that point, but the edifice constructed around Victoria Cave was not built on a single bone but on several interconnecting lines of evidence. As Tiddeman's BAAS report for 1878 explains, remove the fibula and the geology still told the same story, the lower bone bed still had a unique thermophilous fauna, human presence was still attested by the (highly dubious) chopped goat bones.[210] Nevertheless, this was a personal and professional disaster for Tiddeman, whatever positives he tried to glean from it. The fibula was probably the only reason the BAAS ever funded the excavations. In closing his report he apologised that the labours of that year had brought little for the monies invested, but was sure this was a blip that would be overcome in future years. He begged for the Committee to be reappointed.

The BAAS did not reappoint the Committee. The funding was gone. The fibula debacle combined with Dawkins' crusade to undo Tiddeman were no doubt factors in this decision, but it is worth noting that among the vice-presidents of the Geological Section of the BAAS that year were William Boyd Dawkins and Thomas McKenny Hughes. The president was John Evans, whose closing remarks as Chair of the RAI debate had not exactly been a whole-hearted endorsement of the lines of evidence relied upon by Tiddeman.

For all the advances he had made in the previous decade, these two episodes reveal that Dawkins was becoming unreceptive to new ideas, or at least to those that disagreed with his own positions. He used his influence to quash perfectly good evidence of complex Pleistocene climate change and in so doing lost the friendship of Richard Tiddeman, prevented Victoria Cave from taking its rightful place among the canon of celebrated British cave sites, and basically held back the progress of Quaternary science. It was probably not his finest hour, but neither was it his worst. As a final insult, Dawkins requested that his dissent from the 1878 BAAS report was fully recorded, obviously not satisfied with the revised version requested of Tiddeman.

Around the World in 138 Days

When offered the curatorship at Manchester, Dawkins had been shrewd enough to negotiate the same holiday entitlement as its academic staff. This allowed him the freedom to continue his many annual museum visits, but also freed up larger blocks of time for foreign excursions. While at the Survey, Dawkins had made only one foreign trip, to the 3rd International Congress for Prehistoric Archaeology in Paris in September 1867. He wisely avoided Paris during the Franco-Prussian War of 1870-1871, when the city had been under siege and the Museum of Natural History shelled, but made another trip to France in the Autumn of 1873, visiting Louis Lartet (son of Édouard) in Lyons, and Professors Gervais and Gaudry at the Jardin des Plantes, Paris. His archive at Buxton Museum contains sketches of antlers and bone made at the time.

On Monday 7 June 1875, Dawkins took the 4.15pm train from Manchester to London, spending the night at the Euston Hotel. There he met Rooke Pennington to whom he entrusted his will. At 8.40pm the following day Dawkins departed for Paris, the first destination on a round-the-world adventure that would last five months (Figure 3.9). Ostensibly the purpose of trip was to assess the prospects of an Australian kerosene mine on behalf of a consortium of Manchester businessmen – one of his earlier forays into commercial geology – for which he was paid £1000 plus expenses.[211]

Dawkins of course took every opportunity to visit colleagues and examine materials. Frances did not accompany him on the trip, or if she did he never once mentioned her presence, although he did note that the weather was smooth.[212] From Paris he took a train to Turin, the first leg of a five-day journey through Italy to the port at Brindisi, which also took him through Alessandra, Bologna, Parma, and Ancona. At Brindisi they boarded a steamer to Alexandria, Egypt, passing on the way Dalmatia, Albania, Zakinthos and Crete, Dawkins rising at 3am to get a glimpse of Mount Ida. Dawkins' diaries also record a game of rope quoits, the excitement of which must have left just as an indelible impression as these geographical spectacles.

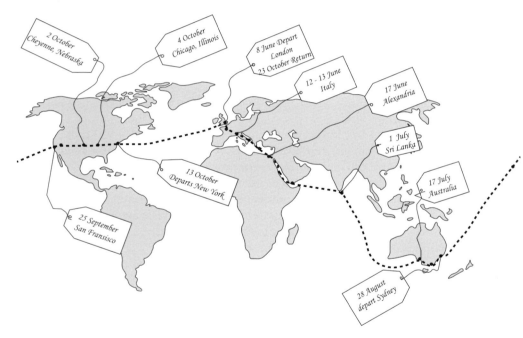

Figure 3.9: Dawkins' World Tour 1875.

He arrived in Alexandria at 5.30pm on Friday 17 June departing on the train for Suez just two and a half hours later, where he was due to board a steamer to Australia. The boat was old but with good deck cabins; the heat, he noted, was considerable. The journey took a full month and after passing the Red Sea he landed only at Aden on 23 June and Sri Lanka on 1 July.

Dawkins' diaries are characteristically spartan: noting the state of the sea, the location of each Sunday's Christian service, and flying fish. On 3 July Dawkins waved goodbye to the Old World as the boat left Sri Lanka and headed out for Australia. His diary for this period records only the temperature, which he found uncomfortable, and the fact that he was ill for the entire week prior to arriving in King George's Sound on 17 July. The steamer trip continued round the coast via Adelaide (21 July), Melbourne (23 July), Sydney (28 July) and Mount Victoria (3 August), Dawkins was greeted at each point and dined by local scholars, dignitaries and politicians. He assiduously noted in his diary every important person he met and every personal expense he incurred – hotels, meals, cabs, trains, boats, porterage, drinks and tips – and on 30 July had a 'fight with Caldwell about £1300'. Two days latter Caldwell paid Dawkins £900, but there is little else to learn of this intriguing episode or indeed who Caldwell was, although given the sums of money involved he was probably a member or an agent of the Manchester consortium.

This lack of archival information is a characteristic of Dawkins' whole life – unless he published it, it is generally lost. A surviving album of postcards and plates of people, places and specimens from Africa, Australia, New Zealand, Hawaii, and North America reveals that he took or was given a lot of photographs and bought guidebooks that he later cannibalised.[213] But he wrote little down, or if he did little has been preserved. It is truly a shame that his diaries for the whole trip record so few details – what we have are really records of appointments. There would definitely have been people at home willing to pay good money to learn more of Dawkins' plight while 'nearly lost in the bush,' as he baldly noted on 19 August, while visiting kerosene oil-shale pits at Hartley, close to the Blue Mountains.

These pits were the reason for the trip, and became one of Dawkins' favourite tales. The story told to many friends and reporters was that while in Australia he was working as a consulting engineer for a group of Manchester businessmen, who had empowered him to offer any sum necessary for the licence to extract the oil.[214] Dawkins inspected the pits, which were presumably genuine, but discovered that the vendors were fraudsters who did not actually own the property. Fearful of exposure and prosecution they offered Dawkins £8000 to keep quiet – 23 times his annual salary – but he refused the bribe. The next day he sent telegrams to the value of £5 10s 0d and spent £8 10s 0d contacting the exchange in London, presumably relaying his report on the incident back to England; although as ever the diary contains only details of his itinerary and personal expenses (£1 15s 0d) and nothing of the fraud. It is at this point that one actually has to ask whether Dawkins realised just what he might have been getting himself into – practically alone, in the bush, presumably unarmed, with a group of con-men he was about to expose. There must have been some truth in the story, for on his return he told it to E.A. Freeman who commented, 'So you have been round the World, gathering great sums honestly and refusing greater sums dishonestly'[215] but if it played out exactly as Dawkins described, he was frankly lucky to escape with his life.

On 28 August Dawkins left Australia for New Zealand, where he spent only one day before heading north across the Pacific Ocean to Honolulu. He arrived on the island at midnight of 16 September and departed for San Francisco just twelve hours later. San Francisco Bay came into view on 26 September; on landing he immediately bought a cross-continental train ticket to New York, at a cost of £30 8s 4d. This epic journey was broken by brief stops in Battle Mountain, Nevada; Cheyenne, Wyoming; Omaha, Nebraska; Niagara; and Boston, Massachusetts. At the latter destination he took a few days out to visit Harvard University, meeting amongst others Oliver Wendell Holmes Sr. (1809-1894), Dean of the Medical School[216] and the geologist Nathaniel Shaler (1841-1906).

His first stop in Nevada lasted little more than forty-eight hours, but during this time he examined argentiferous deposits and was offered the chance to purchase his own silver mine for £350. He personally verified that the ore was of good quality, but decided he could not leave his work in Manchester to run a mine. When the price of silver plummeted the following year, to levels so low that the crisis was discussed in the Commons, Dawkins could be argued to have had a narrow escape, although his letter to the *Pall Mall Gazette*[217] shows it was nothing of the sort. Dawkins knew that the silver reserves in the mountains were vast, a fortune, but also guessed that when 'progress' had overcome the present obstacles to extraction – poor transport links, lack of wood, and hostile native Americans – the price could only collapse. Dawkins was shrewd, not lucky.

He arrived in New York on Sunday 10 October 1875 in a state of excitement – 'NEW YORK' – he impressed heavily into his diary. The American adventure ended on 14 October, when he left for Europe on the steamer 'Russia'. They landed in England on Saturday 23 October, after 138 days away, finally reaching Manchester on Friday 29 October. The entry for the following day records the sum of £845 10s 11d, presumably the total cost of the journey, of which the prudent Dawkins could account for every penny.

Dawkins returned to Britain a famous and now well-travelled geologist, with every reason to be optimistic that 1876 and beyond would bring even greater triumphs. His spirit would perhaps not be disappointed to know that it is for the events of the next five years at Creswell Crags that he is mostly remembered today. In fact, the names Creswell and William Boyd Dawkins are almost indivisible in geological and archaeological circles. He would probably be horrified to learn, however, that it is not fame but infamy that drives this legacy.

Chapter 4

Creswell Crags, 1875

The Hamlet of Creswell and its Gorge

Creswell in the 1870s was nothing more than a rural hamlet on the north-eastern boundary of Derbyshire. Houses spread out over both banks of the river Wollen, the south-eastern part belonging to the parish of Elmton, the north-western part to the parish of Whitwell. The 1881 Census lists just 338 men, women and children occupying sixty-five homes, 90% of them belonging to Creswell-with-Elmton. Most of its denizens were agricultural and industrial workers (quarrymen, stokers and miners), craftsmen (blacksmiths, cordwainers, masons, wheelwrights, tailors) or shopkeepers. Creswell had its own school and schoolmistress, but no Post Office, the nearest being in Whitwell.[1] In 1875 Creswell got its own railway station, part of the Midland Line running between Worksop and Nottingham, connecting this otherwise obscure location to the nexus of Victorian transportation.

About a third of a mile to the east of Creswell village is a stunning gorge known as Creswell Crags, which cuts through the Magnesian limestone to form low cliffs that reach heights of 50 ft. The gorge is narrow, about 150 ft at its widest point, and runs roughly north-east to south-west for about a half a mile – the northern side being in Derbyshire, the southern side in Nottinghamshire. The river Wollen once flowed through it, but was dammed at the eastern end by the Duke of Portland in the 1860s to form a small boating lake, which still exists today.[2] The Crags were a well-known local beauty spot, and had been used as a backdrop for a series of paintings by the eighteenth century artist George Stubbs, most of which, of course, included horses. Until 2007 the road from Worksop to Welbeck ran on the northern side of the gorge, so it was not exactly off the beaten track in local terms.

The cliffs, then and now, are beautifully wooded, and heavily fissured; twenty-four openings are currently known, six of them forming reasonably large caves. The gorge probably represents a collapsed phreatic system (formed by dissolution of the limestone below the water table) and the caves share a similar origin.[3] The earliest Pleistocene sediments in the caves date to the Last Interglacial (the Ipswichian Interglacial or Marine Isotope Stage 5e, spanning the period 128,000-120,000 years ago), so the collapse would date at the latest to the preceding glacial period, although it could have conceivably occurred earlier, with all traces of more ancient sediments having been flushed out.

In 1875 the residents of Creswell could hardly have suspected what was in store for their romantic gorge.

The First Explorers: Mello and Heath

Creswell Crags was a relative latecomer in the Victorian exploration of Pleistocene caves. As we have seen, excavations at Kent's Cavern, Kirkdale and Paviland began as early as 1821; Brixham Cave was explored in 1858; Wookey Hole was investigated by our main protagonist in 1859; many others were already known, even in remotest North Wales and darkest Yorkshire. According to Rogan Jenkinson the absence of an earlier interest was in part due to Creswell's obscure location and lack of a decent transport network.[4] Although the Worksop-Welbeck road ran through it, the limestone gorge at Creswell was considered by many to be wild and impassable. Even its owner, the Fifth Duke of Portland, remarked that the route through the Crags was not even wide enough for a carriage to pass through (Plate 6), although as Mick Jackson revealed in his wonderful novel *The Underground Man,* the Fifth Duke of Portland was a dangerously eccentric man. It may be no coincidence that Creswell gained national and international renown just as it got the railway.

The first documented discovery at Creswell was made at Yew Tree Cave by W.H. Ransom, a local doctor, who gave a report on the occurrence of Lynx at the 1865 meeting of the BAAS;[5] although Pleistocene fossils had been found in what is now the Creswell Limestone Heritage Area[6] four years earlier, in a cave at Pleasley Vale. The real story, however, began in 1873 when Mr Frank Tebbet, supervisor at the Creswell Crags limestone quarry, found fossils eroding from a cattle byre at the mouth of Church Hole Cave, on the Nottinghamshire side of the Crags. Tebbet brought his finds to the attention of two people.

The first was Reverend John Magens Mello (1836-1914) (Plate 11). Mello was the eldest son of John Arnold Mello, a member of the banking dynasty Dorrien, Magens, Mello and Co,[7] which descended from eighteenth century German immigrants.[8] This heritage is obviously where Magens Mello got his highly distinctive preferred name. Mello was partly educated in Paris,

103

before going up to St John's College, Oxford in June 1854, aged 18.[9] He graduated in June 1859. Later the same year he married Charlotte Nottidge (the service was conducted by her brother Rev. George Nottidge) and took up his first curacy at All Saints, Derby.[10] Mello left Derby in 1863 – with a handsome golden handshake of 35 guineas – to take up the role of Perpetual Curate at St Thomas' Church, New Brampton, Derbyshire.[11]

Mello remained at Brampton for twenty-four years. The parish was large and straggling, and Mello took charge during a period of rapid expansion.[12] Local industrialisation had brought more workers and their families, which generated a demand for new homes and attracted new businesses. This left the parish church caring for a greatly increased flock. In August 1867, an order of the Queen's Council raised the benefice of Brampton to a Rectory with Mello as its first Rector, on an income of £310 per annum. *Kelly's Post Office Directory* for 1876 lists 6,277 residents, served by St Thomas' plus Wesleyan and Primitive Methodist Chapels. This large population would certainly have kept Mello busy, but he had a parish clerk and a curate to share the burden, and his duties did not prevent him from pursuing a full range of other interests, particularly geology, archaeology and art: for which he 'displayed considerable versatility and rare ability, and almost every year travelled either to the continent or English lakes'.[13] He was also a Member of the Société Scientific de Bruxelles, Fellow of the Geological Society, Honorary member of the Chesterfield and Midland Institute of Engineers, Member of the Burton Archaeological and Natural History Society and Corresponding Secretary of the Victoria Institute. He also served as Chaplain to the local British Volunteer Force (after 1908 the Territorial Force), a part-time riflemen, artillery and engineer corps that had originally been formed in the late 1850s to counter the growing concern for home security at a time when the regular army were positioned in numerous localities across the Empire and beyond.[14]

Mello can also be credited with the creation of a museum in Brampton, which opened on Chatsworth Road in 1868. The museum, which included many of Mello's own antiquities, seems to have been a curious mix between a library and working men's club. As Mello wrote in his parish magazine, for an annual fee of two shillings per year members had access to all leading newspapers, could borrow books or play all manner of games. When the museum was demolished in 1932, the incumbent rector Hubert J Sillitoe remarked that 'the museum was a landmark … a reminder of the days when the Church throughout the land was the largest helping hand to those who sought knowledge and culture'.[15] Available sources all comment on Mello's generous and caring nature, whether acting as an artist, author, geologist, polyglot, archaeologist or pastor. Armitage tells us that 'Mr Mello was full of fun in his own house, writing a comic "History of England" for his girls, and he and his wife and two daughters added much jolly picnicking to the arduous Creswell explorations, often turning these gatherings of the learned into merry meetings'.[16] Altogether Mello seems to have been a jolly nice fellow, although a difficult one to trace in the historical records, possibly owing to the frequent misspelling of his surname.

The second person contacted by Tebbet late in 1874 was Thomas Heath, curator and librarian at Derby Museum and Art Gallery. Heath was the youngest and least privileged of the Creswell triumvirate, and certainly never had the benefits of the Oxford education afforded to Dawkins and Mello. He was born in the ecclesiastical parish of Oughtibridge, Yorkshire, the eldest of the eight children of Mr Joseph Heath and his wife Thirza.[17] His father was a file cutter and by the age of twelve young Thomas was apprenticed in the same profession.[18] By 1870, Heath had abandoned this trade and moved to Sheffield where for a time he worked as a gardener. On 13 August 1870 he married Lucy Swallow, a blind seamstress thirteen years his senior, and by 1871 the couple were living in Bramwell Street, Sheffield, with two lodgers; Heath's occupation at this time was listed as warehouseman.[19]

In Dickensian style, Heath's prospects then underwent a sudden and rapid advancement. In 1872 he was appointed branch librarian at Upperthorpe, Sheffield and in 1873 won his position at Derby Museum. Like many museums at the time, Derby was in transition. The Burgesses of Derby had agreed in 1870 to adopt the Free Public Libraries Act, but the original building at the Wardwick was not fit for purpose.[20] While the newsroom was opened in 1871, only a small part of the museum was ever opened to the public; it eventually closed entirely in 1875 awaiting a new building. The museum finally got its building in June 1879, funded by the MP for Derby, Michael Thomas Bass, whose brewery was at the time the largest in Britain.[21] The ultimate task of filling the museum with specimens and organising its displays would fall to Heath as principal curator. As early as 1874, Heath was looking for new opportunities and was shortlisted for the post of curator at Sheffield Museum, which he did not win[22]. He remained in post at Derby for 12 years. The position did not leave Heath a particularly wealthy man compared to his colleagues – his salary in 1875 was £100,[23] less than a third of Mello or Dawkins' incomes. He lived in a tied house at 3 Wardwick, Derby, by 1881 having been joined by his 16 year-old brother, Herbert .[24] His job was thus his livelihood and his home. When the Creswell excavations began, Heath was just 28 years old. His credentials had been given a much needed boost by his election to a Fellowship of the Royal Historical Society in January 1874, but of the three men associated with Creswell in the 1870s he had the most to gain and the most to lose.[25]

The First Explorations: April-June 1875

Neither Mello nor Heath acted on Tebbet's information immediately, but local geologist Dr Bergener and his students continued to pick up miscellaneous finds until April 1875.[26] This delay was to be to Heath's lasting regret. Magens Mello eventually visited the gorge in April 1875, and immediately thereafter applied to the Duke of Portland for permission to work the caves. At about the same time, Thomas Heath applied to the Duke for permission to explore the caves on behalf of Derby Museum, but was informed that permission had been given to Mello 'only a few days before'.[27] As a result, in his first paper on Creswell, read before the Geological Society on 23 June of that year, Mello was at pains to lay claim to far longer intellectual priority:

'Some years ago I had formed the strong wish to examine the fissures in this locality, but until lately could never find the opportunity. Last April, however, I was enabled to pay a preliminary visit to the spot. A very brief inspection sufficed to show me that it was one well worth careful exploration; and in answer to an application to His Grace the Duke of Portland, he kindly gave me leave to carry on the work'.[28]

(Dawkins was absent from the reading, being at that point somewhere off the coast of Aden).

Mello returned in May, accompanied by two 'non-scientific friends', one of whom he named as Mr C White of Chesterfield.[29] Mello and his colleagues explored three separate openings in the rocks, which he named Fissures A, B and C – although then, as today, these were known locally as Pin Hole Cave, Robin Hood Cave and Church Hole Cave respectively. The first cave investigated was Church Hole, on the Nottingham side of the gorge, which presented a large entrance that contracted after a very short distance into a narrow fissure. Mello dug a 'small hole' at the entrance, where he found a fragment of a woolly rhinoceros leg-bone at a depth of 3-4 inches. More substantial work was undertaken at Pin Hole. From its tall, narrow entrance Pin Hole 'penetrates some 40-50 yards … it is moderately lofty throughout a good part of its course; but a short distance from its entrance it bifurcates and becomes very narrow, the western fork being inaccessible beyond a yard

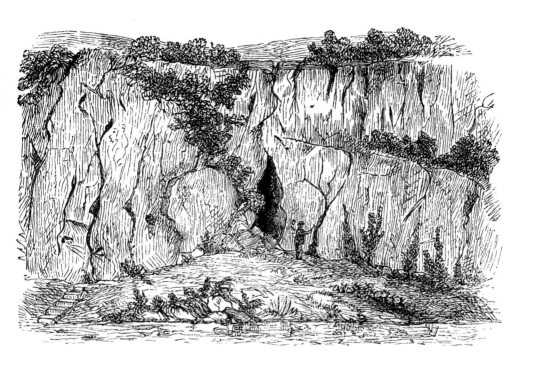

Figure 4.1: a) Mello's Drawing of Fissure A (Pin Hole Cave) before excavation; b) his early section drawing (after Mello 1875).

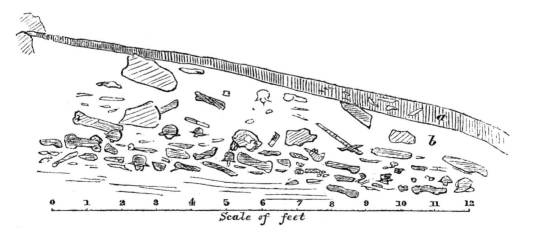

Scale of feet

or two; and the other one can only be pursued by a sidelong motion'[30] (Figure 4.1). Several large roof falls were noted, and 40 yards into the cave the passage was almost completely blocked by a mass of stalagmite and rock. Mello recorded a simple geological sequence: 4 inches of surface soil, underlain by a 3 ft thick seam of fossiliferous red sand, beneath which lay a lighter coloured sand of unknown depth. In the space of three days, a trench 25 ft long by 2 ft wide (the latter being the entire width of the cave) was excavated to exploit the bone-bearing bed. As he was not an expert in Pleistocene mammals, Mello invited Professor George Busk to identify the fauna. The results were beyond his expectations. Busk confirmed that the mammals were Pleistocene in age, and included bear, hyaena, wolf, horse, woolly rhinoceros and mammoth, many of which bore traces of carnivore gnawing. He also identified wolverine (*Gulo gulo*), a very rare animal in Britain, and arctic fox (*Alopex lagopus*), the first ever record of this animal in the British Isles. For Mello, these were exciting times and with newspapers syndicating reports of his first paper, read before the Geological Society of London on 23 June 1875. The site and its discovery quickly achieved national celebrity.[31]

That same season Mello made a superficial cutting in Robin Hood Cave. The largest cavern in the gorge, Robin Hood Cave was wider and more accessible than the others and was divided internally into four or five chambers separated by buttresses of rock. In its virgin state, the cavern was about 30 yards long and almost equally as wide. On the right hand side the roof was 'tolerably lofty' but on the left it was low, being joined to the floor by stalagmite in several places.[32] The cutting revealed a sedimentary sequence similar to the other caves, with fossiliferous red sand just below the surface-soil. This cave also yielded numerous flint chips, and some quartzite pebble tools, the first hints of Palaeolithic humans in the gorge.

There are two things that seem peculiar about the early days of the explorations. The first is the timing of Mello's reconnaissance visit and application to the Duke, and its coincidence with Heath's own letter. Living just outside Chesterfield and eight miles from Creswell, Mello had easy access to the Crags; he could have walked there in less than three hours. Although his flock at New Brampton was a large one, this never stopped him pursuing external interests, including writing the *Hand-book of the Geology of Derbyshire*, a small book of seventy-nine pages completed in 1875. Can we blithely accept that there is nothing suspicious in the fact that he apparently did nothing for years, only to act coincidentally just as Heath was told of the site? Heath and Mello cannot have been complete strangers: both lived locally, both were keen geologists, both attended lectures at learned societies and even if unknown to each other their networks must have overlapped. It is not, therefore, entirely beyond belief that Mello found out about Heath's interest and intentions and this finally drove him into action.

The second question is why Mello asked Busk and not Dawkins to assist him with the fauna. We have already met George Busk (1807-1888), one of the great polymaths of Victorian science. He had started his career as a naval surgeon, during which time he had worked for the Seaman's Hospital Society on diseases such as cholera, scurvy and smallpox.[33] On retiring from service in 1855, he concentrated his efforts on his other passion, natural history, becoming an authority on palaeontology and zoology.[34] He had authored monographs on the Polyzoa (primitive multicellular organisms), was involved in the Brixham Cave excavations, and played a key role in the recognition and interpretation of the earliest-discovered Neanderthal skulls. He also held Fellowships of the Royal Society, the Geological Society, the Linnaean Society, and Royal College of Surgeons, among others, and was President of the Anthropological Institute (1873-4). He was a member of the infamous X-Club, the exclusive and powerful fellowship of eminent Darwinists who had set out to transform Victorian science into a visionary world-leading powerhouse,[35] which numbered among its ranks John Lubbock (archaeologist), Joseph Hooker (botanist), Herbert Spencer (philosopher), William Spottiswode (mathematician), John Tyndall (physicist), Edward Frankland (chemist), Thomas Hurst (mathematician) and Thomas Huxley ('Darwin's Bulldog'). One might suggest that Busk was too high up the food chain to bother with a pilot excavation conducted by a rural vicar.

Dawkins was equally renowned, however, and being a master self-publicist perhaps even more famous than Busk, especially locally. A short train ride away in Manchester he would have been a much more obvious choice to study the Creswell fauna than the London-based Busk. Mello and Dawkins must have known each other from the Geological Society of London (both were fellows) and other local societies, and Mello almost certainly would have owned and read Dawkins' works. Although no documents have been found to prove it, I suspect that Dawkins would have been Mello's first choice, and he may well have asked Dawkins to assist during the summer of 1875, only to find that the Professor was due to leave England on 8 June to embark on his round-the-world tour. Maybe it was Dawkins who initially suggested Busk or approached him on Mello's behalf. Dawkins and Busk were old colleagues and they sat on many of the same committees (Settle, Kent's Cavern); as palaeontological specialists they were rather interchangeable and it was not unusual for one to replace the other on a project depending on availability, interest and social factors. The very fact that Busk remained involved in the Creswell Crags Exploration Committee formed in 1876 implies that he bore no resentment at being replaced by Dawkins. This is entirely in keeping with the character of a man described as being 'of unaffected simplicity and gentleness, without a trace of vanity'[36] and whose 'self-effacing (and perhaps even diffident) manner prevented him achieving a higher profile'.[37] That said, he clearly had issues with some of Dawkins' ideas and was not afraid to speak his mind.

If he did not know of it before, Dawkins was certainly made aware of the excavations on his return to England. Writing on 5 November 1875, Augustus Wollaston Franks (1826-1897) told Dawkins he had met Mello at Sheffield and that he was digging at Creswell: 'I think you know him,'[38] Franks remarked.

Working In Perfect Harmony: July 1875

If Heath was disappointed by the negative response from the Duke, he soon took steps to rectify the matter. The Duke's letter had contained a vital piece of information – Mello had been given permission to dig.[39] Heath wrote to Mello offering to assist him in the work, and Mello replied positively on 18 June. Heath was overjoyed at the 'very much more liberal terms than I could have expected'.[40] For Heath, Creswell was a means of obtaining a large collection of Pleistocene fauna for Derby Museum,[41] which granted him a leave of absence in 1875 to participate in the excavation and authorised him to cover one-third of the costs.[42] It is fair to assume that the Museum Committee expected a return on their money in the form of an outstanding collection and kudos. As events will show, they got neither.

Heath joined the excavation early in July and for the rest of the season the two 'worked together in perfect harmony'.[43] Excavations began with renewed effort in Pin Hole Cave, but this was soon abandoned as the deposits became increasingly barren: 'All the front of the cavern was thoroughly searched, the chief bones found being two perfect pelves of *Rhinoceros tichorhinus* [woolly rhinoceros] and also two atlases [neck vertebra] of the same animal, together with a few reindeer and other bones of no particular interest. As we worked our way further into the fissure the number of bones found was very small indeed; the bed of red sand, which at the entrance of the cave had proved so rich in its contents … was nearly destitute of bones; and we determined to desert that cave for the time and begin the exploration of a neighbouring one a little lower down the ravine, and in the same side of it'.[44]

They then turned their attention to Robin Hood Cave. The first day was spent removing large limestone blocks from the cave entrance, after which Heath and Tebbet cut a trench across the mouth down to the limestone bedrock. Heath's account contains significant details that are missing from Mello's 'official' one, as well as a number of discrepancies.[45] While Mello described a section at the entrance some 8 ft thick, Heath reports that the deposits in the trench were 'for some distance' only 2 ft deep and 'suddenly' ran out. The whole area had been recently disturbed, and although remains of hyaena and woolly rhinoceros were recovered, these lay alongside Roman pottery, a human incisor and bones of modern animals. On the east side of the entrance they encountered a fissure covered by a large block of limestone – this they blasted (with the aid of workers from the quarry)[46] to reveal a cave earth full of the bones of extinct Irish elk (*Megaloceros*). They then began to excavate inside the cave, working back the section until, at a point 25 ft from the mouth, they finally revealed a full sequence of deposits: basal sands overlain by cave earth and capped with stalagmitic breccia, all highly variable in thickness (Figure 4.2-4.4) This continued with little variation up to the

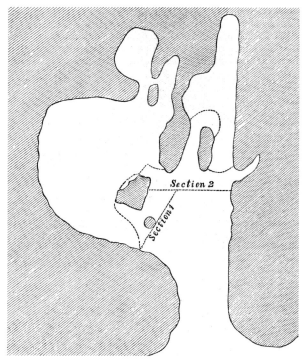

Figure 4.2: Plan of Robin Hood Cave as it was understood in 1875. The two geological sections (Figures 43a & b) are denoted by the dashed lines 1 & 2. The dotted line indicates the extent of the area worked out (after Mello 1876).

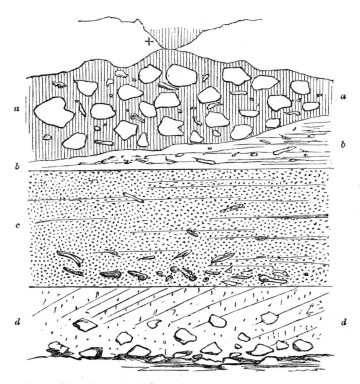

+ Stalactite uniting breccia with roof.
a. Stalagmitic breccia, with bones and implements, 18 in. to 3 ft.
b. Cave-earth, with bones and implements, of variable thickness.
c. Middle red sand with laminated red clay at base, containing bones, 3 ft.
d. Lighter-coloured sand with limestone fragments, 2 ft. ?

Figure 4.3a & b: Mello's 1875 Geological Sections, along lines 1 and 2 (Mello 1876). The sections show a full geological sequence in the cave as it was published in 1876. This described a few inches of topsoil (a) underlain by a heavily cemented breccia of varying thickness (b) that locally came into contact with the roof. It was so hard in places that it frequently had to be removed by blasting. Below this was a cave earth (c), again of varying thickness, being thinnest where the breccia was thickest, and vice versa; the breccia was almost absent from the centre of the cave (Mello and Heath 1876). Both deposits contained bones and stone implements. The cave earth was underlain by a red sand (d), also fossiliferous, with the base of the sequence being a light sand with limestone fragments (e – not shown).

a. Surface-soil and thin breccia, 2–3 in.
b. Cave-earth, with flint and quartzite implements, teeth, bones, angular limestone fragments, and charcoal, 3 ft.
c. Red Sand with laminated clay, few bones, 3 ft.
1. Fox-hole ?

entrance of Chamber C. Moving deeper into the cave, examining each
stratum in turn, Heath and Tebbet worked out Chambers A and B to within
the entrances of Chambers C and F, and partly worked out Chamber G (see
Figure 5.1 for a key to the Chamber names).[47] The further they penetrated
into the cave, the further they moved from the daylight zone; after only a few
yards they would have been entirely reliant on candle light.

The cave earth and red sand in Robin Hood Cave produced abundant
fossils of Pleistocene mammals, unequivocally proving that the deposits were

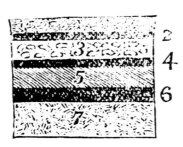

1. *Surface Soil.*
2. *Stalagmite.*
3. *Breccia.*
4. *Stalagmite.*
5. *Cave Earth.*
6. *Stalagmite.*
7. *Red Sand.*

Figure 4.4: Heath's version of the 1875 section, situated 7.6m from the entrance of the cave on the West side (equivalent to Mello's section 1). While the main units are the same, in Heath's account there are three separate stalagmite deposits. At the top of the sequence, the whole of the west side was encrusted with a stalagmite up to 2ft thick over a distance of ~10 yards. None of this appears in Mello's version, which mentions stalagmite only once - at the top of the section in Chambers A and C (Mello 1877).

formed during the severe conditions of the ice age. Horse, woolly rhinoceros, bison and hyaena dominated the assemblage, with reindeer, mammoth, bear, wolf, elk (*Alces alces*) and lion present in decreasing numbers. Dawkins later opined that the herbivores were dragged in as carcasses by hyaena, whose occupation of the cave was interrupted by floods and by humans, a conclusion bolstered by the fact that the mega-herbivores – woolly rhinoceros and mammoth – were dominated by young individuals of a size more easily hunted by hyaena and susceptible to infant mortality.[48] Hare bones were the most abundant fossils in the overlying breccia, where they were associated with Late Upper Palaeolithic artefacts; the fact that most were split or broken suggested that they had formed the principal diet of the ice age hunter-gatherers, and a valuable source of furs.

Associated with the fauna were ~390 Middle and Upper Palaeolithic stone tools. Of those from the cave earth (~107) nine were made of flint, one of ironstone, and the remainder of locally available quartzite: they included hand-axes, flakes and worked quartzite pebbles (Figure 4.5).[49] The objects in the breccia showed the opposite, only four quartzite artefacts compared to 284 of flint. There were clear technological differences between the flint and the quartzite artefacts too. The quartzite objects were considered to be the 'ruder' of the two series and were compared with those assigned by the

Figure 4.5: Artefacts from Robin Hood Cave. a) Middle Palaeolithic hand-axe made on ironstone; b & c) Middle Palaeolithic hand-axes made on quartzite; d & e) Early Upper Palaeolithic blade points made on flint; f & g) Late Upper Palaeolithic Creswellian Points made on flint (after Dawkins 1877).

Parisian archaeologist Gabriel de Mortillet to the age of Le Moustier or St Acheul, while the flint objects were seen to correspond with the age of Solutre, largely on the basis of two lance heads (now identified as Early Upper Palaeolithic leaf-points[50]). An antler awl was also described, made from a tine that Dawkins suggested had been ground down to a fine point, along with a piercer made of mammoth molar. Both were later rejected as natural objects.[51]

During the same period Heath conducted the first proper investigation of Church Hole Cave.[52] Church Hole comprises two chambers, A and B (Figure 4.6). Chamber A has an inviting entrance some 20 ft high and 8 ft wide, but this quickly narrows into a long straight fissure that runs in a north-south direction 155 ft into the cliff, where it rises steeply for another 41 ft before ending in a blocked-up crack (this may extend as a fissure on the plateau above). Chamber B, to the west of Chamber A, is 45 ft long from its entrance through a small fissure in the cliff face to its rear wall. Inside, the two Chambers join some 30 ft from the cliff face. At the start of the excavation, Mello noted that the front of the cave had been used as a stable or cattle byre, and that for a distance of about 20 ft from a newly installed door or gate (see Figure 4.6) the sediments were disturbed to a depth of 3 ft.[53] This was probably the result of earlier wildcat explorations but according to Mello the majority of the bones had gone unnoticed.[54] At 25 ft from the door the passage had been completely walled-up to 'keep out foxes'.[55] When first explored, the long passage (Chamber A) was covered with angular and slightly worn fragments of limestone, a number of quartzite pebbles and a large quantity of animal bones brought in by foxes. The roof was low, in places barely 12 inches from the floor although there were a number of 'lofty' cracks and chimneys, 'one of which apparently open[ed] into a passage overhead'.[56]

At 4am one fine July day, Heath began work at Church Hole, clearing a jumble of cave earth, breccia, straw and litter from inside the 'entrance', by which he almost certainly meant inside the new gate. He found no trace of Pleistocene animals until 10.20am, when he uncovered a large mammoth molar 12 ft from the gate. Three others lay in close proximity. When he reached a point adjacent to the junction with Chamber B, Heath discovered three bone needles; he stopped when he reached the wall.[57] For the rest of the day he worked out Chamber B, assisted by his friends, W.B. Sellars, S.H. Burrows and Dr. Claudius Buchanan Webster (the United States Consul at Sheffield).[58] This too had previously been disturbed, to a depth of 8 inches. As the group started working this side chamber, the deposits suddenly dipped away and in the centre about 18 inches from the surface it was one mass of

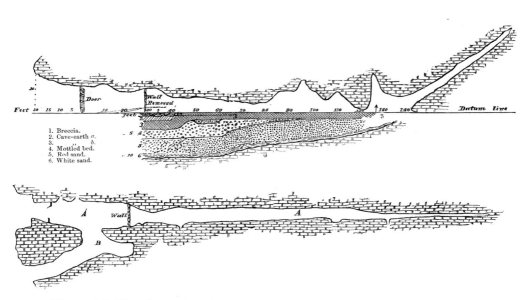

Figure 4.6: Plan (bottom) and section (top) through Church Hole (after Mello 1877).

fossils: rhino, horse, young mammoths (including many milk teeth), bear, wolf and reindeer: all heavily gnawed. Of 'over a cart-load' of bones, 'the result of that day's work'[59], only four were whole – two phalanges, a tarsal and a metatarsal. The remains of 116 different individuals were recovered, seventy-two of them hyaena. There was no trace of human presence; the low-roofed Chamber B was clearly a hyaena den. The next day Heath finished Chamber B, with the exception of a thick tough breccia adhering to the wall.

The presence of his friends might explain why Heath chose to start before dawn; he so desperately wanted to create a good impression that he felt the need to prepare the site for their arrival and ensure that their day produced a wealth of fossils for them to go home and talk about. If that was his purpose, he could not have hoped for better results. However, Heath's observations also suggested that the rhinoceros pelvis found by Mello in April had come from disturbed deposits, while the absence of significant finds for a distance of 12ft from the gate indicates that Mello was mistaken in the suggestion that the fossil content had gone unnoticed.[60]

By the end of 1875 Heath had spent upwards of fifty days working at the Crags, but the Derby Museum Committee was pleased with their investment.

Announcing Derby's share of the finds, William Hobson, the chairman of the Committee, applauded Heath's 'indefatigable research' and described the Pleistocene fossils as 'one of the most important additions that could be made to the Museum'; he also noted that Rooke Pennington had promised a collection from other Derbyshire caves.[61] Heath was thus cleared to return to Creswell, although the weather from November 1875 until February 1876 was awful enough to put him off visiting the caves. He returned in early March 1876 with his Friend Rev. W.H. Painter, and excavated the entrances of Chambers C and G in Robin Hood Cave. This work carried on until the latter part of June, when the responsibility for the site passed to a newly formed exploration committee.

The First Chords of Dissonance: April 1876
At the meeting of the Geological Society of London on 5 April 1876, Mello delivered his second report on the excavations, concentrating on the work in Robin Hood Cave: 'During the past summer I have been able to carry on the work of exploration, assisted by Mr. Thomas Heath, F.R.H.S., Curator of the Derby Museum, who has been able to devote a good deal of time to it, and whose skilful help has been of great value in carrying on the researches; and I must also acknowledge the energetic assistance given us by Mr. F. Tebbet, superintendent at the Creswell quarries, who from the beginning has taken much interest in these discoveries'.[62]

Mello's paper was immediately followed by a report on the mammal remains and traces of man from Robin Hood Cave, given by Dawkins, the newest member of the Creswell team. As a hint of things to come, Dawkins referred to Heath as Mello's 'coadjutor' (an assistant to a bishop),[63] thereby creating a distorted picture of the relationship between the two men that marked Heath as Mello's inferior. Of the three men, Heath had spent most time at the site 'assisting' in the excavations, Mello had visited rarely and Dawkins had not at that point even seen the site. Otherwise, the session past rather uneventfully, the subsequent discussion dominated by questions relating to the absence of coprolites (Dawkins asserted that the cave was too wet for their preservation), and whether the quartzite implements were necessarily older than the flint ones, a recurring theme.

Things soon took a turn for the worse. On 8 April 1876 *The Pall Mall Gazette*, a popular London evening newspaper with a circulation of 10,000 copies a day, carried an anonymous article on the '*Recent Discoveries in Caves in Derbyshire*'. The author painted a vivid picture of life in the ice age, describing the habits and prey of savage hyaenas and the rude tribes of hunters who left behind tools similar to those used by Eskimos and North American Indians. The discovery was lauded as the most significant since Brixham Cave in 1858, and Mello and Dawkins were credited with bringing it to the attention of the scientific world. Thomas Heath was not mentioned once. He was understandably upset and embarrassed; such a blatant snub would not go down well with his employers at the museum. To make matters worse, the story was not confined to London but was picked up by local newspapers over the course of the following week, including the *Sheffield Independent, Nottinghamshire Guardian, Derbyshire Times* and *Chesterfield Herald*. Mello regretted the omission but did not think it was a deliberate slight. He was apparently under the impression that John Evans was the author of the offending piece, in which case he must be excused as he could have had no knowledge of Heath's true role.[64] The real author of the piece was Dawkins.[65] Heath was furious, although felt powerless to do anything about it.[66] The stage was now set for a bitter feud that would long outlast the excavations and set in motion a convoluted cycle of vitriol and acrimony in which no party was wholly innocent.

First into the fray was John Plant, who still bore a grudge over the disputed discovery of Windy Knoll Fissure. He was more than happy to intervene on Heath's behalf. At the meeting of the MGS on 25 April 1876 Plant interrupted proceedings before ordinary business could commence to call the members' attention to discoveries at Creswell Crags.[67] He went on to describe the stratigraphy, mammals and artefacts recovered from Robin Hood Cave the previous year, stating that 'the excavations have been, for the most part, carried out by Mr Thomas Heath, curator at the Museum of Derby, and chiefly at the expense of a member of the Derby Museum and Library Committee'.[68] His speech could barely have lasted more than two minutes, but its effect was magnificent.

In the Chair for the meeting was William Boyd Dawkins, who immediately expressed 'considerable astonishment' at the communication for a number of reasons. Foremost among Dawkins' concerns was that Plant was in possession of specimens from Creswell, which more properly belonged with Mello's collection, and that he had omitted to mention Mello at all. He went on to warn that it was a 'very serious mistake for any person to interfere with an excavation which is being carried on as admirably as Mr Mello is carrying on this...[and] which is not in any degree complete,' pointing the audience in the direction of more 'official' announcements such as *The Times* and *Pall Mall Gazette*.[69]

A short report of the meeting was published in the *Manchester Guardian* for 26 April 1876. This contained details of Plant's reply to Dawkins, which were not reported when the Society published its own record of the meeting. In answer to Dawkins, Plant had said that 'his object had been accomplished. He wished to get from Professor Dawkins what his knowledge of this "find" was. He had been requested by Mr Heath and another gentleman to mention the matter at the Manchester Geological Society, so that he [Mr Heath] might give a denial to what Professor Dawkins had just stated'.

If Plant thought he was acting selflessly and in the best interests of Heath, in the latter's eyes he was actually making things worse. Heath acted quickly to distance himself from the whole affair, fearing perhaps that he could be removed from the Creswell excavations altogether. On 28 April, Heath sent a letter to the *Manchester Guardian* in which he denied having ever communicated with Plant over Creswell 'or any other subject' and stating that 'Professor Dawkins's remarks are substantially correct'.[70] This rather irked Plant, who was now being cast as an unwelcome *agent provocateur*. Furthermore, Plant's actions had come at personal cost, for Dawkins' 'considerable astonishment', reported in the TMGS in a pleasant and almost genteel fashion, had manifest itself not as a measured response but as a verbal assault. Plant wrote to the *Manchester Guardian*:

'Mr Thomas Heath is literally correct in saying he "never had any communication with Mr. Plant upon that or any other subject"; but it is only a quibble, so to put it. At the Geological Society's meeting, in replying to the uncalled-for attack on me by Professor Dawkins, I did not weigh my words very carefully, or I should have said, to be strictly accurate that a gentleman at Derby [Frederic Stubbs, who had worked in the caves with Heath in October 1875] had written to me on the part of, and with the consent of, Mr Heath, to take up the cudgels in his behalf, &c. Mr Heath is not ignorant of the details of the whole matter, and he knows very well that whilst suffering from the grievance of neglect, he agreed with his friend that I should be written to, and it was suggested to him by this friend that a letter from me to a leading London journal would perhaps give him a chance of stating how much his work had been overlooked in all the accounts of the Creswell Crags discoveries. I did not think it proper to write to a London journal, as suggested, but took my own course by reading a short paper to our Geological Society on the specimens I had from the Cresswell Cave, and took the opportunity of praising the important work done by Mr. Heath. It is with satisfaction that I now see the results of my speaking, as I think it will also be to Mr Heath on mature reflection. Before I opened my mouth, Mr. Heath, being unknown, was badly treated, as I was given to understand, and was desirous that his own large share of the work should be known. I made this known for him, and all was at once changed. He will be sure of honourable mention in all future pages, although in the papers already read by Mr Mells [sic] and Professor Dawkins he was quite forgotten. "All is well that ends well" and my object has been accomplished'.[71]

Whatever Plant's motives he certainly derived considerable delight in annoying Dawkins. Not so for Heath, who was now more embarrassed by the letters going to and fro in the *Manchester Guardian* than by the original slight. He should have left it there and he was clearly complicit in some form, having encouraged Stubbs to act on his behalf, regardless of whether or not he had prior knowledge of John Plant's precise plan. Yet he now sought to deny everything, digging himself even deeper:

'Mr Plant's letter requires some explanation from me as he considers some parts of my former letter a quibble. It was not intended to be, neither do I think it is. The circumstances from which the controversy has arisen are as follows: – On the 8th Ultimo an article appeared in the *Pall Mall Gazette* on the cave explorations at Creswell, from which my name was entirely omitted. Gentlemen connected with this institution [Derby Museum] – one of whom defrayed my expenses – were aware I spent upwards of fifty days at the said explorations, and in consequence, after the lapse of a few days, I found myself in quite a labyrinth of embarrassments. On talking over the matter with a friend from Owen's College, he said "If you won't write to the Pall Mall and relieve yourself of this embarrassment, I'll ask Mr Plant to do so." I replied, "Since I've got the name of the writer I fear it is intentional, and I do not care who does now. I regretted having prevented others doing so, only I will not." This is the only time I have named the subject out of my own household, consequently that must be what Mr Plant refers to, and I must say had Mr Plant or anyone else written to the *Pall Mall* I should not have complained; but no one could be more astonished than myself to find the thing had been dragged before the Manchester Geological Society, and that professedly at my request, or even with my consent. I may add that the writer of the article has since expressed his regret to me at the omission, especially since it placed me in such a false position, and assure me he was quite unaware of the amount of time I had devoted to the explorations'.[72]

Soothing Words

Heath's belief that the MGS was a more incendiary forum then the *Pall Mall Gazette* was probably based on the proximity of the damage. Few readers of the London paper would have known Heath or cared precisely who was tinkering in the ancient hyaena dens of remote Derbyshire, but the Society was close to home and his local reputation, maybe even his job, was at stake. Thankfully, after a month of silence, Magens Mello gave his side of the story on 8 May 1876, in a letter that appeared immediately above Heath's in the 10 May edition of the *Manchester Guardian*. He came to the front line as a peacekeeper:

'Sir – Having seen Mr. Plant's letter in your issue of the 5th on the subject of the Creswell Caves, you will, I trust, allow me to make a few remarks in reply, as my name, although misspelt, is brought into the correspondence … It was an unfortunate oversight that the London papers should have omitted to mention Mr. Heath's name in connection with the last paper I read at the Geological Society. The large share he had in the work was duly acknowledged by me at the meeting, and had Mr Plant but the patience to wait till the paper was published he would have avoided such as misstatement as he is guilty of in saying that Mr. Heath was quite forgotten in it. I have had the greatest pleasure in stating how ably Mr Heath has co-operated with me; and through the history of the Robin Hood exploration I have throughout made use of the plural "we" uniting Mr. Heath's name to my own. I should not like it to be thought that there is any wish on my part to with-hold from Mr. Heath the honour to which he is so justly entitled'.[73]

Mello also noted Heath's involvement in the excavations in his *Hand-book of the Geology of Derbyshire*, published in 1876 but written in 1875. This acknowledgement takes the form of a *nota bene* at the end of the discussion on Creswell, and simply states that the explorations were ongoing with Heath's assistance. Dawkins' involvement is not mentioned, and one wonders whether the 'NB' was part of the original text or a hastily added afterthought. Whichever is true it is clear that Mello had no intention of expunging Heath from the history of the excavations.

A new scientific article describing the 1875 excavations, this time under the joint authorship of Mello and Heath, was read before the Manchester Geological Society on 30 May 1876.[74] Dawkins delivered it. As the paper contains no new information, and is little more than a précis of the London communication, it is clearly another good will gesture aimed at salving increasingly strained relationships before the onset of the 1876 season, due to begin the following month. Several local newspapers ran the story, all giving Heath his due credit.[75] A piece in the *Manchester City News* contained useful details of the day's discussion not found in the TGMS, the most telling comment coming from G.E. Greenwell who expressed concern that the paper was read at all. He understood that given all that had 'previously taken place' Mello was forced to act in 'self-defence', but nevertheless thought that the society was put in an 'invidious position with the London Geological Society who were in the process of publishing Mello's '2nd Paper' on Creswell (i.e. that read in London on 5 April 1876).

Sadly, while Mello was trying to placate Heath and secure a peace settlement, Dawkins was busy stirring things up. Mid-May brought a number of identical reports in the local and national press entitled 'Professor Dawkins and the Discoveries at Cresswell Crags', describing a field trip for Owens College students to the gorge.[76] This is likely to have been one of Dawkins' earliest trips to the crags, although we know from his diaries and notebooks that he had previously visited on 27 April in the company of Mello and Heath – probably so that they could prime him for his forthcoming field school. The title is provocative, but while Dawkins almost certainly provided the copy, the headline was most likely supplied by an editor. The piece provided the usual description of the gorge, the caves and their contents, and gleefully told how the remains of wolf, bear and other animals had been picked up in the rubbish heaps thrown out of the cavern – which one might cynically view as an oblique criticism of Heath's excavation methods. These reports also contained the first hint that a committee was to be formed to superintend the work. This would have been worrying news for Heath who, incidentally, is not mentioned once.

Chapter 5

Under the Auspices of the Creswell Committee, 1876

The Exploration Committee

From March 1876 Heath and Tebbet intermittently worked the Creswell caves until official explorations resumed in late June. Two major changes took effect for the 1876 season: first, Dawkins had assumed a major role as site palaeontologist; second, the work was no longer conducted solely under the licence granted to Mello but under the auspices of a newly formed exploration committee. The Victorians loved committees and formed them around every major project. The BAAS was literally overrun by them. In 1876 alone, twenty reports from committees were presented to the BAAS, including the explorations at Kent's Cavern and the Settle Caves. Boyd Dawkins sat on both of these, plus another commissioned to study the location and nature of erratic rocks. For every new question a new committee, but on every new committee the same old faces. Far from encouraging free-flowing science, these committees were a more a mechanism for control and power among the scientific elite.

The Exploration Committee for Creswell Crags comprised:

John Lubbock, MP, FRS, FGS, FSA – President
William Boyd Dawkins, FRS, FGS, FSA – Secretary
F. Longdon – Treasurer
Prof. G. Busk, FRS, FGS,
W. Bragge, FGS
R.D. Darbishire, FGS
John Evans, FRS, FGS, FSA
Rooke Pennington, FGS
Prof. Joseph Prestwich, FRS, FGS
Rev. J.M. Mello, FGS – director and reporter
Prof. W. Boyd Dawkins, FRS, FGS, FSA – superintendent
Mr. Thomas Heath, FRHS – superintendent

By any standards this is a remarkable group. At its core were five giants of nineteenth-century Palaeolithic archaeology: John Lubbock, author of *Prehistoric Times* and originator of the term Palaeolithic; John Evans, author of *the* book on ancient stone implements[1] who along with Joseph Prestwich had helped smash the 'time barrier' to human antiquity in 1859; and the original site palaeontologist George Busk. Most were Fellows of the Royal Society, the Geological Society, the Society of Antiquaries, the X-Club and/or part of the Evans-Lubbock network: elite groups that dominated and powered Victorian science for three decades.[2] All were personal acquaintances of Dawkins, the senior University academic on the team. The rest were all fellows of the Geological Society, except for Frederick Longdon, a manufacturer of surgical bandages and hosiery who had served as Mayor of Derby from 1866-1868; as an alderman of the city he had authorised the finances for Heath's involvement with the Creswell explorations.[3] There can be little doubt that it was Heath who insisted Longdon was a member of the Committee, to protect the interests of Derby Museum. Dawkins had cleverly sold the idea of a committee to Mello and Heath on the grounds that 'the work had become too great for individual exertions' and that 'a committee of scientific gentlemen [could] prosecute it on a larger and more efficient scale'.[4] In reality it was a badly disguised coup to take control of the excavations. The Committee never had any official status, was not sanctioned by the BAAS or any other scientific body, and was never convened – it existed solely to serve Dawkins.

The most accessible accounts of the 1876 excavation season are the back-to-back papers by Mello and Dawkins in the *Quarterly Journal of the Geological Society*.[5] The most informative record, however, is to be found in Heath's two incredibly rare pamphlets,[6] privately published after attempts to have his work disseminated in high profile journals had been thwarted. These provide significant details of Heath's work in Church Hole in 1875 and Robin Hood Cave in 1875-6. His accounts differ substantially from those of Mello and Dawkins and it requires a value judgement to determine whose is more accurate; one certainly cannot assume that as a lone voice Heath cannot be trusted, quite the opposite in fact. Dawkins' original notebook for the excavation still exists in Manchester Museum.[7] Mello's is lost, as is Heath's. The recovery of Heath's notebook, lost for over 130 years, would do more for our current understanding of Church Hole and Robin Hood Cave than any amount of re-excavation. By contrast, Dawkins' notebooks are remarkable only for their lack of detail. Two typical entries will illustrate this point (square brackets are my insertions):

'22 June
Worked in main passage [of Church Hole]
3. Stalagmite 1 foot
2. Dark C.[ave] E.[earth] 1 foot
1. Red sand 5 feet
Flint impl.[ements] in 2.3.
Quartzite in 1
Large scapula of [?] in 1'

'27 June
worked with 3 men at passage 1 of Notts
few bones & remains
west side of Robin Hood & n. end worked [next word unreadable]
many remains'

While containing little of value when interpreting the contents of the cave, the notebook entries do serve to show that Dawkins was present for much of the time from 19 June until at least 7 July, the date on which his entries for Creswell end. He spent the last few days taking measurements of Church Hole and Robin Hood Cave, both rather cryptic and barely coherent plans of the caves or their surroundings. His vertical measurements from the entrance, for example, used the surface level of the spoil heap and a large yew tree as reference points. On 10 July, Dawkins' notebook recorded 'W.W Matlock Bath 3/2'.[8] He then went on to Yoredale. Other than a few outstanding payments on 11 July, there are no further Creswell entries, suggesting that after visiting Yoredale he did not return. One highly curious matter is that his personal diary for 1876 – the key year in the Creswell saga – is missing from the collections at Manchester Museum, the only gap in a run that spans 1864-1912.

Throughout both seasons, Mello still had considerable parochial obligations. Unlike Heath who was on leave of absence or Dawkins who was no doubt enjoying a long summer vacation, Mello visited infrequently. This did not stop him claiming an extortionate £10 in personal expenses from the exploration budget, much to Heath's disgust.[9] Work began on 19 June 1876 and finished on 21 July. For the 1876 season the excavation campaign operated on two fronts with simultaneous work in Robin Hood Cave, supervised by Heath, and Church Hole, under the direction of Dawkins and Mello. These two caves sit diagonally opposite each other in the gorge, separated by a narrow artificial lake and its feeder stream. It is possible to maintain verbal communication between the two (albeit by shouting), and it takes barely two minutes to walk from one to the other around the western side of the gorge. With the levels of animosity that now existed between Dawkins and Heath, it is more likely that the two superintendents stood glaring at each other from the mouths of their allotted caves, while workmen toiled away in the gloom.

Robin Hood Cave 1876
A considerable amount of sediment remained in Robin Hood Cave at the beginning of the 1876 season, although Chambers A and B, closest to the entrance, had been pretty much worked out. According to Dawkins, 'unauthorised' digging had despoiled the cave between seasons,[10] presumably a reference to Frederic Stubbs, who had provided the material displayed before the MGS by John Plant. Dawkins complained that such activities left the archive incomplete. The published plan for 1876 (Figure 5.1) showed the

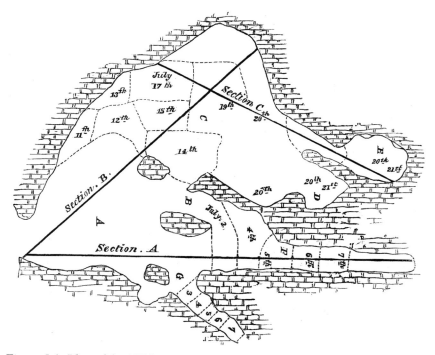

Figure 5.1: Plan of the 1876 excavations in Robin Hood Cave, showing Chamber Designations and daily progress (after Mello 1876).

areas excavated each day, based on an identical plan, hand-drawn on graph paper. The plan is now housed in Buxton Museum (Plate 8). Though not a complete record this can be used to reconstruct the pattern of work, although it must be remembered that Heath later suggested that the dates and sections had been made-up or bastardised from his notebooks. This might be true, for although Dawkins' notebooks contain measurements that conceivably relate to a rough sketch plan, he could not have known the location of the section at any precise date because Heath directed the work; another point of contention that later boiled over.

The summer of 1875 had been wet in central England, like many other years of that decade, but 1876 was notably drier if relatively cool. The weather, of course, mattered little when excavating inside a cave. According to Mello the 1876 season commenced with the cutting of a trench through the talus outside the entrance. This trench revealed 1 ft of cave earth above white sand with limestone blocks[11] and produced objects of various ages, including flint chips, bones of woolly rhinoceros and hyaena, pieces of Roman earthenware and sheep, all testifying to recent disturbance. Heath makes no mention of this trench, and the scene bears an uncanny resemblance to the work undertaken at the start of the previous season. Something must have occupied their time for the first ten days, though, as the first record of excavations into intact sediments inside the cave was not made until 29 June, and the earliest date on the plan is 3 July. Work on these dates began where the previous season's excavations had stopped, so beyond perhaps a bit of cleaning no intervention appears to have been made earlier. One source of delay may have been the 2 ft of cemented breccia that occurred between Chambers A and C, where both Mello and Heath agree that work began. This obstacle had to be removed by blasting. The first new areas to be excavated were Chambers F and G, which were worked back in tandem from 2-7 July. The work was hurried and conducted with pick and shovel; the plan has no scale, but at a minimum they were removing sediments from an area 3 ft by 6 ft and to a depth of 3-6 ft each day. This equates to ~3-4 tonnes of compact sediment every day. From 11-19 July they pushed on into Chamber C. Here the daily rate of excavation seems to have picked-up even further, a minimum of 6 ft^2 and a maximum of 10 ft^2, the volume depending on whether one follows Mello given depth of sediment (8 ft) or Heath's (4 ft). The final areas to be explored were Chambers D and E, which were emptied between 20-21 July 1876: a phenomenal area for just two days digging.

The published plan agrees with the archival one on all but two points: a change of date for work in the bottom right-hand corner of Chamber C (from

19 to 20 July), and a record of two additional day's work on 27 June and 7 July between Chambers B and C, where Mello records 'line of old w' on Figure 5.1. Each is fairly trivial, and there are no obvious instances where the inked text disagrees with the original pencil annotations. There are also two unexplained and rather cryptic notes, one stating 'face of work 29.30' the other a curly bracket pointing to the words 'upper 3 feet excavated 30.1.2.3. Lower Mottled Sand'. Assuming that these numbers are all dates, they imply that work had reached the end of Chamber G by 29-30 June and that the rear of Chamber F had been excavated to a depth of 3 ft between June 30-July 3 both of which make no sense in terms of the published plan. We shall return to this below.

Seven sections showing lateral variation throughout the cave sediments accompanied the plan (Figure 5.2). The basic sequence (from bottom upwards) comprised: red sand, cave earth, breccia, stalagmite, surface soil. The breccia, formed by the precipitation of calcium carbonate (stalagmite) within the cave-earth to produce a hard cemented structure, was present only where adequate lime-rich water could percolate; it thinned towards the back of the cave and was absent on the eastern side except at the mouth of Chamber G. The cave earth, however, was distributed throughout the cavern, although it varied greatly in thickness, being very thin at the entrance and reaching depths of 5 ft or more in the interior. Immediately below the breccia at the mouth of the cave was a thick red conglomerate of pebbles in an iron/lime cement (a continuation of a pebble-bed noted the previous year), which Mello took as evidence that a stream of running water had flowed through that part of the cave at some point. Another highly localised bed was found at the front of Chambers F and G, where a 'mottled bed' comprising 1-2 ft of silt with numerous angular limestone fragments parted the cave earth; this quickly thinned and died out towards the rear of both chambers. The red sand was uniformly distributed across the whole cave, with an average thickness of about 3 ft.

The breccia again produced a few Pleistocene fossils and flint chips, slim pickings compared to the richer cave earth. However, because Dawkins believed the cave earth and breccia to be localised facies of the same deposit he combined everything together in his report, making it impossible now to determine the actual degree of difference.[12] Hyaena, horse, reindeer and woolly rhinoceros were particularly numerous throughout, but bison was nowhere near as abundant as it had been at the front of the cave. Lion and wolf were again reported among the carnivores from the cave earth, and the 1876 excavations added two important new species: leopard[13] and the lesser

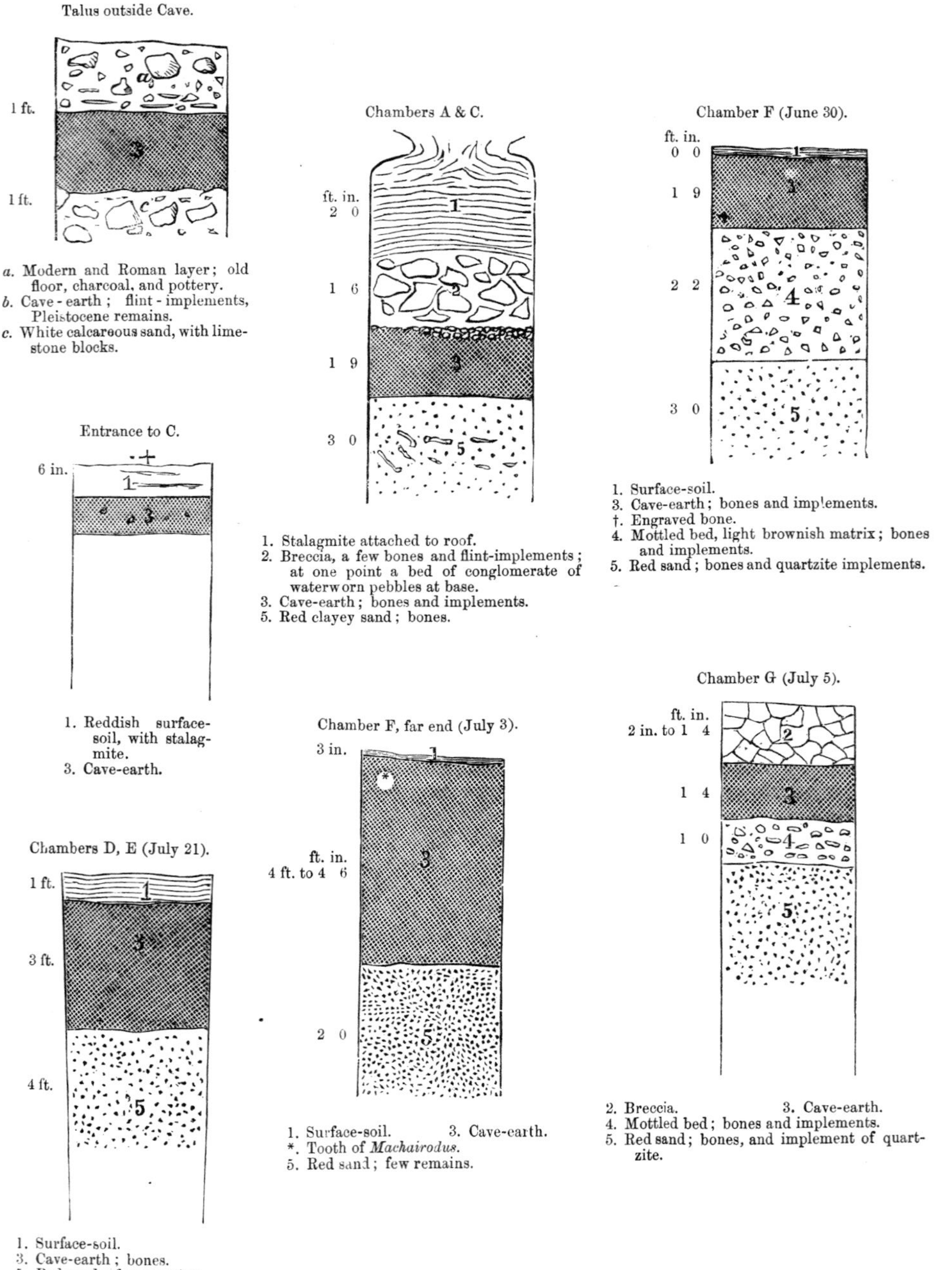

Talus outside Cave.

1 ft.

1 ft.

a. Modern and Roman layer; old floor, charcoal, and pottery.
b. Cave-earth; flint-implements, Pleistocene remains.
c. White calcareous sand, with limestone blocks.

Chambers A & C.

ft. in.
2 0

1 6

1 9

3 0

1. Stalagmite attached to roof.
2. Breccia, a few bones and flint-implements; at one point a bed of conglomerate of waterworn pebbles at base.
3. Cave-earth; bones and implements.
5. Red clayey sand; bones.

Chamber F (June 30).

ft. in.
0 0

1 9

2 2

3 0

1. Surface-soil.
3. Cave-earth; bones and implements.
†. Engraved bone.
4. Mottled bed, light brownish matrix; bones and implements.
5. Red sand; bones and quartzite implements.

Entrance to C.

6 in.

1. Reddish surface-soil, with stalagmite.
3. Cave-earth.

Chambers D, E (July 21).

1 ft.

3 ft.

4 ft.

1. Surface-soil.
3. Cave-earth; bones.
5. Red sand; few remains.

Chamber F, far end (July 3).

3 in.

ft. in.
4 ft. to 4 6

2 0

1. Surface-soil.   3. Cave-earth.
*. Tooth of *Machairodus*.
5. Red sand; few remains.

Chamber G (July 5).

ft. in.
2 in. to 1 4

1 4

1 0

2. Breccia.   3. Cave-earth.
4. Mottled bed; bones and implements.
5. Red sand; bones, and implement of quartzite.

Figure 5.2: Seven sections through Chambers A, C, D, E, F and G at Robin Hood Cave, excavated between June-July 1876 (after Mello 1877).

130

scimitar-toothed cat. Fossils and artefacts were also recovered from the mottled bed below the cave earth in Chambers G and F. Chamber C, where the deposits were thinnest and the roof and floor were at their closest, produced the fewest finds. Mello thought that his postulated stream might have run through this portion of the cavern too.

Evidence of human occupation in the cave was now proven to occur in all the major deposits: breccia, cave earth, mottled bed, and red sand. In terms of British cave assemblages the haul of 1040 stone objects was (and still is) massive. Eight came from the red sand, and 1032 from the breccia, cave earth and mottled beds, which, like the fauna from these beds, Dawkins lumped together into a single assemblage. This is an unfortunate and now irreversible decision, as no depths below a fixed datum were recorded or noted on the artefacts for us to disentangle the original assemblages, although there is no reason to doubt the anecdotal observations of Mello and Dawkins that the flint artefacts occurred higher in the sequence than the quartzite ones. Flint implements were also greatly outnumbered by those made on local quartzite, which occurred in in all stages of wear and in such abundance that Mello suspected the cave served as a stone tool 'manufactory'. Two hand-axes of ironstone were also found associated with the quartzite artefacts. In addition to the stone tools, a bone awl and forty-three pointed antler tips were recovered. Dawkins had become cautious about the latter, no longer accepting them as tools but suggesting that they may have been produced by the action of 'carbonic acid' wearing away the 'bruised surfaces'.

The quality of the Creswell excavation requires careful comment. When compared with the systematic work undertaken by Pengelly at Kent's Cavern or the meticulous excavation and recording standards of the irascible Augustus Pitt-Rivers just about anywhere,[14] they were slapdash. The pace at which deposits were removed alone is enough to raise alarm bells. That said, Heath claimed to have carefully recorded everything, each change in the stratigraphy being described in his notebook: 'I was most careful in taking my sections whenever any layer altered six inches or run out, or where anything particular occurred – we worked about one yard at a time, and each yard sections were checked and the least alteration noted – I was equally careful in taking my notes'.[15] Mello was also keen to emphasise the careful methods used, with each bed worked independently and the sediments sieved as they were removed from the cave to ensure that nothing of importance was missed (although the number of finds recovered from his spoil heaps during recent excavations shows this to be a rather spurious claim).[16] The objects found each day were separately packed and labelled. Dawkins adds 'our method of work was to put up into calico bags, properly labelled, the results of the labours of each day; and these were, from time to time, sent off in hampers to Owens College, where they were spread out, cleaned, gelatinized, and arranged, each date, corresponding with the day's work, being marked on the plan. This was continued until, in six weeks, the caves were worked out as far as we cared to pursue them.'[17] If this was true the information is now lost, and not properly used at the time.

For the reasons behind their relatively 'potato-digging' approach we really need look no further than time and money. To use Pengelly's method, with which we know Dawkins was familiar, would have exhausted both resources without the quick rewards wanted by all. To make matters worse the labourers employed from the quarry and village had little or no training. Dawkins' notebooks – which contain more relevant information about the finances of the dig than scientific data, including the cost of calico, string and candles, etc – show that in the course of the six weeks' excavation no fewer than sixteen 'day cleaners' were employed, at four shillings per day. Heath also records that 'night cleaners' were employed to clear away the earth examined during the course of the day.[18] The dig ran for twenty-nine working days (excluding only Sundays), during which a total of £41 17s 0d was paid in wages, an average of £1 3s 0d each day (or about four day cleaners and two night cleaners).[19] This is important because assuming a fair rota between the workmen giving equal earning opportunities, then each man would have worked in the caves for only seven days, which can hardly qualify them as experienced excavators. Compared to Charles Keeping and George Smerdon at Kent's Cavern, who worked in the caves for two years and seventeen years, respectively, they had no experience at all.

A Game of Cat and Horse
The two most important finds from Robin Hood Cave have yet to be discussed. The first, found by Mello on 29 June 1876 was an engraved bone fragment of Late Upper Palaeolithic age (Plate 11). Mello records the find thus:

'In the cave-earth, about the middle of Chamber F, a small fragment of a bone (the rib of some animal) was observed by the writer to have marks of engraving upon it. These, on being brought to the light, we examined carefully; and Mr Tiddeman, who was present at the time with Prof Dawkins, at once noticed the rude picture of the fore part of a horse exactly similar to the Palaeolithic figurines that have been found in some of the continental caves. The value of this discovery, the first of its kind made in this country, need scarcely be insisted upon.'[20]

Dawkins provided a fuller description of the piece:

'… the head and forequarters of a horse incised on a smoothed and rounded fragment of rib, cut short off at one end and broken at the other. On the flat side the head is represented with the nostrils and mouth and neck carefully drawn. A series of fine oblique lines show that the animal was hog-maned. Indeed the whole is very well done and evidently a sketch from the life. As is usually the case, the feet are not represented. On comparing this engraving with those of horses from the caves of Perigord and from the recently described cave of the Kesslerloch, near Thayingen, in Switzerland, the identity of style renders the conclusion tolerably certain that the Palaeolithic hunters who occupied the Creswell cave during the accumulation of the upper part of the cave earth were the same as those who hunted the Reindeer and Horse in Switzerland and the south of France'.[21]

Given a find of this magnitude – and it might not be too much of a stretch to say that figurative art is a holy grail to British prehistorians both then and now – it is somewhat perplexing that Dawkins' notebook says no more than: 'found sculpt. rib in RH in cave earth in D'[22] (Plate 10). There are no measurements, sections, drawings of the find spot, celebratory photographs, nothing except that one bald statement. In fact, the majority of his notebook entry for 29 June relates a tragi-comic tale of a goose that got stuck in Pin Hole Cave and came out without a feather, which I can only presume was Dawkins amusing himself with a variant of the 'absurd' local tradition of an old woman's goose that flew into Eldon Hole and came out in Peak Cavern, Castleton.[23]

The second major find was a canine of *Machairodus latidens*, the lesser scimitar-toothed cat, found by Dawkins at the rear of Chamber F on 3 July 1876 (Plate 11). This was a remarkably rare fossil, and at the time of the discovery was generally believed to be a Pliocene animal that had become extinct long before humans arrived in Britain. The only other known British examples were from Kent's Cavern, Torquay, Devon, found by the Rev. John MacEnery in 1825-1829, and the Pliocene Crags of the Norfolk Coast.[24] The animal was equally rare on the continent, with a handful of occurrences at

Val d'Arno, Italy; Mt Perrier, Pay-de-Dome; the Jura in France and Darmstadt, Germany. The excitement at this amazing find must have been palpable, but it ended in controversy. Because of this it is worth rehearsing the various surviving statements concerning the circumstances of its discovery.

Mello, who was not in the cave at the time, recorded only what he had been told by Dawkins:

> 'At the far end of Chamber F, in the same cave earth [as the horse engraving], at a depth of about 1 foot, Prof Dawkins had the good fortune to see extracted, by a workman, a canine of *Machairodus latidens*, an animal whose remains, as all will be aware, have only twice before been found in England … The discovery, therefore, of the *Machairodus* at Creswell in the undisturbed cave-earth is one of the greatest interest, which will be dwelt upon, in conjunction with all the details relating to the various remains found in these caves, in the accompanying paper by Prof W. Boyd Dawkins'.[25]

Dawkins again provided a fuller account of the find and its significance:

> 'The discovery of the incised drawing of a Palaeolithic Horse is rivalled in value by that of the rare animal *Machairodus* in the same stratum at a short distance away. On July 3, while I happened to be superintending the work, one of our men dug out, before my eyes, the crown of a fine upper canine quite perfect. It lay about one foot below the stalagmite in the cave-earth; and in association with it were a fine flint flake and remains of Bear, Woolly Rhinoceros, Reindeer, Horse, and Mammoth … The tooth was probably introduced into the cave by the hand of man, since it is broken short off by a sharp blow, and is without marks of the teeth of hyaenas; a few scratches at its base may have been made by a flint flake. Its singular shape and sharp, serrated cutting-edges would certainly strike the fancy of any rude huntsman who might be fortunate enough to meet with the carcass or skeleton of its possessor, or who might have had the rare luck to kill so formidable an animal … Whether, however, the Creswell tooth was collected or not, its mineral condition agreeing with that of the other associated teeth forbids the supposition that it was obtained from the [Cromer] Forest-bed, or from any Pliocene strata on the Continent, in which the remains, so far as I have yet seen, are in a totally different

state of preservation and of a different colour. As the evidence stands, it is in favour of the animal having been a contemporary of man in the neighbourhood'.[26]

Heath, in characteristic fashion, added yet further detail to the story:

'On Tuesday 4th July at 2.10pm, and while Mr Dawkins was chatting to my friend and myself, one of the men struck his pick at an angle, causing a small fall of earth, which left a clear escarpment. In this escarpment could be plainly seen a canine of what proved to be *Machairodus*. Mr Dawkins took this treasure outside the cave to examine it by daylight. As was my wont I began to examine the place where it was found and its surroundings. It was exactly 10 inches from the surface, and 14 inches from the wall at the extreme end of Chamber F'.[27]

He later revealed:

'Now, Mr Dawkins made his appearance in the Robin Hood Cave for the first time that day at 2pm. At 2.10 pm when Mr Dawkins was chatting with my friend and me, the men laid bare a small escarpment, when we saw a canine, which Mr Dawkins immediately recognized and exclaimed, "Hurrah! The Machairodus".'[28]

Without these two finds, the Creswell excavations would have assumed an important place amongst the canon of British Middle and Upper Palaeolithic sites. With them, however, they gained mystery and notoriety.

Church Hole 1876
The spectacular finds Robin Hood Cave (and the furore that later surrounded them) makes it easy to forget that the excavations in Church Hole were equally successful. There are four sources available to us now – Mello and Dawkins' published papers, Dawkins' notebook in Manchester Museum[29] and a series of hand-drawn plans and sections in Buxton Museum. The latter provide the daily progress through the deposits (Figures 5.3 & 5.4, and Plates 10 and 12)

Work began on 19 June, when Dawkins' notebook records: 'Worked at Nottingham Cave. Made Plan. Under wall on E at entrance underneath the level of the plateau about 6 inches is a layer of charcoal – a bronze brooch,

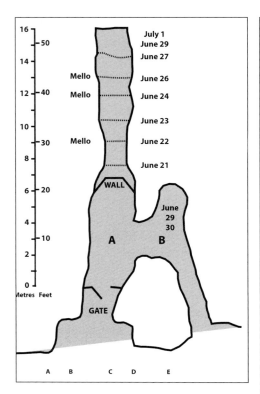

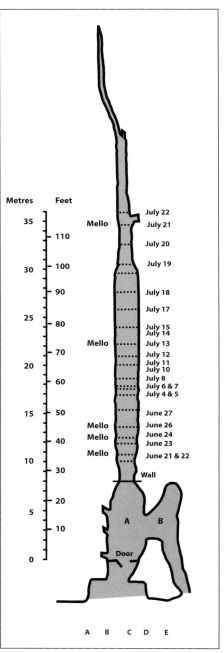

Figure 5.3a & b: Plans of the June and July excavations at Church Hole 1876, showing daily progress. 'Mello' indicates days on which Magens Mello was on site and drew the section. Re-drawn versions of Plates 10 & 12.

a human cal[caneum], frag[ments] of coarse pottery – were found nearly on cave [illegible] – Here animals. Many burnt sheep and a thing made of bone on the wall – Roman. Two men at work'. Mello's record is similar, although he is more specific about the location: 'When we resumed work this year we began, as we had done at the Robin-Hood Cave, by making an examination of the talus at its mouth … on the left-hand side, close to the extreme edge of the entrance, a very fine and perfect bronze fibula was found'.[30] The following day, Dawkins noted the section exposed in this left hand corner, which comprised 19 inches of fossiliferous red cave earth underlain by unfossiliferous sand. This corresponds well with Mello's published section for 20 June (Figure 5.4), from which they recovered the bones of rhinoceros, bear, hyaena, horse, reindeer, giant deer (*Megaloceros)* and badger from the cave earth, the latter a modern intrusion.

Towards the end of the day they began to work inside the cave to a depth of 6 ft.[31] Their first tasks involved clearing the detritus from the front of the cave as far as the wall, establishing a decent barrow run to empty the spoil from the interior, and recording the sections left by Heath the previous year. On 21 June, the cleaning operation produced flint flakes and another bone needle from undisturbed cave earth 'opposite to inner side of branch' (Chamber B).[32] The following day, they established a 9 ft deep section 31 ft from the gate, near to where Heath had stopped working in 1875; this turned out to be the most complete representation of the Church Hole deposits (Figure 5.4). The published and unpublished records allow us to reconstruct variation in the sedimentary sequence as they progressed deeper into the cave, and also estimate the daily digging rates.

On 24 June Dawkins and Mello reached a point about 42 ft from the gate, an advance of 11 ft through the thickest part of the sedimentary sequence in just two days. On 26 June they had advanced to 50 ft, having excavated another 8 ft in just one day (no work took place on Sunday 25 June). The duo stayed in Church Hole until 29 June, when in Heath's absence they annexed Robin Hood Cave, which they occupied until 3 July. Workmen must have carried on in Church Hole, for on 29-30 June they worked at the face of Chamber A and emptied the remaining sediments from Chamber B, there revealing a fissure in the floor full of red sand. Mello recorded that they dug this out to a depth of 11 ft, at which point it was deemed too unproductive to continue; Dawkins' notebook recorded a cut-marked bone from the bottom of the red sand. By 4-5 July they had reached a point 57 ft inside the cave. The final entries in Dawkins' notebook are for 6-7 July, when he recorded measurements for a north-south running fissure in the quarry above Church

137

Outside entrance.

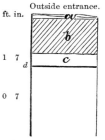

ft. in.

1 7

0 7

a. Surface-soil Brit-Welsh; variable.
b. Reddish cave-earth or sand; pleistocene remains.
c. Whitish sand.
d. Black band (manganese?).

120 ft. from Gate (July 21).

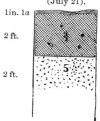

1in. 1a

2 ft.

2 ft.

1a. Stalagmitic film.
3. Cave-earth; few bones.
5. Red sand; few bones.

Pot-hole, Chamber B.

5 ft.

6 ft.?

1. Breccia; bones.
2. Red sand; bones.

31 ft. from Gate (June 22).

ft. in.

1 0

1 0

1 8
to
2 0

2 0

3 0

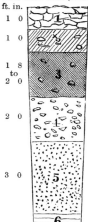

1. Stalagmitic breccia, with charcoal, worked flints, and bones.
2. Reddish cave-earth, with charcoal fragments, layer of ditto, flint implements, bones, and blocks of limestone.
3. Lighter cave-earth, with similar remains.
4. Mottled cave-earth, more sandy and mottled, with small angular fragments of friable limestone; quartzite and flint-implements, and bones.
5. Light-reddish sandy earth; bones, but no implements.
6. White calcareous sand and rock.

71 ft. from Gate (July 13).

1in. 1a

2 ft.

2 ft.

3 ft.
to
4 ft

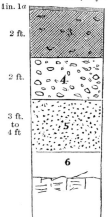

1a. Stalagmitic film.
3. Cave-earth; few bones.
4. Mottled bed; few bones, a bone implement.
5. Red sand; bones numerous.
6. White calcareous sand and rock; no bones.

About 42 ft. from Gate (June 24.)

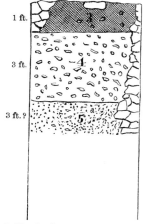

1 ft.

3 ft.

3 ft.?

1. Nearly absent.
3. Cave-earth, with loose breccia lining right side of cave; charcoal, bones, and implements.
4. Mottled bed; bones, and implements of stone, flint, and bone.
5. Red sand; bones &c.

About 50 ft. from Gate (June 26).

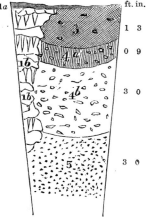

ft. in.

1 3

0 9

3 0

3 0

1a. Surface-soil and stalagmite, 2–3 in.
1b. Open breccia, with stalactites, lining left side of cave.
3. Cave-earth.
4a. Brown mottled bed.
4b. Red mottled bed.
5. Red sand.

138

Hole (presumably the continuation of the chimney at the back of the cave) and a series of measurements in Robin Hood Cave that are not only almost impossible to read but which make little sense even once tentatively translated. Dawkins left the excavations on or shortly after 7-8 July, having made little further progress in Church Hole beyond cutting the sections back another 18 inches. Dawkins was probably of the opinion that Church Hole had already given up the best of its spoils and with Heath back in Robin Hood Cave he was not inclined to stay. Work must have continued after Dawkins' departure, with Mello keeping notes as and when he could visit. This was probably not often; only two geological sections exists for the final 50 ft stretch of the cavern, one drawn on 13 July at 71 ft and one on 21 July at 120 ft from the gate, the last day of the excavations. Here the cave was declared to be worked out to all practical purposes, the team obviously not fancying the rock-jammed fissures that rose at the very back of the cave.

Faunal remains in Church Hole were recovered from every layer except the white sand. Dawkins divided them into two groups, with 639 specimens from the red sand and 1199 from the cave earth and breccia.[33] A further 219 fossils from the 1875 season were added to the tally, but their origin is puzzling. Mello excavated only a small sounding in April 1875, from which he pulled a rhinoceros pelvis. Heath and his friends conducted the main work in July, which as we have seen produced a cartload of bones from at least

Figure 5.4: Sections from Church Hole: The geology of Church Hole was similar to that in Robin Hood Cave. At the top of the sequence was a capping of stalagmite breccia, a hard dark-brown earth with blocks of limestone at the top, but softer at the base where it gradually blended into the next bed. It was usually no more than 1ft thick, but reached up to 5 ft in places, where it had grown down a gap between the sediments and the cave wall. The breccia was underlain by three facies of cave earth (reddish, lighter and mottled) with a total thickness of 5 ft, mantling a 3 ft bed of light red sand. At the base was white calcareous sand, probably an in situ weathering product of the limestone. The distribution of the deposits varied from front to back. The breccia disappeared about 6m from the door, where the conditions necessary for its formation ceased to operate. Fragments on the walls showed that it must have once been present almost to the outside, but this had been destroyed in more recent times. Cave earth was found throughout the entire length of the cave, as were the red sand and white sand, although like the breccia the reddish facies disappeared 18 ft from door, while the mottled facies carried on until 95 ft from the door where it tapered out.

139

116 individual animals including seventy-two hyaenas. Neither of these figures is compatible with Dawkins' sample from 1875, which listed 219 specimens and only ten hyaena bones. This anomaly notwithstanding, the species represented and their relative abundance was similar to Robin Hood Cave, only without scimitar-toothed cat. Dawkins saw them as part of groups that 'spread over Central Europe, from the Pyrenees as far north as the Elbe, and swung to and fro according to the season. They would naturally find their way from the low grazing-lands now occupied by the German Ocean up the line of the Trent to Creswell'.[34] In a nice example of early taphonomic inference, he further argued that the condition of the bones reflected three different agents: 1) gnawing by hyaena; 2) deliberately broken and sometimes burnt by humans; 3) chemical attack by carbonic acid.

The 1876 excavations produced almost all of the known artefacts from Church Hole, the given figures reporting twenty-three or twenty-four from the red sand and 211 or 213 from the cave-earth/breccia.[35] The cave earth/breccia contained artefacts of flint, bone and antler. The latter two materials included another eyed-needle (to add to the three found by Heath in 1875), two bone awls, three rounded rods of antler that may have served as javelin foreshafts, and a denticulated flat disc made from the transverse process of the vertebra of a horse or bovid (Figure 5.5). The red sand and base of the cave earth contained only cruder implements of quartzite, the division in the artefacts mirroring that seen in Robin Hood Cave. All the strata above the red sand contained charcoal and calcined bones, suggesting that hearths were built and food cooked within the confines of the cave, but the age of these remains speculative. In addition, the surface soil and the mixed uppermost deposits contained the remains of domestic animals, relatively recent human skeletons, Romano-British and Medieval artefacts, both inside and outside of the cave.

Even accounting for losses, translating the field records into the published papers, for Church Hole in particular, must have involved alchemy. Dawkins' Creswell notebook is, to put a positive spin on it, impressionistic. It contains neither sketches from which master copies could later be compiled nor enough data to do the same. There is no indication that Dawkins kept other more comprehensive notes either; Manchester Museum houses a large number of field notebooks from various parts of Dawkins' career, and they are all equally superficial.

There is, furthermore, barely any resemblance between the published accounts and Dawkins' notebooks. This can be illustrated by comparing Mello's section for 22 June (Figure 5.4), with Dawkins' record of that day.[36]

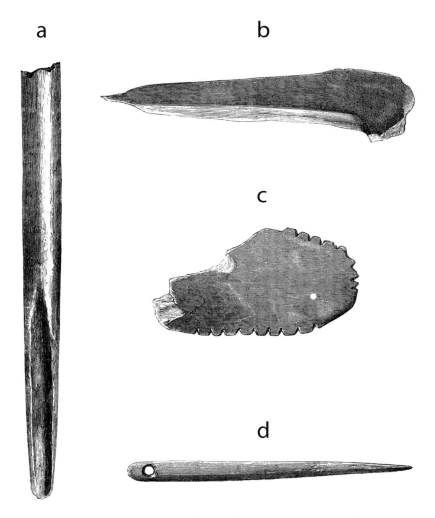

Figure 5.5: Organic artefacts from Church Hole a) antler sagaie; b) bone awl; c) denticulated bone object; d) bone needle (after Dawkins 1874a).

Far from the complete sequence Mello presents, Dawkins' notebooks recorded a partial set of deposits, comprising from bottom to top 5 ft of red sand, 1 ft dark cave-earth and 1 ft stalagmite. Who should we believe? Dawkins recorded nothing on 24 June, and nothing on 26 June other than the fact that he was away in the afternoon and Mello took notes. Dawkins was equally silent on the geological profiles drawn by Mello on July 13 and 21, as he had left.

A few surviving drawings on loose pieces of plain and re-purposed graph paper, some by Mello, some by Dawkins are all that remain of a, presumably, once larger site archive (Plates 10, 12 & 13). This is certainly implied in the surviving exchanges between the three protagonists, and we know Mello made notes and drawings when he was present at Creswell, but as this was infrequent – perhaps no more than 16 visits over the course of two seasons – they can only ever have been a partial and unsatisfactory record. Mello cannot have based the Church Hole reports or diagrams on Heath's records, as he later claimed, because Heath had not worked Church Hole in 1876. The web of lies surrounding the excavations is impenetrable.

The archival drawings from Church Hole require comment. The geological sections (Plate 13) are obviously those on which the final published versions are based, a few minor differences in dimensions and scale arising between the pencil drafts and the woodcuts. But they are far from being original field-sketches. They are generally too clean, both in the sense that they show no traces of having ever been in a dank muddy cave and that they contain no revisions, strike-throughs or rubbings-out. They have obviously been re-drafted, but whether from original field-sketches, notes or memory is unknown. Similarly, the sketch-plans (Plates 10 & 12) provide an outline of the cave and a series of dates showing the position of the working face at the end of each day. One plan covers the work for 21 June – 4 July, when Dawkins was almost continuously present. The other the entire excavation. They are both to scale and dates are recorded, even on days when neither Mello nor Dawkins were present. Of the two, the shorter (June) section is more likely to be a field-original that has been carefully looked after, or an early copy of such. It is dog-eared, contains struck-through errors, corrections and amendments. It was originally drafted in pencil and later inked-up, some parts being left undone. Dates were first pencilled in the margins (in both Mello's and Dawkins' hand) and later transcribed in ink adjacent to the plan. Ink annotations overwrite some of the original marginalia and the position of the drawn sections, labelled 'Mello', are likely to be later additions. All of the inked text is in Dawkins' hand. The longer plan has also been inked from a pencil outline, but this time in Mello's hand. This drawing is just too perfect to be a working copy; it is too clean for an item used in the cave for several weeks and totally free from error or revision. I suspect Mello redrew it from a field-worn original.

So what does all this tell us about the recording protocols followed by Dawkins and Mello? Dawkins kept few and poor records in his notebooks, but recorded the days' work for June and early July on a pencil-drawn plan;

for the few days he was absent he either left it to Mello or guessed where the face should have been based on an average daily work-rate. Mello drew the geology whenever he managed to visit, with the drawings putting him in Creswell on at least 22, 24, 26 June and 13 and 21 July; he was also in Creswell on 29 June, the day that the engraved rib was found. The whereabouts of Mello's notebooks is unknown; they probably survived until the 1930s, when his daughter Katherine gave the photos in Plate 7 to Harold Armitage to use in his book *Early Man in Hallamshire*. For most of the period between 6-7 July and 21 July, both Mello and Dawkins were absent and we can only assume that the ground plans were left with a 'responsible other' who pencilled in the position of the face at the end of each day. This is unlikely to have been Heath, who clearly stated he did not work in Church Hole during 1876, so it might have been Tebbet or another literate workman. That the daily terminuses are irregularly spaced effectively rules out the possibility that they are guesses based on an average digging rate.

In the final analysis, one can only conclude that much of what is contained in the reports came from hearsay or memory, the notebooks being little more than aide memoirs. This is an argument that Heath used to great sarcastic effect. It is also worth remembering that Heath spent a total of ninety-five days at the Crags in 1875-6, far more than Dawkins and Mello combined.[37]

Heath Departs

On 11 April 1877, Mello and Dawkins read the results of the 1876 excavations before the Geological Society of London, published in the Society's quarterly journal later the same year.[38] Heath is credited as a member of the Exploration Committee and, along with Dawkins, superintendent of the excavations, but despite directing the entire seasons' work at Robin Hood Cave and having the greatest working knowledge of that cave, he was not given joint authorship.

With the main excavations finished, Mello returned to his parishioners and Dawkins to his students. First on the agenda for the Professor, though, was a trip to Italy, where he examined the material from Val d'Arno in Florence Museum, which allowed him to finish another epic paper on the Miocene and Pliocene deer of Europe.[39] Both Dawkins and Mello remained active at Creswell, but Heath had no further involvement here or at any other excavation. For the next three years Heath funnelled his energies into his job at Derby. The Museum was undergoing a major overhaul, and a brand new building was to be erected on the Wardwick to replace the existing library and museum on the site. In preparation the collections were being mothballed, the Committee deeming it impractical to exhibit them until their new and permanent home was ready. As curator and librarian, Heath was central to the success of the move. He oversaw that everything was 'carefully packed and removed to suitable premises', which turned out to be the lower room of the Old Grammar School in St Peter's Church Yard.[40] His time was otherwise occupied restoring existing objects, sourcing new acquisitions to fill gaps in the collections, designing new displays and organising bespoke air-tight cases to house them.

On 25 October 1876, Mr Michael Thomas Bass, the benefactor who had already given the town a recreation ground, school of art and swimming baths, laid the foundation stone for the new Derby Museum. The sheer importance of these municipal projects to towns such as Derby is revealed through contemporary newspaper reports. The day was one of spectacle and grandeur, conducted with full masonic honours. A circular marquee had been erected on the site of the new building, its interior magnificently decorated with flags, evergreens and flowers, and the internal seating, arranged like an amphitheatre, was draped in elegant coloured cloth. A procession left the Town Hall at 12.30pm, arriving at the site to the sound of music and the ringing of bells. The train was led by Michael Bass, followed by 300 masons of the Grand Lodge of Derby, the Mayor and Corporation of Derby, members of the local magistracy, the Free Library Committee, representatives of various 'friendly' societies, and halberdiers in full regalia. They arrived to a marquee packed with the 'principal inhabitants' of the borough and neighbouring areas; Sir John Lubbock was in attendance, and although not directly named Heath as Head Curator and Librarian was almost certainly lurking among the Free Library's representatives. After the hymn 'Let the Lord conduct the plan' was sung, Mr Bass was presented with a silver trowel and the stone was lowered by pulley; attended by masonic rituals and a blessing by the Archdeacon of Derby, Edward Balston. Several addresses and heartfelt plaudits later, the ceremony was closed with a rendition of the National Anthem led by members of Lincoln Cathedral choir. At 3pm a congregation of 1000 guests repaired to the drill hall for luncheon. The reception room had again been lavishly ornamented: the upper end of the hall had been decorated in such a profusion of trees and plants that it resembled a tropical forest; hundreds of flags hung from the curves of the arched roof; the walls were draped with lace and cloth; while evergreens and textiles of many colours surrounded the fine orchestra, whose music created a fitting soundtrack to the splendour. The feast concluded around 6 o'clock, and judging by the long series of loquacious toasts and the accompanying laughter

Dawkins following his appointment at Manchester, circa 1870 (Courtesy Derbyshire County Council – Buxton Museum).

Magens Mello's watercolour of Creswell Crags, the site with which Dawkins' name is inextricably woven. Through the personalities of Dawkins, Mello and Heath, this tranquil idyll would become a crucible of hostility (Reproduced Courtesy of Manchester Museum).

Buttington Parsonage, Dawkins' Childhood Home (side elevation, photograph by the author).

Hyaena Den, Wookey Hole. The mill leat (stream) – the cutting of which exposed the cave – is visible in the foreground (Photograph Paul Pettitt).

William Boyd
Dawkins ca. 1862, on
joining the Geological
Survey (Reproduced
courtesy of the British
Geological Survey).

John Richard Green
(Reproduced courtesy
Derbyshire County Council
– Buxton Museum).

The Erith Explosion, witnessed by Dawkins (London Illustrated News 8 October 1865)

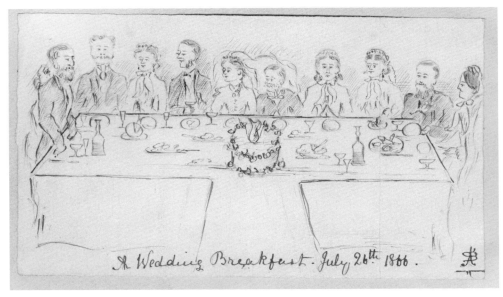

'The Wedding Breakfast'. (Reproduced Courtesy of Manchester Museum: PDW/7/3)

James Geikie (1839-
1915: reproduced
courtesy of the British
Geological Survey).

Richard Hill Tiddeman
(1842-1917;
reproduced courtesy of
the British Geological
Survey).

Victoria Cave, Friday July 15 1870. The figure in the centre of the photograph is Joseph Jackson, site superintendent for the excavations from 1870-1878. The planks in the foreground mark the datum-line, along which the parallels were measured and from which distances left or right were recorded. This was extended into the cave by the rope seen disappearing through the horizontal wooden slats. (Reproduced with kind permission of Tom Lord).

Photograph of Creswell Crags (ca. 1900-1910, in possession of author).

Photographs of the 1876 excavations in Church Hole. Note the massive spoil heaps outside of both caves (Reproduced courtesy Derbyshire County Council – Buxton Museum).

Photographs of the 1876 excavations in Robin Hood Cave (Reproduced courtesy Derbyshire County Council – Buxton Museum).

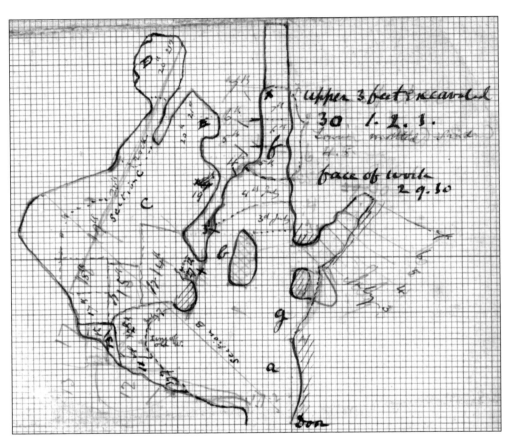

Hand-drawn plan of the 1876 excavations in Robin Hood Cave, showing daily progress. See Figure 5.1 and the text for differences between this and the published version (Reproduced courtesy Derbyshire County Council – Buxton Museum: DERBS 71901).

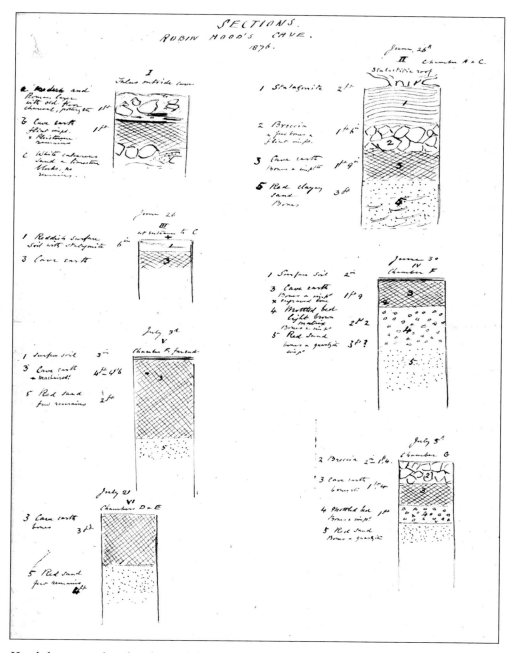

Hand-drawn section drawings of the 1876 excavations in Robin Hood Cave (Reproduced courtesy Derbyshire County Council – Buxton Museum: DERBS 71903).

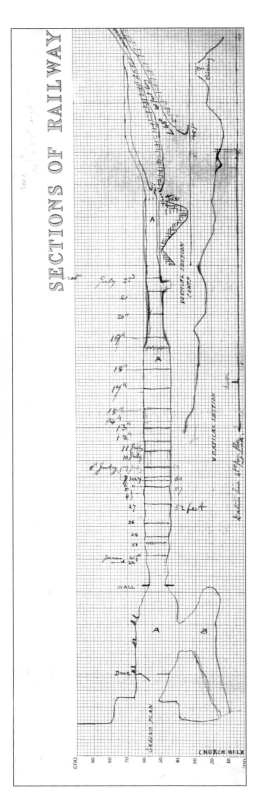

Dawkins' Notebook Entry for 29 June 1876
(Reproduced courtesy of Manchester
Museum).

Hand-drawn plan of the
June-July 1876 excavations
at Church Hole, showing
daily progress. (Reproduced
courtesy Derbyshire County
Council – Buxton Museum:
DERBS 79100).

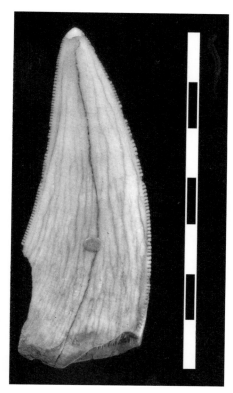

The canine of *Machairodus latidens* (=*Homotherium latidens*) from Robin Hood Cave. Scale in centimetres. The round plug in the middle of the tooth is presumable filling Oakley's sampling area (Courtesy Trustees of the British Museum).

The Reverend John Magens Mello (Courtesy of the Trustees of the British Museum).

The engraved rib from Robin Hood Cave showing a depiction of a horse Dimensions: 73mm x 23mm (Courtesy Trustees of the British Museum).

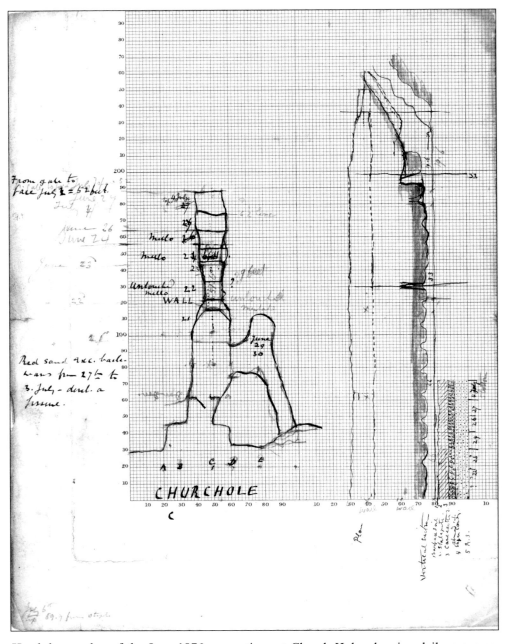

Hand-drawn plan of the June 1876 excavations at Church Hole, showing daily progress. 'Mello' indicates days on which Magens Mello was on site and drew the section (Reproduced courtesy Derbyshire County Council – Buxton Museum: DERBS 71902).

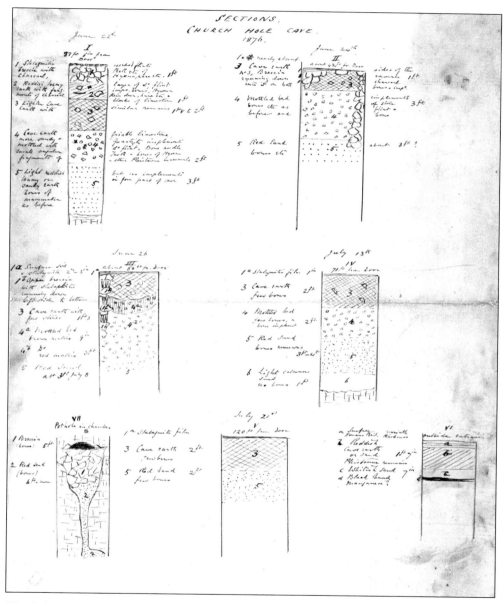

Hand-drawn section drawings from the 1876 excavations in Church Hole (Reproduced courtesy Derbyshire County Council – Buxton Museum: DERBS 71904).

William Boyd Dawkins in his geologising outfit with trusty hammer. Probably late 1870s/early 1880s and looking far more battle worn than a decade earlier (Reproduced courtesy Derbyshire County Council – Buxton Museum).

Edward A Freeman (1823-1892) (Reproduced courtesy of the National Portrait Gallery).

Ella Selina Dawkins (1881-1969), the Dawkins's only child. She married the Rev. Samuel Taylor in 1915 (after Bishop 1982, courtesy Mike Bishop & Buxton Museum)

Frances Dawkins (1839-1921). She and Dawkins were married for 55 years (after Bishop 1982, courtesy Mike Bishop & Buxton Museum).

William Boyd Dawkins, probably mid 1880s (Reproduced courtesy of the Royal Society).

The Heading for the 1882 Channel Tunnel at Shakespeare Cliff, 1882 (from The Million, 4 June 1892).

Inside the 1882 Channel Tunnel, with the tunnelling machine in the background (from The Million, 4 June 1892).

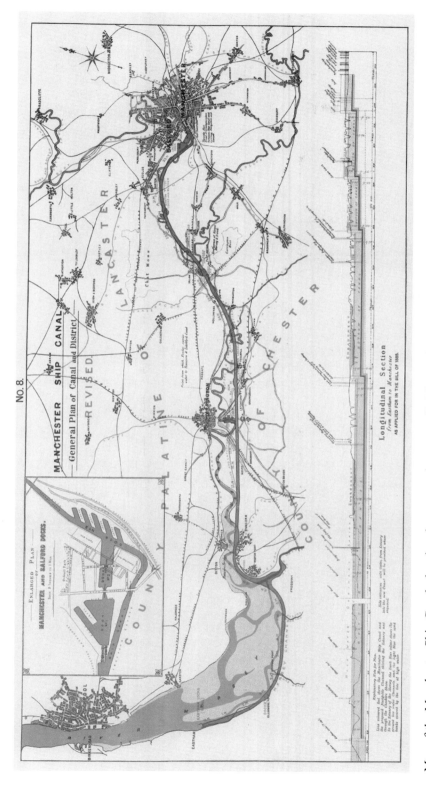

Map of the Manchester Ship Canal, showing the proposed route applied for on the 1885 Bill (after Leech 1907).

Navvies excavating the Manchester Ship Canal, 1890 (Reproduced courtesy of the Institute of Civil Engineers).

Waterhouse's 'monumental' building housing Manchester Museum (reproduced Courtesy of Manchester Museum).

Photograph showing the northern end of Doveholes, filled with clay and blocks of limestone. The spade and pick standing between the two groups of workmen mark the location of the ossiferous clay (after Dawkins 1903).

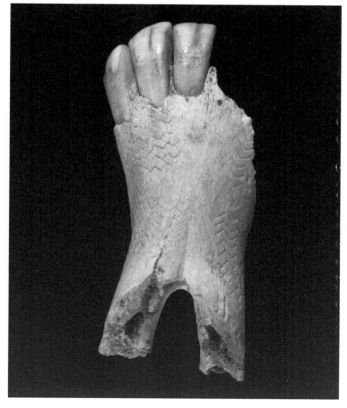

Horse maxilla with engraved chevron designs from Kendrick's Cave (Reproduced Courtesy of the Trustees of the British Museum).

William Boyd Dawkins in 1899
(Reproduced courtesy Derbyshire
County Council – Buxton
Museum).

William Boyd
Dawkins, looking
particularly stout.
Photograph by Sir
Benjamin Stone, 1901
(Reproduced courtesy
of Birmingham Library
Services).

Dawkins' Creswell notebook entries for 30 June–5 July 1876, in the order that they appear in the notebook. The dates are out of sequence, and the notebooks appear to have been tampered with (Reproduced courtesy of Manchester Museum).

Dawkins' Creswell notebook entries for 30 June-5 July 1876, in the order that they appear in the notebook. The dates are out of sequence, and the notebooks appear to have been tampered with (Reproduced courtesy of Manchester Museum).

William Boyd Dawkins ca. 1914. The photo is undated, but the similarity to this picture and one published in the Manchester Evening Chronicle in February of that year suggests a similar period (Reproduced courtesy Derbyshire County Council – Buxton Museum).

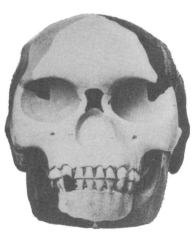

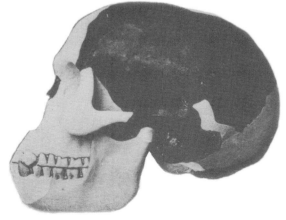

The Piltdown Skull (from a contemporary photograph in possession of the author).

Sir William Boyd Dawkins,
photograph by Walter Stoneman,
1920 (Reproduced courtesy of the
National Portrait Gallery).

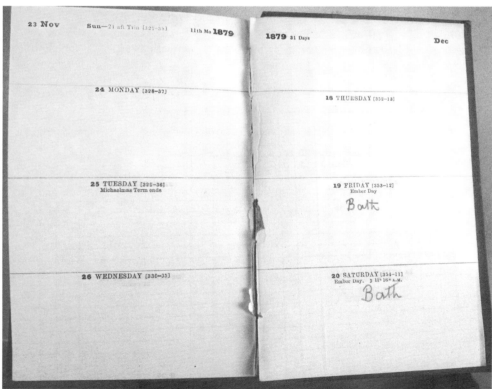

Dawkins' diary for 1879 showing the missing pages between 26 November and 18
December 1879. This coincides with the beginning of Heath's renewed campaign to expose
the *Machairodus* as a fake (Reproduced courtesy of Manchester Museum).

and applause, the event was probably well lubricated; exactly what one would expect from an event honouring a master brewer.

The opening of the museum on Saturday 28 June 1879 was a similar gala event and medals were struck to commemorate the occasion. On arriving at Derby's Midland Railway Station, Mr Bass was 'entertained to luncheon' by the Mayor and Corporation in the Shareholders' Room, before travelling by carriage to the museum. Huge crowds lined the roads along the mile-long route, and the vista was resplendent with flags, banners and flowers hanging from houses and street furniture on either side of the road. The procession moved slowly in the direction of Market Street, accompanied by church bells, cheers from the assembled populace, and several brass bands. At the head of the were four mounted policemen, followed by Synyer and Gilmer's band, and the Derby fire engine drawn by horses; behind them were the Corporation, headed by an officer waving the borough banner. Then came the carriages containing the Mayor and Mr Bass, alongside aldermen, town councillors, MPs, magistrates, officials and special visitors. The tail of the procession was made up of several bands and representatives of over 20 societies, companies and orders. Even the weather co-operated to make the day a high holiday. The actual ceremony took place in the Guildhall, in which the 79 year-old Bass handed over the title deeds of the property to the Mayor; Bass was then escorted to the building for a tour, returning to the steps to declare the building open. [41]

The new museum building was majestic, constructed in red brick and stanton stone in the Victorian Gothic style, to a design by Richard Knill Freeman.[42] The entrance, a tall arch nestled beneath a central clock tower, led to a hall, off which were the secretary's office, general reading room, ladies' room, students' room, the lending library and the reference library. Flights of stairs on either side led to the first floor, housing the museum and a committee room. The latter was ornamented with old oak panels from Exeter House, the seventeenth century mansion house in Full Street, Derby that had gained notoriety as the head quarters of the Young Pretender, Charles Edward Stuart, during the 1745 Jacobite uprising and which had been demolished in 1854. Heath's home, the tied curator's house, was situated at one end of the main building, with the caretaker's house at the other. Both were designed to sympathetically blend in with the main museum. It was estimated that the building and fittings cost Mr Bass in the region of £15,000, almost twice the original tender.

Heath's efforts in the renovation, classification and display of the collections and the negotiation of important loans did not go unremarked; he was lauded in the Museum Committee's annual report, which noted the approval of the 'principal' museums of England and Germany, and proudly stated that the museum was not merely of casual interest but of scientific significance above that of a normal provincial museum.[43] His currency at home could not have been higher, but as events would show, Heath was still a very bitter and disillusioned man.

Mother Grundy's Parlour 1878

At the end of 1876, with Robin Hood Cave and Church Hole 'practically' worked out and Pin Hole previously given up as a lost cause, only one small cave remained to be explored. Known as Mother Grundy's Parlour, after an old gypsy woman who had supposedly dwelt there, the cave was situated within an isolated outcrop of limestone at the eastern end of the gorge, on its Derbyshire side. The cave comprised a shallow, semi-circular chamber some 35 ft deep and 22 ft wide, with a small cavity (4 ft wide by 2 ft 6 in high) towards the rear on the eastern side, blocked to the roof with fragments of rock and earth (when unblocked this proved to be another long passage[44]; Figure 5.6).

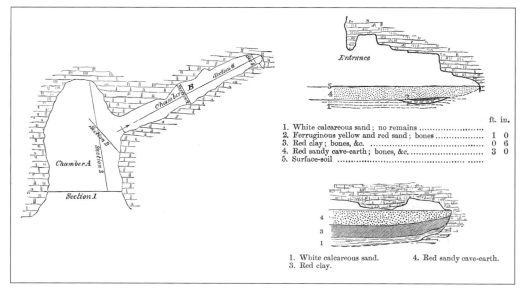

Figure 5.6: Mother Grundy's Parlour 1878, showing floor plan (left), and transverse sections along lines 3 (top right) and 6 (bottom right) (after Dawkins and Mello 1879).

Like many caves in the gorge the deposits had been disturbed, according to local tradition by a local man searching for buried treasure his wife had seen in a dream. Undeterred, Dawkins and Mello made some exploratory soundings in the cave in 1876, but quickly abandoned the work when they found only sterile sand;[45] that it went totally unrecorded at the time is unsurprising.

Two years later a Mr John Young contacted Dawkins concerning a hippopotamus tooth he had bought in London, the former property of Messrs Duffy and Gain of Tuxford, a dubious pair of no further renown who no doubt came into possession of the tooth through illicit means (Tuxford is a village about 15 miles from Creswell which despite its diminutive size was on the Great Northern Railway main line). Hippopotamus had not previously been found at Creswell, and in that instant Mother Grundy's Parlour assumed new significance for Dawkins. New work began at Mother Grundy's Parlour in November 1878, superintended by Mr Knight of Owens College, one of Dawkins' students. According to the published article, Dawkins and Mello visited 'from time to time to direct the work', although Dawkins' personal diary tells a different story. He visited only once, on Wednesday 20 November, when his diary reported: 'Went to Cresswell, found hippo bones. Labour etc. } cost – £2-0-0'.[46] The previous day records a lecture and visit to J. Alexandra in Sheffield, the following day merely that he lectured. The documentary evidence, on which Dawkins would later put so much emphasis, therefore points to a single visit. Mello's movements are unknown.

Under Knight's supervision, the excavations commenced with a trench on the right-hand (eastern) side of the main Chamber (Chamber A). Most of the surface soil had been mixed-up or removed by earlier ransacking, with only a few inches remaining intact, and then only in localised patches.[47] From this layer came charcoal, burnt clay and bones, a considerable number of flint chips and a few flakes; if an old gypsy woman had ever lived in the cave she left little behind her other than the remains of a few cooked meals (work on the talus slope outside the cave was similarly devoid of her presence). Beneath the surface soil was a red sandy cave earth, which contained a familiar set of animals – bison, reindeer, bear, wolf, fox and hyaena; the dryness of Mother Grundy's Parlour compared to the other caves had also facilitated the preservation of a large number of hyaena coprolites. Horse, so frequent in the other caves, was represented by just two teeth in Mother Grundy's Parlour, and conversely the bison, which was relatively rare and heavily gnawed elsewhere, was found in great profusion and mostly intact.

A small number of artefacts were found in this deposit, including quartzite flakes, flint objects, pot-boilers (stones assumed to have been heated and thrown in water to boil it, in fact mostly natural stones) and one ironstone hand-axe. As observed in the other caves, the flint artefacts were stratigraphically higher in the cave earth than the quartzite and ironstone objects, again suggesting that they were of different ages.

Over much of Chamber A, the red sandy cave earth lay directly on sterile white sand, the weathered remains of the limestone bedrock. Near to the entrance of Chamber B, however, it sat on two strata not seen elsewhere – red clay underlain by ferruginous sand. These were the source of the warm-climate fauna, the ferruginous sand giving up fragments of a hippopotamus skull and other bones alongside the teeth of the forest or narrow-nosed rhinoceros. The hippo skull was fragmentary, not because it had been gnawed by the hyaenas that originally dragged the dead animal into the cave, but because it had been smashed by the illicit excavations that had first alerted science to its presence. The ferruginous sand was restricted to this one area,[48] but the red clay extended into the protective arm of Chamber B, where further remains of hippo, narrow-nosed rhino, hyaena and bison were found. In total the remains of at least three hippos, none fully adult, and one narrow-nosed rhinoceros were recovered from the cave.

The cave also produced the partial skeletal remains of four humans. Those from Chamber A were identified as being from portions of red sandy cave earth that had been disturbed in recent times, the proof being the head of an iron hammer at the bottom of the strata; this presumably also means that we can dismiss the claim that these same deposits were in situ, made eight pages earlier in the same article. The skull found in Chamber B would at face value appear to be a much better candidate for a Palaeolithic burial. It was found in the red sandy cave earth in a small recess in the cave wall 19 ft 6 in from the entrance of the Chamber and at a depth of 2 ft 6 in below the surface, which here was touching the roof. There were no obvious signs of disturbance and the chamber had been completely blocked up in places, but the bones of domesticated animals were found scattered throughout. Dawkins pointed to rabbit, badger, foxes and humans as the prime suspects, declaring the skull to be Neolithic in age. Later authors would cast doubt upon this conclusion, although in this, and in his assertion that humans did not co-exist with the hippopotamus fauna, Dawkins was ultimately proved correct.[49]

Summing up their paper, Dawkins and Mello presented just three conclusions covering almost fours years work in four caves:

1   That during the period when the waterlain red clay and ferruginous sand was deposited in Mother Grundy's Parlour, 'the hippopotamus and [narrow-nosed] rhinoceros, the hyaena and bison 'haunted the wooded valleys of the basin of the upper Trent.'[50] Humans, horses and reindeer were absent;

2   This was followed by a time, represented by the red sand in all the caves, when the arctic species including mammoth, woolly rhinoceros, horse and reindeer frequented the district around Creswell, sometime falling prey to the hyaena and sometimes to the human hunters who left evidence of their presence in the form of quartzite artefacts similar to those found in the river gravels of Britain and Europe;

3   Finally the caves were occupied by Upper Palaeolithic hunters, who left in the upper cave earth and breccia flint implements of a 'higher order', as well as implements of bone and antler and the incised figure of a horse that could link them with similar finds in Europe.

The British Association Goes to Creswell, August 1879

Mello and Dawkins read their paper on Mother Grundy's Parlour before the Geological Society of London on 11 June 1879. They were back at Creswell six weeks later, on Saturday 23 August 1879, leading a field excursion for the 49th Annual Meeting of the BAAS in Sheffield. The excursion turned out to be quite a jamboree event, *The Derbyshire Times* for 30 August painting this picture of the spectacle:

'The party which went to Cresswell Crags on Saturday had a most enjoyable and instructive outing. It was originally intended to limit the party to 100, but the known picturesqueness of the chosen locality induced such a plentitude of applications that the Committee of Management decided to extend the number. The excursionists left Victoria Station at Noon in a special train comprising several saloon carriages. The arrangements of Professor W. Boyd Dawkins, M.A., F.R.S., and the Rev. J. Magens Mello, M.A., F.G.S, the directors were all that could be desired. Arrived at Cresswell, a walk brought the party to the Board Schools, where luncheon was partaken of. They then wended their way to the Crags, and on arrival there all were charmed with the lovely spot, which on the programme was correctly described as "a romantic glen in the Permian rocks. On both sides, towering far above the head of the spectator, are the crags, grand in all their ruggedness, and rich in all that the geologist holds dear, while between them runs a winding stream. Shortly after arriving at the crags, Professor Dawkins delivered a short speech, in which he referred to the formation of the glen

CRESSWELL

Figure 5.7: Reconstruction of Creswell Crags showing a naked human hunter stalking a reindeer, by Rowe. Robin Hood Cave maybe shown in the background, with smoke billowing from a hearth (British Museum Jacobi Archive, Courtesy of the Trustees of the British Museum).

and its general characteristics. This formed a sort of introduction to a geological address by the Rev. J.M. Mello, who dealt in detail with the foundation of the scheme for the working of the caves in the crags and the discoveries that have been made. The Pin Hole, Robin Hood's cave, and Church Hole were then severally visited. In these and other caves in the Crags the Rev. Mr Mello has discovered numerous Romano-British remains, and also abundant traces of the occupation of the caverns by hyaenas, whose varied prey consisted of the mammoth, rhinoceros, bison, reindeer, horse, and many other animals. The rude implements and the works of man were also frequent. The caves were lighted by candles and the magnesium light, and the view presented was a very pleasing one. The digging out of "Mother

Grundy's Parlour", one of the caves, was shown, and the party were also afforded an opportunity of witnessing "cave hunting". At five o'clock they returned to the school room at Cresswell, where dinner was partaken of, and the directors were accorded the hearty thanks of those who, under their guidance had spent a thoroughly delightful day. The party returned to Sheffield at 7.15" (see figures 5.7-5.8).

For Dawkins and Mello, their work at Creswell Crags was over. Or at least, that's what they must have thought. But there was one man at Creswell that day who would not have enjoyed the occasion, one for whom Creswell would 'ever be a source of pain and much disappointment'[51] and who was not prepared to remain quiet any longer.

Figure 5.8: Another reconstruction by Rowe showing a naked human hunter stalking a reindeer, this time closer to Robin Hood Cave. Judging by its shape the cave in the background may be Mother Grundy's Parlour, although in reality it is further from Robin Hood Cave than depicted. The river is higher in the landscape, and the scene is possibly meant to represent an earlier period of occupation (British Museum Jacobi Archive, Courtesy of the Trustees of the British Museum).

Chapter 6

The Suspicions of Mr Heath

An Abstract Description

Heath kept his silence for three years, during which time he busied himself getting Derby Museum's collections ready for display. With the opening of the new building at the end of June 1879, he was freed from the stress and turmoil of the Museum's transformation. This period of relative mental idleness coincided with the lecture on Mother Grundy's Parlour, reports of which were all over the local press, and the BAAS excursion to Creswell, was another case of bad-timing in the life of Thomas Heath. He still harboured strong resentment towards Dawkins and, encouraged by an unnamed colleague (who we later learn was John Plant),[1] he threw together a 'hastily written pamphlet',[2] giving his version of the history of the excavations and correcting 'one or two errors'. He advertised the pamphlet in newspapers and took copies to the Sheffield BAAS meeting, where they were offered for sale to members.

Entitled *An Abstract Description and History of the Bone Caves of Creswell Crags* (Figure 6.1) and priced at four old pence, the pamphlet was very factual in design. It laid out Heath's account of the work at Creswell during 1875 and 1876, all drawn from notebooks kept at the time. In general it agreed with the published versions of Mello and Dawkins, but added considerable detail and texture. In one or two places the accounts differed, but Heath was never hostile and in his opening lines was almost apologetic:

'I hope … to contribute additional information to that which is already known. Had it not been that I believed the errors were calculated to mislead future scientific investigators, I should have left the course and conclusions adopted by my late colleagues unchallenged, rather than referred to that which must ever be to me a source of pain and much disappointment. I have delayed doing this until now, hoping that time would displace the unfortunate spirit which then characterized the proceedings and discussions by one more consistent with the promotion of scientific truth and interests'.[3]

The critical point of departure lay with the facts surrounding 3 July 1876

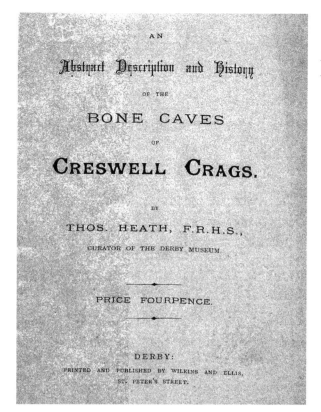

Figure 6.1: Heath's First Pamphlet.

– the day the *Machairodus* was found. Heath's main concern was that the geological descriptions and sections published in the 1877 report did not tally with those in his own notebooks, from which they may have been copied. Heath had been present on site for almost the entire season and by arriving on site at the same time as the workmen (usually four hours before Dawkins) he had witnessed every section first-hand. Although he was absent for three working days prior to the discovery in question, he was there when it had been uncovered and had recorded the geology for the days before and after; in any case Mello's published plan showed no work in Chamber F until 3 July.

Contrary to Mello's record (see Figure 5.2), the only deposit Heath found in Chamber F was a 'conglomerate of cave-earth', cream-coloured angular fragments of limestone that crumbled to the touch. This was usually 2 ft thick

Figure 6.2: Heath's section through Chamber F. An asterisk marks the point at which the canine was supposed to have been found. 1) Conglomerate of Cave Earth, angular fragments of limestone and surface. 2) Silt.

and attained a maximum of 4 ft; nowhere in Chamber F did the deposits reach the 6 ft thickness reported by Mello. Even the surface soil here was not the usual black colour found elsewhere in the cave. In Heath's opinion the whole area had been disturbed by a stream, which had flowed out of Chamber C, around B and along F, exiting through a fissure at the rear of the latter chamber, which it had filled with silt (Figure 6.2). According to Heath, Mello shared this opinion and had postulated that water had flowed in through a pothole in the roof in Chambers B and F; Mello had, in fact, openly reported that the terminal fissure was filled with an 'independent' waterlain bed deposited by a stream flowing through Chamber C.[4]

The records of precisely where the tooth was found were also confused.

According to Mello it was found 1 ft below the *surface soil* in cave earth, while Dawkins has it 1 ft below *stalagmite* in cave earth. Heath is once again more precise: 'it was exactly 10 inches from the surface and 14 inches from the wall at the extreme of chamber F" and was adamant that there was no stalagmite or any cemented material in Chamber F. One might think that Heath was simply being difficult and pedantically quibbling over differences in geological description, but he understood that the value of the find depended very much on whether the deposits containing it were intact or not, so the nature and integrity of the sediments immediately above it mattered enormously. A capping layer of intact stalagmite would more-or-less guarantee the find was in a secure context that had not been recently disturbed. Heath had other reasons to be suspicious:

'The first thing that attracted my attention was a perpendicular polished surface of the escarpment, about one inch wide, immediately over, and six inches beyond where the tooth was found. In my opinion it had been made by some implement, probably a pick…I feel most reluctantly obliged to decline to classify [*Machairodus latidens*] in the Creswell fauna … By what agency it got here I do not even care to conjecture; but nevertheless, I should not be surprised if, left unchallenged, some wag was discovered to be having a laugh at our expense at the hoax that had so successfully exposed our carelessness in a matter of so much importance'.[5]

Even more curiously, Heath also related a discussion with Mello in which the cleric had told him that the engraved rib was found in Church Hole not Robin Hood Cave.

Now War is Declared

As brave as Heath's course of action might now appear, it is difficult to see what he hoped to achieve. If a quest to expose the truth, he could surely not have expected a tidal surge in his favour – his testimony was circumstantial at best and Dawkins had far too many friends and far too much influence. Heath had made himself a quixotic figure, tilting at Dawkins' windmill, and if the pamphlet had been a cathartic act to rid himself of the turbulent professor, it tragically backfired. He succeeded only in opening a whole new round of hostilities, although the fact that Dawkins and Mello did not move immediately to rebut the pamphlet's claims suggest that the next sordid series of events might have been avoided, if not for the actions of the old stirrer

John Plant. Almost two months after the Sheffield meeting, Plant published a letter in the *Manchester City News* under the provocative headline 'Creswell Crags Bone Caves: Fraud or Hoax?'.[6] It later transpired that the headline had been added by the editor and was not of Plant's devising,[7] although he was no doubt thrilled with it. Plant drew the readers' attention to Heath's pamphlet and called into question, before a wide audience, the authenticity of the tooth *and* the engraved rib. This was the first time that the authenticity of the rib had been questioned, Plant's doubts derived in the main from its association with the tooth rather than any firm facts. It was Mello who responded first.

Mello's rebuttal was that of a man whose patience had finally run out.[8] His letter in the *Manchester City News* was not long, only four column-inches, but presented a sustained personal attack on Heath. He opened by calling into question the propriety of Heath's pamphlet, suggesting that when it was being 'hawked' about at Sheffield the BAAS had banned its sale, and that the president of the Geological Section (Professor P. Martin Duncan) had condemned the piece in 'very strong language' as a libellous and ungentlemanly attack. Mello was also perplexed as to why Heath had 'suffered years to pass in silence' rather than doing his scientific duty and standing up at the Geological Society, or indeed the BAAS meeting, and airing his concerns. The undertone was clear: the pamphlet was a cowardly and treacherous way of bringing forth serious charges, which, if made in public, could be quickly and easily refuted.

Having satisfactorily assaulted Heath's social graces, Mello turned his attention to the two finds under scrutiny. He rejected out of hand the suggestion that he had changed the find locality of the engraved rib, and mocked the 'minute' description Heath provided of the discovery of the tooth, doubting that he was even in the cave at the time. He closed with what he intended to be assassination of Heath's scientific standing, but which to modern eyes is simply academic snobbery: '[the finds] have been examined by the highest authorities and *no one whose opinion is of any value* has questioned their authenticity ... My friend Professor Boyd Dawkins' character as an honest and experienced investigator stands far too high to require defence against the attacks of *such a man as Mr. Heath*' (emphasis mine).

Heath's reply, published a week later, showed none of the restraint he had managed in the exchanges of 1876.[9] Then he was trying to limit the damage that John Plant's interference might have done to his relationship with Mello, which in the worse case could have seen him removed from the exploration team. Now he was fighting for his reputation as a scientist and a gentleman. The letter was fuelled by rage and oiled with sarcasm, opening with an assault against the 'spirit and disingenuity' of Mello's missive which 'place[d] his example outside the pale of emulation'; although it is a shame that Heath could never seem to emulate one of its key characteristics – brevity. Heath was certainly not impressed with the impoverished and negative evidence that Mello and Dawkins now relied upon to back up their claims, or their refusal either to explain or accept the errors they made in the field. How, he asked, was it enough for Mello to blankly deny that he changed his story about the find locality of the engraved rib or the accounts of its identification without some explanation? Was this not one gentleman's word against another?

There are in fact three different versions: the published one that Richard Tiddeman noticed the engraving immediately it was found in Chamber F; Dawkins' notebook that stated it was from Chamber D; and Heath's lost notebook entry that said it came from Church Hole and was recognised by Mello at his home four days after it had been removed from that cave. Such inconsistencies intensified Heath's indignation, especially the jibe that his account was 'ridiculously minute'. Using this as a weapon, Heath mockingly assumed (quite rightly in Dawkins' case) that his erstwhile colleagues would never be troubled with noting the details of their work, preferring instead to rely on their 'phenomenal memories'. Memories were tricky things to rely on and Heath had proof. Dawkins, for example, had claimed after the *Pall Mall Gazette* episode that he had quite forgotten that Heath was even involved in the excavation, while Mello persisted in peddling the notion that John Evans had authored the article a full four days after a member of Mello's own household had admitted to Heath that everybody there knew Dawkins had written it. Furthermore, Heath had unquestionably been in the cave when the tooth was discovered: Dawkins knew it, Mello knew it, Heath knew it and the workmen knew it – so why was this fact now in question?

Mello's memory about the events that transpired at the BAAS meeting was also suspect. The President of the Geological Section denied ever making the statement Mello attributed to him, in private or in public. Comments had been passed at a committee meeting about certain passages in the pamphlet, but Duncan would not be drawn, stating that 'for a gentleman to pass such an opinion upon the results or conclusions of scientific men without any knowledge of the work was most libellous'. As Heath obviously had exceptional knowledge of the work, this could not apply to him, meaning that Duncan's comments were aimed elsewhere, at the very people who were commenting on the pamphlet. Heath also asked two other attendees about the supposed banning of his pamphlet, but neither had heard anything about it. The truth was that the BAAS had no authority whatsoever to prevent its sale. Heath therefore accused Mello of trying to evade answering the real questions by wriggling behind the president and setting-up the Associations' supposed actions as the ultimate arbiter in the matter.

Turning to the reasons for his three-year silence, Heath's letter took on a more sorrowful tone. He had not replied before the Geological Society all those years ago because he was not a Fellow. He had been tempted with the offer a life-fellowship early in 1876, proposed by Henry Clifton Sorby (1826-1908), the famous Sheffield geologist and microscopic petrologist, with Dawkins promising to second the motion. When Dawkins spitefully withdrew his support and turned to active opposition, the nomination was withdrawn. This meant that without an explicit invitation to speak from the President, Heath was rendered silent; or at least this was what Heath believed. He had therefore gone to Creswell on the day of the BAAS meeting with every intention of substantiating his claims, but was carefully 'guarded' from the opportunity to do so by Dawkins and Mello. Heath closed his letter with a rejection of arguments based solely on authority, pointing out that such savants as Conrad Merk and Professor Leopold Rütimeyer had been fooled by two engraved bones from Kesslerloch near Thayngen in Switzerland that had later been proved to be forgeries.[10]

This was an apposite parallel. Conrad Merk, a schoolteacher, had discovered the cave at Kesslerloch in 1873 and subsequently excavated it with the assistance of his older pupils. One of Dawkins' friends, Ludwig Rütimeyer, prehistorian, palaeontologist and physician at the University of Basel, was enlisted by Merk to identify the animal remains. The site produced tens of thousands of Late Pleistocene fossils, 12,000 flint artefacts, bone javelin heads, bone harpoons, personal ornaments of tooth and bone, and bone needles, dating to a similar period as the Upper Palaeolithic (Magdalenian) levels at Creswell. It also produced a number of engraved antlers and bones portraying reindeer, horse and musk-ox. After the main excavation had finished, another prehistorian, Jakob Messikomer (excavator of the famous Stone Age lake dwelling at Robenhausen in Switzerland) was given permission to sieve the spoil heaps, which resulted in 'an abundant harvest' of flint tools and bones. It was during this phase of the work that one of Messikomer's workmen, Alfred Stamm, apparently returned to the heaps on his own and discovered two engraved bones – one depicting a bear in profile, the other a fox in portrait. These were included in the site report, but as they were found after it had gone to press they were barely discussed, so Merk only commented on the fact that they were created by a less accomplished artist than the other engravings. Rütimeyer's glowing appraisal is given in a new appendix John Lee added to his English translation of the report, where he also revealed that the great Swiss archaeologist Ferdinand Keller thought them genuine, suggesting that the crudeness of the images was due to the unforgiving nature of the materials; Lee himself believed that at least one of them was certainly genuine. Embarrassingly for all concerned, the German prehistorian and portable art sceptic Ludwig Lindenschmidt later discovered that the two images had been copied from a popular children's book on zoo animals published in 1868. After interrogation, Stamm confessed that his cousin had engraved them and that his only motive had been the expectation of being paid a premium for them.

Heath's long letter offered no comment on his opinion of Professor Dawkins.

And Battle Come Down

Unsurprisingly, the following Saturday's edition of the weekly *Manchester City News* contained Mello's response.[11] For the interested Victorian gentlefolk, this must have been as good as a serialised novel, and while perhaps not up to the late Charles Dickens' standard of prose was looking to give him a run for his money in wordage and drama. Mello's reply was an exercise in blunt contradiction based on authority, containing no evidence or any new testament to support his assertions. As such it is only worth summarising the points made in his long letter. Mello insisted that, regardless of what Heath now claimed:

1 The sale of the pamphlet had been banned by the BAAS;
2 Duncan had made the comments attributed to him;
3 Dawkins had confirmed that Heath was not in the cave when the tooth was found;
4 He had never said that the engraved rib was from Church Hole;
5 Heath could have spoken up at the Geological Society as any visitor was able to speak, and nothing stopped him from speaking at Creswell;
6 As a superintendent at Creswell it was Heath's bounden duty to bring any matters to the director or the Chairman;
7 Heath's suppression of the evidence was cause to doubt the veracity of his notebooks.

He also accused Heath of only speaking out because he was still resentful of the fact that Dawkins and Mello would not support his election to the

Geological Society, in consequence of certain representations [i.e. Dawkins] calling in question his fitness; but this had happened over three years earlier.

On 22 November, a new witness came forward. Moses Hartley, one of the men employed to assist in the excavations, wrote to the *Manchester City News* with his eyewitness account of events in Robin Hood Cave on 3 July 1876. It represents the only independent account of what happened in the cave on that day, and confirmed Heath's story. It is worth repeating verbatim:

> 'Mr Mello, in your last issue, asserts that he has Mr Boyd Dawkins' authority for saying that "Mr Heath was not in the Caves at the time" when the *Machairodus* tooth was found. I beg to say that both Mr Heath and I were present on that interesting occasion, and I distinctly remember the remarks made to me by Mr Heath at the time. I called his attention to the fact that the tooth in question was most unlike all the other finds I had seen in the Caves, inasmuch as it was perfectly dry, and had no sand adhering to it. I remember distinctly, too, the remarks made by Mr Boyd Dawkins. He said "Oh, my! Pengelly will go wild when he hears of this! It will spread like wild-fire over Europe!" I also remember calling Mr Heath's attention to the beautiful serrated edge of the tooth, which appeared quite clean. Not being able to account for such phenomena was cause for my calling Mr Heath's attention to them.'[12]

Heath had a letter in the same issue, which by his own admission was largely a repetition of his first letter. He asked for clarification on a few specific points:

1   Mello's omission of the stalagmite floors from parts of Robin Hood Cave, where Heath recorded three
2   The presence of a stalagmite floor described by Dawkins in Chamber F, which never existed
3   The sections that Mello described from Robin Hood Cave, which never existed
4   Proof of the errors that Mello insisted were present in Heath's account of the finding. Heath had been there at the time, Mello had not.

In the end Mello had little aptitude for fighting, and he wrote just once more, declaring his involvement finished. His final word on the matter, published in the *Manchester City News* for 29 November, simply dismissed Heath's account as irrelevant, misleading and erroneous. He refused to defend the accuracy of his sections until it became a necessity, which he deemed it was not, and insisted that he must leave it to those who heard Duncan's remarks to say whether they were connected to the pamphlet. From this we may infer that Duncan had made no direct comment, but Mello had interpreted what he had said as a slur on Heath. His final line passed the fight to his more pugnacious friend: 'Professor Dawkins will doubtless be able to defend his position … if he cares to do so'.

Around this point, another eyewitness entered the debate, Frederic Stubbs.[13] Stubbs had worked in Robin Hood Cave in October 1875, and had worked out part of Chamber F. He was able to categorically state that there was no stalagmite in the chamber, nor any signs of an intact stratigraphy. He described the sediments as a mixture of brownish sand and clay, with angular pieces of limestone, a few bones, teeth, flint flakes and chips, and mentioned the discovery of a piece of pottery a few inches from the cave floor. This would indicate that the area had been disturbed, as Heath maintained. He went on to mention that the engraved rib and cat's tooth were unlike any other fossils from the site, being clean and dry rather than brown, damp and discoloured. He closed with the rather optimistic hope that his first-hand account would help settle the matter.

A Letter to Nature

That Dawkins would respond in print was inevitable. One might even suppose that Heath deliberately provoked him into action though his comment that Mello's attack had been more injurious to their cause than anything Heath could have orchestrated himself, knowing that it could not and would not go unanswered.[14] Dawkins responded with an open letter to the scientific journal *Nature,* published on 4 December 1879. *Nature* in 1879 was only 10 years old,[15] but it already aspired to bring science to both general and specialist audiences. Its weekly circulation was fairly small, although as many libraries and gentlemen's clubs took it the actual readership was far greater. The journal's first editor, Norman Lockyer, boasted that it was becoming 'more and more widely recognised as the organ of science the world over,'[16] but the truth is that *Nature* just did not have the academic clout it enjoys today. Lockyer was also steering *Nature* into controversy, its 'Notes' and 'Letters to the Editor' sections taking articles that bordered on the offensive. As such, Dawkins' choice of outlet for his rebuttal was inspired. With one letter, Dawkins plucked the argument from the parlours of

Manchester, and thrust it onto an international stage where it could be read by a larger number of people from all walks of life.

Dawkins' letter was factual and disciplined, yet the subtext bristled with contempt and indignation. Dawkins first attended to the 'insinuation' that the engraved bone and *Machairodus* canine were not bona fides discoveries but were planted in the cave by persons unspecified and derived from a place unspecified. He summarily dismissed the issue of the engraved rib: Heath had not been present, but Dawkins had and could thus vouch for the veracity of Mello's account. He then turned to the *Machairodus* canine, carefully avoiding any statement as to whether Heath had or had not been present in the cave when the tooth was discovered and rejecting the claim that the tooth was dry and clean. The fact that it had split during the drying process and the red cave earth that could still be seen in the pulp cavity was proof enough.

Having discharged all questions of authenticity to his own satisfaction, Dawkins turned his attention to Heath's professional integrity. According to Dawkins, Heath was never a member of the Exploration Committee, merely a sub-ordinate of Mr Mello. He therefore had a duty to report any problem or fault, and was honour bound to hand over any notebooks relating to the work, which were the property of the Committee. He had done neither, even though he had ample opportunity to do so, at MGS meetings, BAAS meetings etc. As a final blow, Dawkins stated that the only notes that had been given to Mello (some measurements inside Robin Hood Cave) had to be done over, implying that Heath's work had been sloppy.

Prejudice and Pride

For Heath the letter was a personal disaster. In just 585 words it assassinated his honesty, professionalism and scholarship before a multi-national and interclass audience. He penned a reply on 9 December and sent it to the Editor of *Nature*. Two weeks later he received the editor's decision, relayed through the sub-editor John Scott Keltie (1840-1927, himself a distinguished geographer). Heath was asked to cut the letter down so that it occupied no more than one column of the journal and was reminded that the editor was only interested in the scientific value of the caves, to which Heath should confine himself. Should Heath accept these conditions, the editor would be happy to publish the letter, although of course Dawkins and Mello would be given the opportunity to reply should they so wish, but there the correspondence must end.[17]

Heath had undeniably produced an over-length diatribe, one that contradicted Dawkins' every point in minute detail, but he found the revisions too bitter to swallow. In a letter dated Christmas Day 1879, Heath remonstrated with Keltie that the journal had allowed Dawkins to make 'groundless and impudent attacks' and now colluded with him to suppress any reply.[18] As for *Nature* only being interested in science, Heath agreed that this was a wholesome principle, but one which the journal had violated by publishing Dawkins' letter in the first place. Dawkins' letter contained only one paragraph dealing with the science; the rest was 'an impotent attempt' to sideline the real issue by bringing forth a series of 'unwarrantable' aspersions. Heath complained that he was not being offered a fair opportunity to defend his character as a 'gentleman and scientist', while his opponents were given the right to reply without answer. It was quite simply an example of class bias and privilege (we also know Dawkins was a personal friend of the publisher, Alexander MacMillan). In closing, Heath informed Keltie that he must refuse the offer of submitting a revised manuscript, which he considered to be nothing more than a 'generous aid to your friend'. He would instead publish it in full elsewhere, along with his correspondence with *Nature*.

Another Letter to the *Manchester City News*

Heath next wrote to the *Manchester City News*, asking the 'old battle ground' to take his letter in its unadulterated state alongside the exchange with Keltie, explaining that he was clearly not of the 'right stuff' to get published in *Nature*. The newspaper accepted and published Heath's lengthy rant on 3 January 1880. Heath would later sarcastically comment that it was his failure to appreciate the 'kind paternal care' and 'disinterested motives' of the editor of *Nature* that led him to publish it instead in the journal in which Mr Mello chose to make his first attack.[19] Heath was rapidly becoming the bête noir of the Pleistocene world; he was certainly not making any new friends and his turgid writing style may have been one of the reasons he failed to influence people.

Heath's 'suppressed' letter emulated the structure of Dawkins' own, dealing first with the facts surrounding the discovery, and then the portrayal of Heath's role in the exploration. Much of the first reiterated details contained in Heath's pamphlet: the fact that there was no stalagmite in Chamber F, and that Dawkins and Mello could not even agree on whether the cave earth was red or light-coloured. This was important, because Heath agreed with Mello, meaning that Dawkins' claim that red cave earth could still be found in the pulp cavity of the tooth made no sense – *there was no red cave earth* in Chamber F to adhere to the tooth. Heath also pointed out that the 'unfortunate split' on the tooth, which Dawkins insisted had occurred as it dried, was present when it was found and is clearly visible on the published engraving (Figure 6.3); besides, splitting meant nothing as perfectly stable bones could split if their environment was suddenly changed. Heath also confirmed Hartley's account that when the tooth was found it was dry and clean with no sand adhering to it – this, and what he had found on examining the find spot, had led him to the opinion that the tooth had been planted.

Heath was most irritated by Dawkins' final throwaway remark, about the measurements in Robin Hood Cave, which brought out his sardonic best: 'the person who [retook the measurements] must be a most wonderfully inventive genius for they are measurements and sections that had for ever disappeared, so that they could only have been "done over again" by such a fertile imagination'. Mello had actually borrowed Heath's notebooks, and when he returned them on 9 October 1876 had said that no measurements had to be done over.[20] Heath makes little of it, but it shows that he had passed his notebooks to Mello immediately after the excavation and had not withheld them. In fact, Heath, Tebbet and the workmen were the only people to see the geological sections illustrated in the paper; without Heath's notes Mello could not have reproduced them, as he visited the cave so rarely and then only for a cursory look and a family picnic. So, it seems plain that the Robin Hood Cave section drawings in the 1877 paper were based on Heath's notebooks, although he was not satisfied that they had been copied faithfully, deeming them 'reckless' or totally made-up. Heath also dismissed the dashed lines showing each day's work, calling them fallacious and pointing out one critical contradiction. According to the dates on the published plan the tooth, which was found at the rear of Chamber F, would have been found on the 7 July; on 3 July they were apparently only just beginning to enter Chamber F.

The answer to the latter probably lies in the annotations on the original plan and the differences in excavation methods. Heath stated that he excavated each face back about a yard at a time, noting changes in the faces as he went. Mello, on the other hand, removed each stratum separately, presumably

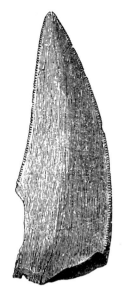

Figure 6.3: Dawkins' original illustration of the Machairodus, clearly showing that the split was already present in 1876 (after Dawkins 1877). Comparison with Plate 11 shows that the split has since extended right up the tooth.

working forward for an unspecified distance before returning to the beginning to remove the next stratum.[21] The inked annotations on the plan highlight the position of the working face in Robin Hood Cave on 29-30 June and reveal that the first three feet of sediment was removed from the rear of the chamber between 30 June and 3 July. Being the days either Mello or Dawkins were in the cave, this fits with their methods. Presumably, the lower deposits were left in place and excavated after 3 July, as Mello's published plan shows. This would help explain the discrepancies between the published and unpublished plans, why Mello records twice the depth of sediment recorded by Heath, and how the tooth could have been pulled from the rear of the chamber on 3 July. Still, something just does not ring true and Heath may have been vindicated in his assertion that the dates were simply made up to create the impression of careful recording, with the inked annotations being added retrospectively to imply the use of methods that supported Dawkins' version of events. Whichever is true Mello made a clumsy mistake in stating in his text that the tooth was found at the rear of the chamber, on a date when the accompanying illustration shows them working the mouth.

The remainder of the letter 'emphatically repudiated' the Mello/Dawkins view of Heath's duties and obligations. Heath and Mello had entered into an agreement 12 months before Dawkins became involved, and Heath had personally conducted the majority of the work. Dawkins has suggested the formation of a committee, telling Mello and Heath that it would add more importance to the work. Dawkins had also assured them that the reports would be in joint names, with the spoils distributed according to the subscribed amount; Heath had been authorised by Alderman Longman to offer one-third of the costs. The Committee, however, was a sham, designed only to shift the balance of power to Dawkins, who appointed himself its secretary. Heath described it as mythical, rejecting the notion that it held any legal or moral rights over his notes, or indeed the specimens. It met only to receive financial reports, and no publications were submitted to it for approval. Far from helping fund the work, only two Committee members had contributed at all, the sum of £5 each. Heath on the other hand had personally spent £41 on the project, including the wages for the two night cleaners. Alderman Longdon had given an additional £25 for Heath's railway expenses and board at the inn. In total Derby Museum or its representatives spent £86 4s 6d, over half the entire excavation budget for the two seasons, yet they never received an equivalent share of the finds. As a further insult Dawkins had the temerity to charge the Committee full price (one guinea) for the copy of *Cave Hunting* presented to Tebbet, while Mello claimed £10 expenses for his few visits from Chesterfield.

In a long outburst about the excavation finances, Heath cryptically stated that on 1 June 1876 an offer was put to him, which he had declined because of the embarrassment already caused by Dawkins' piece in the *Pall Mall Gazette*. The nature of the offer or by whom it was made is not known, but Heath was sufficiently affronted to take the matter to the Duke of Portland. According to Heath's account, the Duke authorised him to talk to Mello and intimate that if the 'expedients to extricate Mr Dawkins' (this is a quote from the seventeenth century theologian and pamphleteer Edward Stephens – meaning to wriggle out of their guilt) were not discontinued, then 'the explorations would be finished under different auspices from those under which they commenced'. In other words the Duke had licensed Heath to issue a threat to the effect that unless Dawkins stopped whatever it was Dawkins was doing, both he and Mello would be removed from running the explorations. Obviously this never occurred and the Committee was formed.

Heath ends with another revelation. Far from not knowing of Heath's concerns, Dawkins had been aware of them since October 1876. At that time, Heath had asked Dawkins if they could quietly discuss the matter and get to the truth without it becoming public, but Dawkins had 'assumed a supercilious air' and asked Heath to present his case in writing.[22] From then until 1879 the two had not communicated at all. The reasons why Heath took so long to publish his notes rings true to modern scholars – his day job just did not leave him enough time to write the volume he was planning.

Heath's own last lines were equally designed to annoy. He first asked Dawkins why he had not acquiesced to the Duke's condition that all unique finds were deposited with the British Museum, although to be fair to Dawkins the only unique find was the engraved rib, and this *was* with the national museum. He then questioned whether the fossils really were the property of the Committee; if this was truly the case, then why, he asked, had an acquaintance of Dawkins' been selling teeth for 5-10 shillings each, months before they were due to be divided among the subscribers?[23]

A Scene at the Manchester Geological Society
The Dawkins family spent Christmas 1879 in Derby, although it is unlikely that they would have been welcomed into the Heath household, where the timing of *Nature's* rejection letter had no doubt dampened the festive spirit. Still, the appearance of his supressed paper and chiding letters to Keltie just three days into the New Year must have brought some satisfaction. If this

was the case, it did not see the month out. On Tuesday 27 January 1880 Mello read another paper before the MGS, entitled 'More Recent Discoveries in the Creswell Caves'.[24] The paper was effectively a re-run of the Mother Grundy's Parlour article for the local society,[25] with a summary of all previous work. Mello painted a romantic picture of man's struggle with hyaenas, wolves, lions and bears, as well as the 'dreaded *Machairodus*'. The latter animal topped the faunal list, and Mello boldly stated that there could be no doubt that the beast was living in England during the Pleistocene and was not, as suspected when it was first found at Kent's Cavern, a fossil from the Pliocene.

The event was should have passed as unremarkable but Dawkins had other plans. Dawkins had brought along a series of specimens to display and discuss, including hyaena and hippopotamus teeth. He used the opportunity to discredit Heath, who was not at the meeting:

'I have no doubt that some here are perfectly aware that certain hard words – which fortunately break no bones – have been drawing attention to these Creswell explorations in the Manchester press; and the hard words have more particular attached to the two things, which have been alluded to this afternoon. One is the discovery by Mr Mello of the remarkable engraved bone; the other relates to the discovery of the *Machairodus* by myself, and in both of these cases it is insinuated that there was a "fraud, or hoax" or "plant" or something of that kind concocted by some one or another'.[26]

To a completely captive audience Dawkins went on to repeat the statements made in his *Nature* paper. Concerning Heath's claim that there was no red earth in Chamber F, Dawkins dug himself a deeper hole, stating that Mello had already disposed of that objection by noting that 'this chocolate coloured deposit, when wet, is frequently red'.[27] Mello had actually made no such statement – or if he had the words were not included in the published text – and he nowhere described the deposits in Chamber F as chocolate coloured. From the account of the discussion published in the Society's *Transactions* one gets the impression that the meeting concluded in good temper, with gentle questions concerning the activity of hippos in the River Wollen, the ability of a hyaena to drag a dead one into the cave, and whether the remains might not have been introduced by water action or a fissure from the plateau above.

A report in the *Manchester City News* for 31 January 1880 revealed otherwise. As soon as the discussion opened, John Plant spoke out, stating that it seemed to him that the intention of the paper had not been to describe further discoveries, but to enflame a well-known controversy before a packed meeting when only one side of the argument was represented. It was 'neither courteous, gentlemanly, nor honest', he continued, to debate the issue in Heath's absence, when he had not been invited and had been given no notice of Dawkins' intentions. At this point the Chair, Edward Binney (1812-1881), interjected, pointing out that every member of the society had been given notice, but Plant was adamant that Heath had received no intimation of the meeting, yet Mello, who was not a member, clearly had. Plant's reasoning is somewhat awry here – of course Mello knew that the paper was to be read, it was his paper. Becoming conciliatory, Binney said that with his forty years experience with the Society, he was sure that after the present paper was published Mr Heath would be given the opportunity to reply.

A number of Dawkins' friends took umbrage at Plant's accusations. Rooke Pennington objected to the base insinuation that the room had been deliberately packed with Dawkins' supporters, while William Horsfall (an invited guest) scoffed at the ludicrous notion that Dawkins and Mello were guilty of fraud. Pennington was also quick to dismiss the possibility that he had known the *Machairodus* would be mentioned, but thought it a perfectly legitimate subject for discussion, a sentiment echoed by the newly-elected member and Dawkins-acolyte Mark Stirrup (1831-1907). Stirrup added that he was certain Heath would receive full justice from the Society and a Manchester audience, and was equally as certain that Dawkins would come out of it untarnished. The discussion ended with a typical retreat from Mello, who said his intention had only been to bring the latest discoveries to the table, not make any form of attack. His last words were the most telling: 'as for the dispute, he would only say that if the time should ever come when these attacks were made in such a form that they required an answer, they would be met'. Precisely what, we may justifiably ask, would 'such a form' be? Clearly not in Mello's mind a privately published pamphlet or a damning letter in a newspaper.

When Heath learned of the meeting, he fired off an immediate reply, which appeared in the following Saturday's edition of the *Manchester City News*.[28] His letter was controlled and factual, but typically long and convoluted. Over half is a rejection of Horsfall's comment that Heath had accused Dawkins and Mello of deceit, reiterating the fact that he had never accused anyone and did not see it as his duty to conjecture on who had perpetrated the hoax, just to lay out the reasons he suspected one. Indeed, the only people who seemed to be making this charge against Dawkins were his own friends. Heath still considered Mello an honest man, and exonerated him from knowingly publishing misrepresentations, although by relying on Dawkins for information he had unwittingly done so nonetheless. Dawkins was clearly the villain in Heath's mind, a cad who continually peddled the same litany of errors and falsehoods, who dishonourably fought the battle without his opponent being present, and who worked behind the scenes to suppress Heath's views and prevent an open and frank discussion. Reflecting on the events of that evening a few months later, Heath was more tempestuous, remarking with scorn that when Plant took exception to Dawkins' 'courageous remarks' it was no doubt due to 'the inexperience of Mr Plant who is evidently unschooled in the privileges and licenses conferred upon Mr Dawkins by his well-earned reputation for such polemical battles, and I am informed that they were very properly suppressed. That they were the only part of the discussion that were suppressed is beside the question'.[29]

Chapter 7

Creswell Crags versus
William Boyd Dawkins

An Audience With Thomas Heath

Closing his letter of 7 February, Heath said he was looking forward to taking up the President's offer to reply in front of the Manchester Geological Society, before snidely thanking Dawkins and Mello for providing him with the opportunity. His day finally came on 25 May 1880, when he read a long paper before the Society, the President Joseph Dickinson (d.1912) in the chair. The text of the paper was published in full in Heath's second pamphlet[1] but for reasons we shall learn was seen nowhere else. It was classic Heath, beginning by chastising the chairman of the January meeting for allowing Dawkins to refer to matters that had no relevance to the paper under discussion. Many of the points Heath raised had been aired before, and for this Heath was duly sorry, although he was unapologetically verbose and convoluted in presenting them: 'I could not avoid emulating my late colleagues by giving in some measure a transcript of what has already appeared. This recapitulation can only be atoned for, so far as it is right to repeat the truth of a controverted fact, until it has wrought conviction.'[2]

Heath's rebuttal concentrated on three key points.

1   The nature of the deposits in Chamber F;
2   The conditions in the cave when the piece was found;
3   The condition and location of the tooth.

Heath's first criticism was one that any close reading of Mello's 1880 paper and the published discussion show to be correct. When taking the floor at the MGS in January, Dawkins had attributed to Mello words that were not contained in the paper – that the chocolate-coloured deposit turned red when wet – which given their importance would have surely been reported had they been spoken. Heath was caustic, asking whether Mello had failed to follow Dawkins' instructions, and whether Dawkins had failed to notice that the expected words had not been uttered. Heath clearly regarded Mello as a marionette, innocently performing the routines determined for him by his nefarious puppet-master, Dawkins. Regardless of whether the words were spoken or not, the whole point was a bluff – Mello never once in print or elsewhere described the deposit as chocolate-coloured – he always said it was 'light'. Regardless of what Mello had said, Dawkins' claim that a chocolate-coloured deposit turned red when wet went against common sense. Heath explained: red sand was simply a calcareous or any other sand that was impregnated with iron oxide. The precise hue depended on the proportions of the staining agent, a chocolate-coloured deposit containing a significantly greater amount of iron oxide than a red one. Mello, being an artist, would surely have known this? It was just ridiculous to state that a darker colour would become lighter when wet.

The deposit supposedly adhering to the tooth also left Heath bemused. Not only was it supposed to be visible in the pulp cavity,[3] but now it was adhering to the serrated edge too.[4] The tooth seemed to be acquiring more red earth as time went on, despite the fact that there was no red earth in Chamber F (and if chocolate-coloured, it must surely have dried after four years). Heath had, furthermore, seen it moments after discovery, when there was no matrix on it at all. Dawkins had also succeeded in fooling everybody at the January meeting. When he asked the audience to compare the appearance and condition of the *Machairodus* tooth with samples found along with it, he was delivering a magical slight of hand, as the displayed specimens and the matrix sticking to them were from Mother Grundy's Parlour, not Robin Hood Cave. That there could be a similarity between teeth from different caves showed that the tooth really could have come from anywhere. The implication was clear: the fossil was foreign to the chamber and was already clean when it was introduced. The fact that the crack in the tooth had been present when it was found meant that the original discoverer had failed to gelatinise it quickly enough. Heath thought it incredulous that an authority such as Dawkins would have made such a fundamental mistake. In other words, somebody else – an amateur – had found / obtained it and afterwards introduced it to Creswell.

The conditions in the cave on the day of the discovery, and the reasons why Heath and Hartley had immediately been suspicious, were finally presented in detail. At about 2.10pm on 3 July 1876, just after the lunch break, Dawkins, Heath and Hartley were watching workmen in Robin Hood Cave when one exposed a small escarpment. From the light of two candles

171

illuminating the area, they could all see a tooth embedded in the cave earth. At a distance of 9 ft 6 in from the working face, Heath was unable to determine the species but Dawkins, standing right next to him, apparently had keener sight. It was at this moment that he uttered the lines Heath and Hartley attributed to him: 'Hurrah! The *Machairodus*. Oh, my! Pengelly will go wild when he hears of this! It will spread like wild-fire over Europe!' (These words, never disputed by Dawkins, seem to be as rehearsed as 'One small step for man…'). Dawkins removed the fossil and was the first to handle it, but everybody had seen it *in situ*, so Dawkins' claim to have been the discoverer was misleading.

Hartley and Heath immediately noticed something was wrong: the condition of the tooth was different to that of anything else from the cave. When Dawkins took the fossil outside, he left Heath and Hartley alone to inspect the find-spot. Heath saw a shaft with a polished surface, 1 in wide and 18 in long, running 6 in beyond the position of the tooth. The impression of the tooth was clearly visible, penetrating the side of the shaft (Figure 7.1). Heath was certain that the polished surface had been made by a pick or iron bar, forming a deep chute into which the tooth had been dropped. Unfortunately for whoever planted it, it had become stuck halfway down; a little push had embedded it into the side wall but to force it further would have likely jeopardised it. The hole was certainly newly formed and nobody had subsequently walked over the area or compressed the sediment. To test this idea, Heath inserted a pick and a walking stick into the cave earth and walked over it; the sides of the cavity bulged, destroying the burnished surface. Hartley witnessed everything, and was by reputation a man of such integrity that 'even Mr Dawkins' temerity [would] not venture to impeach' his statement.[5] Yet, at the moment of discovery Dawkins was in such a state of high excitement that nobody dared question the circumstances. They were afraid of Dawkins, a fact more damning to the Professor's cause than his opponent's.

A detailed deconstruction of the nature and integrity of the deposits at the rear of Chamber F provided Heath with his coup de grâce. Not only was there no stalagmite or even breccia in Chamber F, but the contour of the roof precluded stalagmite formation within 15 ft of the find spot. From the entrances of Chambers G and B there were no intact deposits. The recent inhabitants of the cave had told Heath it had been used for storing straw and fodder, and had occasionally been used as a makeshift cowshed because it was so dry. This would explain why several inches of the surface were composed of fine straw debris and the rest a dirty cream-coloured bed that

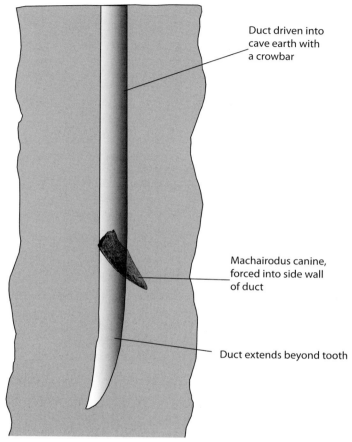

Duct driven into
cave earth with
a crowbar

Machairodus canine,
forced into side wall
of duct

Duct extends beyond tooth

Figure 7.1: Heath's version of the section where the Machairodus canine was recovered, showing a duct made by bar or pick and the tooth jammed into the side (redrawn after Heath 1880).

had been disturbed in modern times. At the entrance of Chamber G this creamy deposit reached depths of 2 ft thick, opposite Chambers B and C it was 2 ft 7 in, and at the point where the tooth had been found it thickened to 4 ft 6 in. This was not just geological pedantry. The absence of stalagmite and the geology of this part of the cave was so important that to 'tender the excuse for the mistake as mere inadvertence, or lack of information that could so easily have been acquired, must render the credibility of the evidence of its author (who so wantonly outrages that observation and care necessary to science) as too imaginary and unreliable to be any serious embarrassment in the comparison he courts, and the importance of his uncorroborated evidence nil.'[6]

This lack of attention to detail carried on through all of Dawkins and Mello's measurements; it was *their* records that were wrong, not Heath's as had been claimed. The apparent doubling of the true depth of deposit in Chamber F had already been reported, but the measurements on the sections drawings for Chambers A and C and Chambers D and E were also a nonsense, being 1 ft 9 in too short and 5 ft too deep respectively. Heath left his audience with no doubt as to the cause of these errors: 'if sections are of any value at all, surely they should at least be approximately correct, and not as if they had been manufactured in a study to corroborate some conclusion it is desired to establish.'[7] Yet why rely on Heath's word alone, when the question could be ground-truthed? Sediment remained in the caves, and the rocks did not lie, Heath scoffed. Heath was so confident in the truth of his testimony that he challenged Dawkins to a wager: a trip to the cave should be organised for three members of the Society along with the three combatants to examine the remaining sediments. If Heath was wrong, he would foot the bill, if he were correct, Dawkins would pay for the trip.

In conclusion, Heath stated that his emphatic repudiations were not a charge against anyone – he had never intended to conjecture whence the tooth came or who put it there. He simply wanted to prevent science making a massive blunder by willingly receiving a fraud or a hoax:

> 'The issues are great, the alleged find unique, and would complete an important page in the History of the Fauna of the Midlands and the geographical distribution in Europe of an important animal, if the *bona fides* were properly established. My disappointment is a great as yours can be, that my first objections have not been dissipated by my learned opponents, whose defence has in such a remarkable manner, not only corroborated them, but raised more serious ones which I venture to think effectively negative the possibility of this tooth being a native of Creswell.'[8]

The room was then opened up for discussion.

A Controversy among the Cave Hunters

The discussion that followed lasted over three hours and descended into what Dawkins described in his diary, with a minimalistic skill not matched by his oration, as a 'scene at Geol. Soc.'. A summary that ran to almost 4500 words was printed in the *Manchester City News* for 29 May 1880, and reprinted in Heath's second pamphlet, where it was augmented by shorthand notes taken at the meeting along with a running commentary from Heath in the footnotes.[9] An account of events follows.

Dawkins took command of the room and turned it into a kangaroo court. He opened with a brief master class in gamesmanship:

'Professor Dawkins: Before I begin my reply, I will ask Mr Heath what evidence he has of the truth of the statements he now makes

Mr Heath: Personal knowledge

Professor Dawkins: You have no documentary evidence of any sort?

Mr Heath: I don't quite understand you. How can we have documentary evidence of a find in a cave? I was there, and saw the same find as yourself.

Professor Dawkins: Then you have nothing further to say on that point?

Mr Heath: I have not

Professor Dawkins: Very Good

Mr Heath: You may take it that the whole of the reasons I have for coming to the conclusions I have arrived at have been given to the society this afternoon, and it is now for you to deal with them.'[10]

Dawkins' motive for this opening exchange was sinister, and Heath had walked straight into the trap. Dawkins had been asking whether Heath had any notebooks from the time, which he had. But by asking in such an obtuse fashion and neglecting to clarify the question when Heath admitted he did not understand, Dawkins had cleverly allowed Heath to imply before the assembled fellows and guests that he had nothing to back up his claims. He was therefore given no opportunity to have them examined by the society. So, with a disingenuous flourish, Dawkins began:

'Before I make my reply to this very remarkable communication, which so far as I know is certainly without precedent – at all events, within the limits of my experience – I should like to put before the Society my extreme regret at such a fuss having been made about a question of bones of this sort. It seems to me that this controversy, which is raised by Messrs. Heath and Plant, is a very poor sort of controversy, a sort of bone dust, and within the last six months there has been a great deal of this dust flying about. This communication is the latest development of *an organised attack* upon Mr. Mello primarily, and upon myself secondarily, by Messrs. Plant and Heath no less than four years ago. In dealing with this attack, I shall venture to put before you documentary evidence which was brought before you then. I shall not pit my assertions against those of the gentleman who has preceded me, but shall give you chapter and verse for them out of Mr. Heath's letters, and such other evidence as would be acceptable in a court of law'.[11]

Dawkins then proceeded to describe the events of April 1876, in which he referred to Heath as a 'paid servant' of Derby Museum and claimed that the motive behind the first controversy was to rob Mello of his due credit, which was blatantly untrue. As Plant had stated at the time, the point was to had to get some acknowledgement of Heath's central role in the work. This is not a subject that need detain us too long, but it is worth noting that Heath had always, personally and in print, recognised Mello's primacy in the excavations, and considered Mello a man of utmost integrity. He also undertook his duties as a paid servant of Derby Museum with great pleasure and pride, and failed to see the difference between being a paid servant of Derby Museum or a paid servant of Manchester Museum.

Moving on, Dawkins claimed to have had no knowledge of Heath until after the Committee was formed, that he was unaware of his earlier involvement, had not used a single note Heath had produced, and in the *Pall Mall Gazette* article had not claimed any credit for the discovery. This was demonstrably a pack of lies: Dawkins and Heath had been in correspondence for months before the committee was formed, until May 24 1876 the salutation had been 'My Dear Heath', after that date a chillier 'My Dear Sir.'[12] (In 1880 Heath still had these letters as proof, but no trace of them can be found today; it is a shame Heath did not follow through with his threat to publish them). Dawkins had also clearly forgotten that he had actually apologised to Heath for omitting him from the article four years earlier, explaining that the letter had been written in a hurry and he genuinely had no idea of the true extent of Heath's involvement.[13]

Plant was next to speak, telling the audience that Dawkins was deceiving them in saying he had claimed no credit for the find, and that he had brought the article with him as proof. The passage was read aloud and although it was true that no credit was directly claimed, the implication was clearly there: 'finds in Derbyshire, brought before the Geological Society as few days since by Mr Mello and Professor Dawkins.'[14] Dawkins had started to respond when Mark Stirrup spoke up and asked whether the time of the society should be taken up with what appeared to be purely personal quarrels in which the members could have little interest, an interjection that was met with a chorus of 'hear, hear'. Dawkins agreed, but pressed on, stating that he regretted having to do so but as the question of bona fides had been raised against himself and Mello he felt honour bound to reply. This included ridiculing the testimony of Frederic Stubbs, who had come out in support of Heath: 'This gentleman, it appears, visited the cave in October, 1875, and he undertook to describe appearances which presented themselves in 1876, so that here they had a witness gifted with the spirit of prophecy'.[15]

Abruptly changing tack, Dawkins next attempted to dismiss the entire controversy, which he felt had no scientific merit whatsoever and was merely a clash of personalities. Appealing once again to his own authority, he told the members that he had the work of twenty years to fall back on to support his position, but he was there to stop himself and Mello from being portrayed as the ravening wolves savaging Heath's innocent lamb. Contained within this smokescreen is one of the most curious statements Dawkins ever made, that: 'He was not there that day to put before them his own case, *for what did he care about what be said as to a bone found here or another found there*'[my emphasis].[16] How is one to read this? Is Dawkins implying that given his vastly superior knowledge he was interested only in the bigger picture, not the details of individual bones? Or is he suggesting that he was not interested where the tooth came from, thereby rejecting the unquestionable primacy of context in all archaeological and paleontological research? It is difficult to tell, and may be nothing more than the result of garbled note taking during a frenetic and heated meeting, but I suspect Dawkins might have been attempting to lull the audience into believing that the precise find spot of the tooth did not actually matter.

This was what Heath took from the statement, as he immediately asked Dawkins if he still stuck to his assertion about the matrix and the presence of stalagmite, to which Dawkins replied that his 'impression was that he was literally correct'. Heath's footnote on this point is incandescent.[17] This was not a matter of impression, but a matter of fact. If Dawkins had seen a stalagmite formation, it would show every statement Heath had made was wrong. It would guarantee the sediments in Chamber F were virgin and undisturbed, and it would be evidence that moisture had dripped from the roof, disproving the statements of the 'old inhabitants' that the chamber was dry and had therefore been used for storing fodder. It would also, Heath sneered, add the use of pottery, the cultivation of straw and other materials used in animal husbandry to the list of Pleistocene finds from Creswell, and exonerate Dawkins of his 'unparalleled recklessness in describing a stalagmitic formation created by himself which the work of neither twenty years or fifty years can redeem or alter. The conflict is not between Mr Dawkins and myself' Heath concluded, '*but between Mr Dawkins and the Rocks*' [original emphasis].[18]

John Plant then took the floor, prepared to deliver a long speech. He began by declaring that the engraved rib was undoubtedly genuine, but that it came from a French Cave, such finds being absent from Britain. That it was unique in a British context was not a valid reason to reject it, he knew, but at this point in his speech it remained unclear whether Plant was implying that it was planted recently or discarded 14,000 years ago by visitors from France. He lauded the rib and tooth as two superb finds, clearly the most extraordinary among the 8000 specimens found in the caves. How serendipitous then, Plant marvelled, that of all the objects in all the caves, it fell to Mello and Dawkins to find the two most treasured pieces on one of their cursory visits. 'The doctrine of chances is acknowledged to be inexplicable,' he conceded, 'but to my mind this is an instance of coincidences and lucky chances beyond all precedent. It would have been a relief to one's incredulity if, in the ordinary daily work of the labourers, it had been their unknown good fortune to have shovelled this bone and tooth with their ordinary finds into the common bag made up each day'.[19] It has to be admitted that this is a good point. Plant also highlighted the contradictions in the pair's accounts. Mello argued that *Machairodus* was a Pleistocene species only, Dawkins that it was found in the Pliocene too (in fact he had earlier maintained that it was exclusively Pliocene in age). Dawkins maintained that there was a stalagmite, yet Mello's section showed none. Mello said the cave earth was light, Dawkins that it was red. Heath was therefore well justified in criticising the accuracy of their reporting, and their memories.

Plant was far bolder than Heath in his accusations, pointing out that *Machairodus* teeth were not so rare or difficult to obtain as Dawkins would have people believe, and could occasionally be found for sale in Europe, South America and the United States. But what could have been the motivation behind such a fraud? For Plant, the pair strained credulity in their efforts to make Creswell Crags a model locality that could be favourably compared in every respect with the richest on the continent. The cat and the engraving were needed to complete the set, although Plant also expressed scepticism over whether the identifications of two other rare species, arctic fox and wolverine, were even correct (he was wrong, and besides, the identifications had been done by Busk, not Dawkins). The difference in opinion was not that the two finds were introduced by the hand of man, but when they were introduced, and how. Plant was only ever going to side with Heath: '[Mr Heath] has stated his facts, the names of his witnesses, and all the data upon which he argues and endeavours to prove his case, and in my opinion and upon other knowledge which it is not yet prudent to reveal, I come to the conclusion that both the tooth and the incised bone were buried in the Creswell Caves not very long before they were found, in 1876.'[20]

It was at this juncture that Mello spoke up, but only to repeat again the circumstances of how Heath came to work with him in the caves, and to ask permission to present extracts and sections from his notebooks. Exactly what was presented was not reported, but Mello pointed out that they stood in direct contradiction to Heath's notes. The veracity of Mello's evidence was immediately and completely destroyed when somebody asked him whether he had been in Robin Hood Cave when the cat was found, forcing him to admit that he was not at Creswell at all on that day. His notebooks were thus a false witness; in fact the sections he claimed to have recorded had ceased to exist thirty hours before he visited the cave.[21] Mark Stirrup, tired of the personal squabbles, again tried to draw things to a close. It was a shame, he said, that Heath and Plant showed so much personal feeling, because when personalities are introduced to the discussion it gives the public the wrong impression of scientists; men of obvious ability should not spend their energies wrangling over matters such as this. Clearly an advocate of Dawkins,' he expressed extreme doubt whether 'some wag' would go to the bother and expense of procuring such a rare fossil when there were so many less costly ways of frustrating scientific explorers. He hoped the discussion could now be dropped, the charges brought against Dawkins and Mello poor reward for all their efforts.

But it did not end there. On the Chairman's invitation, Frederic Stubbs explained that he shared the opinion of many others in doubting the authenticity of the tooth, and gave his version of the events of October 1875.[22] He was not gifted with the spirit of prophecy as Dawkins had sarcastically suggested. He had worked with Mr Heath before Dawkins had even seen the caves or any of their contents. On the last day of work before closing down for the winter, all the soil removed over several days was thrown back over the working escarpment, so that if any unwanted visitors managed to break into the cave they would be met with disturbed spoil. This was close to where Dawkins claimed to have found the tooth. Had there been a stalagmite, decomposed or otherwise, he would have seen it in the careful examination he made during his time in the cave. The whole of the area he was involved in excavating had been disturbed relatively recently, as shown by the pottery close to the floor.

The meeting then descended into a bickering farce. Plant remonstrated with Mello for falsely telling a 'gentleman of Sheffield' that he had stolen bones from the caves, when in fact he had never been near the place. Mello denied this, stating that he had only told the gentleman of Sheffield that there were bones in the Peel Park Museum, Salford that he had not authorised to be sent there. In what followed it was established that the bones had been found by Stubbs, and sent by him to Peel Park.

Heath took the fight to Stirrup, saying that if his correspondence had evinced 'warmth' (i.e. aggression) it was because of extreme provocation by his opponents who had, basically, lied at every turn.

The Chair finally stepped in and closed the meeting, saying that: 'if there had been a want of temper amongst the disputants in this controversy, there had certainly been no want of ability on either side in putting their case before the society. He must, however, express his regret that such a subject had come before them at all, for that Society was only interested in two subjects – geology and mining – and he contended that a bone cave was neither one nor the other. Ripples of laughter spread through the audience, many no doubt relieved that the ordeal was over.

An Air of Corruption
News of the debate was syndicated in the local press. The full discussion was published in a supplement of the *Manchester City News* for 29 May 1880, accompanied by an editorial in the main paper which opined that: 'the debate ought not to be let die out at the present point. A careful examination of all who might be witnesses, and of the place itself, would probably elucidate much that is now inexplicable'. The author also stated that Heath had introduced the question in a purely scientific manner, and deserved an answer in the same spirit, but that, sadly, Dawkins had put science aside and embarked on a personal crusade. It concluded that Dawkins had provided nothing destructive against Heath's criticisms, and that he should use his twenty years' experience to put aside prejudices and recall opinions shown to be doubtful. The piece was anonymous but could

be said to contain all the hallmarks of John Plant were it not for a rejection of comments Plant had made at the meeting; although this could just have been subterfuge.

Dawkins was certainly of the opinion that Plant was behind the piece. Writing in a private letter to R.D. Darbishire,[23] Dawkins thanked his colleague for kind words, but passed the whole thing off as an elaborate attack on his bona fides that was too acrimonious do any harm, implying that no one who mattered would give much credence to such ungentlemanly behaviour. The rest of the letter rehearsed the contents of the *Nature* paper, including the attack on Heath's character. Here Heath was accused of being 'a man of... many falsehoods', whose only witnesses were 'casuals' who could not have seen what they claimed to have seen, and who was making a series of charges for his own ends. Dawkins ended with an indignant statement that no London Society would allow such baseless attacks of this sort, and offering Darbishire access to the fabled notebooks. 'Life is far too short to enter into a question opened and closed nearly four years ago and now reopened on purely personal grounds, and developed by a series of afterthoughts,' he concluded. The letter is important because it was not to a friend, but to a trustee of Owens College, and provided only a summary of what could be derived from the literature – it is frank but guarded. Presumably Dawkins was genuinely concerned that he was in danger of bringing the institution into disrepute, and one wonders whether a letter to a friend such as Green would have been less restrained. Sadly, no such letters have been traced.

Regardless of Dawkins' bluster, others came out in support of Heath. A short piece about the meeting published in the *Sheffield Independent* for 27 May 1880 was considered so unrepresentative that Dr. T. Carter Wigg, a local GP who had attended the event, acerbically likened it to 'the Decalogue, without the word NOT'. He took it upon himself to inform the readership of Heath's six main treatises. Wigg's letter must have crossed Heath's own in the post, but the paper quickly tired of the affair, stating in their 1 June issue that they had received a long letter from Mr Heath, but 'decline to be further deluged on a matter that has descended into a paltry personal squabble'. How far Dawkins had instigated this response is unknown.

Despite the local press having tired of his dogged pertinacity, Heath had every right to expect the MGS to make good on its promise and publish his paper in full. However, to the eternal shame of that once august body it reneged on its commitment, when on 29 June the MGS Council decided that it was not desirable to print Heath's paper or the discussion in its *Transactions*. Instead they would insert a short notice. William Boyd

Dawkins, ex-officio vice-president of the society and de facto member of Council, was present at the meeting.

On receiving the news, Heath entered into a correspondence with the editor and secretary, Joseph S. Martin, a mining engineer from Prestwich and later H.M Inspector of Mines for the south-west. In his first letter of 4 July 1880 Heath simply asked for the return of his manuscript and an explanation for its rejection; it was, after all, a reply to a previous paper by a member of Council, which the President had led him to believe would be accepted.[24] Martin duly returned the manuscript along with a cordial letter,[25] although his explanation for the rejection of the paper can hardly be called explicit. Martin revealed that after the talk he had received representations from several members of the society concerning its publication, and in order to keep himself individually clear from any accusations of wrongdoing had decided to refer the matter to Council, which had unanimously decided not to print. Dawkins' hand in this is not difficult to spot, but Martin then made a terrible mistake, confiding to Heath that he was personally relieved the manuscript had been withdrawn completely, as he nursed reservations about how an abbreviated version could have satisfied both sides and left the honorary secretaries of the Society blameless.

Writing again on 12 July, Heath expressed thanks for the return of the manuscript, and assured Martin that he did not hold him personally to blame. Nevertheless, he failed to see how the Council had acted with equity or justice, or even in a disinterested fashion, especially given the fact that Dawkins had been on the deciding panel. He had withdrawn the paper, he explained, because he feared that the task of editing it would be given to Dawkins and he preferred 'extinction' of the truth rather than 'mutilation'. Threatening to publish the whole debacle privately, Heath again asked for the reasons behind the rejection.[26]

Feeling himself dragged into a crisis not of his own making, Martin became more defensive. His next letter reiterated to Heath that the Council had no intention of suppressing his views, and assured him a fuller explanation of the rejection would be sought at the next meeting of Council, scheduled for September.[27] He also refused to be baited by the intimation that the preparation of a short communication would be left to Dawkins, emphasising his own professionalism and the fact that proofs were automatically sent to all parties before publication, including those mentioned in the discussion, precisely to avoid giving grounds for such 'baseless' accusations and to avoid implicating the honorary secretaries (i.e. him) in any 'unpleasantness'.

Heath's patience could not last until September, and he read into Martin's failure to supply the information requested an admission of guilt. His next letter was long, aggressive and agonisingly doctrinaire, accusing Martin of abdicating his responsibilities as editor, and the Council, by allowing other members to interfere in the its decision, of violating the Society's own regulations.[28] Who, he demanded to know, had made the supposed representations against his paper, and what, precisely, had these entailed? In the absence of any facts, Heath supplied his own answers. It could not be because the chairman had said bone caves were of little interest to the society, as Mello and Dawkins had seen their paper published without question. It could also hardly be the fact that the paper was 'too humble a production', because what better way for Dawkins to prove his point than by allowing Heath to publish a lame duck of a retort that he could easily and summarily dispense with? It was surely not the fact that Heath was not a member of the MGS, as neither Mello nor Heath were members when their 1876 joint article was published in the *Transactions*. There was only one conclusion: all of the previous papers agreed with Dawkins, this one alone opposed him. Given that the Society and its Council was dominated by Dawkins and his friends, alongside a few coal engineers who knew nothing of the affair other than Dawkins' own skewed version, it did not take much to work out who was behind the whole thing. Working through the medium of Council, Dawkins rendered himself 'bereft of responsibility' and 'unembarrassed by scruples'. In closing, Heath informed Martin that he would have been happy with an abridged version if he could have believed that Dawkins would not have interfered, and dismissed the professional set of rules Martin described as irrelevant because nobody had seen fit to follow them. Martin's fifty-eight-word answer merely informed Heath that he would not be drawn into a controversy, that he would supply the reasons for rejection when the information became available, and that Heath's threats and assumptions counted for nothing.[29]

Shortly after this Heath was sent proofs of the abridged version, as Martin had promised (Figure 7.2). Heath was unable to stop himself. Taking the article as justification for all his 'assumptions' he ironically praised its uniqueness and superlative excellence, and again threatened to expose the affair in his private printing.[30] By this time poor Joseph Martin was exasperated, and in a letter of 31 July told Heath that he failed to understand why he was being dragged into the dispute and repeated that he simply was not in possession of the information Heath now demanded – he did not know the reasons for the rejection and was waiting for a reply from Council.[31] The

Manchester Geological Society.

CRESWELL CAVE.
DISCOVERY OF THE MACHAIRODUS TOOTH.

A discussion on this subject (see page 299) took place. Mr. Heath and Mr. Plant read notes alleging the discovery of the above-named tooth to have been the result of a hoax or fraud. Professor Dawkins and the Rev. Mr. Mello controverted and denied the allegations.

Mr. Mark Stirrup also took part in the discussion.

(This reference to the discussion, &c., of the 25th May last is what is intended shall now appear in the Society's Transactions.)

For perusal; and please return to

JOSEPH S. MARTIN,
Park Villas, Prestwich,

20/7/80.   MANCHESTER. *

Figure 7.2: The proof of the abridged version of Heath's paper from the Transactions of the Manchester Geological Society, sent to Heath 20 July 1880 (after Heath 1880).

correspondence concluded on 9 August, when Heath reiterated his suspicions that Dawkins was behind the whole scandalous affair and, in a manner redolent of Uriah Heap, excused Martin of any wrongdoing.[32] Martin remained silent.

Heath had no other recourse than to privately publish another pamphlet, carrying out his threat to make the full account available to the scientific world. He prefaced his work thus:

'I am conscious of the prejudice excited against anyone upon whom circumstances impose the unenviable duty of taking exception to any proposition or alleged discovery by an eminent savant. It generally resolves itself into a contest of might and right. The latter is too often vanquished because of the vortex of every-day life, which produce superficiality, the painful destruction of ideals, and the alienation of associations and friends, which make men cowards. Even at the risk of incurring the charge of being factious and perverse, it is my intention to recur this object until it has been officially removed from every standard work into which it has found access.

I have published this brochure in consequence of the peculiar coincidence of the fate of each of my replies. The bungling audacity of the attacks resists serious treatment, and consistency left me no alternative as to the nature of my replies.'[33]

An editorial in *The Derbyshire Times* for 11 September, by their regular correspondent 'The Impartial Observer', presented an opinion on the pamphlet. Among musings on angling, climbing in the Peak District, Buxton Spa and other anecdotes of Derbyshire life, the Observer noted how Heath's pamphlet provided the first full exposé on the subject. Unless Professor Dawkins could bring some very striking evidence to the table, it stated, his claims of authenticity remained an insult to one's common judgement, and with his position so seriously assailed the writer looked forward with undisguised glee to Dawkins' next bout of defensive posturing. 'The *Machairodus* has turned out to be a very troublesome tooth, indeed; and has caused more aching pain than the whole dental economy of the prehistoric animal to which it belonged ever experienced'. Such a testimony would be very damning indeed if only it were truly impartial. But the *Derbyshire Times* was published by Edward Clulow junior who had also published Heath's pamphlet, and at the bottom the Impartial Observer calls for 'tickets &c' for his column. The writer was close to Heath, maybe Plant, Stubbs or even Heath himself.

Thomas Heath (1847-1886) and John Magens Mello (1836-1914)
At various points during this unpleasant series of exchanges, the anger and exasperation evident in Heath's letters show a man whose sense of perspective was beginning to unravel; he was clearly not able to ignore Dawkins' bluster and belligerence with the same stoic disregard publicly aired by Tiddeman. But with his cathartic and acknowledged rebuttal now in the public arena, Heath allowed the matter to rest. He did not return to Creswell, at least not in any official scientific capacity, although he did write about it on one other occasion. Volume 4 of the *Journal of the Derbyshire Archaeological and Natural History Society*, of which he was a founding council member, ran an article entitled *Pleistocene Deposits of Derbyshire and its immediate vicinity* by Heath. It was a perfectly balanced piece that provided a summary of Pleistocene occurrences at Dream Cave, Waterhouses, Thor's Cave, Bakewell, Middleton, and Windy Knoll, in addition to Creswell Crags. For the latter, he gave a short and factual overview, set out the details

as he understood them and mentioned the work of Mello. He ignored Dawkins' contribution. His only reference to the debate was a footnote to his table of Creswell fauna, which read: 'I have deliberately omitted *Machairodus latidens*, because of the impossibility of its really belonging to the Creswell fauna, as stated by Prof B. Dawkins, since the reasons there adduced have been sufficient to justify Dr. Geikie in omitting it from his work, *Prehistoric Europe*.'[34] Heath had moved on.

Despite any fears he may have held about the safety of his position at Derby, he remained in post. July 1881 saw the denouement of his long-running efforts in transforming the Museum galleries, with glowing reports in the local press heaping praise on his method of providing guidance for further research on each exhibit while adopting the only effectual method of drawing in the masses – simplifying the attainment of knowledge and mixing amusement with instruction.[35] He continued to build the Corporations' collections: in 1882 alone he received a collection of minerals from the Natural History Museum in London and for the opening of the new Art Gallery organised a loan of historic English watercolours, The Duchess of Edinburgh's collection of Old Masters and a panoply of objets d'art from South Kensington.[36] He also threw himself into public education, with at least one highly successful lecture series in the spring of 1882 advertised and reported throughout the local press.[37]

In March 1884, Heath resigned his post at Derby to take up the curatorship of the new museum and art gallery at Queen's Park, Manchester, the Derby press lamenting that his dedication and flair would be much missed.[38] His tenure in Manchester – his 'learned opponents' stomping ground – did not last long, and later in that same year he left England for New Zealand, in a state of ill health. By February 1885, New Zealand's eighth premier, Julius Vogel, had appointed Heath as the head of the industrial section of a large exhibition illustrating the arts, manufactures and produce of the colony.[39] The exhibition was to open in March 1886, but Heath never saw the project to completion. He returned to Derby later in 1885, where after a few months suffering, he died of tuberculosis on 5 February 1886 at the age of 38.[40] It was a tragic loss. A brief obituary in the *Derby Mercury* noted that there would be 'much genuine sorrow for his untimely demise,'[41] although it is doubtful whether this would have extended as far as Owens College. His wife and both his parents, who in 1891 were still living in Four Acres, Oughtibridge with two of their younger children and an adopted son, survived him.

Mello's life after Creswell was significantly longer. He would never again direct a Palaeolithic excavation, but his interest in geology never waned. He continued to write articles on geological matters for the local Yorkshire and Derbyshire journals, including a summary of the history of Creswell Crags.[42] A second edition of his *Hand-book to the Geology of Derbyshire* was also published in 1891; in this and the former publication all mention of Heath has been removed, the only credit going to Dawkins. As Heath had been dead for five years this was a churlish and unbecoming act for a man of God. In 1887 he left Brampton and took up a new post at Holy Cross, Mapperley, Nottinghamshire. Compared to his previous parish, the living was modest, a net yearly value of just £128, but the population was less than a tenth of that at Brampton,[43] and one might suspect that as he approached his mid-fifties Mello was looking for a change of pace. As he retained two servants even into retirement,[44] it is unlikely that Magens Mello, descended as he was from an elite banking family,[45] had ever wanted for money. He retired in 1901, and moved to Warwick, where he continued to be active in geology and took up the role as curator of the museum. In 1906 he lost his wife of forty-seven years, Charlotte, although his daughter Katherine Inez Mello (b. 1871) remained living with him until his death, on April 14 1914, aged 78.

I will return to the Creswell case in Chapter Ten

Chapter 8

Early Man in Britain

The Promise Satisfied

Throughout the second battle of Creswell, Dawkins was otherwise busy finishing his second book, *Early Man in Britain and His Place in the Tertiary Period,* fulfilling his half of the pact made with Johnny Green over twenty years earlier.[1] Whether by coincidence or design, the two old friends were in synchrony: Green's *A Short History of the English People* appeared in 1874, as did *Cave Hunting*, while the fourth and final volume of *A History of the English People* was published in 1880, the same year as *Early Man*. *Early Man* overshadowed everything else in Dawkins' working life for the better part of two years, a fact revealed by the dramatic reduction in his public commitments and journal articles – just four papers appeared for 1879-80 most extracted from the text of *Early Man*.[2] The archive is likewise peppered with communications about the book, including tense messages to and from his engraver[3] and publisher, and consent from friends and colleagues to whom Dawkins had written asking permission to use their published images and existing clichés.[4] Given this consuming project, one can sympathise with Dawkins' frustration at being dragged away to deal with Heath's nonsense, as he saw it, and can perhaps understand the brutality of his retorts; but words spoken or penned in anger do not excuse Dawkins the Machiavellian schemes he employed to silence Heath in the scientific press. The book was released in April, Dawkins receiving advanced copies on 25 March.[5] He wrote several lists of people to whom he wanted to send them.

It has to be said that *Early Man* is a rather strange volume. Dawkins explained in the introduction that the book bridged geology, archaeology and history, which together formed a seamless continuum from the earliest phases of the earth to the present. This is true enough, but even a continuum must be divided for heuristic purposes and Dawkins made some cuts in the wrong places. Chapters II-IV, 80 octavo pages, dealt with the geology, landscapes and faunas of the Tertiary Period, which Dawkins believed to have been totally devoid of humans on both theoretical and empirical grounds. During the Eocene there were no placental mammals at all, while in the Miocene no members of the animal community to which humans belonged were to be found – it was absurd, he reasoned, that the highest form of animal could have existed alone, when all of its conspecifics were absent. Dawkins conceded that some man-apes might have been present, but not humans as we know them – if humans had been in the Miocene why had they not gone extinct or evolved to a different form like other animals (Figure 8.1)? He also found the claims for Miocene artefacts from France unconvincing, such as the stone tools from Thenay or the notched rib from Pouancé: if they were artificial they were probably the work of an anthropomorphous ape, a view shared by his friend Alfred Gaudry (until the latter changed his mind).[6] Dawkins put up no such theoretical barriers to the presence of humans in the Pliocene, yet rejected all of the claims of such from France and Italy because their contexts were simply not secure enough. He could not have anticipated it, but the question of Tertiary humans would become a very hot topic within the scientific community in later decades.

Next came the inevitable chapter describing the Pleistocene fauna of Europe. Only in Chapter VI, after 133 pages in which Dawkins had, Genesis-like, prepared the Earth to receive God's finest creation, did the titular *Early Man* appear. The remaining chapters dealt with the Palaeolithic, Neolithic, Bronze Age and Iron Age, but in the end Dawkins was not sure where to stop, and like a train out of control crashed into the 'English Conquest' of the first millennium, finally grinding to a halt with the extirpation of Wolves in the eighteenth century. Only Chapters VI on the river drift and VII on the caves contained much of Dawkins' own research, the rest relying, as he acknowledged, on the work of his British and European peers. This makes it all the more interesting, then, that these two chapters contained almost nothing that had not been discussed, dissected or rejected in *Cave Hunting* and few, if any, of the ideas presented in *Cave Hunting* and his numerous papers before or since had changed. He had just found new ways to bolster previously held opinions against his critics.

For example, his debate with Searles V. Wood Jr in 1867 (Chapter 2) had failed to alter his opinion that the 'trail' in the Lower Thames was evidence for glaciation, because, as he now crowed, if not a glacial deposit itself it nonetheless showed evidence of cryoturbation (disturbance by freezing and thawing) during a glacial period and was, ergo, pre-glacial. He was also much clearer on explaining the modified version of seasonal migrations, which in 1874 he had hurriedly 'hashed-up' to deflect Geikie's objections that the hippopotamus could not walk from Perpignan to Pickering and back in one

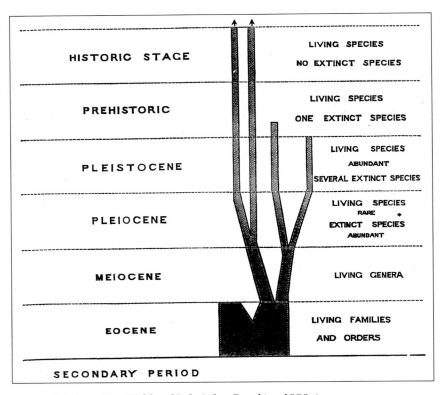

Figure 8.1: Dawkins' Table of Life (after Dawkins 1880a).

season (Chapter 3). In the revised version Dawkins appealed to a series of secular (long-term, directional) climatic changes. When the cold was at its maximum, arctic animals extended their range south, and when at its minimum, hyaenas and hippopotamuses moved their range north. In between these two limits was a middle or frontier zone into which both groups encroached on a seasonal basis, and where their remains would be found intermingled. So hippopotamus would be found in Britain during the same years as the reindeer only when the limit of its range extended sufficiently far north for it to reach Britain during the summer months, and, presumably, vice versa for the northern species. This might have been a more clearly articulated mechanism but it was still no more coherent, because climatically-controlled range expansion and contraction would presumably just shift two parallel borders north and south, without necessarily drawing them any closer together. With cold at its minimum the range of the hippopotamus might have been sufficiently far north that it could reach the Thames in June, but what about the musk-oxen, whose range must have been pushed north by a commensurate amount? And how did hyaena ever meet reindeer, let alone gnaw on their freshly killed bones? Geikie was quick to seize upon the illogicality of it all: 'Professor Dawkins seems to have lost faith, to some extent, in the theory of seasonal migrations, and to have partially adopted that of secular migrations; see especially *Early Man in Britain*, where, if I do not misunderstand him, he now endeavours to maintain both views at once'.[7] Geikie was treated to his own share of scorn, though, Dawkins refusing to allow the idea that the glaciation of northern Britain would have any effect on southern England or France 'pass unchallenged'; the geological evidence was purely local and was 'useless for determining the flora and fauna of wider landscapes'.[8]

Strange and contradictory too were Dawkins' ideas on the presence of humans within interglacials, or his own peculiar version of them. He had long recognised that his own Thames Valley data might mean that humans were pre-glacial as well as post-glacial, suggesting that they moved in and out of the country in response to climate, just like the fauna, although his opinion changed several times. In the same year that *Early Man* appeared, Flaxman Spurrell discovered an in situ flint 'workshop' at Crayford, where refitting groups of flint artefacts occurred alongside the Lower Thames faunal group.[9] The find came too late for Dawkins to include it in *Early Man* – he mentioned it in his 1882 Presidential address to the BAAS[10] – but it merely confirmed not altered his opinion. By a very odd logic, this also made humans interglacial in Dawkins' mind, especially in light of the emerging evidence from East Anglia (e.g. High Lodge) where artefact-bearing strata apparently occurred between two boulder clays. This evidence was still doubted or held 'in a suspense account' by many, yet Dawkins rather uncharacteristically accepted it. To reconcile this with everything else he held to be true, one must return to his three-phase model for the glacial period. This included a warm marine period, during which the 'middle drift' accumulated around an archipelago of islands, chronologically and geologically sandwiched between two eras of glaciers and ice. Humans must have existed somewhere in neighbouring areas of Europe during the more extreme periods, making fleeting visits to East Anglia before the upper boulder clay had accumulated. In hindsight it would have just been easier if everyone concerned – Dawkins, Evans, Prestwich, Hughes and all the others – had just realised that, uniformitarianism aside, there was really only one logical conclusion – Geikie was right, climate change was cyclical. But they had all built careers on monoglacialism and too many deeply entrenched opinions would have to be jettisoned to drop it now.

The book was not a wholly stagnant pool. Dawkins did further develop some of his ideas on the Palaeolithic, driven by the evidence from Europe. Since 1866 he had been nursing a hunch that 'river-drift people' were earlier than the 'cave people', had occupied a different geographical range and were probably a different race. Evidence of this could be found in Kent's Cavern, and in the quartzite implements from Creswell Crags. From the distribution of their artefacts, Dawkins surmised that the river drift people were a southern race – wandering over the whole of Europe from southern England, to Spain, Italy, Greece, the Levant and India. They belonged with the southern group of mammals. The cave people were a northern race, from England, France and Germany, who belonged with the northern species. He still rejected the cultural sub-divisions of de Mortillet – except for that in the river drift, the Acheulean – insisting that the cave people belonged to the same stage of culture but to different tribes. The evidence was now sufficient to give a detailed ethnographical account of this culture, especially their artistic talent and hunting prowess, alongside a reprise of his belief that the Eskimo were living members of this group, casual racism that may offend contemporary sensibilities but would have fazed the Victorian reader not one bit. He was also more receptive to Palaeolithic human remains (from Arcy-sur-Cure, Naulette, Laugerie Basse, La Madeleine in France, and Pontnewydd in Wales), but still rejected all putative burials. He accepted the Palaeolithic age of the skull from Duruthy in the French Pyrenees, which had been found 6 ft down in intact cave sediment and in association with the canines of bear and lion, some decorated and all perforated to form a necklace. What he could not accept was that it was a burial, agreeing with Édouard Lartet that the individual had been killed in a rock fall, the bits of the body sticking out of the rubble having been eaten by animals. That is where the concord ended, and he rejected their idea that the skull belonged to the race of Crô-Magnon, or that it was racially the same as the Neolithic burials found 6 ft above it. He believed it was too badly damaged to determine to which race it belonged. Any similarity between the Neolithic skulls and those at Crô -Magnon did not suggest that the 'race of Crô -Magnon' survived into later prehistory, but rather that the Crô -Magnon skulls *were* Neolithic, as he had argued in 1874.

Early man was generally well received, the reviews in newspapers and magazines mainly positive and polite (Dawkins should have taken note). Some were over-the-top in their gushing praise;[11] most contained little of interest other than the reviewers' personal bugbears; none of those retained in Dawkins' scrapbook was openly hostile. The reviewer for *Nature* saw no evolutionary reasons why humans should not have existed in the Miocene,[12] while the *Scotsman's* didn't like the use of the term Tertiary in the sub-title, when the actual evidence for 'early man' in Britain was wholly Quaternary.[13] The reporter for *The Athenaeum* suggested the book should have been called 'Early Man in Europe', and implied it was too paleontological, while *The Standard's* correspondent thought Dawkins ignorant on the most important works on the Eskimo, but awarded it third place in the best book on human antiquity stakes, after Lyell's *Antiquity of Man* and Lartet and Christie's *Reliquiae Aquitanicae*.[14] More insightful comments came from the *Princeton Review*, which criticised Dawkins' reasoning on the differences between the people of the drift and the caves, his consistent yet flawed logic in separating the various internments at Duruthy, and the carelessness with which he used ethnographic analogy – scarcely worthy of his reputation the reviewer exclaimed.

Despite most reviewers recommending it as a fine read and a handsomely stout tome, *Early Man* did not sell particularly well. In the three months from July-October 1880 (its second quarter on the shelves) it sold just eighty copies globally.[15] Dawkins was probably disappointed with these weak sales, if not for his reputation for the damage it was doing to his royalty cheques – he even wrote to MacMillan asking why his share of the US sales amounted to so little. Alexander MacMillan informed him that 25% duty was excised on all English books sold in America, and that as a result they could not pay him the same rate. 'Don't you see?' MacMillan implored.[16] Not prepared to be swindled by the US Government, Dawkins asked MacMillan to find an American publisher; MacMillan suggested Appleton & Co of New York, but warned Dawkins that the copyright laws there were 'somewhat amusing', a mess that lay at the door of British publishing houses, he admitted. Dawkins would have done well to listen to the advice of his old pal Johnny Green and publish a popular primer aimed at a wider audience – when Edward Clodd produced *The Story of Primitive Man* in 1895 it sold 5000 copies in the first few months after publication.[17]

Boston, Massachusetts

With the summation of his life's work wrapped up between the blue octavo boards of *Early Man*, what could Dawkins do now? His diary for 1880 shows only a modicum of teaching and few social events: a dinner at the Geological Society in April, a soiree with students from Owen's College in May, the odd evening with friends such as Edward Freeman (Plate 14) and R. Angus Smith (1817-1884, the Owen's College chemist who discovered what we now call acid rain). In March he had met with R.A. Eskrigge to examine Kendrick's Cave, near Landudno, a site that produced an engraved jawbone of a horse of Palaeolithic age (Plate 19) and prehistoric human skeletons,[18] but there was no ongoing excavation, few field trips, no controversy, in fact there was almost nothing to use up his seemingly inexhaustible stores of energy. Fanny must have found him murder to live with, especially as she was mourning her mother, who died in June aged just 60.

After a summer of relative indolence, Dawkins set off on a three-month trip to the USA (just as a new academic year was about to commence in Manchester), where he had been invited to give a series of lectures to the Lowell Institute in Boston, Massachusetts, following in the footsteps of Lyell and Agassiz. He departed from Liverpool on the *S.S. Atlas* at 11pm on 6 October.[19] The voyage was marred by gales, the magnificent sight of spouting whales not enough to compensate for the high seas and frightful rolling of the ship that caused Dawkins' portmanteau to fly about his cabin, put him off his food and prevented him from sleeping. It was thus to great relief that the ship docked at Boston at 9am on 18 October. On Wednesday 20 October, Dawkins gave the first of 12 lectures to the Lowell Institute entitled *Fragments in the History of the Earth.*[20] Other titles in the series – *The Question of Man's Existence in the Miocene Period; The Flora and Fauna of the Pleistocene Age; Important Discoveries in the Caves of Europe; The People of the Neolithic Age, etc., etc.* – show that Dawkins worked his way through the highlights of *Early Man*. He was a huge success in America. His talks were enthusiastically received by increasing large crowds and the local press. The latter described Dawkins' 'felicitous delivery' as winning 'golden opinions' and printed each lecture verbatim.

Dawkins' lectures took place every Monday, Wednesday and Friday from 20 October–15 November. Outside of this small commitment, his social calendar was hectic. He lunched and dined with new people every day, engaging both scientists and society. He attended the theatre 'enjoyed *School for Scandal*, acting very good, theatre pretty like the Prince's in M[anchester'],[21] he visited the Union Electric Works, watched a one-legged boy playing football in the snow, went to Cambridge, Massachusetts to view collections in the Peabody Museum, and had a bout of flu. Given his celebrity, it was most probably on this trip to America that Dawkins was supposedly offered the headship of the University of California, apparently on his own terms, which he nevertheless refused because he had no desire to leave

Manchester.[22] (One does have to wonder whether these fireside tales of derring-do had much basis in reality – Nevada silver booms, Australian Kerosene scandals, Headships of major international universities – they seem more in keeping with the escapades of George MacDonald Fraser's fictional antihero Sir Harry Flashman, than a Welsh geology professor from Manchester.)

Dawkins left Boston on 17 November, travelling on to Trenton, New Jersey with two new companions, the archaeologist Henry Williamson Haynes (1831-1912) and mineralogist Henry Carvill Lewis (1853-1888). He stayed there two days with the archaeologist Dr C.C. Abbott (1843-1919) before travelling on to Philadelphia, where he examined the palaeontological collections of Dr. Joseph Liedy (1823-1891). He sailed for home from a snow swept New York on 8 December aboard the *S.S. Cynthia*, a 'good ship' on which he had a good berth – Stateroom 238. He had arrived at the Buckingham Hotel, New York a few days earlier to deliver a lecture to the Academy of Science, coming via Washington, New Brunswick and New Haven, where he spent four days and nights with no engagements, presumably recuperating or saving money. The journey home was smoother, the ship docked at Liverpool at 1.20pm on 18 December. Dawkins was at his own front door by 5.20pm. Mello arrived the following Monday. In 1882 Dawkins was elected a fellow of the American Philosophical Society.

Glacial Wrangling Part 3

New Year 1881 saw the publication of James Geikie's second book – *Prehistoric Europe: A Geological Sketch*. It covered much of the same ground as Dawkins' *Early Man*, spanning the Palaeolithic to the Iron Age, and provided an account of climate, floras and faunas, fluvial sites, cave sites (some excavated by Dawkins), as well as later settlement by farmers, potters and metallurgists. But, it was a far better and more forward thinking book than Dawkins' offering. It even started in a more logical place – with the appearance of humans rather than in the Miocene – and adopted a framework of glacials and interglacials, heresy to most of his contemporaries but totally orthodox today. Following on from the second edition of *The Great Ice Age*[23] Geikie situated the Palaeolithic record within a sequence of at least three glacial-interglacial cycles, reserving the term post-glacial for the current warm period, beginning after the end of the *last* ice age, its modern usage. For Geikie, Palaeolithic peoples had arrived in Britain during interglacial periods, and had stayed for a long time, leaving their tools in both cave and river deposits. He was also sympathetic to Lartet's faunal division for the Palaeolithic, seeing faunal turnover driven by climate change as the reason for different mammalian assemblages, not human hunting preference or prowess.

These were but a few of the many points on which Geikie and Dawkins disagreed, and Geikie certainly did not shy away from reaffirming his criticisms of Dawkins' ideas. Up until this point the two combatants had managed to maintain some civility. In 1875, Dawkins had signed Geikie's certificate for election to the Royal Society,[24] and when expressing his disappointment at the outcome of the Royal Anthropological Institute 'conference' on the question of human Antiquity in Britain, Geikie had nonetheless lauded Dawkins as 'my able opponent'. Things changed with the publication of *Prehistoric Europe*, because almost everything in it could have been designed to rile Dawkins. Geikie even used the engraving of a feeding reindeer from Kesslerloch, Switzerland to illustrate his front cover (Figure 8.2), the very image that Dawkins had praised as the 'highest example' of the cave man's artistic achievements.

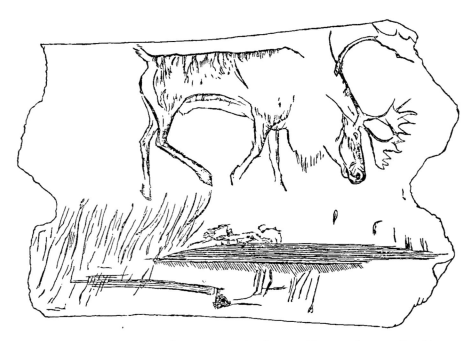

Figure 8.2: Geikie's Cover Illustration for Prehistoric Europe, showing Dawkins favourite piece of Palaeolithic art, from Kesslerloch, Switzerland (after Geikie 1881).

Given his known opposition to Geikie's ideas, it seems astonishing that Dawkins was allowed to review the book for *Nature* and almost unbelievable that the geological editor who let the review through was Geikie's own brother, Archibald.[25] Dawkins began his review by noting that the 'appearance of man and his progress in culture, combine to form a subject which cannot, in our opinion, be treated satisfactorily on the present state of knowledge. New facts are being daily brought to light, the speculations of yesterday are being tested by the discoveries of to-day...'[26] clearly implying that Geikie – who he labelled an advocate – had minimal evidence and was largely arm-waving, especially when compared to the Marquis de Nadaillac's 'humble' book which he gave a one paragraph review alongside it. This is pure hypocrisy, coming from a scientist who a mere eight months earlier had published these words: 'The materials necessary for this task [of writing prehistory] are perplexing in their abundance ... the progress of discovery is very swift, and there are great blanks in the story yet to be filled in. Nevertheless, after a preparation of many years by researches in this country and on the continent, it seems to me to be better to attempt to perform the task, however imperfectly, rather than to wait for that perfection which perhaps might never come'.[27]

Anybody who has followed Dawkins' story this far can probably guess what followed. He set to work undermining Geikie's main thesis, ridiculing *Prehistoric Europe* as an attempt to throw a glacial net over the whole of Europe while standing on a mountain in Scotland. Dawkins disputed much: the geological basis for interglacial-glacial cycles; the notion that ice sheets not icebergs deposited most glacial sediments; Geikie's use of the term post-glacial; the evidence from Victoria Cave, which ignored the all-important reindeer; the flora and fauna that Geikie took to be evidence for warm conditions. Regarding the latter he appealed to the rotten old chestnut of an argument that hippopotamus and rhinoceros survived perfectly well in London Zoo, and that the Mediterranean fig tree and Judas tree could both survive 'a spell of hard frosts'. When not rejecting new ideas, he was boldly reaffirming old preconceptions and when not doing that he was just being belligerent. He accused Geikie of basing his arguments on 'ice, and ice alone', of selecting only evidence that suited his theory, and of naively drawing on Pliocene and Neolithic examples. He also called on another favourite tactic – appealing to the (when it suited him) unimpeachable authority of Lyell, Prestwich, Evans, Hughes, and company, who as fellow monoglacialists generally agreed with him, and who as history would reveal were all, to a man, absolutely wrong. He finished with the crushing remark that he could find in *Prehistoric Europe* no 'addition to what has already been known'.[28]

Geikie's reply[29] corrected Dawkins on several points of facts, and remarked that he genuinely did not recognise in Dawkins' outline any trace of his own argument. As for the data, Tiddeman had confirmed the account of Victoria Cave as written, while the sites thought by Dawkins to be Pliocene had been proved by more recent work to be Pleistocene or contain horizons of Pleistocene age. Geikie was, furthermore, just as experienced and just as well-read as Dawkins, and while he might not have the paleontological expertise he had a very wide knowledge base. Just a glance at the contents page was enough to show the falsehood behind Dawkins' 'ice, and ice alone' comment – a barb that might be turned around and aimed at Dawkins with his 'bones, and bones alone' attitude. Of everything Dawkins had said, though, it was the accusation that Geikie had selectively used evidence that supported him, ignoring all else, that cut deepest. It went beyond a disagreement of interpretation and challenged his honour as a scientist. In concluding, Geikie asked whether Dawkins had fully understood his work, which he felt had been totally misrepresented. 'I have met with many forcible statement of opinion by Mr Dawkins that he does not agree with me; but I may remind him (and not for the first time) that mere expression of opinion, however emphatic, proves nothing save, as a rule, the sincerity of him who utters them,' wrote Geikie in a superbly cutting remark that reveals much about Dawkins' blusterous tactics.

The scene was set for another round of tit-for-tat replies. Dawkins' arrived on 17 February, again in *Nature*.[30] It did little more than re-affirm previous statements, almost as though Dawkins had tired with the whole thing. Its contents can be summed up as: Geikie had said the words attributed to him, perhaps not in the book under review but certainly in his earlier work; Tiddeman's views on Victoria Cave had never been reliable and reindeer had been deliberately omitted; Geikie's continental sources were simply wrong on the age of the Pliocene fauna (Dawkins had seen the material in question, so there could be no argument). This, he declared, was to be his last communication on the subject. Geikie's second response[31] was much angrier than the first. His private correspondence from the time shows just how enraged he had become. In letters to Peach he labelled Dawkins 'a vain cocky humbug, who has endured so long simply because no one has been examining the evidence derived from foreign sources,' before going on to complain that Dawkins had waged a smear campaign in anonymous letters and notices of blatantly obvious authorship, and decrying how 'monstrous' it was 'that such a nincompoop in physical geology should be allowed to strut about as an authority'.[32] Further abuse came when the editor of *Nature* (presumably not Archibald) tried to veto Geikie's reply, leading the silver-tongued geologist to call the journal the 'kiss-my-arse of Macmillan & Co,'[33] Dawkins' publishing house whose proprietor was his personal friend. Geikie threatened to send an expanded version to *The Athenaeum* and *The Academy*, two highly popular magazines, but *Nature* capitulated. In the published letter Geikie protested that Dawkins was still putting words in his mouth, and was totally unjustified in repeating the offensive accusation that the evidence of reindeer at Victoria Cave had been suppressed. Geikie had not suppressed it, he had rejected it, because it had been found only during Dawkins' gung-ho shaft digging phase, and never in the more careful work of Tiddeman. The rest of the letter confirmed the veracity of the new evidence provided by his continental colleagues, suggesting that Dawkins' refusal to accept it was simply a sign of ignorance. At this point, Geikie too left the field – the affair had left affected him badly, leaving him shaken and unable to eat or sleep.[34]

Published alongside Geikie's letter was a reply from Richard Tiddeman,[35] who was not especially delighted at having his name tainted by Dawkins once again. Tiddeman's letter confirmed what had been established years before: reindeer had been found 'associated' with the lower hyaena-hippopotamus fauna at Settle but only during Dawkins' shaft digging exploits, otherwise it was not a member of that group. The same division was true at Dawkins' own site at Mother Grundy's Parlour, so he had no right to accuse Tiddeman of founding his opinion 'on a mistake' or to accuse Geikie of suppressing evidence. The arrival of this new combatant pulled Dawkins back into the arena,[36] where he rehearsed the standard routine about the fibula, goats, landslips and reindeer (see Chapter 3), informing the readership that when Tiddeman had been chastised for leaving the latter off the relevant faunal lists, he had capitulated and described its presence as 'noteworthy'. Tiddeman was in no mood to be bullied any longer, pointing out that Dawkins had previously been a firm believer in the fibula, that the goat bones were in the same condition as the others, and that there had never been frequent landslips – Dawkins' own visits were too infrequent for him to ever have known what had occurred on site.[37] Concerning the reindeer, Tiddeman merely repeated what he had said five years earlier, that Dawkins had worked at the end of the section where the chances of admixture between the upper and lower fauna were high, Tiddeman had worked in the middle where the chances of admixture were practically zero. He had found no reindeer – that was what he had thought 'noteworthy'.[38] Viewed from the perspective of modern Quaternary science, what is even more noteworthy is that though almost a decade had passed since the start of the argument, in which time 'new facts were daily being brought to light,' Dawkins was immovable. His presidential address to Section H (Anthropology) of the BAAS in Southampton the following year showed his opinion had not changed. In Dawkins' mind, nothing had changed. Geikie was wrong and he was right. That, as far as Dawkins cared, was that.

Chapter 9

Industrial Disputes

Ella Selina

William and Frances' only child, a daughter Ella Selina Boyd, was born on 13 April 1881. Shortly after, the family moved to a new home in Woodhurst, Fallowfield. Dawkins was 43, and for the first time truly responsible for someone other than himself. Such reckonings often bring new perspectives (Plate 15).

By the time Ella was born, Dawkins had achieved practically everything he had set out to do in archaeology and palaeontology. *Cave Hunting* and *Early Man in Britain* had been published to almost global acclaim, fulfilling the precocious pact he had made with John Green when both were just students. (Dawkins would sadly soon lose 'Dear Johnny', who passed away in Italy on 7 March 1883; on hearing the news a distraught Freeman wrote to Dawkins 'how strange that I never saw you and him together since that one time in 1868, when you fought').[1] His work was recognised nationally and internationally, his status marked by prestigious Fellowships of The Royal Society (1867), The Geological Society (1861), The Society of Antiquaries (1873), and the American Philosophical Society (1880) and he had served roles from secretary to president for a host of national and local institutions. He had failed to secure the chairs at Oxford or Cambridge, but in 1880 became one of a select number of University professors, when Owens College became part of the new Victoria University, Manchester. The following year, 1882, he was given an Honorary Fellowship of his alma mater, Jesus College Oxford[2] and E.T. Newton named a species of extinct Pleistocene deer after him: *Cervus (=Megaloceros) dawkinsi.*[3]

Dawkins loved his work, relished each new discovery, and strived to push the boundaries of knowledge, which he had successfully accomplished many times in the years since leaving Oxford. He was also something of a workaholic. His friend E.A. Freeman admonished him to his face: 'I don't wonder at your being knocked up. When you gad about like a canon of Poules and write letters on trains';[4] as well as behind his back: 'Dawkins is very

201

cheery as usual but, as usual full of work'.[5] This is not entirely atypical in the self-absorbed academic whose work defines them. Dawkins work also brought him the celebrity he craved, both in scientific circles and in the public eye through his ceaseless round of lectures, newspaper interviews and other public engagements. By 1881, though, he was no longer the brilliant young parvenu. He was *the* authority on Pleistocene mammals in Britain – *THE Dawkins* as Geikie termed him, the definitive article – a status he adored. New facts may have kept rolling in as he continued to be active as a cave hunter, but new ideas were now much harder to come by. He had spent years revising preciously defended models and had long since become entrenched behind positions that he was unable to relinquish even in the face of compelling evidence. His intractable nature and total inability to walk away from a fight left him battling on several fronts at once with Geikie, Tiddeman, Heath, Plant, Wood and others taking potshots from all angles. It must have been stressful and exhausting, merely opening the pages of a journal or venturing into a society lecture could bring forth another salvo, but nobody could doubt that he had brought it upon himself. He had been the one who refused to listen; he had been the one who each time had lowered the tone, turning polite comments on points of fact into acrimonious defences of points of honour.

Devotion to his discipline was not accompanied by financial reward. I have mentioned on several occasions that in his field notebooks and diaries Dawkins seemed obsessed with expenses. His salary at Owens College and the Museum left him comfortable, able to live in a good sized-house in a nice area and to employ a housemaid and a cook, but he was hardly rich. His starting salary as curator at Manchester in 1869 had been £400. On his appointment to a lectureship this had been reduced to £200 from the museum and £140 from the college, plus a share of the student fees. Mello earned almost as much and he had no rent to pay. Not until 1886 would Dawkins' college salary rise above £200, by which time he had been professor for twelve years and Owens College had been incorporated into the federal Victoria University of Manchester (established 1880). While a free round-the-world trip is hard to pass up the £1000 consultancy fee must have been the main incentive for his 1875 tour. It would certainly have opened his eyes to the opportunities that lay in the commercial sector.

It is perhaps no coincidence then that 1881 marks a rubicon in Dawkins' life. This was the year in which he gave up almost all original paleontological and archaeological research and ceased to be active in the field – he would conduct no new fieldwork for twenty years, working just

DISCOVER MORE ABOUT MILITARY HISTORY

Pen & Sword Books have over 4000 books currently available, our imprints include; Aviation, Naval, Military, Archaeology, Transport, Frontline, Seaforth and the Battleground series, and we cover all periods of history on land, sea and air.

Keep up to date with our new releases by completing and returning the form below (no stamp required if posting in the UK).

Alternatively, if you have access to the internet, please complete your details online via our website at **www.pen-and-sword.co.uk**.

All those subscribing to our mailing list via our website will receive a free e-book, *Mosquito Missions* by Martin W Bowman. Please enter code number ACC1 when subscribing to receive your free e-book.

Mr/Mrs/Ms ....

Address..

....

Postcode.................... Email address...

Website: www.pen-and-sword.co.uk Email: enquiries@pen-and-sword.co.uk
Telephone: 01226 734555 Fax: 01226 734438
Stay in touch: facebook.com/penandswordbooks or follow us on Twitter @penswordbooks

Freepost Plus RTKE-RGRJ-KTTX
Pen & Sword Books Ltd
47 Church Street
BARNSLEY
S70 2AS

one further cave, Doveholes near Buxton, in 1902. Make no mistake, he was still a commanding force in the world of geology and archaeology, and continued to defend his views wherever and whenever he felt them challenged. He remained active in the London and local societies and in 1883 was a founder member and first President of the Lancashire and Cheshire Antiquarian Society. He continued to haunt the BAAS, served on numerous of its committees and used the 1884 meeting in Toronto as an excuse to tour Canada.[6] He never stopped teaching college students, lecturing to public audiences, leading field excursions and having his say on topics of the day through newspapers and magazines; people from all walks of life still sent him information or enquiries. He also published articles on a range of archaeological topics – cave burials;[7] early man in Britain,[8] Maltese cart ruts,[9] and the archaeology of Wales and the Welsh.[10] The latter interest, if anything, grew during this period; Dawkins concentrated on the archaeological aspects, complementing the work of his friend John Rhys (1840-1915), fellow Jesus alumni and the first Professor of Celtic Studies at Oxford. The two would often exchange letters quizzing each other on their specialist fields. Nothing could drag Dawkins away from his beloved mammals,[11] the most unusual new record during the period being *Ailurus anglicus*, a type of red panda, from the Red Crag of East Anglia. But such papers were few and infrequent compared to his earlier career, and he often reported rather than proselytised.

In place of purely academic endeavours Dawkins threw himself into commercial geology, acting as a consultant and advocate on projects ranging from the Channel Tunnel, the Manchester Ship Canal and Dover Coal. It was a different life, which gave Dawkins new goals and new directions. Such high profile projects guaranteed his name would be emblazoned all over the national news and they were certainly more lucrative. With millions of pounds at stake Dawkins charged up to 100 guineas for a report, and occasionally requested sums of £500 just to retain his services;[12] these were not, however, always forthcoming. So he spread himself widely and also began to take on more paid writing, providing popular accounts on geological topics for the general reader, the *North American Review* paying handsomely for contributions of 4000 words.

The rest of this chapter highlights Dawkins' career from 1881-1929, a period we might call the Industrial Years for both archaeological and geological reasons, as will become clear. Admittedly, a single chapter to cover forty-eight years – over half his life – seems totally inadequate, shamefully following the trend to remember famous geologists only for their scientific or 'pure' work rather than their applied or industrial endeavours.[13] This is arguably because industrial geology was regarded as a lesser pursuit in Victorian England, apparently frowned upon in academic circles (ironic given that it was the science that quite literally fuelled the country), Dawkins' work in this area described in one obituary as 'an incidental activity and success'.[14] This description was simply not true, and as we shall see Dawkins was proud of his achievements in this field. I suspect there is another reason this bias persists. The stories of the pioneers of geology and archaeology are almost always written by dabbling archaeologists (such as myself), academic geologists or historians of science, scholars who are largely interested in the scientific development of their subject or the scientific researches of their protagonists. This rarely extends too far into the commercial activities that applied rather than generated knowledge, so beyond a summary and a few anecdotes the details are safely left to others. In this vein, as interesting as a complete account of Dawkins' later years might be to the student of industrial geology, as an archaeologist concerned with his work as a cave hunter and palaeontologist, it is simply outside my remit or expertise.

Of Tunnels and Waterways, Coal and Canals

The idea of a tunnel joining England to France beneath the Channel had been mooted since Napoleonic times without much action, but in 1874 a joint Anglo-French scheme for a submarine railway became a real possibility, with the Government authorising the South Eastern Railway Company and the London, Chatham and Dover Railway Company to apply £20,000 each towards the cost of borings and shafts in connection with the tunnel.[15] This led to the formation of two companies: the Submarine Continental Railway Company (SCRC), of which Sir Edward Watkin (1819-1901) was chairman, and the Channel Tunnel Company, led by Lord Richard Grosvenor (1837-1912). Yet as the French happily busied themselves with 7,672 soundings from Dover to Calais and 1668m of tunnel,[16] the British descended into a wave of xenophobic paranoia, people of all ranks and callings banding together in opposition to the scheme, convinced that such a tunnel was a grave threat to national security.[17]

The South Eastern Railway Company (and later its subsidiary SCRC) nonetheless dug three shafts: Shaft No.1 at Abbot's Cliff near Folkestone, and Shafts No.2 and 3 at either end of the Shakespeare Tunnel, beneath Shakespeare Cliff at Dover. At Shafts 1 and 2 the company began excavating tunnels 7 ft in diameter, with plans to widen the headings to 14 ft and line them with 2 ft of concrete. In the meantime, the Military refused to support two bills submitted to Parliament, and in 1881 the Board of Trade tried to have the tunnelling stopped. They first invoked Section 77 of the South Eastern Railway Act of 1881 that forbade tunnelling below low water mark, but work was only suspended for a short period because the tunnelling machine also provided ventilation to the workmen.[18] When the Board of Trade demanded to inspect the tunnelling, Watkin prevaricated, forcing the Board to get a High Court Order. The Board demanded that the tunnelling stop immediately, although Watkin may have continued with clandestine operations. By the end of 1882 Watkin was forced to stop altogether, having achieved two tunnels: the first 897 yards, the second 2040 yards.[19] (Plate 16)

Dawkins became geological advisor to the SCRC in 1882. He had extensive knowledge of the area from his days on the Survey, and also knew Edward Watkin, a prominent Mancunian. Dawkins produced a report confirming that the company's heading was laid in the best location, prepared recommendations for Parliament and spoke openly about the scheme,[20] rebuffing geological objections and warning that future generations would resent the lack of vision and submission to fear prevalent at the time. Although work was suspended (as it turned out for over a century) Watkin retained the services of Boyd Dawkins, hoping that the Government could eventually be persuaded to allow tunnelling to resume.[21] In 1887, Dawkins reported on the status of the Shakespeare Cliff heading, which he found to be in good repair and drier than when it had been abandoned, an excuse for another round of public lectures and open support for the scheme.[22] Dawkins also acted as consultant to the aborted Humber Tunnel Project during 1882-1884, netting himself several hundred guineas.[23] Despite support from many merchants in Hull, who were dissatisfied with the ferry service and speed and which trade could be conducted, the scheme was rejected due to political pressure from the railway companies.[24]

An interest in preserving the historic environment led to a long association with the Isle of Man. In 1884, Dawkins was invited by Phillip M.C. Kermode (1855-1932) to accept an Honorary Fellowship of the IoM Natural History and Antiquarian Society. Members of the society were active campaigners, and in 1885 Kermode and Rev. E.B. Savage, in the context of presenting the Governor with a draft 'Act for the Preservation of Wild Birds', expressed the need for legislation to protect the Island's antiquities.[25] The Governor convened a committee the same year and invited Dawkins to prepare a report on Manx antiquities. Dawkins visited the island in the autumn of 1885, and with Savage as a guide examined a large number of sites and objects. His report, coming in the wake of Lubbock's 'Ancient Monuments Protection

Act 1882' for Britain and Ireland, is a model of archaeological preservation. Dawkins urged legislation and highlighted a series of measures aimed at protecting/recording existing antiquities and place names on Ordnance maps.[26] He was particularly concerned that Runic Crosses, prehistoric and historic alignments, habitations, camps, places of assembly and tombs, many away from main roads and improperly recorded, were being left to weather to dust, deliberately vandalised or were being used for unsuitable purposes – Runic Crosses as gateposts, for example. He recommended that everything should be published and finds deposited in the Government Office or in the Museum. His visit sparked in him a more general interest in the Island and he became a frequent visitor, producing papers on its archaeology and mapping the geology on the six-inch Ordnance maps.[27] In 1896, while working as a consultant looking for coal on the island, he stumbled upon important salt fields in the Triassic marls of Ayres, which later developed into a major industry to provide preservatives for the Island's fishing industry.[28] The truth is, though, that while Dawkins may have inspected a few rocks much of his time was spent fishing. His diaries for each visit record days and days of sea fishing, with proud tallies of the species, number and weight caught.

Dawkins' coal explorations on IoM were not his first. He had been involved in prospecting for coal since the BAAS Sub-Wealden Committee's borehole of 1871, but it was his involvement with Watkin, who by 1886 had decided to turn his attention from tunnelling to the search for Kentish Coal, that would earn Dawkins the popular epithet 'King Coal'.[29] The prospect of a coal field in south-east England had been proposed on geological reasoning by Richard Godwin-Austen (1808-1884), although at the time his views were vehemently opposed by Murchison.[30] When both men gave their opinions before the Coal Commission in 1866-67, the resulting report by Prestwich accepted Godwin-Austen's position, but Murchison went to his grave refusing to believe it.[31] It was on the basis of this report – tardily published in 1871 – that the Sub-Wealden Exploration Committee put down their trial boring at Netherfield near Battle, Sussex. After three years of drilling, to a depth of 1905 ft, the borehole was abandoned when the lining pipe failed and the drilling-bit was lost at the bottom, but the effort was not wasted. The stratigraphy revealed that the overlying beds in the chosen locality were too thick and that the predicted ridge of coal must lie further north, towards the North Downs. On 20 March 1886, Dawkins was asked to meet with the South Eastern Railway Company (SERC), to discuss making borings for coal between Tonbridge and Godstone; he replied by sending Watkin a report recommending that a boring should be made nearer to Dover, and suggesting the abandoned Channel Tunnel site at Shakespeare Cliff as the best prospect.[32]

Watkin acted with his 'usual energy' and started work the same year.[33] Dawkins was retained as geological consultant, with the SERC chief-engineer, Francis Brady, supervising the boring operations. By 1890, one seam of coal measures had been struck at a depth of 1204 ft from the surface, 100 ft deeper than on the French side of the channel. Based on comparisons with continental and Somersetshire coalfields, Dawkins speculated that tens of seams totalling 98 ft or more of workable coal might be expected.[34] Cause for great confidence indeed, but when he presented the discovery to the MGS on March 11 1890, he ended with an appeal for a change in the mining laws in Britain. In France, he explained, borings were fostered by investment from Government, who owned the mineral rights and could grant concessions to developers for a relatively small royalty. In Britain landowners retained all mineral rights, but it was usually left up to the 'philanthropic enterprises' of men such as Watkin to explore them. This was a risky business because when and if such explorations hit coal, the philanthropists had borne all the cost, but the landowners and their neighbours reaped the rewards. Dawkins was certainly not advocating that the Government should assume ownership of British mineral resources, and he strongly opposed the idea that they should take control of (i.e. Nationalise) the coal industry. This could not be done without interfering with the sacred rights of property; he merely wanted explorers to get some pecuniary return from their work. As borings continued six further seams were discovered, sufficiently promising to warrant Dawkins and others to advise a trial shaft.[35] Feeling that the project had now become one of testing the commercial value and of practical mining, Dawkins ended his association with it. Watkin, in failing health, did not proceed with the shaft.

The Company's rights were instead sold to a new organisation formed in 1896, the Kent Coalfields Syndicate Ltd, chaired by Arthur Burr, a bankrupt with a dubious past in other coalfields.[36] Without Dawkins on board, they relied on Brady's experience as an engineer, but he failed to take into account that some of the strata above the coal measures were saturated with water. The first shaft, 'the Brady', flooded, the second ruptured suddenly after six months, tragically drowning eight men. Burr subsequently brought Dawkins back as consultant geologist, and he would continue to act for various incarnations of Burr's companies until 1908.[37] Throughout this period Dawkins' success rates in predicting the location of coal measures were variable and he became increasing concerned with some of Burr's sharp practices, which included doctoring his geological sections for company reports, dodgy financial practices and deliberate deceiving the shareholders. In the end Dawkins became vexed about how money was being transferred around various subsidiaries and feared he was becoming involved in a fraudulent conspiracy.[38] He threatened legal action, but nothing came of it. Dawkins later became involved in a further venture with the Medway Coal Exploration Company, under the auspices of Lord Harris. Borings at Sittingbourne and Chilham came to nothing.

Despite the fact that the Kent Coalfield was a failure, it was a noble one that did nothing to harm Dawkins' reputation – he considered his discovery one of the country's greatest assets that gave him the international acknowledgement his paleontological work had never quite achieved. He was always willing to lecture or talk on the work. It was thus inevitable that he would not stand idly by when Brady, who resented the accolades given to (or taken by) Dawkins, tried to claim priority for the original Dover borings. Dawkins adopted his usual battle tactics: taking his own claim to the societies, journals and newspapers.[39] In 1905 he complained to the *Manchester Guardian* that the Consolidated Kent Coal Corporation was practically ignoring the massive contribution made by himself and Watkin,[40] and he was still going strong in maintaining his priority in 1913.[41]

Dawkins eventually built up a diverse practice as a consulting geologist. He acted as advisor to diamond mining companies in South Africa (his diaries contain no evidence he ever visited the country, although he was acquainted with Cecil Rhodes),[42] to Carrara marble quarries in Italy, and to Australian oil companies.[43] He provided advice to water boards and Parliamentary bodies on the effect of geology on the water supply in London, Manchester, Bolton, Hull, Huddersfield, Lincoln, Dover, Eastbourne, Brighton, and Buxton, amongst many others. Water quality was of course a major source of concern in an age that suffered the Great Stink of 1858, when a hot dry summer had left London reeking from all the human effluent in the Thames, and the growing evidence linking contaminated water with deadly diseases such as cholera left Britain in urgent need of quality-controlled, fresh, clean water. During 1878 Dawkins travelled to London to advise on water several times each week, travelling first class at a cost of £1 5s, staying in fine hotels and charging a daily fee of 10 guineas, before rushing back to Manchester to lecture.[44] One commentator believed in cases of water supply Dawkins was engaged as an expert witness by the Law Courts more than any other geologist of the day,[45] while Anthony Trollope, in introducing Dawkins to Oliver Wendell in Harvard, quipped: '…do not let him get hold of any Boston water, or he'll analyse it all and persuade you that you are going to be poisoned'.[46]

In April 1891, Dawkins acted on behalf of the Cheshire town of Northwich in the House of Commons, his purpose to secure compensation for the subsidence in the town caused by brine pumping in the Cheshire salt fields (as mining salt became increasingly uneconomical, hot water was instead flushed through the deposits and the brine pumped out, causing collapse). This ultimately resulted in the Brine Pumping (Compensation for Subsidence) Act of 1891, although the actual extraction of compensation led to dispute between neighbouring areas.[47] Such was his growing reputation in his new area of pursuit, that in 1898 he gave the James Forest Lecture at the Institute of Civil Engineers. Dawkins also used his vast experience in applied geology to introduce a greater element of practice-led teaching into the Manchester curriculum.

The most successful of all Dawkins's civic ventures was the Manchester Ship Canal (Plates 17 & 18), a waterway connecting the city of Manchester directly to the sea that was vital to restore Manchester's fading fortunes.[48] Dawkins provided the original geological report that allowed the scheme's instigator, George Hicks, to get the project underway, was an active campaigner in favour of the scheme when it was touted round various trade union halls, and assisted Daniel Adamson, the Manchester Ship Canal Company's first Chairman in assessing waterways along the Mersey-Irwell.[49] This is not the place to discuss how the scheme was navigated through regional opposition to the eventual Parliamentary Bill of 1885, but Dawkins was there at the outset, campaigning and advising on geological matters throughout, and although the construction, which began in 1887, was largely an engineering project he was on hand to offer geological advice, probably whether it was wanted or not.

Principled Politics

For twenty-five years, from 1904 until his death, Dawkins served Manchester as a Justice of the Peace, a duty in which he had been 'most assiduous'.[50] He also sat on the Court of Governors at Manchester University. Politically, he was a Liberal Unionist, having split from the Liberals in 1886 in opposition to Gladstone's Irish Home Rule Bill, views he shared with Lubbock, and he served as the President of the South Manchester Liberal Unionists Association until 1909.[51] He later accepted office in the Manchester Conservative and Unionist Association and in 1918 took the presidency of the newly formed Manchester University Constitutional Association, a role he held until his death. He was also asked to stand as Conservative candidate for the Northern Universities, but he declined this and all other offers of political advancement. Dawkins was acutely aware that the First World War would change the social landscape forever, and urged reform. At a meeting of the Manchester and District Working Men's Club and Institute Union he warned that the war had heralded the end of Victorian 'slothful ease' and that every person rich or poor, high or low would have to face self-denial if the war effort were to succeed.[52] He believed that while the country was facing the impoverishment of the middle class, it was vital that the working classes be given a living wage. The old order was dead, their political parties with them. In a letter to T.G. Bonney at Cambridge, Dawkins expressed his annoyance at MPs preaching thrift when they had awarded themselves £400 without consulting the nation. 'Cutting down expenditure often means sending people adrift who could not find other employment' replied Bonney in a sentiment ringing with modern significance; 'the more I reflect upon the last government, the more I doubt whether knavery or tomfoolery predominated among them' he sneered.[53]

As Dawkins got older he never lost his sense of social responsibility. He wanted to use the Museum at Manchester to educate the populace. It was not enough that miners dug coal, he wanted them to understand coal; so too in other real-life situations that touched upon scientific endeavours such as petrology, palaeontology and botany.[54] British museums, he felt, were a century behind the continent, and he deplored the habit of the aristocracy to view these centres of learning as convenient storehouses for their junk. In 1903 he was the most vocal advocate for using the old infirmary site at Manchester Piccadilly as a new Museum, Art Gallery and Public Library, going as far as drawing up a scheme of operations.[55] In 1908-10 he was a driving force behind the petition to prevent the break-up of the India Museum at South Kensington and arrange it by material in the new Victoria and Albert Museum. For many such an arrangement would have been disastrous, breaking up the cohesion of India's unique culture and art, and mixing it among the relics of Europe. Working closely with the renowned interior designer J.D. Crace (1838-1919) Dawkins crusaded against the proposal, recruiting to the cause some important and influential figures including Rudyard Kipling, Sir John Lubbock, Sir Benjamin Stone, Sir Henry Howorth, and Sir Mancherjee Bhownagree (one of only two Victorian era Indian MPs) Prof F. Simpson (University College), Henry Balfour (Pitt Rivers Museum). Several key institutions also opposed the move, the British Empire League, the Royal Asiatic League, the East India Association and Oxford University among them.[56] Lord Curzon, the ex-Viceroy to India, was persuaded to champion the campaign, a two-year struggle involving meetings with the Board of Education, a newspaper campaign and petition to Parliament. Eventually, the plans were dropped and the collections remained were they were until the 1950s, when the building was demolished and the collections finally transferred to the Victoria and Albert. But for now, Dawkins had won another victory.

A Crisis at Waterhouse's Museum

In 1880, Alfred Waterhouse, the architect who had designed the new Owens College buildings on Oxford Road, was asked to prepare sketches for a new Museum and Department of Natural History. The project finally came to fruition in 1888 with a 'monumental Gothic building' that comprised four floors of galleries, a herbarium on the top floor, and a three-storey atrium.[57] (Plate 18) The internal arrangement of the collections was largely Dawkins': the ground floor housed the mineralogy collection and displays on the earliest history of the earth, showing fossils from the first organisms to ice age mammals; other floors contained displays of animals in a 'vaguely' evolutionary sequence, with botany displays in side rooms.[58] The Museum's focus was natural history, although its displays included Palaeolithic and Neolithic stone tools, archaeology from Ancient Egypt and the Mediterranean, and ethnographic items. The collections were regularly enhanced by donations from staff and collectors. Dawkins had been Head Curator for nineteen years, and had moved and arranged the collections into new homes on three separate occasions. This move would prove more permanent, but Dawkins would not remain in post long enough to see the new Museum open its doors to the public.

The task of running the new Museum raised questions in the mind of Joseph Greenwood, Owens College Principal, about the future role of the curator. Dawkins had for years been fulfilling three different offices – Professor of Geology, Curator-in-Chief of the Museum and consulting geological engineer – and Greenwood wrote as a friend wondering whether he felt this was sustainable.[59] It was for Dawkins an unexpected turn and he reacted badly, totally mistaking 'the drift' of Greenwood's words, seeing the letter not as pastoral concern for his future wellbeing but an insinuation that he was disloyal and under-performing. Greenwood acted quickly to calm Dawkins, assuring him that he was held in the highest regard and that there was no conspiracy; in fact Greenwood knew nothing of other's opinions.[60] Nobody was questioning the energy, loyalty and ability Dawkins had given to each of his roles, but when the new building was finally opened to the public and students on a six-days a week basis, the curator would be faced with a vast increase in his administrative and scientific work. However, if the Council Committee felt that the existing arrangements were satisfactory, then the matter would rest; Greenwood would not use his position as Principal to interfere.

Fearing that the Council Committee could not be trusted to arrive at a sensible decision, Dawkins, Williamson and Marshall (the retired and incumbent Professors of Zoology) wrote to the chairman Joseph Thompson petitioning for the management of the Museum to remain unchanged. Before presenting the letters to Council, Thompson passed them to Greenwood, who urgently wrote to Dawkins reminding him of their previous discussions, particularly the fact he did not think it the business of the Principal to influence Council on the matter.[61] If Dawkins had thought that Greenwood would intercede on his behalf, he was mistaken.

The disappointment did not end with this betrayal by inaction, for the Council agreed with Greenwood's initial thoughts that new arrangements would have to be made. Dawkins cooperated with the Council for a while, and professed to generally approve of their new scheme. He did not, however, think it proper for him to implement it and on 29 November he resigned the curatorship. He spent at least two days perfecting his resignation letter, of which three drafts survive.[62] The first surviving iteration warned Council how long it would take his replacement to learn the business of the museum, offered suggestions for future staffing arrangements, and informed them that he had spent months holding his tongue. This bitterness was dropped for drafts two and three. He decided to leave not in spite but in glory, reminding them that during his twenty year tenure he had consolidated the collections of the College, the MGS, the MNHS, and many others, transformed the museum from one whose future hung in the balance into a 'going concern', and would leave it a 'new force in education and a pattern to other museums'. This knowledge was reward enough for the years of waiting and preparation. Dawkins therefore exited craftily cocking-a-snook, his pride intact and with all his bridges surprisingly unsinged.

He stepped down in March 1889, the month after he had received the Lyell Medal of Geology from the Geological Society of London (on February 15) and offloaded a large collection of fossils onto the museum. In May, Greenwood wrote informing Dawkins that during a discussion with the Treasurer it had been proposed to raise his Professorial salary from £200 to £300, to award him £50 per annum for museum duties, in line with monies given to the Professors of Botany and Zoology, and to offer an additional stipend of £150 if he were willing to continue giving Museum lectures.[63] Amazingly, Dawkins had managed to shed half his workload and secure a pay rise into the bargain. It is interesting to note, however, that for the next five years Dawkins was involved in a greater number of public lecture series than previously, through the Museum, the University, the Royal Institute and other organisations. Clearly he needed another outlet for his energies now that his beloved Museum had gone.[64]

Eoliths and Other Archaeological Fancies
The question of when humans first appeared in Britain took another turn during the 1880s. As we have seen, most of the pioneers including Dawkins rejected Geikie's work and were still monoglacialists; most, including Prestwich, Hughes and Evans, still believed that humans had appeared after the 'Great Glacial' (although Prestwich began to change his mind on the latter after the 1877 RAI Conference, and later claimed to have believed it all along).[65] Dawkins had bucked the trend somewhat, for contained within his assertion that the Thames Valley group of mammals belonged to (at different points in his career) either pre-glacial, 'middle-drift' or Middle Pleistocene times was an acknowledgement that humans might also be pre-glacial. But the reading of these papers had met with stern opposition. The one thing that everybody apparently agreed on was that there was no evidence whatsoever of humans in the equivalent of the Forest Beds of East Anglia (late Pliocene or Earliest Pleistocene) or earlier in the Tertiary Period. This comfortable situation was challenged in the late 1880s, leading to a debate that would simmer for decades. Dawkins was involved throughout, but his contribution was not novel and principally involved defending the long-held positions of himself and his closest allies.

The first claim came from one of Dawkins' oldest haunts – the Clwyd Valley in North Wales. In 1884 local doctor Henry Hicks (1837-1899) began to excavate at Ffynnon Bueno and Cae Gwyn, two new and largely undisturbed caves.[66] The sequence within Cae Gwyn showed human/hyaena occupation beneath a broken stalagmite, in turn overlain by what Hicks interpreted as marine sand. Accordingly, he suggested that the stalagmite had been broken by violent wave action during the mid-glacial submergence phase. Following this phase, the seas retreated and glaciers deposited boulder clay in the valley, sealing the cave. This meant that the archaeological material beneath the stalagmite must be pre-glacial, even Early Pleistocene. A BAAS committee was almost inevitable, but the excavator found himself

213

at loggerheads with other members, particularly Hughes, who responded at the same meeting with a confusing array of geological smoke and mirrors[67]. Even his old colleagues at the Survey lambasted Hughes for his behaviour.[68] Dawkins had no a priori problem with Hicks' favoured date and had identified some of the original bones from Cae Gwyn and Ffynnon Bueno in the house of Mr. E Bouverie Luxmoore. He still found himself subject to a gratuitous slight from Hicks, who questioned the migration theory and promoted the idea that different parts of the same country could experience different glacial climates depending on geographical location. Convinced by the stratigraphic arguments, Prestwich supported Hicks.

The next development opened a farcical episode in British prehistory that took generations to resolve. Benjamin Harrison (1837-1921) was a shopkeeper from Ightham in Kent, although like many of the businessmen-antiquarians of his era he spent more time than he should on his hobbies.[69] Exploring the landscapes around his village, Harrison began to collect from the surface of the High Level Plateau gravel of Kent ochreous stones with apparent retouch. These came to be known as 'eoliths' (dawn-stones), although Harrison affectionately nicknamed them 'brownies' (Figure 9.1). The eoliths derived from gravels above 340 ft O.D., deposits that could not be related to the post-glacial drainage patterns and had to relate to more ancient river courses. Furthermore, the crude character of the objects arguably put them at the beginning of the evolutionary sequence of human culture.[70] The validity of the eoliths split the scientific community with the many fervent opponents, including Evans, Dawkins, Worthington Smith (1835-1917), Flaxman Spurrell (1842-1915), William Whitaker and Augustus W. Franks matched by an equal number of zealous believers, W.J. Lewis-Abbot (1850-1933), A.J. Montgomerie Bell (1845-1920), T. Rupert-Jones and Joseph Prestwich chief among their number.

Figure 9.1: A selection of eoliths drawn by Benjamin Harrison (original in possession of author).

It was the recruitment of Joseph Prestwich to the cause in 1889 that set the eolith debate ablaze,[71] commencing with a paper read before the

Geological Society on 6 February 1889.[72] In presenting eoliths to the scientific community, Prestwich adopted the same approach as he had done in 1859 – emphasising the context and character of the objects.[73] This time, however, he was on the opposite side of the chamber to John Evans who, along with William Whitaker, raised immediate objections about the age of the gravels, and of assigning any age at all to surface finds. At the reading of a second paper on 21 January 1891, these doubts were echoed by several members of the Geological Survey.[74] The objects used to illustrate the reading of both papers raised fewer comments, being a mixture of eoliths alongside genuine Lower and Middle Palaeolithic finds. A third paper was read before the RAI on 23 June 1891, this time accompanied by a display of tools.[75] These finally brought Dawkins to his feet, to argue that the presence of finer and cruder artefacts merely demonstrated that drift period hunters walked across the landscape where they discarded tools, and that wave damage could mimic retouch of the kind found on the eoliths. Evans too had by now decided that the eoliths were natural debris, pointing out the near-uselessness of the objects. Prestwich was dismissive of these objections, and was disgusted at the behaviour of both men when they interrupted Harrison's part of the talk to ask questions, unable to wait until the end because they each had to catch a train. 'Their objections are puerile and they don't even wait to have them replied to', Prestwich whispered to his neighbour as the pair left the room together.[76] Harrison was equally annoyed, referring to Dawkins as Evans' 'esquire'.[77] Dawkins would not have been amused.

Evans, like Dawkins, had long since become intractable in his views and both would continue to oppose eoliths till the end of their lives. At the 1894 BAAS in Oxford, where a debate took place between Section C (Geology) and Section H (Anthropology), lead by William Whitaker (against) and T. Rupert Jones (for), both predictably spoke out against the supposed artefacts. Dawkins' main point was that he could match most of the tools geologically, which John McNabb[78] interprets as meaning that Dawkins thought the eoliths were flakes, and had thus missed the point. This inference is based on a talk given by Dawkins to the RAI,[79] where he showed hand-axes, splinters and 'rude forms' from Creswell and flakes from Cissbury to demonstrate that the material on the Plateau could easily have been produced during the manufacture of known types and need not represent an earlier form of culture.

I believe that the solution lies elsewhere, and Dawkins' apparently puzzling statements[80] stem from the fact that Harrison and Prestwich continued to include both genuine artefacts and natural debris in their high-level artefact group. In a letter to Darbishire, Dawkins explains his position: 'My Objection to the conclusion based on the *whole group* of Kent Plateau implements is:

1. That there is no evidence that any of those which are undoubtedly artificial are older than the Palaeolithic age
2. That most of those which have been found are identical to those which occur elsewhere, under the basalt of Ireland – under the boulder drift of Norfolk and Suffolk, under conditions which render it most unlikely that they have been made by the hand of man. I found them, for example last month at Barton Mere, near Bury St Edmunds *in* the chalky boulder clay. If you look for them in any flint gravel, of any age I believe that you would find them
3. Most of the flints are surface finds, and are not necessarily of the age of the gravel on which they rest, or in the upper part of which they have been found. Under these circumstances it appears to me unfortunate to do anything with them except to put them to a 'suspense account'
PS. I ought to add that rudeness of form has nothing to do with age'[81]

Dawkins clearly did not think they were waste flakes. He doubted the artificial nature of most, and refused to accept that the real ones were as old as the gravel beneath. He was correct on both counts. The letter to Darbishire also makes it hard to believe that Dawkins privately confessed to the archeolithophile A.J. Montgomerie Bell that he believed in eoliths but could not admit it in public.[82] Dawkins was many things: he was probably a liar, and he was probably a cheat but he was nobody's fool and if he was true to anything it was himself and his beliefs.

While the eolith debate raged into deadlock, Dawkins and Evans found themselves having to defend their views at the opposite end of the time scale – the relationship between the Palaeolithic and the Neolithic. Both men had long argued that there was no continuity between the two periods: Evans could find no bridging series of artefacts, Dawkins saw only an abrupt change in the Mammalia with the mega-fauna and southern species replaced by domesticates.[83] In a paper read before the RAI in 1893, John Allen Brown (1831-1903), whose previous work at Creffield Road in Acton had revealed a remarkable Early Middle Palaeolithic workshop,[84] argued that he could detect a developmental sequence in axes from Palaeolithic types, through transitional 'Mesolithic' forms to Neolithic axes.[85] His proving ground for these ideas had been the Chalk Downs around Eastbourne, East Sussex, where material had been recovered from chalky rubble and colluvium in dry valleys, on or just below the surface, with other examples coming from Cissbury, near Worthing. Brown then gave instances where caves preserved evidence of increasingly sophisticated knapping techniques and tools through time – at Creswell, Kent's Cavern, and a range of French sites – the last series in each case transitional or approaching Neolithic forms. For Brown, if these had not been associated with extinct animals they might never have been classed as Palaeolithic, and he was able to marshal examples where the animals in question (reindeer, mammoth etc.) might actually have lived on into later periods. This was just one of the problems of using caves – the taxa present depended on regional availability and hunter preference, as Dawkins had said years before. Another difficulty was that Neolithic people were not troglodytes, but lived in open-air settlements, so transitions would often be absent from caves but some could be found in the Pyrenees and elsewhere.

It did not take long for Dawkins to respond,[86] reiterating before the RAI that profound differences in climate, geography and animal life separated the two periods, precisely as he had stated twenty-six years earlier. Vast numbers of species had become extinct during the Palaeolithic, and while a few survived into historic times (aurochs, red deer, roe deer, horse and wild boar) domesticates appeared suddenly, as if by magic, in the Neolithic. After a brief rehearsal of the migration theory and a gratuitous poke at Geikie, Dawkins took issue with the idea that because different periods were found in stratigraphical order in caves there was continuity, when in fact there was often a long hiatus, in some caves long enough for a considerable depth of stalagmite to be formed. They formed a fragmented sequence, not a continuous one. Assuming Evans' mantle, Dawkins then dealt with the artefacts. Brown's materials from the South Downs were mostly surface finds from ploughed fields, ranging from roughly chipped blocks to Neolithic axes. He summarily dismissed them as were worthless 'waifs and strays' when it came to dating, but agreed with Brown that a similar range could be found in the old refuse heaps at Cissbury and also at Grimes Graves. But these were both Neolithic flint mines and contained evidence of domestic animals, pottery, and dolichocephalic people, and the supposedly different types of axe were all simply Neolithic axes in different stages of manufacture, he argued. The perfect forms were conspicuous by their absence, while those unfinished forms closest to completion were clearly Neolithic. To illustrate his points he brought along a series of finds from Cissbury showing all stages of manufacture. In the thick of it all, Dawkins' mother, Mary Anne, died, aged 84.

Into this already tempestuous mix E.T. Newton threw Galley Hill Man, a partial skeleton comprising the brain case, right mandible and post-cranial elements of a single individual discovered in the autumn of 1888 at Galley Hill, near Northfleet, Kent (Figure 9.2).[87] The initial find was made by a quarryman, Jack Allsop, who had concealed the discovery until local antiquarian Robert Elliott could investigate it on one of his fortnightly visits to the Swanscombe and Northfleet quarries. The skeleton had come from gravel of the 100 ft terrace, a known source of hand-axes, at a depth of 8 ft beneath the surface. Elliott and his son had examined the section carefully, and could find no evidence that the gravel had been disturbed, a conclusion 'confirmed' seven years later by William Topley and Clement Reid (1853-1913) of the Survey, even though the actual section had long since disappeared. Examining the human material, Newton observed a peculiar combination of characteristics: the skull was dolichocephalic, but of a form more exaggerated than found in the Neolithic; the jaw had a chin and was

Figure 9.2: The skull of Galley Hill Man (after Keith 1915).

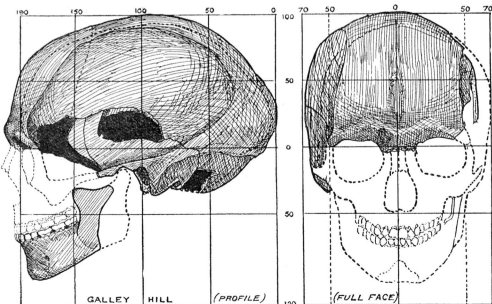

218

gracile, but the face was prognathous with thick brow ridges like the Neanderthals. Newton argued that it did not conform to any known race past or present, but considered it to bear greatest affiliation to the Eskimo, the race Dawkins believed was a direct descendent of Palaeolithic Europeans. Newton, now suggested that the Galley Hill skeleton was a Palaeolithic ancestor of the Neolithic people of Britain, rejecting the Dawkins-Evans notion of a cultural and genetic rupture. Sitting in the audience, Evans commented that the length of time between the original discovery and the examination of the find spot by a geologist meant the context could not be certain, and noted inconsistencies between the eyewitness accounts. He suspected the skeleton was an intrusive burial, a feeling shared by Dawkins, who admonished Newton for not comparing it with the Scandinavian barrow burials.

Time would prove that Galley Hill was a Neolithic intrusion[88] but that Brown was quite correct in defining his Mesolithic period. Numerous Mesolithic forms do indeed occur on the South Downs around Eastbourne, but this was not widely accepted at the time. The 1902 British Museum Guide to the Antiquities of the Stone Age suggested that no convincing transitional forms had yet been found.[89] Priced at one shilling and available to over 1740 daily visitors,[90] this view would have circulated far more widely than papers read to even the most august Society, much to Dawkins' delight when he reviewed the book.[91] He was less happy with the inclusion of eoliths in the Palaeolithic – if they were real, which they were not, then they were Pre-Palaeolithic, he insisted – and questioned the author's acceptance of Skertchley's interglacial, on which he must have changed his opinion since *Early Man*.

The End of the Hunt

Dawkins' final cave excavation took place in 1902, at the Victory Quarry, Bibbington, between Doveholes and Buxton, the first Pliocene cave to be discovered in Britain.[92] The local area had periodically yielded an occasional specimen of late Pleistocene fauna, including a mammoth tusk in the collections of the Manchester Museum. Then, in 1902, a cave was exposed in the side of the quarry that contained fossils of mastodon, hyaena, Etruscan rhinoceros, southern mammoth (*Mammuthus meridionalis*), extinct horse and *Machairodus crenatidens* (=*Homotherium crenatidens*), the precursor of the troublesome cat from Creswell. Master Hicks, a local schoolboy, and the Buxton antiquary Mr M. Salt, first brought the site to Dawkins' attention, after which he made arrangements to monitor that site and collect specimens.

The cave was part of a complex and ancient system incorporating a vertical swallet and a horizontal passage 90 ft long and 4 ft wide. Bones and teeth were found pell mell throughout the cave infill, some very rolled, others sharp, some hyaena gnawed, some not. Dawkins' description of the fauna shows that none of the old skills had left him, treating the reader to a description of the finds and, where appropriate, a summary of its taxonomy and distribution. He concluded that the fossils were undoubtedly Pliocene and had been derived from an old hyaena den at a higher level, moved by the action of water through fissures in the limestone to their present position (Plate 19). The article demonstrated that throughout his industrial years Dawkins had kept abreast of developments in Quaternary palaeontology, but that nothing had moved him to alter his earlier opinions. The Pliocene geography of Britain was but slightly modified from his 1880 map, the ancient seas were still awash with icebergs, and all the Pliocene caves with the single exception of Doveholes had been destroyed by denudation of the land surface, just as he had said in *Early Man*. The discussion afterwards was courteous. Woodward and Andrews agreed with every word, but Clement Reid wondered why Dawkins had brought up matters not arising from the discovery at hand – an extremely good point that somebody might have raised earlier in Dawkins' career. Dawkins invited Salt to hear the Doveholes paper read before Geological Society, where he would be given full credit for the discovery, but it is unknown if he accepted. Around the same time, Dawkins began corresponding with Nina Layard about her excavations at Foxhall Road, Ipswich, where he commended her geological work. In 1904 he was received as an honoured guest at the site, visiting on 20 December with Frances Eld, as Layard recalled: *'Rookwood at 2.10, looked over my flints and other 'finds', and then all drove to the Foxhall Road Palaeolithic site and stayed there watching the excavating and examining the site till about 9.15'.*[93] Dawkins shared Layard's scepticism that Palaeolithic pygmies used the miniature implements from the site; she and Evans thought them tools for children.

Dawkins retired as Professor of Geology at Manchester University in March 1908, a landmark event in the history of the University worthy enough to be reported in the *Manchester Guardian* and *Pall Mall Gazette* (The former bizarrely stated that for two years Dawkins had studied medicine at Oxford, a claim recorded nowhere else).[94] Shortly before Dawkins' retirement J. Wilfred Jackson (1880-1978) took up a junior curatorial-post at Manchester Museum; Dawkins acted as a mentor to the young conchologist, helping him learn his curatorial and research duties and establishing a friendship that would shape Jackson's career.[95] Retirement was greeted, as it often was, by a rash of honours and awards. In 1909, he was conferred the award of Doctor of Science by Manchester University,[96] and profiled in the *Geological*

Magazine's 'Eminent Living Geologists' series.[97] His old student D.M.S. Watson named a species of marine reptile from the Upper Lias at Whitby after him: *Sthenarosaurus dawkinsi*.[98] A year later he was invited to give the Huxley Lecture for the RAI, the greatest accolade the Institute could confer (see below). Further honours came in 1911, when a portrait of Dawkins was revealed at the University Galleries at Whitworth Hall, leading to another round of plaudits and potted biographies in the local and national news.[99] The 'vain cocky humbug' must have loved it, although he perhaps did not so much enjoy the University Chancellor's anecdote of a Scotchman [sic] who said of Dawkins: 'Mon, he has a great head, it's like a geological specimen', or the column inches given over to the ladies' dresses.[100]

Dawkins 1910 Huxley Lecture[101] began almost inevitably with a brief account of how the speaker had known Huxley personally, and what a major influence the great naturalist had exerted on his career. Dawkins explained how he had sat at the feet of Huxley at the Survey, how he had heeded the Master's advice and took the job at Manchester, and how Huxley had continued to act as guide, philosopher and friend for many years afterwards. Dawkins then moved on to the main subject of the talk 'The Arrival of Man in Britain'. It served as the final major synthesis of Dawkins' ideas, but the audience could have been excused for believing they had been transported back in time to 1880, 1874 or even 1867.

Dawkins opened with a brief summary of the periodisation of the Tertiary, refusing to accept the newly coined Oligocene period because it merely merged animals from either side. He then reiterated his rejection of eoliths as natural objects, describing the Belgian archaeologist Aime Rutot (1847-1933) as the chief of the 'cult', but accepted the Javan hominin fossils *Homo erectus* found by Eugene Dubois in the 1880s-90s as a missing link, more human than ape. He was positively delighted that the mammalian species associated with the Javan human fossils were either extant species or extinct species of firm Pleistocene age. Pliocene man was still anathema, and he rejected Abbott's claimed artefact from the Cromer Forest Bed. In terms of material culture, Dawkins had by now come to accept de Mortillet's classification, which by 1910 had grown to include Chellean, Acheulean, Mousterian, Aurignacian, Solutrean and Magdalenian, but he saw them as largely regional in significance and, as in 1880, did not think they applied to Britain. On these shores, the first three occurred together in fluvial deposits and on the hilltops of Bedfordshire, while the later three were found mixed in cave deposits in a way that left 'no reasonable doubt' that they belonged to the same period of occupation. He instead follows Evans' forty-year old division into river-drift men and cave men. (Once again, Dawkins' lack of attention to stratigraphy and taphonomy, unless it suited him, had let him down). Lartet's divisions were rejected for reasons he had discussed many times before. The bulk of the paper is taken up by faunal divisions and distributions, which follow *Early Man* to the letter, and although mentions of the sites at Swanscombe and Wolvercote show he had kept up with new finds, these only served to show that his Thames Valley group defined in 1867 was still valid.

He was similarly unrepentant on the 'glacial controversy'. The point was, he argued, that the southern margin of the ice sheet had fluctuated back and forth throughout the whole of the Pleistocene period, glaciers surviving in Scotland until the Neolithic. In the Alps this was represented by four glacial advances named by Penck and Brückner as Günz, Mindel, Riss and Würm, separated by three interglacials delineated by the cold periods either side (Günz-Mindel, etc.).[102] Dawkins explained that he used the term post-glacial in the sense that the animals and humans he documented were later than the boulder clays of England and Wales, but that for Geikie this was just another interglacial because there were still glaciers in Scotland and another glacial advance followed. He bemoaned the confusion of terms (which was actually mostly his own) and thought the evidence of interglacials reflected only local conditions. In a footnote he confessed that he still believed in a period of submergence in Britain as shown by Lyell in 1863. He also reaffirmed his belief that hippopotamus and narrow-nosed rhinoceros were contemporary with the reindeer fauna, and that seasonal migration provided the best explanation for this strange mixture of animals in caves. The French might think they indicate an earlier period and an interglacial, he acknowledged, but in Britain they were associated with the typical river-drift implements during the mid and late Pleistocene. They were not, though, associated with the tools of the cave men. Had Dawkins interrogated this or been prepared to abandon his most cherished theory, he could not have helped realising that they were in fact a succession, exactly as he had found at Mother Grundy's Parlour. Instead he repeated the notion that the river-drift people were southerly folk who followed the migrations of the animals, and who occupied Britain south of a line from the Humber to the Severn, with an outlier in North Wales. What he had really mapped, however, was the extent of the Last Glacial Maximum. The cave people were still considered a northern tribe, probably of Neanderthal type, and he still saw close similarities to the Eskimo although no longer thought they were directly descended. To the last he harboured doubts about Crô-Magnon.

Prelude to Piltdown

Retirement quashed none of Dawkins' fight, and he was more than ready for round two of the eolith controversy, as instigated by Reid Moir and championed by Ray Lankester. James Reid Moir (1879-1944) was by trade a gentleman's outfitter, apprenticed to the family business on the Butter Market, Ipswich.[103] It was a calling to which he was never committed and from which his father threatened him with dismissal for neglecting his duties. His consuming interest lay in archaeology, a field in which he was, it is fair to say, something of a maverick.

In 1909, Moir discovered some crude flints in gravel heaps at Boulton and Loughlin's Pit, Ipswich, stones derived from the base of the Pliocene Red Crag (Figure 9.3). In an audacious letter to *The Times* on October 17 1910, Moir claimed that these were irrefutable human artefacts that pushed

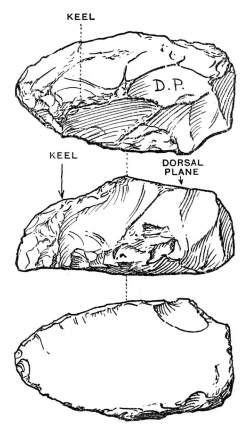

Figure 9.3: The 'Norwich Test Specimen', a prime example of Moir's rostro-carinate implements (after Moir 1927).

human antiquity back beyond the age of the Norfolk and Suffolk Forest Beds deep into the Pliocene. This opinion plunged him into a fractious debate, but also brought him the support and friendship of Sir Edwin Ray Lankester (1847-1929), whose illustrious career had seen him hold chairs in natural history at University College London and Oxford, and the directorship of the Natural History Museum.[104] Moir invited a party of geologists from the Geological Society to visit the site, and a Special Committee of the newly formed Prehistoric Society of East Anglia (PSEA) was convened to pronounce upon them. Under the guidance of their first President, William Allen Sturge (1850-1919), the PSEA declared that Moir's flints – which came to be known as rostro-carinates, 'eagle-beaks' or pre-palaeoliths – were genuine artefacts.[105] (Sturge, who had retired to Ipswich from Nice in 1907, was another man with reason to despise Dawkins, having been on the receiving end of his legendary bite; according to one of Weiner's sources, Dawkins had 'stuck his knife into poor old Sturge with his usual ferocity, which so upset him that it brought on one of his heart attacks').[106]

Dawkins was hostile to Moir's claims, but at 75 he preferred to leave the proof up to Samuel Hazzledine Warren (1872-1958: geologist), Frederick Nairn Haward (1871-1953: engineer and friend of Warren) and William Johnson Sollas (1849-1936: Professor of Geology at Oxford) while taking his own potshots in the Societies and papers. Yet he left Moir in no little doubt of his opinion during an exhibition at Burlington House, when he told him his stones were natural, nothing more, and he similarly clashed with Lankester at a Royal Society soirée.[107] Dawkins put the burden of proof on Moir and Lankester, refusing to accept them unless the pair could demonstrate the stones were not produced naturally; the hot-headed Lankester, for his part, dismissed Dawkins' attitude as unscientific and said that nobody any longer attached any importance to his opinions.[108] Dawkins pleaded with Sollas to stamp down on Moir and Lankester whenever rostro-carinates came up at the Royal Society, fearing they were lowering the tone of their *Philosophical Transactions* and conning people into thinking the society gave them its stamp of approval. Henry Hoyle Howorth (1842-1923), ex-MP for South Salford, fellow Rossall alumnus[109] and British Museum Trustee was similarly appalled,[110] implying that the geological committee of the Society was frightened of Lankester and so accepted everything he submitted.[111] In the meantime, Dawkins found time to give an interview to the *Manchester Guardian* on Oliver Cromwell's head.[112]

It will be recalled that at the beginning of his professional career, Dawkins had joined a team surveying the geology of the Weald, which before he resigned had been extended to include the drift. None of these exercises ever mapped the small remnant of River Ouse gravel at Barkham Manor, near the small village of Piltdown in Sussex, where between 1908-1912, in a small pit used for road metal beside the drive up to the manor, Uckfield solicitor and antiquarian Charles Dawson discovered a series of fossils belonging to a new type of human, one with a large human-like skull and robust ape-like jaw. The jaw was associated with eoliths and a bone tool shaped like a cricket bat, along with a mix of Pliocene and Pleistocene fauna. The cricket bat may have been a little Edwardian whimsy, but the association of 'dawn stones' with 'dawn man', *Eoanthropus Dawsoni* (Plate 23), was something far more devious. The story of Piltdown Man, the hoax that fooled British science for over 40 years is too well-known to need much explanation;[113] I am here not concerned with who was guilty of the hoax but with Dawkins' involvement in the affair.

Dawson's scientific partner in the investigations at Piltdown was Arthur Smith Woodward (1864-1944), Keeper of Geology at the Natural History Museum, London. Woodward was the son of a dye merchant from Macclesfield, who had won a scholarship from Macclesfield Grammar School to attend University. These awards were usually made to a student destined for Oxbridge, but Woodward had chosen to attend Manchester, where he studied under Dawkins between 1880-1882. Dawkins' local celebrity may have influenced Woodward's decision and although he left to take up a junior post at the NHM before completing his degree, he always remained good friends with his old master. Dawkins was rightly proud of his student's success and was one of Woodward's inner circle throughout the Piltdown affair.

Piltdown man was officially unveiled to the world on 18 December 1912, but Dawkins had been given a preview; letters to Woodward on 6 October and 7 November indicate that he had gone to the museum while on other business in London.[114] In a familiar twist, the story leaked in the *Manchester Guardian* on 21 November, which despite containing little information forced Woodward to hold a press conference to limit the potential damage and curb speculation. Dawkins gave an interview to the same newspaper on 23 November where he admitted he knew much about the find but would not be drawn on the details before the official announcement at the Geological Society. What is most interesting about the interview is that Dawkins obviously anticipated the arguments that would arise from the find and tried to pre-empt them by dismissing the skeletons at Galley Hill and Ipswich as recent remains buried in ancient deposits. He further gave the game away when the reporter asked whether the finds would require him to re-write *Early Man in Britain*, to which Dawkins (rather amusingly and entirely predictably) responded 'Not at all, I may have something to add; I shall have nothing to correct,' drawing the reporter's attention to page ninety where he stated that there was no inherent improbability of humans being present in the Pliocene.

The reason for Dawkins' pre-emptive strike was an on-going quarrel with Arthur Keith (1866-1944, Hunterian Professor of Anatomy at the Royal College of Surgeons), which had started in 1912 with a confrontation at the BAAS meeting in Dundee. Keith was a keen eolithophile and believer in Pliocene humans. In 1911 he had published his first book on palaeoanthropology, *Ancient Types of Men*, and his views on a deep antiquity for the modern human form, descended from much earlier Neanderthal races, were becoming well known. Of the two skeletons dismissed by Dawkins, Keith had readily accepted both. The putative pre-glacial age of 'Ipswich Man', discovered in 1911 in Boulton and Loughlin's Pit beneath intact boulder clay[115] (Figure 9.4), provided a comparison for the earlier Galley Hill find, a skeleton Keith saw as very recent in form but very ancient in date; the oldest in England in fact. Such a position was bound to bring him into conflict with Dawkins eventually, and Dundee was as good a place as any. Dawkins knew he was on safe ground. Moir had published accounts of the geology at Boulton and Loughlin's Pit where he claimed that John E Marr (1857-1933, Hughes' successor to the Woodwardian Chair) and William Whitaker had confirmed the integrity of the deposits, but Whitaker had privately told Dawkins that he did not really understand the situation. He had not seen the skeleton *in situ* and the geology of the pit was complicated, with patches of boulder clay and decalcified remnants of the same. He could not explain how the skeleton got there but was sceptical about a pre-glacial age.[116]

Keith was scheduled to give the keynote lecture to the BAAS on the evening of Monday 9 September 1912, advertised in the programme as being on 'Modern problems relating to the Antiquity of Man'. This put Dawkins on his mettle. The Friday before Keith's address, Dawkins read a paper by William Duckworth on a piece of maxilla discovered inside Kent's Cavern in 1867, which the author concluded was of the Palaeolithic type.[117] Rather unconventionally, having read the paper, Dawkins then savaged it. He argued that there was only one type of human in Palaeolithic Europe, the river-drift type of which Neanderthals were the archetype and all others more or less assimilated. Everything that deviated from this was surrounded by vague context or other reasons to be suspicious, and all examples of modern skulls from caves were worthless, he declared. Dawkins' timing was exquisite: as

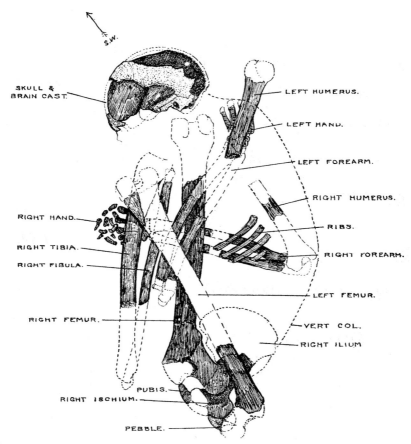

Figure 9.4: Ipswich Man, shown with the parts of the skeleton placed in their original positions (after Keith 1915).

the evening was drawing on the President immediately closed the session, regretting that they had no time to discuss Dawkins' provocative remarks. This brought Keith to his feet, protesting strongly that the whole thing was ridiculous and not even scientific.

Keith had the weekend to orchestrate a reply, which came at the opening of his lecture. He thus began his lecture by praising the men who had first unlocked the truth about human antiquity, before rounding on Dawkins:

'That splendid movement of the nineteenth century, which knocked the shackles of tradition from the problem of man's origin, was led by men of courage, conviction, and sound judgment. It was a progressive

227

and victorious movement they initiated; but in every movement of that kind there comes a time when those who cleared the way turn circumspect, cautious, and more critical than constructive. Opinion tends to become fixed and conventionalised, and then a new heterodoxy raises its head. That is the phase which we, who make a special study of the facts relating to man's origin, seem to have reached now. I cannot cite a more stalwart or distinguished representative of the orthodox opinion of to-day than Professor Boyd Dawkins, of Manchester'.[118]

Keith's understanding of variation and evolution demanded greater lengths of time than suggested by most geologists. Sollas had estimated that the Pleistocene lasted for 400,000 years, which was just not long enough for Keith (Dawkins thought it pointless to measure the distant past in years, and that only cycles of geological events and animal life made any sense).[119] Gibbons and apes with minimally changed forms occurred in the Miocene and earlier, and Keith expected that humans would be found in the Miocene and even the Oligocene. He had at this point in his thinking reached the conclusion that modern humans and Neanderthals were from different stock. Ancient humans equal in development and brain size to the 'australoid' form had existed deep into the Pleistocene, living alongside other forms that had since gone extinct. But only one type was found in Palaeolithic Britain – the modern forms at Galley Hill and Ipswich – Neanderthals had been absent. There is much in Keith's words recognisable in modern ideas – multiple forms of co-existing *Homo*, modern people emerging from a single line and all others going extinct, a deep human ancestry – but he arrived at the conclusions using spurious evidence and questionable ethics. It is also clear that everything Keith had said in the September lecture was informed by prior knowledge of Piltdown and aimed to set the scene for his opinion on it,[120] precisely like Dawkins.

When the day of the Piltdown presentation finally came, the Geological Society was unusually packed, the rumours that something special was afoot drawing the fellowship out of their warm parlours and clubs on a bitter December evening to hear Dawson and Woodward present the details of the site, the fossils and the associated artefacts.[121] Dawkins' colleague at Manchester, Grafton Elliot Smith (1871-1937), also spoke on an endocast of Piltdown man's brain, which showed an incipient power of speech, although the jaw made actual speech impossible.[122] In the discussion, Keith queried Woodward's reconstruction of the cranium, and asserted without reservation that the remains were associated with the Pliocene mammals rather than the Pleistocene beasts – the height above the river, the eoliths and simian jaw demanded it. As he linked tool making with language, he also sensed a problem with the reconstruction of the jaw.

Dawkins was delighted with his student's great discovery, but irritated by Keith. For Dawkins, associating the human remains with the oldest and not the youngest mammalian fossils simply ignored good geological practice. The modern looking skull just confirmed what he had said forty years previously: that human evolution took place in the Pleistocene, by remodelling a basic form.[123] He was equally dismissive of Keith's opinion of the reconstruction, remarking that the case for tool use and language was speculation – 'examples in the political world show that the power of speech and actual capacity to act in the practical things of life are unrelated,' he told a reporter in the *Manchester Evening Chronicle*.[124]

Keith set to work on his own reconstruction, which included a larger and more modern looking cranium, fulfilling his own beliefs in the course of human evolution that placed Piltdown within *Homo* and not a new genus. Dawkins was desperate for Elliot Smith to counter with his own reconstruction, and grew increasingly impatient when a promised set of casts failed to arrive, even though Keith had obviously received his. He wrote to Woodward in January urging for the casts to be sent with haste, and sent reminders until at least August, the last a terse 'can you hurry up the casts'.[125] Realising that he may lose the anatomical arguments, Dawkins chose to fight the more critical battle – chronology. If he won this fight, then Keith could have his reconstruction.

Writing in the *Daily Express*, Dawkins was emphatic: 'No traces of modern types of man have as yet been found in any undisturbed deposit of [Pliocene or Early Pleistocene] age in any part of the world. Those relied upon by Dr. Keith are certainly proved in the case of Ipswich to have been an internment that may be of any age, from the Neolithic times down to to-day, and in other cases [e.g. Galley Hill] are not of clearly defined geological age'.[126] This inevitably brought Reid Moir and William J. Lewis Abbott (1853-1933) into the fray who along with the rest of their cult almost unanimously supported Keith. Moir was in no mood to have his work so summarily dismissed in the press, and quickly challenged Dawkins' assertion that the Piltdown gravels were Pleistocene and that the case against the Ipswich skeleton had been proven.[127]

Abbott was a jeweller from Hastings, described by Alfred Kennard as 'a short, stocky man with a ferocious moustache, nearly always wore a boater in the field, came from a remote part of Essex, the Dengie Hundred ... a frequent speaker at outdoor meetings, defending orthodox religious views'.[128] His archaeological beliefs were anything but orthodox, and he credited himself with wonderful discoveries of 'new races and new things in flint'.[129] By his own estimation he was an overlooked genius, but others found him eccentric, a reckless enthusiast and 'immune to modesty'.[130] Even his long-time friend and correspondent, Benjamin Harrison found him temperamental, troublesome and mentally unbalanced,[131] while Keith described him as bold and resolute in formulating scientific explanations of past events, and perhaps more occupied with the contributions which he himself had made to his favourite subjects of study than those made by his fellow-workers.[132] He was also not above deception, which is why his name has frequently been linked to the Piltdown fraud.[133] His numerous personal and published letters frequently bordered on abusive, Kennard drily noting that they were best classed under fiction.[134] Abbott and Dawkins had a history of animosity; Abbott particularly hated the Professor's unswerving belief in his own infallibility. He was not the only person to resent this, but was one of the most publicly outspoken. His own letter to the *Daily Express* was simply rude, comparing Dawkins' conviction in the finality of his opinions to: 'The historic mussulman who closed the Koran and declared that any book that supported it was unnecessary and should be destroyed, and that any that differed from it should be similarly treated'.[135] In a letter to Rutot, the Belgian High-Priest of the continental eolith movement, Abbott quipped 'We have a large number in this country who think perfect Pleistocene man dropped from the clouds, such people look up to Boyd Dawkins'.[136]

After a year of bitter sniping by all concerned parties, a second report on fresh discoveries at Piltdown was read before the Geological Society on 17 December 1913. Dawkins had by now visited the site, which he found rather disappointing and not as imposing as he had hoped.[137] Dawson and Woodward presented new details on the geology and fauna, and revealed the discovery of an ape-like canine tooth, which conveniently removed one of the main anatomical obstacles.[138] Dawson, perhaps acting on Woodward's advice, was clear that the gravel of the skull level was a Pleistocene deposit made up of reworked Pliocene sediments. Latching on to on the fact that the artefacts from Piltdown had been found in the layer above the skull, Keith commented that had no human remains been found then few would hesitate to assign the deposit to the Pliocene, strongly implying that the whole thing reeked of hypocrisy. William Sollas objected, pointing out that the presence of derived fossils in gravel was one of the commonest geological facts and that the geologists had been correct in following their usual method of dating the gravel on the basis of the youngest specimens. Dawkins agreed, adding that the presence of red deer, a species unknown in the Pliocene but abundant in later periods, confirmed it.

The next day's *Morning Post* covered the meeting, the reporter astutely highlighting the fact that the debate was not really about anatomy but about antiquity. Dawkins was delighted with the paper's insightfulness, but the old pugilist wrote to complain that the article had failed to mention whether the 'fight was fought to a finish, or whether one of the principals was knocked out,' a prelude to informing the readership that the fight had been won and that he had personally delivered the decisive blow.[139] His letter also elaborated on his reasons for preferring a Pleistocene date for the finds: '...it [cannot] be maintained that *Eoanthropus* is of Pliocene Age, although the Pliocene mammals occur in the gravel. Their bones and teeth are all in the condition of pebbles and have obviously been derived from the destruction of Pliocene deposits like the Norfolk crag then existing in the district. They offer, therefore, no information as to the age, except that the gravels of which they form a part were accumulated later than those strata'. It seems odd that after a lifetime of dismissing putative Palaeolithic burials, some of them perfectly legitimate (e.g. Mentone [Grimaldi] in Italy], Dawkins was totally taken in by this hoax, to the extent that he felt the need to defend his positions using all his geological powers.

Dawkins' geological points were enough to win the argument, but he could not resist overstating his case by appealing to the archaeological evidence as well. Dawkins claimed that the tools associated with the skull were identical to those found in the older gravels of the Thames Valley and that this pointed to an Early Pleistocene date. Abbott was first to seize the opportunity to embarrass Dawkins, in a letter to the *Morning Post* of 1 January 1914 challenging him to produce just one implement characteristic of the Chellean. The corresponding silence gave Abbott cause to crow, telling Rutot that he had given the professor his 'eternal quietus'.[140] Abbott went on to criticise Woodward for failing to come clean about his secret belief in eoliths, stating that Dawkins seemed to have Woodward in some sort of hypnotic trance that had made him distort the true age of the Piltdown finds. For Abbott, Dawkins' behaviour was an outrage, and he suggested that had he been a physician or lawyer he would have been struck off; if he makes 'no attempt now to retrieve his honour, it will be forever lost, and no one can look upon him as a man, let alone scientist,' he ranted.[141]

The 'eternal quietus' was hardly eternal and certainly not quiet. Dawkins thought Abbott and Moir to be peddlers of fallacy in a moribund debate, their beliefs on the antiquity of man of little consequence. They were beneath his contempt. For Dawkins, younger workers such as 'Hazzy' Warren and Fred Haward had demolished both Harrison's brownies and Moir's rostro-carinates, demonstrating that they were nothing more than natural debris with no possible function.[142] The pre-eminent French scientists, Marcellin Boule (1861-1942) and Henri Breuil (1877-1961) reached the same conclusions following a visit to Moir and Lankester in September 1912,[143] and Boule's 1915 account of his findings in *l'Anthropologie* provided Dawkins with an excuse to air his well-known objections once again.[144] Sollas and Breuil would later changed their minds and accept some of Moir's implements, although his cherished rostro-carinates were not among them; Dawkins never wavered.[145] Most eolithophiles shared the same opinion of Dawkins, thinking him arrogant and dogmatic. On reading Dawkins' introduction to Herbert Balch's Wookey Hole monograph,[146] Moir told Keith 'Fancy old Dawkins still believing Cheddar man is Neolithic – but I suppose he stated this many years ago and being infallible what he said is true for all time'.[147] Reviewing the Wookey book in *Nature* Keith sarcastically makes the same point, applauding Dawkins' gallant fight for ideas and opinions put forward fifty years earlier.[148]

However important these things seemed prior to August 1914, when it was not all over by Christmas, a scrappy piece of skull from Sussex quickly lost lustre. Following Dawson's death in 1916, no further human remains were found, over the decades Piltdown became increasingly out of step with genuine finds in other parts of the world, and finally, in 1953, it was exposed as a fraud.[149] By then eoliths had long been consigned to the dustbin. In fact, doubts about Piltdown had begun to be sounded before 1914, and if war had not occurred, it is likely that it would have been exposed far sooner.[150] Before 1916 was out Moir was also forced to admit that he had been mistaken about the age of the Ipswich skeleton, although he remained convinced it was Palaeolithic, perhaps Aurignacian.[151] It would take a little longer for Galley Hill to be refuted, but here too Dawkins was proved correct.[152] Had he exercised his usual reserve with regard to the human skeleton at Piltdown, he might today be credited as an early doubter. Instead he trusted Woodward's faith in the find and like everybody else was totally taken in.

Death of an Eminent Scientist
Reminiscing in 1915 with T.G. Bonney, who Dawkins had first met in Sussex in the early 1860s, the two old men remembered those who had 'passed

within the veil': they were among the last of the old crowd of geologists still standing (Plate 23).[153] Unlike Dawkins, Bonney had accepted the concept of multiple glaciations, and at 82 was trying to reconcile this system with British terrestrial deposits, although he was struggling and not yet in a position to make a public statement. Dawkins quizzed him on his conclusions, and must have been heartened by Bonney's obvious confusion[154] when writing his final opus: a major review article for the *Edinburgh Review* in 1916.[155] The tale is by now all too familiar to repeat, save to say that Dawkins took Henry Fairfield Osborn to task because in his book, *Men of the Old Stone Age,* he not only adopted the Alpine sequence, the application of which outside of the Alps was still in not proven in Dawkins' mind, but dared to use it as a dating method. Keith's attempt at putting a chronological age on the Pleistocene using sediment thickness was similarly upbraided.

In recognition of a lifetime's achievement in Pliocene and Pleistocene palaeontology, the Geological Society awarded Dawkins the 1918 Prestwich Medal. He was only the fifth recipient of the tri-annual award (the others being 1903 – John Lubbock; 1906 – William Whitaker; 1909 – John Evans [posthumously]; 1915 – Emile Carthillac). The following year came an even greater prize, when on 18 August 1919 King George V knighted Dawkins at Buckingham Palace. Two years later, in June 1921, Lady Frances Dawkins, William Boyd's wife of fifty-six years, died aged 81. In May 1922, Dawkins married Mary Lilian Congreve [nee Poole, 1864-1954], widow of Hubert Congreve.[156] Dawkins was 84, Mary 58. The two had known each other for several years, and Dawkins first mentioned her in his diaries on 3-4 September 1918, when he recorded a visit to some Neolithic settlements in Keswick with Mary and Miss Twentyman.[157] One might speculate that there been other outings before and after. We should not judge Dawkins' unseemly haste to remarry too harshly – his closest friends certainly didn't. On hearing the news, Sir Arthur Evans (1851-1941) wrote from Knossos congratulating Dawkins and hoping that together he and Mary could find comfort and happiness.[158]

Through his eighties Dawkins showed no sign of slowing down (Plate 24). In 1921 he was busy with several BAAS committees, one set up to obtain Kent's Cavern for the Nation, another to co-operate with the RAI on explorations in Derbyshire caves. Dawkins was back at Creswell. Although Leslie Armstrong led the excavations, Dawkins was highly supportive – he had obtained permission from the Sixth Duke of Portland to renew excavations and chaired the Committee.[159] He also showed no diminution in his fighting spirit. When in 1924 a modern sect of Druids staked a claim to bury their dead at Stonehenge, Dawkins, then President of the Royal Archaeological Society, wrote to the Ancient Order of Druids pointing out all their mistakes, not least the fact that Stonehenge was Bronze Age, the Welsh and Irish druids described by historical sources late Iron Age.[160] The Grand Secretary replied informing Dawkins that his order had nothing to do with the Society of Druids, and it was the latter with which he should 'endeavour to cross swords'. Arthur Evans shared Dawkins' animosity to this new breed of 'sham druidism', but he went further blaming the Welsh politician David Lloyd George for having paid homage to them, and referred to the Eisteddfod as a new 'stunt'.[161]

A short time later it was Prof. William Sollas who bore the brunt of Dawkins' ire, for making the rash claim that the Creswell horse engraving was a fake (see Chapter 10). Dawkins' involvement with Creswell would never cease. When more art, in the form of incised figures of bison, rhinoceros and reindeer, was discovered by Armstrong and Garfitt at the front of Mother Grundy's Parlour (Figure 10.2),[162] the case seemed closed. Initially enthusiastic, Dawkins later changed his mind, believing that the engravings were nothing more than root marks.[163] Dorothy Garrod, Disney Professor of Archaeology at Cambridge, was equally cautious, accepting the reindeer as crude but of human origin but doubting the other two – even if some of the marks were humanly incised, they were so mixed up with root marks as to make them indecipherable.[164]

In August 1925, Breuil wrote to Dawkins with his interpretation of the Creswell artefacts in French terms,[165] suggesting that they included the latest Aurignacian and Azilio-Tardenosian. It is unlikely that Dawkins agreed with this prognosis, as the Azilian was regarded by some to be a transitional industry between the Palaeolithic and the Neolithic, and he wrote to Boule expressing the fact that he felt the Azilian to be Neolithic, a sentiment to which Boule was not entirely opposed.[166] Still, he received Breuil warmly at Manchester when the latter visited the Creswell excavations in May 1927.[167] As late as 1926 Dawkins was looking for new projects, writing to Davidson Black (1884-1934), the Canadian palaeontologist who had spent six-months in Manchester in 1914, offering to help identify the bones from the Chinese caves that had yielded 'Peking Man'. Black politically thanked him, saying had he known earlier he would have certainly have accepted the offer, but that the fossils had now been sent off to other people.[168]

The Centenary of the Geological Society Club, a dining club founded in 1824, was a poignant event, Dawkins being the only member from the Club's Golden Jubilee in 1874 still alive.[169] Lamplugh noted the curious coincidence that John Evans was president in 1874, and John W Evans was president in 1924. In his ninetieth year Dawkins and Mary moved from Fallowfield to a new home in Richmond Lodge, Bowden, Cheshire. In August 1928 Dawkins wrote to Wilfred Jackson explaining that he had been laid up for six months and intended to resign the Chair of the Creswell Committee;[170] there being no hope of him attending the BAAS meeting. He invited Jackson for tea, enticing him with tales of his garden in full beauty, 'the roses and sweet-peas at their best'. In September he wrote again,[171] relaying his pleasure that the engraved human figure recently found at Pin Hole Cave[172] was genuine. Dawkins' final public engagement was the opening of the new Buxton Museum in September 1928, where he gave an extempore address that lasted forty minutes, regaling the audience with tales of Creswell, Romans and the value of the Buxton collections. He had already decided to bequeath his archive to Buxton. Sir Arthur Evans wrote in late December, telling Dawkins he was going to send some plant cuttings by passenger train.[173] The plants were delicate and not ready for planting out. Dawkins would never do it.

Sir William Boyd Dawkins, FRS, FSA, FGS, died at his home in Richmond House, Bowden on 15 January 1929. He was 91. Obituaries flooded into the newspapers and scientific journals. Other than potted summaries of his scientific career, they tell of a man who was both charming and amusing to friends and colleagues, a man with a wicked sense of humour and infectious chuckle. An anonymous obituary in the *Geological Magazine* described a man whose 'sunny nature and delightful personality' endeared him to a large circle of acquaintances of all rank, while John Gregory, remembering deceased fellows in the annual presidential address to the Geological Society, called him 'a delightful companion, with an inexhaustible store of racy stories'.[174] Similar platitudes can be found in most contemporary profiles and obituaries, but what else would one expect? As we have seen, there was another side to Dawkins, best summed up by Edward Freeman, who described him as a 'lobster with a vengeance';[175] and his second wife Mary, who remarked that he had a 'taste for notoriety' and ' waged war against certain scientific theories and went for opponents with the ferocity of a cave man'.[176] He often would not stop until he was gnawing on their bones and extracting their marrow.

Dawkins' memorial service was held on 15 January 1929 at Holy Innocents' Church, Fallowfield, where he was a trustee. The service included Psalm 90 (Lord, though hast been our refuge: from one generation to another) and the hymn 'O God, our help in ages past'. At the reading of his will it was revealed that his estate was worth £24,500. He left £100 to his executors,

£100 to his gardener Joshua Hammett, and annuities of £65 to each of his servants Eliza Given and Fanny Normansell. To his wife he left his collections, books, letters, manuscripts, money at the bank and £1000 Great Southern Railway Stock, much of which (barring the money) went to Buxton Museum. Provision was made to disburse funds around charities of Mary's choice, but everything else, including his properties, went to Ella Selina.[177] The previous year he had donated a collection of old English furniture, enamels, cloisonné work from the Ming Dynasty, and reproductions of cave painting and engravings illustrative of the 'dawn of art in Europe' to the City Art Gallery in Manchester, his home of sixty years.[178]

The last of the great pioneers of human antiquity was gone.

Chapter 10

Three Men in a Cavern: A Cold Case Revisited

Sollas Puts His Foot In It

I could not end this book without providing some assessment, however speculative, of what I believe happened at Creswell in 1876. After Heath retreated from a battle he would never win, the Creswell question was allowed to sleep. Both the cat and the horse passed into the canon of British Palaeolithic archaeology and the controversy faded from memory. Any doubts that remained were seemingly dispelled in 1914, with the discovery of another engraving of a horse on a rib from Sherborne, Dorset,[1] (Figure 10.1) apparently picked up in a old heap of quarry debris by two boys from Sherborne School – A.S. Cortesi and P.C. Grove. Arthur Smith Woodward, who published the object, speculated that it had probably originated from a rock shelter on the slopes of one of the many dry valleys thereabouts, even going so far as suggesting that the spot would have been south facing and admirably suited to human habitation. The remarkable similarity of the image with that at Creswell was taken as an indicator of its authenticity and in the discussion following the paper's reading at the Geological Society a number of the assembled expressed their firmest support for a Palaeolithic age. For a time this corroborative evidence seemed at last to lay to rest the doubts raised by Heath.

A decade later, the story took another turn. In the third edition of his book *Ancient Hunters*, William Sollas wrote in a footnote that the Creswell horse 'is, I am assured, a forgery, introduced into the cave by a mischievous person', while the Sherborne engraving was similarly dismissed as 'a forgery perpetrated by some school boys'.[2] On discovering this slight in December 1924, Dawkins wrote to Sollas: 'I presume you have grounds for your assurance and write to ask you on what evidence it is based. I shall be obliged if you will give me an early answer that the question may be settled as soon as possible in the interests of science'.[3]

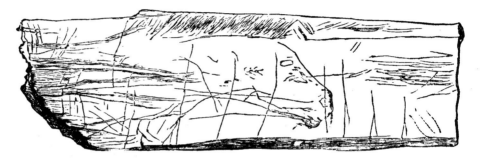

Figure 10.1: The Sherborne horse engraving (top), with the Creswell horse engraving (bottom) for comparison (after Dawkins 1880a and Woodward 1914). Dimensions: the Creswell specimen is 73mm long, the Sherborne one 85mm long.

Sollas sent Dawkins a postcard from France saying that he was away and would give an answer by the end of the January.[4] In the meantime, Dawkins complained about Sollas to Woodward, who had equal reason to be aggrieved with Sollas over the slur on the Sherborne horse.[5] Dawkins threatened to deal with the matter in *Nature* or *Man*, and complained that the drawing Sollas used to illustrate the rib was inferior to his own original woodcut, which made it very difficult for the reader to judge the detail on the piece. With a wonderful stroke of illogicality, Dawkins insisted that it would be impossible for the two forgeries to be identical in style if two different people had made them in modern times.

Sollas replied on 21 January, explaining that in 1919 Rev. E.H. Mullins of Langwith-Bassett had called on him several times concerning some discoveries he had made in Langwith Cave, where the cleric was excavating.

In one of their many conversations, Mullins told Sollas that he knew of the circumstances under which the Creswell engraving had been introduced surreptitiously into the cave. He would give no names nor enter into any details, but gave Sollas assurances that its presence in the cave was a prank. Although failing to satisfy his natural curiosity, Sollas had no reason to doubt Mullins, and would have asked for clarification had Mullins not since died.[6]

Dawkins was satisfied with the reply and easily rebuffed the accusation.[7] He had known Mullins well and informed Sollas that as the man had not been involved with the Creswell explorations he could know nothing about it from personal knowledge. Once again, Dawkins placed much store on personal knowledge, strange for an academic whose life's work depended on imparting and receiving information. In closing, Dawkins assured Sollas that Mullins had provided misleading information that had resulted in the introduction of an 'old canard' into his book. Under the circumstances, Dawkins felt he had no recourse other than go to the press.

Not a man to do anything by halves, Dawkins published his letter in both *Nature* and *Man*; at 87 he had lost none of his old pomp.[8] Opening with the fact that he was Chair of the resumed British Association Committee for Creswell, where new excavations were being undertaken by A. Leslie Armstrong and G.A Garfitt, he told the readership that the piece had been examined by Sir John Evans, Sir Augustus Franks, Lord Avebury (John Lubbock) and General Pitt-Rivers at the time that *he* had found it. Sollas' remarks, on the other hand, were based on gossip from a dead clergyman and he had not a shred of evidence to support his claim. Dawkins also reproached Sollas for his 'equally unfortunate' and sweeping claim that no art at all existed in the British Palaeolithic, as the new work had already uncovered incised figures of bison and reindeer (Figure 10.2). He was confident that as the work progressed there would be further proof that Creswell had been the seasonal home of peoples from the south of France.

Horrified by the gaff, Sollas immediately issued a retraction in *Nature,*[9] rueing that the new Creswell finds had not been made before his latest edition of *Ancient Hunters* had appeared. Sollas' letter explained what Mullins had told him and revealed that more than one person was implicated. He too would have been outraged at such a slur on his old friend Mello, had it not been for the earnest manner in which Mullins imparted the news and the fact that it agreed with what most people believed. He withdrew the statement and promised to delete it from the footnote at the earliest opportunity.

There is much to comment on here. First, Dawkins' memory was clearly failing him, for the acknowledged discoverer of the engraved rib was Mello

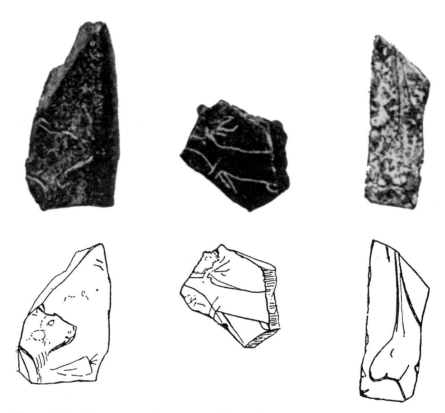

Figure 10.2: The supposed engravings from Mother Grundy's Parlour. Top row: photographs with images enhanced by china-white applied by Armstrong (after Armstrong 1925). Bottom Row: Drawings of the supposed images (after Bahn 2007, reproduced with permission Paul Bahn). Scale: the largest fragment is ~5cm in length.

and not Dawkins. Second, Dawkins used his well-worn tactic of appealing to authority, calling on an all-star cast of Victorian polymaths who could vouch for the authenticity of the Creswell find, if it were not for the awkward fact that they were all long dead by 1925. They were therefore no more use to Dawkins' cause than Mullins was to Sollas'. If that were not bad enough, it was a similar group of savants who forty years later had validated the Sherborne horse, since shown to be an undoubted forgery.[10] The engraving was carved onto old bone of medieval age that had been taken from

240

Sherborne School's collection. Cortesi, who by all accounts was a decent enough artist, probably executed it in 1914. Its similarity to the Creswell piece undoubtedly stems from the fact that it was copied from a published image of it – a copy of Dawkins' *Early Man in Britain* in which it is figured was held in the school library. The whole thing was a prank that went too far to be stopped without several well-known scientists losing face. Although undoubtedly a great scientist and world-renowned palaeo-icthyologist, Woodward it seems was rather too credulous of discoveries outside his own field. Regardless of this, the case of Sherborne shows that Dawkins' appeal to authority was and always has been bogus – scientific standing is really no measure of judgement or credulity, people believe what they want to believe. Similarly, the 1924 discoveries of engravings at Creswell were later shown to be nothing more than the etchings of plant roots onto which willing minds had projected deliberate carvings.[11]

What is of most interest from Sollas' statement is that forty-nine years after its discovery, questions still remained over the authenticity of the Creswell rib, despite it having since passed into the anthropological literature. Dorothy Garrod did not share these doubts and firmly believed the find was genuine.[12] According to Garrod, the nature of the markings showed that had been engraved while still fresh, and she deemed it improbable that it had come from a French cave. Dawkins had won, again.

A Stir in the Derbyshire Countryside

Twenty-seven years after Dawkins' death, the April/May 1956 edition of *Derbyshire Countryside* carried an article by Geoffrey Grigson (1905-1985) entitled 'Caves, Crags and Coal Mines'. The publication was a popular county glossy that ran articles on picturesque villages, angling tips, the utility of estate cars and women's fashion, alongside advertisements for the must have gadgets of the day and local events: altogether the epitome of the 1950s English idyll, and not a vehicle to incite disharmony.

Grigson was a well-known writer, critic and naturalist, and in the spirit of the magazine his article on Creswell was designed to inform and entertain. It had originally been broadcast as a talk on the BBC's North of England Home Service. Grigson began with tales of 'Leather Breeches' the eccentric Fifth Duke of Portland who dug rooms and tunnels beneath Welbeck Abbey, of preparations made in the eighteenth century for a visit by two 'bluestockings' (elite educated ladies of the day), and of his own visit to Creswell to discover more about the mysterious 'Creswellian'. He described the history of the discoveries and the prehistory of the gorge, before finally turning his attention to the rib and the tooth. Describing them as a minor Piltdown, he confidently stated that the engraving was genuine, probably bought from a continental dealer and originally from France, and along with the canine had been planted in the cave. There was nothing new in any of this, but Grigson took the unprecedented next step, accusing either the 'Derbyshire parson or Manchester professor' of perpetrating the hoax in a quest for 'Victorian self-glory'. In closing, he lamented the poor condition of the Crags in 1955, the caves boarded up, barbed wired, and padlocked, the whole area stinking of smoke and sewage. The Victorians would have been ashamed of what the new century's custodians had allowed to happen: on the boards shuttering Mother Grundy's Parlour, some comedy genius had scribbled 'Vacant Possession. Mod. Con.'

In British law you cannot libel the dead, but this is exactly what Leslie Armstrong (1879-1958) accused Grigson of doing in a very passionate reply in the October/November issue of the same magazine. According to Armstrong, Grigson's article was false and misleading, from the stink (apparently caused by work on a sewage pipeline during 1955) to the accusations of fraud. There is nothing new in Armstrong's vitriolic attack. It is merely a reiteration of the same old arguments, appeals to authority (this time his own) and he does not help himself with a long series of factual errors. He dismissed Heath's claims as based on supposition and unscientific reasoning; the reason Heath had seen a pick mark was because such things are normal when using picks. This is certainly true, but then we have an even more difficult problem – how did a pick pass by (or through) the tooth and not destroy it or damage it in any way? Not even a scratch? Armstrong's assertion that the position of the tooth shown in Figure 7.1 is impossible is equally pure nonsense; drop a tooth down a hole, get it stuck and push with a stick, and this is the result. In fact, Armstrong's reply is so full of his predecessors' brand of class prejudice and authoritarian bluster as to be worthy of no further consideration, for whoever's wisdom he called upon, there was nobody left alive who was there when it happened.

In the same issue, Wilfred Jackson, Dawkins' protégé and successor at the Manchester Museum, wrote to refute the accusations against the parson and the professor, which he correctly points out were never made at the time (although John Plant insinuated it enough times). His assessment of the finds is measured and clear – the question over the authenticity of the rib remained unsettled, but he had been assured that the tooth was planted. In 1910 an unnamed eminent geologist had visited Jackson at the Museum and whilst there had informed him that a man from the Castleton district had confessed that he and a friend had put the tooth in as a joke, and had fully intended to expose the prank later, had things not gotten so out of control. Jackson did not reveal his source or the names of the two men, but John Tym, who ran the fossil shop, and Dawkins' old friend Rooke Pennington fit the profile. It is unknown, however, whether either man could be classed as a practical joker, or why Pennington would do such a thing to his friend. There are also no records that either man was at or near Creswell in June-July 1876.

In his response, Grigson was unrepentant. There were three motives for fraud in archaeology, he wrote, amour-propre (self-love), national pride, and jealousy. A critical reading of the evidence weighed against these motives clearly showed that only Mello and Dawkins had anything to gain, and even if they had been subject to a hoax had only themselves to blame. When the finds were doubted they replied by being 'evasive and lofty'; if they were not guilty then they were certainly foolish. It had been their duty not to bullishly maintain the authenticity of the finds, but to prove it, and they should themselves have worked to ascertain the culprits without 'hoity-toity gestures'.

Science in the Humanities
The final word in this story thus far belongs to science. In the 1950s and 1960s Kenneth Oakley of the British Museum (Natural History) was refining the use of fluorine, uranium and nitrogen as relative dating tools. These techniques work on the principal that once buried a bone or tooth will react chemically with ground water, resulting in an increase in fluorine and uranium through external uptake and a decrease in nitrogen through decay of the bones' organic protein, collagen. Bones from the same context theoretically have the same burial history and the levels of the three elements they contain should be very similar; intrusions of different ages or from different locations should therefore be detectable on the basis of different signals. Oakley's most famous success with these techniques was in exposing Piltdown man as a hoax, with a series of tests beginning in 1948.[13]

In the early 1960s Oakley[14] applied these tests to the Creswell *Machairodus* tooth, which he compared with samples from Europe and Britain (Table 10.1). Oakley was able to demonstrate that the tooth was not from two well-known Early Pleistocene localities in Italy and France, as some unnamed 'authorities' had been arguing (although without reference to which 'authorities' these were or why they suspected they had come from these particular caves this strikes me as something of a straw man: build him up and knock him down). Nor had they come from Kent's Cavern or Doveholes,

Site	Nitrogen (%)	Fluorine (%)	Uranium (ppm)
Val d'Arno, Italy	0.2	1.6	35
Mt Perrier, France	nil	1.9	30
Doveholes, Derbyshire	nil	2.5	68
Kent's Cavern, Devon	1.2	<0.01	5
Creswell Crags, Derbyshire	2.1	0.2	<1

Table 10.1: Fluorine, nitrogen and uranium content of Homotherium teeth from Creswell Crags and other European sites (after Oakley 1963).

Buxton. The latter had not been discovered until 1902, but Oakley included it on the premise that Palaeolithic peoples may have discovered the fossil there and introduced it to Creswell as a treasured object. This is a plausible supposition, as Oakley explains using the example of the Grotte du Trilobite, France where humans had deposited an exotic Silurian trilobite fossil, but the subtext here must be that a Victorian fossil hunter might also have been exploiting the Doveholes deposits without announcing them, probably for reasons of profit. But nonetheless, the Creswell tooth was not from Doveholes.

In all, the chemical signature of the Creswell tooth, with high nitrogen, and negligible fluorine and uranium 'agreed' with that of other local Upper Pleistocene mammals. This strongly implies that the *Machairodus* survived into the Late Pleistocene and was not exclusively a Pliocene or Early Pleistocene animal; a discovery that has since been supported by specimens from the floor of the North Sea dated to 28,000 years BP.[15] Oakley never revealed which particular materials the chemistry of the tooth agreed with, but it is worth noting that between 1963 and 1980 Oakley added an adverb so that the material now 'closely' agreed, even though no new tests had been conducted. 'If it were to be maintained that the Creswell canine had been fraudulently planted in the cave', Oakley concluded, 'its composition could only be accounted for by supposing that it had been obtained from some other similar cave deposit elsewhere'.[16]

Fifty years after the original work, these tests need repeating to re-assess their cogency. In the 1970s Oakley conducted similar work on the Sherborne horse, comparing its chemical signatures with that of known Pleistocene horse from Gough's Cave, Cheddar Gorge. The results implied that it was of similar age, and had derived from a similar limestone environment. More recent work has shown the bone to be of seventh-century AD date, the engraving probably no older than 1914.[17] The case needs to be retried. New key pieces of evidence can now be brought forwards, uncalled witnesses must be examined, and a new and better set of techniques exist to those used all those years ago.

The Silence of Richard Tiddeman

In the furore that followed the 1879 BAAS meeting, one key witness was never called: Richard Tiddeman.

It will be recalled that Thomas Heath never openly questioned the validity of the engraved rib because he was not present on the day of its discovery; it was John Plant who insinuated Mello and/or Dawkins was guilty. But as we have seen there were three accounts of its provenance: Mello's published version that it came from Chamber F, Dawkins' notebook record that it came from Chamber D; Heath's account that Mello had told him it came from Church Hole. In the first account, Richard Tiddeman was supposed to have immediately recognised it as an engraving of a horse. So, given the public nature of all that followed, it is intriguing that Richard Tiddeman did not speak out in support of Dawkins and Mello's version of events. If he had done, surely any doubts surrounding the rib would have been forever extinguished.

While Tiddeman was not a member of the Manchester Geological Society, he was a Fellow of the Geological Society of London, and his role in the BGS involved mapping North Lancashire, West Yorkshire and Westmoreland. He was therefore well connected in both local and national geological circles. It is inconceivable that he would not have been aware of the controversy. His name had been associated with the discovery of the rib since Mello and Dawkins' 1877 publication. Typically Dawkins also used the occasion of that paper's reading at the Geological Society to dismiss Tiddeman's opinions on the relative ages of cold versus warm animals at Victoria Cave. Shortly after that, Tiddeman had been craftily out-manoeuvred by Hughes and Dawkins during the RAI Conference of 22 May 1877, yet letters in Buxton Museum show the two men had managed to retain a cordial relationship until at least until May 30 1877, when they exchanged opinions on the significance of reindeer on dating sediments.[18] After this, the situation appears to have become more heated, Dawkins using guerrilla tactics designed to undermine Tiddeman's credibility. Tiddeman also bore the brunt of Dawkins' diatribe during the presentation of the Mother Grundy's Parlour paper on June 11 1879, which was unnecessarily used as a vehicle to attack the work at Victoria Cave. By 1880 there was no love lost between Dawkins and Tiddeman.

Professor Dawkins' Notebook

The superficial nature of Dawkins' note keeping has been mentioned on many occasions. A few relevant entries have already been drawn upon to assist the narrative, but as it was the intention of the earlier chapters to allow the events surrounding the Creswell controversy to unfold as they happened, the entire notebook – the 'documentary evidence' on which Dawkins placed so much weight – has not yet been interrogated in much detail. It is now necessary to redress this as the notebook contains a number of anomalies relevant to making an informed judgement on what actually happened in the cave between 29 June and 3 July 1876.

However many times he may have threatened to bring it forth, Dawkins never actually produced his notebook at any point in the debate. If he had done, the audience may have been shocked. Dawkins recorded the 1876 excavation in a soft bound flip-top notebook measuring 4x6 inches, which he had already used throughout the year to record other sites he excavated or visited, including an earlier trip to Creswell on 27 April with Mello and Heath.[19] The pages are unnumbered but it is worth noting that the entire record of the 1876 Creswell season (19 June – 21 July) runs to twenty-six pages. Three pages are financial statements, consisting of a list of workmen and their remuneration, plus the cost of petty sundries such as calico bags and candles. Two others are journey plans between Manchester to Creswell. Only 644 words pertain to the excavation, fewer than Dawkins' opening gambit during the May 1880 debate. If Dawkins had spent as long recording his excavations as he did plotting the fall of his opponents, then the whole story may have been quite different.

The critical issue at stake here is what Dawkins recorded in his notebooks for the period 29 June to 3 July (Plates 21 & 22). As noted in Chapter 5, the entry for 29 June is devoid of any detail at all and even manages to confuse the Chamber in which the rib was found (citing D, Mello claimed it was F) as can be seen in a reproduction of the page in Plate 10.

The next two entries are both dated 30 June, although the date on the first has been amended and originally read 29 June. This contains a list of measurements for a plan of Robin Hood Cave, with distances from points A-F seen on Figure 5.1 to points within the cave interior. The second is a crude plan and description of the sequence in Church Hole. Neither of these is controversial.

Flipping the page, on 1 July, Dawkins recorded the geology of Chamber F in Robin Hood Cave:

'Surf[ace] soil + stones +R.R. Dent – 4 inches
Cave earth red + stone + fl[int] + quartzite = 3 feet
Cave earth = st[one] frag[ments] decalc[ified] + decomp[osed] 8 inches

――――
Redd. Cave earth?
Quartzite, bones etc. '

Below this in the notebook is another entry, the figure 30 appearing top centre, which reports:

'Robin Hood
Work carr[ied] on in F
Cut bones
5 feet from surface
ironstone implement

――――――
The top is composed
of dark surface soil cont. Black Roman
pottery, flint strike-a-light,
B.[os] l.[ongiforns], capra, hog etc.
about 4 inches thick in F'

These entries make it clear that at least 3 ft of sediment was removed from Chamber F during Heath's absence, but makes no mention of a stalagmite. If Heath or any other discussant had ever asked Dawkins actually to produce the evidence, the truth is he would not have been able to do so. Dawkins was clearly confused or lying about both the presence of a stalagmite, and his ability to prove it was there; Heath had called his bluff in challenging him to go to Creswell and point out where the stalagmite met the wall, which is why Dawkins had refused.

The next entry is at the bottom of the same page and is dated 3 July, (Plate 21) three days later. It reads:

'Robin Hood 3 July
Fine worked flint

Machairodus latidens at end
of cave in cave earth at left side
Quartzite, fl.[int] flakes'

There is no mention of a stalagmite, but what makes this entry odd is that it occurs completely out of sequence. Turning to the next page, the 'subsequent' entry is a continuation of the work undertaken on 1 July followed by a note on 2 July (a Sunday), the date of which has been altered from 3 July. The rest of the notebook runs in date order from the 4 July. Not only is it out of sequence, but the entry for 3 July is also in a darker pencil than all the other records, as is the amended 2/3 on the 2 July entry and the addition of Church Hole to the record for 1 July (the name having been inserted between two contiguous lines). It is my belief that these critical parts of this key witness have been tampered with, Dawkins entering the discovery after the fact when it became apparent that he might have to produce his notebooks. He still neglected to mention a stalagmite.

Two other anomalies regarding Dawkins' pocket diaries need to be noted. As mentioned in Chapter Five, the diary for the critical year of 1876 is missing from the archive, the only absentee in the whole run. This might plausibly be a coincidence were it not for the second irregularity: the pages for November and December 1879, just as Heath began his campaign, have been torn from the diary (Plate 24). I suspect that Dawkins' diaries, like his archive, have been expurgated.

Three Men in a Cavern
There are basically four ways of interpreting the historical evidence:

1) That both objects were found in the cave exactly where described, and that Heath and Plant were simply making trouble for Dawkins because of personal vendettas against him.
There are a number of problems with this proposition, not least the fact that Dawkins' notebooks – his treasured documentary evidence – had been tampered with in the manner described above, and that Richard Tiddeman failed to speak up in support. What is one to read into his silence? Did Tiddeman know that both Mello and Dawkins were lying, but being already embroiled in a debate on the divisions of the ice age mammals, elected to remain silent, lest he was accused of ulterior motives? Or did he know that their account was true, but had no desire to come out in support of his confrontational colleague? Another possibility is discussed below.

I also see little reason to doubt the testimony of Thomas Heath, who was clearly a very meticulous worker, and on whose behalf at least two independent witnesses spoke out. A man from humble beginnings, he had risen to a position of some standing. He obviously wanted to have his moment to shine, and to lay claim to the glories coming out of Creswell, and he may have been so furious that he had not been the one to find the two prize specimens that spite caused him to cast doubt over them. He certainly had little liking for Dawkins, but was the personal cost involved in his crusade, having his name dragged though the mud of the Victorian media, really worth it? There are certainly points in the affair where Heath might be suspected of having been mentally ill, but was this the cause or the effect of the long running and nasty controversy?

2) That one or both objects were planted in the cave by Dawkins and/or Mello, for reasons of personal glory and the keen desire to find the British equivalent of Laugerie Basse or Le Madeleine.
Contrary to Mark Stirrup's 1880 opinion, that acquiring a genuine tooth and engraving was an awful lot of trouble to go to just to perpetrate a hoax, Dawkins certainly had the contacts to have acquired these objects. His world tour of 1875 had taken him to France, Italy, and the USA, countries where these items had either been found, or where they resided in museums. Mello likewise was a keen Francophile, a member of at least one European Society and a frequent continental traveller.

Both had the means and the opportunity, but did either really have a motive? Mello was a parish Rector and geology was a hobby, one among many. When the controversy broke, he was very backwards in coming forwards, and his only motive for speaking out appears to have been as peacemaker, to maintain his priority over the site and to limit damage to his reputation. He ultimately disagreed with Heath's version of events, but his presence at the site was so infrequent that he was really unqualified to pass judgement on anything other than the day he found the rib, and then accounts are muddled.

Dawkins would appear to have even less of a motive. He was an FRS, FGS, FSA and University Professor. His reputation as an international scholar was already sealed and he had no obvious reasons to put his whole career in jeopardy by planting evidence. He was a seasoned field campaigner, with several excavations under his belt or ongoing, although he was somewhat careless in his recording and relied too much on memory. One might maintain that he protested too much, in an effort to hide the truth, but the fact that he was still willing to make the same arguments 50 years later, and discuss it earnestly with his good friend Sir Arthur Smith Woodward, makes me believe otherwise. Dawkins firmly believed that the objects came from Creswell.

3) That one or both objects were planted in the cave by an unknown third-party, perhaps as a joke that went too far, perhaps as something more sinister.

There is practically no way of fully assessing the validity of this proposition at present. Although it is clearly the solution favoured by Heath, mostly because he had no desire to libel Mello or Dawkins by accusing them directly, nobody ever claimed personal responsibility at the time and no letters of confession were found later. We have already seen that Dawkins gave very short shrift to the Mullins/Sollas claim that the engraved rib had been introduced as a prank, damning it twice in the literature. The only other reason we have for suspecting trickery is the 1956 published letter in which Jackson stated that forty-six years earlier an eminent geologist had told him that two men from Castleton claimed to have planted the tooth. If this is true then Tym and Pennington are possible suspects, with the caveats expressed above, but really both Jackson's and Sollas/Mullins' testimonies count for little more than gossip at three removes – 'a friend of a friend told me that…' As both Jackson and Mullins chose not to reveal the names of their sources or the supposed perpetrators, we cannot be sure how or when the original information may have been passed, or even if the supposed culprits would have been alive to have met the claimed recipient of the information. The two accounts are probably nothing more than bluster: either somebody claiming to be party to secret information to laud themselves and get one over on Dawkins, or somebody claiming to have perpetrated a great hoax, for the same reasons. In the case of Jackson one wonders if he ever discussed these doubts with his friend and mentor directly, or whether he demurred to save an old man's feelings or prevent unnecessary tensions.

Oakley's fluorine data might currently refute this suggestion for the tooth, but it certainly needs reanalysing, as his later assessment of the Sherborne horse gave an erroneous result.

4) That both objects genuinely came from the Creswell Caves, but were found out of archaeological context. Mello and/or Dawkins later conspired to construct one.

What if the engraved rib really had have been found in a day bag, amongst bits and pieces of later material, and the tooth among straw and disturbed soil? While still interesting finds, there would have been persistent doubts over their age, their origin and their value. Finds of such importance need a firm provenance. Dawkins knew this more than anybody despite the smokescreen he cast around the fact, including the notebooks and the 25 May address. So, did Dawkins and/or Mello (or conceivably an unknown third-party) conspire to concoct a firm context for these spectacular, but insecurely provenanced, finds? I offer this as my preferred interpretation, and the one that helps explain how of the thousands of objects amassed during the Robin Hood Cave excavation, these two were found in situ by a very occasional visitor and a man who spent most of the season working a different cave.

If both objects were genuinely unprovenanced finds from Creswell, then the only guilt that potentially can be laid at the feet of Dawkins and Mello is in tricking the world into believing they came from a specific context. It is easy to imagine the plots: having pulled exceptional finds from a calico sack or the floor of the cave, Mello and/or Dawkins hid them for a few days before taking Heath's short absence as an opportunity to return them to the ground and fabricate a secure context, all achieved away from prying eyes. Yet, to be fully convincing they needed unimpeachable witnesses who could vouch for the veracity of the discoveries.

Tiddeman was apparently present at the finding of the rib. We know very little about the exact circumstances of the find, only that Mello noticed it was marked, and Tiddeman recognised it as a horse. Tiddeman never denied nor confirmed this. By 1880 Tiddeman had come to resent Dawkins, who had repeatedly and consistently worked to undermine the credibility of his results from Settle, and who had done great damage to his reputation as a consequence. Knowing what he had come to know about Dawkins, how he manipulated the truth for his own ends, Tiddeman might also have started to nurse doubts about what he had actually witnessed. Reflecting on that day in the light of subsequent events did he begin to suspect that the whole thing had been staged for his benefit, his role just a patsy in a larger game, with Mello conveniently 'spotting' some markings he already knew were there and passing it to Tiddeman for confirmation and identification? These seem like very good reasons not to speak out. If the rib had originally come from Church Hole, as Heath had claimed, then very few were ever fully complicit in that deceit.

An almost identical deception can be imagined for the tooth, but here Heath was chosen as a witness, to avert any suspicions he might harbour of Dawkins' honesty. While Heath was safely out of the way, Mello and Dawkins arranged for the tooth to be inserted a short distance behind the working face. When all the superintendents were back on site, Dawkins orchestrated a chat inside the cave, but all the time he was closely monitoring the work to ensure that it was he who would discover the find and Heath who would bear witness. Under such circumstances, how could Heath possibly have any doubts? Unfortunately for Dawkins, whoever had reinterred it had bungled the job, leaving a gaping pick/bar mark and the tooth embedded halfway down. If this is really what happened, then the plan went spectacularly wrong, and cast more doubt over the tooth than if Dawkins had just picked it up off the floor and suggested it came from somewhere on the face. Here too probably lies the reason why Dawkins insisted that a stalagmite floor had overlain the cave earth in Chamber F, all part of a post-excavation revision to make stratigraphic integrity of the tooth appear beyond doubt.

If this is the case, then it is still uncertain whether Mello and Dawkins colluded, whether only one of them was responsible (in which case Mello's absence on the 3 July rules him out), or whether both men acted independently, each having found a different stray object.

All the witnesses are long gone, but the objects remain, and if we are to ever resolve the mystery it is the testimony contained in their chemistry to which we must turn, using twenty-first century science to unlock their history [20]. The final chapter in the case of Creswell Crags versus Professor William Boyd Dawkins may yet to be written.

Notes

Chapter 1

1 Sommers 2003.

2 Gamble and Kruszynski 2009.

3 See Grayson 1983 and Van Riper 1993 for excellent detailed accounts of the establishment of human antiquity. Here I give a potted summary only.

4 Buckland 1823.

5 Jacobi and Higham 2008.

6 See Sommers 2007 for a full treatment of the 'afterlife of the Red Lady'.

7 Grayson 1983; Van Riper 1993.

8 White and Pettitt 2009.

9 Godwin-Austen, cited in Pengelly 1868.

10 Falconer, letter to Geological Society published in Prestwich 1873.

11 Pengelly 1873; Prestwich 1873.

12 Grayson 1983.

13 Lartet and Christy 1875.

Chapter 2

1 Boyd was his second, but preferred, Christian name and not a double-barrelled surname as often assumed.

2 Montgomeryshire Records MR/PR/94.

3 Lewis 1833.

4 1841 Census of England and Wales HO 107/1442/

5 Jones 1981.

6 Lewis 1849.

7 Lewis 1849.

8 Lewis 1833; Lewis 1849.

9 Gardner 1929.

10 Mike Bishop, personal communication, January 2015.

11 Wood 1987; Mike Bishop Notebooks, Buxton Museum.

12 Ashworth 1895.

13 Rowbotham 1901, 49.

14 Rowbotham 1901, 48.

15 'Old Rossallians. Dr Dawkins' Ferocious Schooldays'. *Manchester Guardian* Dec 16 1908.

16 Jackson 1966.

17 Foster 1888.

18 John Phillips (1800-1874) was born in Marden, Wiltshire (Morrell 2004, 2005). Orphaned at the age of seven he was raised by his uncle William Smith (1769-1839) - the 'Father of English Geology' - whom he accompanied on many surveying projects

from an early age. In 1825 he was appointed Keeper of Geology at the Yorkshire Museum, where was able to establish himself as a geologist and lecturer in his own right. In 1834 he was elected FRS and took up the Chair of Geology at King's College London. From 1836-1849 he served as part-time palaeontologist to the Geological Survey, and from 1843-45 held the Chair of Geology and Mineralogy at Trinity College, Dublin. Phillips was appointed as deputy reader in geology at Oxford in 1853, reader in 1856 and professor in 1860. His published works include: *The Geology of the Yorkshire Coast* (1829); *A Treatise on Geology* (two volumes, 1837-39); *Palaeozoic Fossils of Cornwall, Devon and West Somerset* (1841); *Memoirs of William Smith* (1844), *Manual of Geology: Practical and Theoretical* (1855) and the *Geology of Oxford and the Valley of the Thames* (1871). He was awarded the Wollaston medal of the Geological Society of London in 1845. He died on 24 April 1874.

19 George Rollaston (1829-1881) studied Classics at Pembroke College, Oxford (BA, 1st Class, 1850) before switching his attention to medicine, earning his B.Med at St Bartholomew's Hospital London in 1854. He served as a physician during the Crimean War. In 1857 he was elected physician to the Radcliffe Infirmary, Oxford and Lee's Reader in Anatomy, where he successfully fought to get biology and chemistry added to the curriculum, and for the building of the University Museum. In 1860 he was elected as the first Linacre Professor of Anatomy and Physiology. Under Rolleston's influence his department also taught zoology, comparative anatomy, anthropology and archaeology. His key published work include *Forms of Animal Life* (1870) and the posthumous collection *Scientific Papers and Addresses* (1884). He was elected a fellow of the Royal College of Physicians in 1859 and FRS in 1862.

20 Gordon 1894, 56.

21 Morrell 2005.

22 Morrell 2005, 252.

23 Blore 1920.

24 Stephen 1901.

25 E.g., Freeman to Dawkins 7 January 1867; Freeman to Dawkins 26 December 1866. Jesus College Oxford, Freeman MSS 1866-1880.

26 Green to MM April 1861, in Stephen 1901, 76.

27 Anon 1908.

28 *The Druid*, Volume 1, preface.

29 Green to Dawkins 22 September 1862. Jesus College, Oxford, Green-Dawkins MSS.

30 Oxford University 1888, 132; Angela Burdett-Coutts had high-profile connections in geology, including Sir Charles Lyell and Hugh Falconer, and was friends with William Pengelly of Torquay, where she had a sea-side retreat, see http://blogs.royalsociety.org/history-of-science/2014/04/10/burdett-coutts/ (accessed 23 August 2015)

31 Manchester Museum Dawkins Archive PDW/3/1.

32 Dawkins 1864; Dawkins and Sanford 1866-1872.

33 Dawkins 1862, 116.

34 Dawkins 1874a.

35 Stephen 1901, 22.

36 Buxton Museum Dawkins Archive DERBS 70630/2.

37 Dawkins 1862.

NOTES

38 Dawkins 1862; Dawkins 1874a.

39 Dawkins 1862.

40 Keith 1914.

41 Dawkins 1862, 117.

42 Dawkins 1874a, 438.

43 Dawkins 1862, 117.

44 Dawkins 1874a, 438.

45 Buxton Museum Dawkins Archive DERBS 70630/2.

46 Bridgewater B/M/D Register 5C/291.

47 Caroline Lam, Geological Society personal communication via email, 6 October 2014.

48 Geological Society GLS/F/1/6, no 1989.

49 Green to Dawkins 15 January 1862, cited in Stephen 1901, 95.

50 Anon 1887.

51 Falconer to Dawkins 9 December 1861, Buxton Museum Dawkins Archive DERBS 70006/1.

52 Green to Dawkins 24 July 1862, cited in Stephen 1901, 96.

53 *The Daily News*, 30 January 1862.

54 British Geological Survey: GSM/1/8, 211.

55 Dawkins 1863a.

56 James Parker, printer, publisher and architect was the son of Henry John Parker, Keeper of the Ashmolean Museum from 1870-1884 - Alison Roberts, Ashmolean Museum, personal communication, May 2015.

57 Henry Catt was a businessman, collector and geologist. He changed his name to Willett in 1863 as a condition of his mother's will (http://brightonmuseums.org.uk/discover/2011/06/10/personality-of-the-month-henry-willett-1823-1905/), last accessed 23 August 2015.

58 Dawkins 1874a, 305.

59 Green to Dawkins 26 August 1862. Jesus College, Oxford, Green-Dawkins MSS.

60 Kenyon 1983, 159.

61 Freeman to Dawkins 7 & 14 July 1867, cited in Stephens 1895, Vol. 1, 388.

62 The original Wookey Hole notebooks, held in Wells and Mendip Museum, record daily work, but only two dates Thursday 1st May and Monday 5th May. Balch's annotations on the manuscript show that he assumed the year to be 1860, but it can only be 1863. The dates corresponds with another notebook in Buxton Museum Dawkins Archive which contains Dawkins notes on Catt's diagrams, with measurements of that relate to progress through Chambers B and D on Figure 2.2.

63 Dawkins 1863a.

64 Dawkins 1863a.

65 Owen 1846.

66 Owen 1846; Dawkins 1863a.

67 Dawkins 1874a.

68 Dawkins 1862.

69 Dawkins 1863b.

70 We now know that both these sites are some 400,000 years older than Wookey Hole.

71 Dawkins 1863b, 216-217.

72 http://www.bgs.ac.uk/discoveringGeology/geologyOfBritain/archives/pioneers/ pioneers. cfc?method=viewRecord&personId=193, last accessed 23 August 2015.

73 Flett 1937.

74 Buxton Museum Dawkins Archive: handwritten transcript, unregistered.

75 Buxton Museum Dawkins Archive DERBS 71803.

76 Green to Dawkins 1 September 1862, cited in Stephen 1901, 100.

77 See Kirkaldy 1975 for a brief biography of each of these men.

78 Kirkaldy 1975.

79 Flett 1937, 63; Kirkaldy 1975.

80 Topley 1875.

81 A.H.Green to T. McKenny Hughes 26 June 1872, Sedgwick Museum of Earth Sciences, University of Cambridge, Hughes Papers - cited in O'Connor 2005.

82 S .V. Wood Jr to T. McKenny Hughes 3 February 1873, Cambridge University Library MS 9557/2 G/26, cited in O'Connor 2005.

83 Dawkins 1864b.

84 Anon 1906.

85 Flett 1937.

86 Bristow 1864.

87 Murchison to Dawkins 20 December 1864, Buxton Museum Dawkins Archive DERBS 70007.

88 S V. Wood Jr to T. McKenny Hughes 3 February 1873, Cambridge University Library MS 9557/2 G/26, cited in O'Connor 2005.

89 Buxton Museum Dawkins Archive DERBS 70934-70940.

90 Walford 1884.

91 Sainty 1975.

92 Census of England and Wales 1851 HO107/1468/817/12; Census of England and Wales 1861, RG9/778/67/10.

93 *The London Illustrated News* 8 October 1864.

94 W.B. Dawkins, *The Watford Observer* 8 October 1864.

95 Anon 1864.

96 Manchester Museum Dawkins Archive PDW/1/2.

97 Powell 1978.

98 Andrew Morrison, BGS Archivist, personal communication via email 21 May 2014.

99 Buxton Museum Dawkins Archive DERBS 70590/1.

100 Dawkins 1865a.

101 Dawkins 1863c; Dawkins 1865; Dawkins 1867a; Dawkins 1868a.

102 Health Warning: Do not read these papers. Unless you are a specialist on extinct rhino, they are terminal. You have been warned.

103 Reports on paper on the dentition of *Rhinoceros leptorhinus*. The Royal Society RR6.6.94-95.

104 Dawkins 1866a.

105 Dawkins 1864a; Dawkins and Sanford 1866-72.

106 The legend of the dog is an apocryphal tale told in most areas of England where caves are found. Its basic form tells of a dog that disappears into a cave only to reappear several days or weeks later in another cave miles away from the first. In this specific

case the dog went from Great Goatchurch Cavern to Wookey Hole. Other variants include a man with bagpipes and a haunch of mutton - Dawkins 1864a.

107 Dawkins 1865b.

108 Dawkins 1867b; Dawkins 1866b.

109 Owen to Dawkins 2 & 9 September 1865, Buxton Museum Dawkins Archive DERBS 70009 & 70011.

110 Reports on a paper on *Ovibos Moschatus*. Royal Society RR6.6.96-99.

111 Dawkins 1872a.

112 Letters from WBD to G.G.Stokes at the Royal Society dated 22 March 1868,1 April 1868 and 12 December 1868. Royal Society MC.8.158, MC.8.162, MC.8.282.

113 Lubbock 1865.

114 Dawkins 1866c.

115 Tragically, the first issue didn't include a free plastic mammoth or build-your-own-hippopotamus, plastic not being properly synthesized until about 1907, and there were years between issues.

116 Lyell 1863, although the idea owes much to Lartet, who communicated his ideas of a northern fauna 'pushed' southwards and a southern fauna 'projected' north to the French Academy in 1858, see Falconer in Prestwich 1873.

117 Volume 1: Dawkins and Sanford 1866-1872; Volume 2: Reynolds 1902-1912; Volume 3.1. Reynolds 1922; Volume 3.3. Reynolds 1929; Volume 3.4 Reynolds 1933; Volume 3.5 Dawkins 1872; Volume 3.6 Reynolds 1939; Treatise Part A Dawkins 1878a.

118 Bevington 1941.

119 Freeman to Dawkins 8 December 1866, Jesus College Oxford Freeman MSS 1866-1880.

120 Dawkins to Willett 21 May 1867, Buxton Museum Dawkins Archive DERBS 70013.

121 Dawkins 1868a-e.

122 For example, from Archaeology: Lubbock, Evans and Franks; Ethnography: Crawford and Tylor; Anthropology: Hunt; Geology: Lyell; Biological sciences: Busk, Hooker and Huxley.

123 Dawkins 1868f-h.

124 Dawkins 1868i & j.

125 Pengelly 1884.

126 Pengelly 1870.

127 Pengelly to Lyell 1 October 1866, cited in H. Pengelly 1897, 174.

128 See Dawkins 1910.

129 Dawkins to Pengelly 8 September 1868, cited in H. Pengelly 1897, 189.

130 Pengelly to Lyell 11 November 1868, cited in H. Pengelly 1897, 190.

131 Pengelly to Dawkins 21 September 1868, cited in H. Pengelly 1897 189.

132 Dawkins to Pengelly 2 November 1868, cited in H. Pengelly 1897, 190.

133 Pengelly 1870.

134 Dawkins 1869, 206.

135 Jackson 1966.

136 Boylan 1998.

137 Dawkins 1867c.

138 Wood to Harmer 11 January 1867: BGS: GSM1/542/51.

139 Whitaker 1889.

140 Wood to Harmer 11 January 1867: BGS: GSM1/542/51.

141 O'Conner 2007, 41.

142 Wood 1867; Wood 1868a & b.

143 Manchester Museum Dawkins Archive PDW/1/4.

144 Translation: 'point before which', i.e. the latest point in time an event could have occurred

145 Dawkins 1867c & d.

146 Wood 1867, 416.

147 Dawkins 1867c.

148 Wood 1868a.

Chapter 3

1 Thompson 1886; Merriman 2013.

2 Thompson 1886

3 ibid

4 Since their foundations the two Societies' collections had been looked after by various distinguished curators, including the naturalist and malacologist Captain Thomas Brown (1775-1862), who oversaw the MNHS collections for 24 years (1838-1862), and Edward W. Binney (1812-1881), a founder member of the MGS.

5 Darbishire to Dawkins 3 July 1868, Buxton Museum Dawkins Archive.

6 Manchester Museum Dawkins Archive PDW 1/5.

7 Dawkins to Darbishire 6 September 1868, Buxton Museum Dawkins Archive DERBS 70024.

8 Thompson 1886.

9 Thompson 1886, 328ff.

10 Thompson 1886.

11 Thompson 1886, 387.

12 Thompson 1886, 416-17.

13 Jackson 1966.

14 Jackson 1966.

15 Thompson 1886.

16 Thompson 1886.

17 Owens College Council Resolution 16 October 1874, Buxton Museum Dawkins Archive unnumbered; J.W. Greenward to Dawkins 16 October 1874, Buxton Museum Dawkins Archive DERBS 70054; J Nicholson to Dawkins 16 October 1874 Buxton Museum Dawkins Archive DERBS 70053.

18 Thompson 1886.

19 Thompson 1886, 509.

20 *Pall Mall Gazette* 20 November 1869.

21 Thompson 1886.

22 Boylan 1998.

23 *Manchester Courier* 9 February 1911.

24 Dawkins 1869b; Dawkins 1871a.

25 Dawkins 1868b; Dawkins 1870a &b; Dawkins 1871b.

26 Dawkins 1871b.

27 Dawkins 1871b, 119.

28 Dawkins 1871b, 120.

29 Dawkins 1871b, 108-110.

30 Stephen 1901, 292.

31 Green to Dawkins 3 July 1860, Stephen 1901, 43-45.

32 Jackson 1966; Buxton Archive Dawkins Archive DERBS 71809, DERBS 71815, 2772/F176 plus unnumbered.

33 *The Manchester Guardian* 16 January 1929.

34 Jackson 1966, Buxton Museum Dawkins Archive DERBS 71812.

35 *Pall Mall Gazette* 18 November 1869.

36 ASW 1931.

37 Anon 1906.

38 O'Connor 2005.

39 Anon 1906.

40 O'Connor 2005, 454.

41 Anon 1901.

42 H.B.Woodward 1897.

43 J.W.G 1891.

44 Davison 1900.

45 Anon 1896.

46 Anon 1906.

47 Anon 1878.

48 *Pall Mall Gazette*, 3 February 1873.

49 Science Gossip, *The Athenaeum* 2363, 185 & 2364, 216.

50 Available from Durham Research Online at http://dro.dur.ac.uk/3780/

51 Dawkins 1873a.

52 Ingleby to Luard 4 February 1873, Cambridge University library CUR 39.17.2, 130, cited in O'Connor 2005, 457.

53 Ibid.

54 Morrell 2005.

55 Rütimeyer to Dawkins 12 May 1874, Buxton Museum Dawkins Archive DERBS 70051.

56 G Prestwich 1899.

57 Darbishire to Dawkins 31 October 1870, Buxton Museum Dawkins Archive DERBS 70043.

58 Dawkins 1870c & d.

59 http://www.darwinproject.ac.uk/ using the search string 'Dawkins'.

60 Dawkins to Darwin 27 August 1867, http://www.darwinproject.ac.uk/

61 Dawkins 1870c & d.

62 Lucas 2007.

63 Dawkins 1870c, 34.

64 Dawkins 1870c, d; Busk 1870.

65 Lucas 2007 328.

66 Dawkins 1871c; Dawkins 1872b; Dawkins 1874a, 156.

67 Cris Ebbs, 2012, Caves of North Wales, an information resource at https://sites. google.com/site/cavesofnortheastwales/06-archaeological-caves-at-llandegla, recovered 17 December 2014.

68 Dawkins 1874a .

69 Walker and Hulse 2012.

70 Enniskillen to Dawkins 17 February 1865, Buxton Museum Dawkins Archive DERBS 70008.

71 Manchester Museum Dawkins Archive PDW/1/5-13.

72 Dawkins 1874a; Walker and Hulse 2012.

73 Pontnewydd has been examined on and off since the early 1870s, the most recent work being that conducted by Stephen Aldhouse-Green between 1978-1996 (Aldhouse-Green 1995, Aldhouse-Green et al 2012). The cave preserves a fragmentary record of infilling and erosion spanning some 250 years, with the evidence of human presence dating to the earlier phases, corresponding with Marine Isotope Stage 7. It has yielded over 1000 artefacts, including hand-axes, scrapers, and cores and flakes representing the use of the Levallois technique. The mammalian fauna from the cave contains a mixture of open/closed and warm/cold adapted species which today we accept as representing different cold and warm sub stages of the Pleistocene but which Dawkins took as evidence in support of his seasonal migration theory. Twenty-three human teeth belonging to between 4-7 Neanderthal individuals have also been found. The archaeology is believed to have originated outside the cave, and been transported into the cave by debris flow.

74 Stanley 1833.

75 Dawkins 1874a, 286-287.

76 Hughes and Thomas 1874 .

77 Currant 1984; Walker and Hulse 2012.

78 Abbott to Smith Woodward 11 February 1903, cited in O'Connor and White 2004, 37. This might be true enough – material can still be found in the Victorian spoil at Creswell today - but as discussed in Chapter 9, Abbott was a bombastic and tactless man, traits clearly in evidence in this instance of 'harsh words' written to Dawkins' friend and ex-pupil, Sir Arthur Woodward. See also Chapter 5.

79 Hughes and Thomas 1874, 387.

80 Dawkins 1871d, Dawkins and Sanford 1866-72.

81 Dawkins 1872c; Dawkins 1874a.

82 Dawkins 1874a; Tiddeman 1873a.

83 Museum of North Craven Life at the Folly "Exhibition 2012: Victoria Cave Revisited." Retrieved 12 January 2015, from http://www.ncbpt.org.uk/folly/exhibitions/ exhibitions_2012/

84 Interestingly, Horner's discovery involved the ubiquitous lost dog. Where would the history of archaeology be without our hapless canine companions?

85 e.g. Roach and Jackson 1848.

86 Dawkins 1870e.

87 Birkbeck, 1869, cited in Lord et al 2012.

88 Pengelly 1871.

89 Mcfarlane and Lundberg 2005.

NOTES

90 Tiddeman 1875a.

91 Tiddeman 1875a; Tom Lord, personal communication, February 2015.

92 Tom Lord, personal communication, February 2015.

93 Dawkins 1870e, Dawkins 1872c, Dawkins 1874a.

94 The biserial bone harpoon is a classic Magdalenian form that was radiocarbon dated in 1992 to about 13,600 years ago (Hedges et al 1992, Murphy and Lord 2003). Dawkins failed to notice this, even when illustrating almost identical forms from La Madeleine and the Gorge d'Enfer, (Dawkins 1874a, 343).

95 Tom Lord, personal communication, 19 January 2015.

96 Tom Lord, personal communication, 19 January 2015.

97 Tiddeman 1872; Tiddeman 1873a; Dawkins and Tiddeman 1873.

98 Tiddeman 1873a.

99 Dawkins and Tiddeman 1873.

100 Tom Lord, personal communication, 13 January 2015.

101 Tiddeman 1873b; Tiddeman 1875b; Busk 1874.

102 Dawkins 1874b.

103 Lord et al 2012.

104 Dawkins 1871e, 110.

105 Dawkins 1871fe; Dawkins 1874c.

106 Pennington 1877.

107 Plant 1874.

108 Dawkins in Plant 1874, 127.

109 'University Intelligence', *The Daily News* 13 July 1866; *The Morning Post* 18 November 1868.

110 Hancock et al 1976, *Huddersfield Daily Chronicle* 29 September 1873.

111 *Lancaster Gazette*, 17 May 1882.

112 Hancock et al 1976.

113 Manchester Museum Dawkins Archive PDW/1/12.

114 Hancock et al 1876.

115 Pennington 1875a; Pennington 1875b; Pennington 1877.

116 Pennington 1875a & b.

117 Pennington 1875a.

118 Pennington 1877, 78.

119 Pennington & Dawkins 1877.

120 Dawkins 1875a.

121 Pennington & Dawkins 1877; Pennington 1877.

122 Dawkins 1875b.

123 Plant 1876a.

124 Dawkins 1876a.

125 As we shall see in later chapters, this comment is itself biserially barbed.

126 Heath 1882, 168-9.

127 Rooke Pennington, Letters to the Editor of the *Manchester City News* 8 November 1879 & 17 January 1880.

128 e.g. Dawkins 1871g, Dawkins 1872d-f.

129 King 1864.

130 Evans 1862.

131 Christy 1865.

132 Evans 1872.

133 Lartet 1861.

134 De Mortillet 1867.

135 Dawkins 1874, 366.

136 Buxton Museum Dawkins Archive DERBS 71385-71406.

137 *The Daily News* 29 October 29 1874.

138 *The Warder* 7 November 1874.

139 *The Athenaeum* 5 December 5 1874.

140 e.g., Letters from W. Dallas 16 November 1874, M.E.C. Walcott 25 & 28 November 1874, M.J. Carey 14 April 1875, C.L. Acland 31 May 1875, J. Duffy 29 December 1878, Buxton Museum Dawkins Archive DERBS 70061-63, 70073, 70078.

141 Wilson 1851.

142 Wilson to Dawkins 18 February 1875, Buxton Museum Dawkins Archive DERBS 70070.

143 Darwin to Dawkins 18 October 74, Buxton Museum Dawkins Archive DERBS 70055.

144 C. Allen to Dawkins 17 May 76; Minland to Dawkins 29 December 1878. Buxton Museum Dawkins Archive DERBS 70088 & 70109.

145 Green to Dawkins 4 November 1874, Buxton Museum Dawkins Archive DERBS 70058.

146 Dawkins 1874, 435ff.

147 Hamlin 1982.

148 Rudwick 1969; Hamlin 1982.

149 Wright 1898; Hamlin 1982.

150 Buckland 1841, 1842.

151 Morrell 2005; Phillips 1853.

152 e.g., Ramsey 1855; Geikie 1874.

153 Today we think that the Earth experienced five glacial epochs over the past two billion years, the most recent, the Quaternary or Pleistocene, witnessing ice-sheets advance across the northern hemisphere on several occasions, each separated by a prolonged period of warm 'interglacial' climate. Yet this understanding was over a century and a half away.

154 Modern workers will recognise Dawkins' plight all too well. Until very recently Quaternary scientists in Britain were labouring under another compressed framework, largely based on pollen records. According to this model the past 500,000 years had witness only two interglacials (previous to the current one) and three glacials, half the number currently recognised. It is small wonder that only now are we beginning - or so we think - to get the fauna and the archaeology in the right order.

155 Dawkins 1867c.

156 Dawkins 1866c.

157 Dawkins 1867c.

158 Dawkins 1874a, 416 .

159 Dawkins 1869a.

160 The opinions Dawkins presents in *Cave Hunting* are identical to those expressed in Dawkins 1872, so predate its publication by at least two years.

161 Dawkins 1872d; Dawkins 1874a, 392.

162 Dawkins 1872d, 445.

163 Dawkins 1872d.

164 Fisher 1872.

165 Dawkins 1874a, 402.

166 Dawkins 1872d & e; Dawkins 1874a; Geikie 1874.

167 Dawkins 1872d, 430.

168 Dawkins 1871g, 393; also Dawkins 1872f.

169 Lyell 1863, 180-181.

170 O'Conner 2007, 46.

171 Wilson 1977.

172 Croll 1864.

173 Hamlin 1982.

174 BGS: GSM1/321/29.

175 J. Geikie to Peach, 1 November 1871: BGS GSM1/321/32; Sedgwick Museum Cambridge MC:THM.

176 Geikie 1872a.

177 J. Geikie to Ramsay 12 December 1871: ICL: KGA/Ramsay8/412/3, cited in O'Connor 2007.

178 Geikie 1872a.

179 Geikie 1872a, 167.

180 Geikie 1872b.

181 Geikie 1872b, 172.

182 Dawkins 1872d, 431.

183 Dawkins 1872d, 430.

184 Geikie 1873, 54.

185 Dawkins 1874, 397-8.

186 Tiddeman 1875b; Tiddeman 1876; Tiddeman 1877; Tiddeman 1878a; Tiddeman 1879.

187 Tiddeman 1873a.

188 Tiddeman 1875.

189 Tiddeman 1876.

190 Tiddeman 1876; Tiddeman 1877.

191 Dearne & Lord 1998.

192 Tiddeman 1876.

193 Tiddeman 1877.

194 Dawkins 1877.

195 Dawkins 1877, 608.

196 Tom Lord, personal communication, 19 January 2015.

197 Dawkins 1877, 612.

198 cf. Lord et al 2012.

199 Dakyns 1877.

200 Stopes to Layard 1 September 1904, cited in White and Plunkett 2004, 23; McNabb 2012.

201 Evans 1878.

202 Dawkins 1878b.

203 Geikie 1877a.

204 Hughes 1878.

205 Tiddeman 1878b.

206 Geikie 1877b.

207 Skertchley 1877.

208 Dawkins' Diary for 16 August 1878, Manchester Museum Dawkins Archive PDW 1/14.

209 Tiddeman to Dawkins May 30 1877, Buxton Museum Dawkins Archive DERBS 70091-2.

210 Tiddeman 1878a.

211 E. A. Freeman to J. R. Green 16 May 1875, Jesus College, Oxford, J. R. Green Correspondence - typescript, IV 1873–1875.

212 Manchester Museum Dawkins Archive PDW/1/12.

213 Manchester Museum Dawkins Archive PDW/4.

214 Jackson 1966.

215 Stephens 1895, 129.

216 To whom he was given an introduction by their mutual friend the famous novelist Anthony Trollope – see Hall 1983, 662.

217 *Pall Mall Gazette* 8 April 1876.

Chapter 4

1 Kelly 1876.

2 Heath 1879a.

3 Jenkinson 1984.

4 Jenkinson 1984.

5 Ransom 1867.

6 Davies et al 2004.

7 Dorrien, Magens, Mello and Co was a private London bank that existed in various guises from 1770-1842, when it merged with Curries and Co; eventually after many more mergers its constituent parts were swallowed up by the modern RBS Group - http://heritagearchives.rbs.com/companies/list/dorrien-magens-mello-and-co.html, accessed May 2015.

8 cf. Beerbühl 2011.

9 Foster 1888; Armitage 1939.

10 *The Norfolk Chronicle and Norwich Gazette*, 18 June 1859, 15 October 1859.

11 *Derby Mercury* 25 February 1863.

12 Armitage 1939; Spooner n.d.

13 Armitage 1939.

14 Brownlow 1900; Cunningham 1975.

15 Brimelow n.d.

16 Armitage 1939, 37.

17 Census of England and Wales 1851 H.O. 107/2335.

18 Census of England and Wales 1861 R.G.9/3450.

NOTES

19 Census of England and Wales 1871 R.G.10/4681.

20 Stanley 1976.

21 Stanley 1976; Hobson 1875.

22 *Sheffield Daily Telegraph* 24 September 1874; *Sheffield and Rotherham Independent* 24 September 1874 & 30 September 1874.

23 Hobson 1875.

24 Census of England and Wales 1881 R.G.11/3399.

25 Despite an extensive search, I can find no photographs of Thomas Heath. He may be one of the figures seen in the mouth of Robin Hood Cave in Plate 7

26 Heath 1879.

27 Heath 1880, 28.

28 Mello 1875, 679.

29 Mello 1875, 679.

30 Mello 1875, 680.

31 e.g., *Sheffield Independent* 26 June 1875; *Derbyshire Times* 3 July 1875.

32 Mello & Heath 1876.

33 Cook 1997.

34 Woodward 2004.

35 Barton 1990; Barton 1998; Owen 2012.

36 Plarr et al 1930.

37 Cook 1997, 99.

38 Franks to Dawkins 5 November 1875, photocopy in the Jacobi Archive, British Museum. Original untraced.

39 Heath 1879.

40 Heath 1880, 28.

41 Hobson 1875.

42 Heath 1879; Heath 1880.

43 J. Magens Mello, 'The Discoveries in Creswell Crags', *Manchester Guardian* 10 May 1876.

44 Mello 1876, 240.

45 Heath 1879; Mello 1876.

46 Plant 1876b.

47 Heath 1879, 8.

48 Dawkins 1876b.

49 Mello 1876; Dawkins 1876b.

50 see Jacobi 2007.

51 Dawkins 1877.

52 Mello 1877; Heath 1879.

53 Heath 1879.

54 Mello 1877, 584.

55 Mello 1875, 679.

56 Mello 1877, 584.

57 Heath 1879; Mello 1877.

58 Herndon 1898.

59 Heath 1879, 10; a passage that brings tears to the eyes of modern archaeologists.

60 Just to Heath's left as he dug was the Pleistocene engraving of deer discovered in 2003, which at the time would have been near eye-level. Even if he had seen it, he would probably have assumed it was graffiti: Palaeolithic art at the time was known only from portable objects, parietal art not being discovered until after the Creswell excavations and then not fully accepted until 1902.

61 Hobson 1875.

62 Mello 1876, 240.

63 Dawkins 1876b, 245.

64 Heath 1880, 20.

65 Dawkins 1880.

66 Heath 1880.

67 Plant 1876b.

68 Plant 1876b, 84.

69 Dawkins in Plant 1876b, 87.

70 Thomas Heath, 'The discoveries in Cresswell Crags', *Manchester Guardian* 1 May 1876.

71 John Plant, 'The discoveries in Cresswell Crags', *Manchester Guardian* 5 May 1876.

72 Thomas Heath, 'The discoveries in Creswell Crags', *Manchester Guardian* 10 May 1876.

73 J. Magens Mello, 'The Discoveries in Creswell Crags', *Manchester Guardian* 10 May 1876.

74 Mello and Heath 1876.

75 *Sheffield Independent* 1 June 1876; *Manchester Evening News* 31 May 76; *Manchester City News* 3 June 1876.

76 *Manchester Guardian* 16 May 1876, *Grantham Journal* 20 May 1876; *Nottinghamshire Guardian* 19 May 1876.

Chapter 5

1 Evans 1872.

2 Owen 2012.

3 Heath 1880.

4 *Manchester Guardian* 16 May 1876.

5 Mello 1877; Dawkins 1877.

6 Heath 1879, 1880.

7 Manchester Museum Dawkins Archive PDW/3/16.

8 W.W. – the most likely interpretation is 'water works', an early consultancy job perhaps

9 Manchester Museum Dawkins Archive PDW/3/16; Heath 1880.

10 Dawkins 1877.

11 Mello 1877.

12 Dawkins 1877.

13 This identification has since been rejected. The specimens in question are probably hyaena – Andy Current, personal communication to Roger Jacobi – British Museum, Jacobi Archive, Creswell Crags.

14 Van Riper 1991.

15 Heath 1879, 13.

16 Mello 1877, 580; Paul Pettitt, personal communication 2015
17 Dawkins 1877, 589.
18 Heath 1880.
19 Manchester Museum Dawkins Archive PDW/3/16 (1876 Field Notebook).
20 Mello, 1877, 582.
21 Dawkins 1877, 592.
22 Manchester Museum Dawkins Archive PDW/3/16.
23 cf. Rooke Pennington 1877, 111.
24 Lankester 1869.
25 Mello 1877, 582.
26 Dawkins 1877, 594-5.
27 Heath 1879, 14-15.
28 Heath 1880, 7.
29 Manchester Museum Dawkins Archive PDW/3/16.
30 Mello 1877, 585.
31 Manchester Museum Dawkins Archive PDW/3/16.
32 Ibid.
33 Dawkins 1877.
34 Dawkins 1877, 607.
35 Dawkins 1877 – the tables on pages 602 and 604 give different figures.
36 Mello 1880, figure 11; Manchester Museum Dawkins Archive PDW/3/16.
37 Heath 1879, 11.
38 Mello 1877; Dawkins 1877.
39 Dawkins 1878c.
40 Hobson 1876; Stanley 1876.
41 See reports in *Sheffield Independent* 26 October 1876; *Nottinghamshire Guardian* 27 October 1876; *Derbyshire Times* 2 October 1876; *Sheffield Independent* 30 October 1876 ; *Sheffield Independent* 30 June 1879; *Derby Mercury* 2 July 1879
42 Kelly 1899.
43 Hobson 1879.
44 Dawkins & Mello 1879; Heath 1880.
45 Dawkins &Mello 1879.
46 Manchester Museum Dawkins Archive PDW/1/15.
47 Mello 1880, 295.
48 Jenkinson 1984, 24 - later work has shown this to be an area where the bed rock was much deeper, thereby trapping and preserving older sandy sediments.
49 Jenkinson 1984; Chamberlain 1996; Ashton & Lewis 2011.
50 Dawkins & Mello 1879, 733.
51 Heath 1879, 3e.

Chapter 6
1 *Manchester City News* 29 May 1880.
2 Heath, 1880, 1, referring to Heath 1879.
3 Heath 1879, 3.
4 Heath 1879, 13; Mello 1877, 583-4.

5 Heath 1879, 15.

6 *Manchester City News* 18 October 1879.

7 Plant in Heath 1880, 25.

8 *Manchester City News* 1 November 1879.

9 *Manchester City News* 8 November 1879.

10 Merk 1876; Bahn and Vertut 1997; Adam and Kurz 1980.

11 *Manchester City News* 15 November 1879.

12 *Manchester City News* 22 November 1879.

13 Like many of the cast members in this particular tragicomedy, Frederic Stubbs is hard to trace in the historical archives, any search for 'Stubbs & Creswell' invariably pointing to George Stubbs and horses.

14 Heath 1880, 34.

15 http://www.nature.com/nature/history/timeline_1870s.html

16 http://www.nature.com/nature/history

17 Keltie to Heath 22 December 1879.

18 Heath to Keltie 25 December 1879, in Heath 1880, 33.

19 Heath 1880, 6.

20 Heath 1880, 8.

21 Heath 1879; Mello 1876.

22 Heath 1880, 8.

23 This is probably a reference to Rooke Pennington or John Tym, or both. Pennington had established a museum at Carlton House in Castleton, which one entered through Tym's Spa and Marble shop, from which he sold fossils, minerals and rocks (Hancock, Howell & Torrens 1976).

24 Mello 1880.

25 Dawkins & Mello 1879.

26 Dawkins in Mello 1880, 299.

27 Dawkins in Mello 1880, 299.

28 *Manchester City News* 7 February 1880.

29 Heath 1880, 8.

Chapter 7

1 Heath 1880.

2 Heath 1880, 10-11.

3 Dawkins 1879.

4 Mello 1880.

5 Heath 1880, 14.

6 Heath 1880, 16.

7 Heath 1880, 17.

8 Heath 1880, 17.

9 Heath 1880, 18-26.

10 Heath 1880, 18-19.

11 Heath 1880, 20.

12 Heath 1880, 20, footnote *.

13 Heath 1880, 20, footnote ‡.

14 *Pall Mall Gazette* 8 April 1876.

15 Heath 1880 21.

16 Heath 1880, 21.

17 Heath 1880, 21, footnote †.

18 Heath 1880, 22.

19 Heath 1880, 22.

20 John Plant, quoted in the *Manchester City News* 29 May 1880; Heath 1880, 24.

21 Magens Mello quoted in the *Manchester City News* 29 May 1880; Heath 1880, 26.

22 Frederic Stubbs cited in the *Manchester City News* 29 May; Heath 1880, 25.

23 Dawkins to R.D. Darbishire 6 June 1880, Buxton Museum Dawkins Archive DERBS 70716.

24 Heath to Martin 4 July 1880, cited in Heath 1880, 35.

25 Martin to Heath 8 July 1880, cited in Heath 1880, 35.

26 Heath to Martin 12 July 1880, cited in Heath 1880, 35-36.

27 Martin to Heath 14 July 1880; cited in Heath 1880, 36.

28 Heath to Martin 18 July 1880, cited in Heath 1880, 36-38.

29 Martin to Heath 20 July 1880, cited in Heath 1880, 38.

30 Heath to Martin 25 July 1880, cited in Heath 1880 38.

31 Martin to Heath 31 July 1880, cited in Heath 1880, 39.

32 Heath to Martin 9 August 1880, cited in Heath 1880, 39.

33 Heath 1880, preface.

34 Heath 1882.

35 *Derby Telegraph* July 8 1881.

36 *Derby Daily Telegraph* October 20 1882; *Derby Mercury* 1 November 1882.

37 *Nottingham Guardian* 14 February 1882; *Derby Mercury* 29 March 1882.

38 *Derby Mercury* 26 March 1884.

39 *Derby Daily Telegraph* February 3 1885.

40 *Nottingham Evening Post* 9 February 1886; *Derby Mercury* 10 February 1886; *Derby Big Red Book* 1887, 150.

41 *Derby Mercury* 10 February 1886.

42 Mello 1881.

43 *Kelly's Directory 1895.*

44 Census of England and Wales for 1901 RG13/3227; Census of England and Wales for 1911.

45 Beerbühl 2011.

Chapter 8

1 Dawkins 1880a.

2 Dawkins 1879b; Dawkins 1880b.

3 James Cooper of 188, The Strand, London.

4 Buxton Museum Dawkins Archive DERBS 70117, 70122, 70140, 70142-50.

5 A. Macmillan to Dawkins 23 March 1880, Buxton Museum Dawkins Archive DERBS 70159.

6 McNabb 2012, 238.

7 Geikie 1881, 65.

8 Dawkins 1880a, 115 & 170.

9 Spurrell 1880a & b.

10 Dawkins 1882.

11 *The Academy* 15 May 1880; *Boston Daily Advertizer* 8 May 1880.

12 *Nature* 27 May 1880.

13 *The Scotsman* 16 June 1880.

14 *The Athenaeum* 24 April 1880; *The Standard* 5 October 1880.

15 A. Macmillan to Dawkins 2 October 1880, Buxton Museum Dawkins Archive DERBS 70185.

16 A. Macmillan to Dawkins 7 June 1880, Buxton Museum Dawkins Archive DERBS 70177.

17 McNabb 2012.

18 Eskrigge 1880; Dawkins 1880c.

19 Manchester Museum Dawkins Archive PDW 1/16.

20 Buxton Museum Dawkins Archive DERBS 21442-71433.

21 Manchester Museum Dawkins Archive PDW 1/16.

22 Jackson 1966.

23 Geikie 1877.

24 Royal Society Archive RSL: EC/1875/22.

25 O' Conner 2007.

26 Dawkins 1881a, 309.

27 Dawkins 1880, 6.

28 Dawkins 1881a, 310.

29 Geikie 1881b.

30 Dawkins 1881b.

31 Geikie 1881c.

32 Geikie to Peach 17 February 1881: BGS: GSMl/321/68.

33 Geikie to Peach 11 March 1881: BGS: GSMl/321/69.

34 O' Connor 2007.

35 Tiddeman 1881a.

36 Dawkins 1881c.

37 Tiddeman 1881b.

38 Tiddeman 1877.

Chapter 9

1 Freeman to Dawkins 12 March 1883, Jesus College, Oxford Freeman MSS 1880-1897.

2 J.D. Harper to Dawkins 16 October 1882, Buxton Museum Dawkins Archive DERBS 70200.

3 Newton, 1882.

4 Stephens 1895, 195.

5 Stephens 1895, 258.

6 Dawkins' Diary for 1884, Manchester Museum Dawkins Archive PDW/1/20.

7 Dawkins 1901a & b; Dawkins 1902a & b.

8 Dawkins 1893; Dawkins 1901c; Dawkins 1902c; Dawkins 1904; Dawkins 1910; Dawkins 1921.

NOTES

9 Dawkins 1918.

10 Dawkins 1882a; Dawkins 1889; Dawkins 1906; Dawkins 1912; Dawkins 1914.

11 Dawkins 1882b; Dawkins 1883b; Dawkins 1885a; Dawkins 1888a.

12 Tweedale 1991.

13 Tweedale 1991.

14 *The Manchester Guardian* 16 January 1929.

15 Watkin 1882; Clifford 1985.

16 Dawkins 1882c.

17 Knowles 1883.

18 Knowles 1883; Varley 1992; Hunt 1994.

19 Knowles 1883; Varley 1992; Hunt 1994.

20 Dawkins 1882c; Dawkins 1883c & d; Dawkins 1901d; interview in *The Million* 4 June 1892.

21 Tweedale 1991.

22 Dawkins 1887, 1891.

23 Dawkins Diaries 1882-84, Manchester Museum Dawkins Archive PDW/1/18-20.

24 Clifford 1985.

25 Flanagan 1982.

26 Dawkins 1885b.

27 Dawkins 1886; Dawkins 1888b; Dawkins 1890; Dawkins 1894a; Dawkins 1895; Dawkins 1896; Dawkins 1902d & e; Dawkins 1913.

28 Dawkins 1896, 1913.

29 Tweedale 1991 has provided a detailed account of all Dawkins many dealings in the coal industry based on published and archival materials held in the John Rylands Library Manchester. This section draws on and acknowledges a debt to his work.

30 Dawkins 1890.

31 Dawkins 1890.

32 Tweedale 1991.

33 Dawkins 1890.

34 Dawkins 1890.

35 Tweedale 1991.

36 Tweedale 1991.

37 Tweedale 1991.

38 Tweedale 1991.

39 Dawkins 1892; Dawkins 1898; Dawkins 1899; Dawkins 1903; Dawkins 1907; Dawkins 1913, plus numerous newspaper interviews in the *Manchester Guardian*.

40 *Manchester Guardian* 23 February 1905 & 10 May 1905.

41 Dawkins 1913.

42 His diary entry for 10 January 1882 says: 'lunched at Albemarle Hotel – saw Mr. Rhodes and his big diamond. W= 600 [units unclear] =£60,000+. Manchester Museum Dawkins Archive PDW/1/18.

43 Jackson 1966; Tweedale 1991.

44 Manchester Museum Dawkins Archive PDW/1/14.

45 Tweedale 1991.

46 Trollope to Wendell, September 1875, in Hall 1983, 662-3.

47 Brine Pumping (Compensation For Subsidence) Provisional Order Bill (by order) (No. 347.), *HC Dec 31 May 1892 vol 5 cc351-61,* retrieved 22 June 2015 from: *http:// hansard.millbanksystems.com/commons/1892/may/31/brine-pumping-compensation- for*

48 Leech 1907; Owen 1983.

49 Correspondence between Dawkins and Daniel Adamson, 1884, Buxton Museum Dawkins Archive 70211, 70212, 70214 plus unnumbered.

50 Manchester Evening News 16 January 29.

51 Lubbock to Dawkins 8 May 1886, Buxton Museum Dawkins Archive DERBS 70221; *Manchester Guardian* 3 May 1905 & May 7 1909.

52 *Manchester Guardian* 16 July 1916.

53 Bonney to Dawkins 6 March 1916 Buxton Museum Dawkins Archive DERBS 70471.

54 Newspaper cutting of 23 October 1887 entitled 'Manchester's New Showplace'. Buxton Museum Dawkins Archive DERBS 71807/01 [original source unknown].

55 *Manchester Guardian* 27 May 1903 & 9 March 1904.

56 Extensive correspondence and newspaper cuttings related the to the India Museum are held in Buxton Museum Dawkins Archive, Boxes 13 and 14.

57 Merriman 2013; Jackson 1966.

58 Merriman 2013, 39.

59 Greenwood to Dawkins 2 June 1888, Buxton Museum Dawkins Archive DERBS 70234/2.

60 Greenwood to Dawkins 5 June 1888, Buxton Museum Dawkins Archive DERBS 70235.

61 Greenwood to Dawkins 29 September 1888, Buxton Museum Dawkins Archive DERBS 70236.

62 Unsent drafts of a resignation letter from Dawkins to Thompson, dated 27, 29 & 29 November 1888, Buxton Museum Dawkins Archive DERBS 70235-7. The last is possibly a copy of the final letter.

63 Greenwood to Dawkins 22 May 1889, Buxton Museum Dawkins Archive DERBS 70240.

64 Buxton Museum Dawkins Archive unnumbered engagement lists 1889-90.

65 McNabb 2012.

66 Hicks 1885; Hicks 1886; Hicks 1887.

67 Hughes 1886.

68 e.g. Jukes-Brown 1887.

69 Harrison 1928.

70 McNabb 2012.

71 McNabb 2012.

72 Prestwich 1889.

73 McNabb 2012.

74 Prestwich 1891.

75 Prestwich 1892.

76 Maidstone Museum Benjamin Harrison Archive Volume 8. Transcribed by Angela Muthana. Accessed on 22 June 2015 at http://www.kent.ac.uk/sac/research/files/ Harrison_Archive_vol_8.PDF

77 McNabb 2012, 235.

78 McNabb 2012.

79 Dawkins 1894b.

80 McNabb 2012.

81 Dawkins to Darbishire 30 October 1899, Buxton Museum Dawkins Archive DERBS 70267.

82 Maidstone Museum Benjamin Harrison Archive Volume 13. Transcribed by Angela Muthana. Accessed on 22 June 2015 at http://www.kent.ac.uk/sac/research/files/Harrison_Archive_vol_13.PDF

83 Evans 1872; Evans 1897; Dawkins 1874a; Dawkins 1800a.

84 Brown 1887.

85 Brown 1893.

86 Dawkins 1894c.

87 Newton 1895.

88 Montagu and Oakley 1949.

89 Read 1902.

90 Coombes 1994 gives this as the 1894 daily attendance.

91 Dawkins 1903b.

92 Dawkins 1903c.

93 Layard, notebooks, 20 December 1904, housed in Ipswich Records Office and cited in White & Plunkett 2004, 36.

94 *Manchester Guardian* March 26 1908; *Pall Mall Gazette* 15 April 1908.

95 Bishop 1982.

96 *Manchester Guardian* 18 November 1909.

97 Anon 1909.

98 Jackson 1966.

99 *Manchester Guardian* February 9 1911; *Manchester Courier* 9 February 1911.

100 *Manchester Courier* 9 February 1911.

101 Dawkins 1910.

102 Penck & Bruckner 1909.

103 White 2004.

104 see O'Connor 2007 for a detailed account of the second eolith debate.

105 Underwood et al 1911; White and Plunkett 2004.

106 Spencer 1990a, 219.

107 Moir 1911; O'Connor 2007.

108 O'Connor 2007.

109 Dawkins and Howorth had been school friends & Howorth had loved Dawkins' 'cheeky laugh': Howorth to Dawkins n.d, Buxton Museum Dawkins Archive DERBS 70487.

110 Dawkins 1923; Howorth to Dawkins 5 January 1922, Buxton Museum Dawkins Archive DERBS 70501.

111 Howorth to Dawkins n.d., Buxton Museum Dawkins Archive DERBS 70943.

112 *Manchester Guardian* 7 April 1911.

113 Blinderman 1986; Spencer 1990a & b; Russell 2012.

114 Spencer 1990b: 1.2.13 DF100/32 & 1.2.18 DF100/32.

115 Moir 1912.
116 Whitaker to Dawkins 30 April 1912, Buxton Museum Dawkins Archive DERBS 70451.
117 Duckworth 1913; *The Times* 9 September 1912.
118 Keith 1913, 753.
119 Dawkins 1870f: many modern Quaternary specialists would agree with him .
120 Spencer 1990a & b.
121 Dawson and Woodward 1913.
122 Smith 1913.
123 *Manchester Evening Chronicle* 19 December 1912.
124 Ibid.
125 Spencer 1990b: 2.2.36 DF116.15.
126 *Daily Express* 16 August 1913.
127 Spencer 1991a & b
128 Kennard 1947.
129 Abbott to Yates 11 March 1914, cited in Blinderman 1986, 195, and Spencer 1990a, 235.
130 Blinderman 1986, 195.
131 Blinderman 1986, 195.
132 Arthur Keith, Obituary of W.J.L. Abbott, *The Times* August 12 1933.
133 Blinderman 1986.
134 Kennard 1947.
135 *Daily Express* August 1913.
136 Spencer 1990b, 101: RP/IRSNB Abbott to Rutot 1 September 1913.
137 Spencer 1990a; Spencer 1990b: 20.3.1913 DF 116/12.
138 Dawson and Woodward 1914.
139 *Morning Post* 23 December 1913.
140 Spencer 1990b, 100: 3.1.1. RP/IRSNB Abbott to Rutot January 1914.
141 Ibid.
142 Warren 1914; Sutcliffe 1913; Haward 1912.
143 O'Connor 2007.
144 Dawkins 1915.
145 Sollas to Dawkins 27 June 1920, Buxton Museum Dawkins Archive DERBS 70494.
146 Balch 1914 .
147 Spencer 1990b, 3.1.38 KP/RCS Moir to Keith 14 December 1914.
148 Keith 1914.
149 Weiner et al 1953.
150 Blinderman 1986.
151 Moir 1916.
152 Montagu and Oakley 1949.
153 Bonney to Dawkins 30 December 1915, Buxton Museum Dawkins Archive DERBS 70469.
154 Bonney to Dawkins 23 February 1916, Buxton Museum Dawkins Archive DERBS 70470.
155 Dawkins 1916.

156 Congreve was chief engineer of the Manchester Ship Canal who committed suicide in October 1911 owing to depression over canal affairs and strikes. He mounted a bridge crossing the canal at a height of 90ft, shot himself in the left breast and dropped into the waters below. *The Evening Post 2 December 1911.*

157 Dawkins Diary for 1918, Manchester Museum Dawkins Archive PDW/1.

158 Evans to Dawkins June 3 1922: Royal Society MM16.74.

159 Jackson 1966.

160 Dawkins to Crozen 26 September 1924, Buxton Museum Dawkins Archive DERBS 70526/1-4.

161 Evans to Dawkins 23 September 1924, Buxton Museum Dawkins Archive DERBS 70528.

162 Dawkins 1925a, b; Armstrong 1925; *The Times* 22 December 1924.

163 Bahn 2007.

164 Garrod 1926, 145.

165 Breuil to Dawkins 13 August 1925, Buxton Museum Dawkins Archive DERBS 70546.

166 Boule to Dawkins 4 November 1926, Buxton Museum Dawkins Archive DERBS 70561.

167 Breuil to Dawkins 16 May 1927, Buxton Museum Dawkins Archive DERBS 70567.

168 Dawkins to Black 21 May 26, Black to Dawkins 27 October 1926, Buxton Museum Dawkins Archive DERBS 70556 & 70559 .

169 Lamplugh to Dawkins 15 August 1924, Buxton Museum Dawkins Archive DERBS 70525; Arthur Evans to Dawkins 23 September 1924, Buxton Museum Dawkins Archive DERBS 70528.

170 Dawkins to Jackson 1 August 1928, Buxton Museum Dawkins Archive DERBS 70615.

171 Dawkins to Jackson 21 September 1928, Buxton Museum Dawkins Archive DERBS 70620.

172 Armstrong 1928.

173 A. Evans to Dawkins 28 December 1928: Royal Society MM16:92.

174 Gardner 1929; Anon 1929; A.S.W 1931.

175 Freeman to Dawkins 20 July 1886, Jesus College, Oxford, Freeman MSS 1880-1897

176 Lady Dawkins, quoted in Tweedale 1991a, 448.

177 *Manchester Evening News* 9 April 1929.

178 *Manchester Evening News* 8 June 1928.

Chapter 10

1 Woodward 1914.

2 Sollas 1924, 536.

3 Dawkins to Sollas 27 December 1924, Buxton Museum Dawkins Archive Box DERBS 70534.

4 Sollas to Dawkins 7 January 1925, Buxton Museum Dawkins Archive DERBS 70535.

5 Dawkins to Woodward 17 January 1925, Buxton Museum Dawkins Archive DERBS 70536.

6 Sollas to Dawkins 21 January 1925, Buxton Museum Dawkins Archive DERBS 70537.

7 Dawkins to Sollas 5 February 1925, Buxton Museum Dawkins Archive DERBS 70540.

8 Dawkins 1925a & b.

9 Sollas 1925.

10 Stringer et al 1996; D'Errico et al 1998.

11 Bahn 2007.

12 Garrod 1926.

13 Oakley et al 1950; Weiner et al 1953.

14 Oakley 1963, 1980.

15 Reumer et al 2003.

16 Oakley 1963, 43.

17 Oakley 1979; Stringer et al 1996; D'Errico et al 1998.

18 Tiddeman to Dawkins 25 May 1877 & 30 May 1877, Buxton Museum Dawkins Archive DERBS 70091 & 70092.

19 Manchester Museum Dawkins Archive PDW/3/16.

20 These two objects are of such importance to the British Palaeolithic that as an offshoot project of this book permission has been granted to employ twenty-first century scientific techniques to the *Homotherium/Machairodus* canine. We might never be able to distinguish between options 1 & 4, or between 2 & 3 but we might at last be able to establish the age and geographical origin of the piece, in life and in death.

Bibliography

Adam, K. D. and Kurz, R. (1980) *Eiszeitkunst im Süddeutschen Raum*. Stuttgart: Thiess.

Aldhouse-Green, S. (1995) Pontnewydd Cave, Wales, a later Middle Pleistocene hominid and archaeological site: a review of stratigraphy, dating, taphonomy and interpretation. In: J. M. Bermúdez de Castro, J.-L. Arsuaga and E. Carbonell (eds), *Evolución Humana en Europa y los Yacimientos de la Sierra de Atapuerca*, pp 37-55. Junta de Castilla y Leon.

Aldhouse-Green, S., Walker, E. and Peterson, R. (2012) *Pontnewydd and the Elwy Valley Caves*. Cardiff: National Museums and Galleries of Wales.

Anon. (1864) The great explosion of gunpowder and the breach in the river embankment. *Journal of the Franklin Institute* 78: 301.

Anon. (1878) Eminent Living Geologists (No. 3) Professor John Morris, M.A. Cantab, F.G.S., etc.; President of the Geologists' Association. *The Geological Magazine* Decade II. Vol. V: 482-487.

Anon. (1887) Obituary: Henry Michael Jenkins, F.G.S. *The Geological Magazine* 87: 95-96.

Anon. (1896) Obituary: Alexander Henry Green, M.A., F.R.S., F.G.S. *The Geological Magazine* Decade IV. Volume III: 480.

Anon. (1901) Eminent Living Geologists: The Rev. Professor T.G. Bonney, D.Sc, LL.D, F.R.S., F.G.S., F.S.A. *The Geological Magazine* Decade IV, Vol VIII: 385-400.

Anon. (1906) Eminent Living Geologists: Thomas McKenny Hughes, M.A., F.R.S., F.G.S., F.S.A. *The Geological Magazine* Decade V. Vol. III: 1-12.

Anon. (1908) William Boyd Dawkins. *The Manchester University Magazine* 4 (30): 155-158.

Anon. (1909) Eminent Living Geologists: William Boyd Dawkins M.A., D.Sc., F.R.S, F.S.A., F.G.S. *The Geological Magazine* Decade V, Vol. VI: 529-534.

Anon. (1929) Obituary: Sir William Boyd Dawkins. *The Geological Magazine* 66: 142.

Armitage, H. (1939) *Early Man in Hallamshire*. London: Sampson Low.

Armstrong, A. L. (1925) Excavations at Mother Grundy's Parlour, Creswell Crags, Derbyshire, 1924. *Journal of the Royal Anthropological Institute* 55: 146-178.

Armstrong, A.L. (1928) Pin Hole Cave excavations, Creswell Crags, Derbyshire: discovery of an engraved drawing of a masked human figure. *Proceedings of the Prehistoric Society of East Anglia* 6: 27-9.

Ashton, N., Lewis, S., and Hosfield, R. (2011) Mapping the human record: population change during the later Middle Pleistocene. In: N. Ashton, S. Lewis and C. Stringer (eds), *The Ancient Human Occupation of Britain*, pp 39-52. Amsterdam: Elsevier.

Ashworth, T. W. (ed.) (1895) *The Rossall Register 1884-1895*. Manchester & London: G. Falkner & Sons.

ASW. 1931. Obituary Notices: Sir William Boyd Dawkins 1837-1929. *Proceedings of the Royal Society of London 107*: xxiii-xxvi.

Bahn, P. (2007) The historical background to the Discovery of Cave Art and Creswell Crags. In, P. Pettitt, P. Bahn and S. Ripoll (eds), Palaeolithic Cave Art at Creswell Crags in European Context, pp1-13. Oxford. Oxford University Press.

Bahn, P. and Vertut, J. (1997) *Journey Through the Ice Age*. Berkeley: University of California Press.

Balch, H.E. (1914) *Wookey Hole: Its Caves and Cave Dwellers*. London: Oxford University Press.

Barton, R. (1990) An influential set of chaps: The X-Club and Royal Society politics, 1864-1885. *British Journal for the History of Science* 23: 53-58.

Barton, R. (1998) Huxley, Lubbock, and half a dozen others: professionals and gentlemen in the formation of the X Club, 1851-1864. *Isis* 89: 410-444.

Beerbühl, M. S. (2011) The commercial culture of spiritual kinship amongst German immigrant merchants in London 1750-1830. In: B. Lee (ed), *Culture and Commerce: Nineteenth Century Business Elites*, pp225-255. Surrey: Ashgate.

Bevington, M. M. (1941) *The Saturday Review, 1855-1868: Representative Educated Opinion in Victorian England*. New York: Columbia University Press.

Bishop, M.J. (ed) (1982) *The Cave Hunters. Biographical Sketches in the Lives of Sir William Boyd Dawkins and Dr. J. Wilfred Jackson*. Derby: Derbyshire Museum Services.

Blinderman, C. 1986. *The Piltdown Inquest*. New York: Prometheus Books.

Blore, G.H. (1920) *Victorian Worthies: Sixteen Biographies*. Oxford: Oxford University Press.

Boylan, P. J. (1998) Lyell and the dilemma of Quaternary glaciation. In: D. J. Blundell and A. C. Scott (ed), *Lyell: the Past is the Key to the Present*, pp145-159. London: Geological Society Special Publications 143.

Brimelow, P. (n.d), The Rev. John Magens Mello MA, FGS (1836-1914) incumbent 1863-1887 and first rector. Brampton History Group. Unpublished manuscript supplied by the author.

Bristow, W. H. (1864) On the Rhaetic or Penarth Beds of the Neighbourhood Bristol and the South-West of England. The *Geological Magazine* 1: 236-239.

Brown, A. J. (1887) *Palaeolithic Man in North-West Middlesex*. London: MacMillan & Co.

Brown, J.A. (1893) On the continuity of the Palaeolithic and Neolithic Periods. *The Journal of the Anthropological Institute of Great Britain and Ireland* 22: 65-98.

Brownlow, R. H. E. (1900) The British volunteer system. *The North American Review* 170: 745-752.

Buckland, W. (1823). *Reliquiae Diluvianae; or, Observations on the Organic Remains Contains in Caves, Fissures, and Diluvial Gravel, and on Other Geological Phenomena, Attesting to the Action of an Universal Deluge*. London: Murray & Co.

Buckland, W. (1841) On the former existence of glaciers in Scotland and the north of England. *Proceedings of the Geological Society of London* 3: 332-337, 345-348.

Buckland, W. (1842) On diluvio-glacial phaenomena in Snowdonia and adjacent parts of North Wales. *Proceedings of the Geological Society of London* 3: 579-584.

Busk, G. (1870) Notes on the human remains. *Journal of the Ethnological Society of London* 2: 450-467.

BIBLIOGRAPHY

Chamberlain, A. T. (1996) More dating evidence for human remains in British Caves. *Antiquity* 70: 950-953.

Christy, H. (1865) On the prehistoric cave-dwellers of southern France. *Transactions of the Ethnological Society of London* 3: 362-372.

Clifford, F. (1985) *A History of Private Bill Legislation, Volume 1.* Routledge: London.

Cook, G. C. (1997) George Busk FRS (1807-1886), nineteenth-century polymath: surgeon, parasitologist, zoologist and palaeontologist. *Journal of Medical Biography* 5: 88-101.

Coombes, A. E. (1994) *Reinventing Africa: Museums, Material Culture and Popular Imagination in Late Victorian and Edwardian England.* Bath: Bath Press.

Croll, J. (1864) On the physical cause of the change of climate during glacial periods. *The London, Edinburgh and Dublin Philosophical Magazine and Journal of Science* 28: 121-137.

Cunningham, H. (1975) *The Volunteer Force: A Social and Political History, 1859-1908.* London: Taylor & Francis.

Currant, A. P. (1984) The mammalian remains. In H.S. Green (ed.), *Pontnewydd Cave: a Lower Palaeolithic Hominid Site in Wales: The First Report*, pp 171-180. Cardiff, National Museum of Wales.

Dakyns, J. (1877) Exploration of Victoria Cave, Settle, Yorkshire. *The Geological Magazine* Decade II Volume 4: 285.

Davies, G., Badcock, A., Mills, N., and Smith, B. (2004), *Creswell Crags Limestone Heritage Area Management Action Plan.* Sheffield: English Heritage.

Davison, C. (1900) Eminent Living Geologists: Rev. Osmond Fisher, M.A., F.G.S. *The Geological Magazine* Decade IV. Vol. VII: 49-54.

Dawkins, W. B. (1862) On a hyaena-den at Wookey Hole, near Wells. *Quarterly Journal of the Geological Society of London* 18: 115-126.

Dawkins, W. B. (1863a) On a hyaena-den at Wookey Hole, near Wells. No. II. *Quarterly Journal of the Geological Society of London* 19: 260-274.

Dawkins, W. B. (1963b) Wookey Hole, Hyaena Den. *Proceedings of the Somerset Archaeological and History Society* 40: 197-219.

Dawkins, W. B. (1863c) On the molar series of *Rhinoceros tichorhinus*. *The Natural History Review* 12: 525-538.

Dawkins, W. B. (1864a) On the caverns of Burrington Combe, explored in 1864, by Messrs. W. Ayshford Sanford, and W. Boyd Dawkins. *Somerset Archaeological and Natural History Society* 12: 161-176.

Dawkins, W. B. (1865a) On the dentition of *Rhinoceros megarhinus*. *The Natural History Review* 5: 399-414.

Dawkins, W. B. (1865b) On the dentition of *Hyaena spelaea* and its varieties, with notes on the recent species. *The Natural History Review* 5: 80-96.

Dawkins, W. B. (1866a) On the dentition of *Rhinoceros leptorhinus* (Owen) (Abstract) *Proceedings of the Royal Society of London* 15: 106-107.

Dawkins, W. B. (1866b) On the fossil British Oxen. *Quarterly Journal of the Geological Society of London* 22: 391-401.

Dawkins, W. B. (1866c) On the habits of the two earliest known races of men. *Quarterly Journal of Science* 3: 333-346.

Dawkins, W. B. (1867a) On the dentition of *Rhinoceros leptorhinus*, Owen. *Quarterly Journal of the Geological Society of London* 23: 213-227.

Dawkins, W. B. (1867b) *Ovibos moschatus* (Blainville) [Abstract]. *Proceedings of the Royal Society of London* 16: 516-517.

Dawkins, W. B. (1867c) Age of the Thames Valley deposits. *The Geological Magazine* 4: 564-565.

Dawkins, W. B. (1867d) The boulder-clay of the Thames Valley. *The Geological Magazine* 4: 430-430.

Dawkins, W. B. (1868a) On the dentition of *Rhinoceros Etruscus*, Falc. *Quarterly Journal of the Geological Society of London* 24(1-2): 207-218.

Dawkins, W. B. (1868b) The variation of animals and plants under domestication. *The Edinburgh Review* 262: 414-450.

Dawkins, W. B. (1868c) The former range of the reindeer in Europe. *Popular Science Reviews* 7: 34-45.

Dawkins, W. B. (1868d) The former range of the Mammoth in Europe. *Popular Science Reviews* 7: 275-286.

Dawkins, W. B. (1868e) On the value of the evidence for the existence of the Mammoth in Europe in Pre-glacial Times. *The Geological Magazine* 5: 316-321.

Dawkins, W. B. (1868f) Early antiquities in Portugal. *International Congress of Prehistoric Archaeology. Transactions of the Third Session, Norwich August 1868*: 82-84.

Dawkins, W. B. (1868g) On the antiquity of iron mines in the Weald. *International Congress of Prehistoric Archaeology. Transactions of the Third Session, Norwich August 1868*: 185-191.

Dawkins, W. B. (1868h) On the Prehistoric mammalia of Great Britain. *International Congress of Prehistoric Archaeology. Transactions of the Third Session, Norwich August 1868*: 269-289.

Dawkins, W. B. (1868f) On a new species of fossil deer from Clacton. *Quarterly Journal of the Geological Society of London* 24: 511-516.

Dawkins, W. B. (1868g) On a new species of deer from the Norwich Crag. *Quarterly Journal of the Geological Society of London* 24: 516-519.

Dawkins, W. B. (1869a) On the distribution of the British postglacial mammalia. *Quarterly Journal of the Geological Society of London* 25: 192-217

Dawkins, W. B. (1869b) The British lion. *The Popular Science Review* 8: 10-158.

Dawkins, W. B. (1870a) Geological theory in Britain. *The Edinburgh Review* 267: 39-64.

Dawkins, W. B. (1870b) Prehistoric times. *The Edinburgh Review* 270: 439-479.

Dawkins, W. B. (1870c) The Denbighshire caves. *Transactions of the Manchester Geological Society* 9: 31-37.

Dawkins, W. B. (1870d) On the discovery of platycnemic men in Denbighshire. *Journal of the Ethnological Society of London* 2: 440-450.

Dawkins, W. B. (1870e) Explorations of caves at Settle, Yorkshire. *Nature* 1: 628-629.

Dawkins, W.B. (1870f) The geological calculus. *Nature* 1: 505-6.

Dawkins, W. B. (1871a) British bears and wolves. *Popular Science Reviews*: 241-253.

Dawkins, W. B. (1871b) Darwin on the Descent of Man. *The Edinburgh Review* 274: 195-235.

BIBLIOGRAPHY

Dawkins, W. B. (1871c) On fresh discoveries of platycnemic men in Denbighshire. *Nature* 4: 388-389.

Dawkins, W. B. (1871d) On the discovery of the glutton in Britain. *Quarterly Journal of the Geological Society of London* 26: 406-410.

Dawkins, W. B. (1871e) On the formation of the caves around Ingleborough. *Transactions of the Manchester Geological Society* 10: 106-112.

Dawkins, W. B. (1871f) The Date of the interment in the Aurignac Cave. *Nature* 4: 208-209.

Dawkins, W. B. (1871g) On Pleistocene climate and the relation of the Pleistocene mammalia to the glacial period. *The Popular Science Review* 10: 388-397.

Dawkins, W.B. (1972a) *The British Pleistocene Mammalia. Part V. British Pleistocene Ovidae.* Ovibos Moschatus *Blainville*. London: The Palaeontological Society.

Dawkins, W. B. (1872b) On the discovery of platycnemic men in Denbighshire. *Archaeologia Cambrensis* 3: 22-32.

Dawkins, W. B. (1872c) Report of the results obtained by the Settle Cave Exploration Committee out of Victoria Cave in 1870. *Journal of the Anthropological Institute of Great Britain and Ireland* 1: 60-70.

Dawkins, W. B. (1872d) On the classification of the Pleistocene strata of Britain and the Continent by means of the Mammalia. *Quarterly Journal of the Geological Society of London* 28: 410-446.

Dawkins, W. B. (1872e) The climate of the Pleistocene Age. *Transactions of the Manchester Geological Society* 11: 45-52.

Dawkins, W. B. (1872f) On the physical geography of the Mediterranean. *Report of the Forty-Second Meeting of the British Association for the Advancement of Science, Brighton 1872*: 100-102.

Dawkins, W. B. (ed.) (1873a) *Testimonials in Favour of W.Boyd Dawkins, M.A., F.R.S, F.G.S., a candidate for the Woodwardian Professorship of Geology.* Cambridge: Cambridge University Press.

Dawkins, W. B. (1874a) *Cave Hunting: Researches on the Evidence of Caves Respecting the Early Inhabitants of Europe.* London: MacMillan and Co.

Dawkins, W. B. (1874b) Report of the Committee, consisting of Sir John Lubbock, Bart., Professor Phillips, Professor Hughes and W.Boyd Dawkins, secretary, appointed for the purpose of exploring the Settle Caves. *Report of the Forty-Third Meeting of the British Association for the Advancement of Science, Bradford 1873*: 250-251.

Dawkins, W. B. (1874c) Observations on the rate at which stalagmite is being accumulated in the Ingleborough Cave. *Report of the Forty-Third Meeting of the British Association for the Advancement of Science, Bradford 1873*: 80.

Dawkins, W. B. (1875a) The mammalia found at Windy Knoll. *Quarterly Journal of the Geological Society of London* 31: 246-255.

Dawkins, W. B. (1875b) On the animal remains in the Windy Knoll fissure. *Proceedings of the Literary and Philosophical Society of Manchester* 14: 5-7.

Dawkins, W. B. (1876a) Note on Mr Plant's fossil sacrum from Windy Knoll. *Proceedings of the Literary and Philosophical Society of Manchester* 15: 149-150.

Dawkins, W. B. (1876b) On the mammalia and traces of man found in the Robin Hood Cave. *Quarterly Journal of the Geological Society of London* 32: 245-258.

Dawkins, W. B. (1877) On the Mammal-fauna of the caves of Creswell Crags. *Quarterly Journal of the Geological Society of London* 33: 589-612.

Dawkins, W. B. (1878a) *Part A. Preliminary Treatise on the Relation of the Pleistocene Mammalia to Those Now Living in Europe.* London: The Palaeontographical Society.

Dawkins, W. B. (1878b) On the evidence afforded by the caves of Great Britain as to the antiquity of man. *Journal of the Anthropological Institute of Great Britain and Ireland*: 7, 151-162.

Dawkins, W. B. (1878c) On the deer of European Miocene and Pliocene strata. *Quarterly Journal of the Geological Society of London* 34: 402-420.

Dawkins, W. B. (1879a) Creswell bone exploration 1879. *Nature* 21: 106-107.

Dawkins, W. B. (1879b) On the range of the mammoth in space and time. *Quarterly Journal of the Geological Society of London* 35: 138-147.

Dawkins, W. B. (1880a) *Early Man in Britain and his Place in the Tertiary Period.* London: MacMillan and Co.

Dawkins, W. B. (1880b) The Classification of the Tertiary Period by means of the mammalia. *Quarterly Journal of the Geological Society of London* 36:379-405.

Dawkins, W.B. (1880c) Memorandum on the remains from the cave at the Great Ormes Head. *Proceedings of the Liverpool Geological Society* 4: 156-159.

Dawkins, W. B. (1881a) Prehistoric Europe. *Nature* 23: 309-310.

Dawkins, W. B. (1881b) Prehistoric Europe. *Nature* 23: 361-362.

Dawkins, W. B. (1881c) Prehistoric Europe. *Nature* 23: 482.

Dawkins, W. B. (1882a) The ancient ethnology of Wales. *Y Commrydor: Embodying the Transactions of the Honorable Society of Cymmrodorian*, etc.,. 5: 209-223.

Dawkins, W. B. (1882b) On the range *of Anadonta Jukesii. Transactions of the Manchester Geological Society* 16: 4pp

Dawkins W. B. (1882c) The Channel Tunnel. *Transactions of the Manchester Geological Society* 16: 20pp

Dawkins, W. B. (1883a) Presidential address to the Department of Anthropology. *Report of the Fifty-Second Meeting of the British Association for the Advancement of Science, Southampton 1882.* pp 597-604.

Dawkins, W. B. (1883b) On the alleged existence of *Ovibos moschatus* in the Forest Bed and its range in space and time. *Quarterly Journal of the Geological Society of London* 39: 575-581

Dawkins, W. B. (1883c) The Silver Streak and the Channel Tunnel. *Contemporary Review February 1883:* 240-249.

Dawkins, W. B. (1883d) Memorandum on the proposed Channel Tunnel project, based mainly in the Blue Books C.1206 and C.3358. Presented to the House of Commons.

Dawkins, W. B. (1885a) On a skull of *Ovibos mochatus* from the sea-bottom. *Quarterly Journal of the Geological Society of London* 41: 242-44.

Dawkins, W. B. (1885b) Report on the antiquities of the Isle of Man. *Manx Notebook* 2: 38-40.

Dawkins, W. B. (1886) Ornamentation of the early Irish MSS and of the Runic Crosses. *Manx Notebook 3: 120-124.*

Dawkins, W. B. (1887) Memorandum on the present aspect of the Channel Tunnel question, presented to the Houses of Parliament 6pp

BIBLIOGRAPHY

Dawkins, W. B. (1888a) On *Ailurus anglicus,* a new carnivore from the Red Crag (Norfolk and Suffolk) Quarterly Journal of the Geological Society of London 44: 228-231.

Dawkins, W. B. (1888b) On the clay slates and phyllites of the south of the Isle of Man, and a section of the Foxdale Mines. *Transactions of the Manchester Geological Society* 20: 53-57.

Dawkins, W. B. (1889) The place of the Welsh in the history of Britain. *Reprinted from The Manchester Examiner.* 48pp.

Dawkins, W. B. (1890) The discovery of coal measures near Dover. *Transactions of the Manchester Geological Society* 20: 502-17

Dawkins, W.B. (1892) The further discovery of coal at Dover and its bearing on coal question. *Transactions of the Manchester Geological Society* 21: 456-74.

Dawkins, W. B. (1893) The Place of the lake dwellings of Glastonbury in British archaeology. *Natural Science* 3: 344-346

Dawkins, W. B. (1894a) On the geology of the Isle of Man. Pt. 1. The Permian, Carboniferous, and Triassic rocks, and the new Saltfield of the north. *Transactions of the Manchester Geological Society* 22: 590-613.

Dawkins, W. B. (1894b) Notes on exhibits. *Journal of the Royal Anthropological Institute of Great Britain and Ireland* 23: 251-257.

Dawkins, W. B. (1894c) On the relation of the Palaeolithic to the Neolithic period. *Journal of the Royal Anthropological Institute of Great Britain and Ireland* 23: 242-251.

Dawkins, W. B. (1895) The geology of the Isle of Man, Pt. 2. *Transactions of the Manchester Geological Society* 23: 147-159.

Dawkins, W. B. (1896) On the geology of the Isle of Man. *Report on the Sixty-Sixth meeting of the British Association for the Advancement of Science, Liverpool 1896.* pp. 155-160.

Dawkins, W. B. (1898) On the history of the discovery of the south-eastern Coalfield. *Transactions of the Manchester Geological Society* 25: 155-60.

Dawkins, W. B. (1899) On the South-Eastern Coalfield. *Geological Magazine* 6: 501-5.

Dawkins, W. B. (1901a) On the cairn and sepulchral cave at Gop, New Prestatyn. *Archaeological Journal* 58: 322-341.

Dawkins, W. B. (1901b) The exploration of prehistoric sepulchral remains of the Bronze Age at Bleasdale by S. Jackson. *Transactions of the Lancashire and Chester Antiquarian Society* 18. 12pp

Dawkins, W. B. (1901c) The influence of Mediterranean peoples in Prehistoric Britain. *Nature* 65: 39-40

Dawkins, W. B. (1901d) The Channel Tunnel. *Journal of the Manchester geological Society* 7: 81-83

Dawkins, W. B. (1902a) Skulls from cave burials at Zakro in Eastern Crete. *Man* 2: 122-123

Dawkins, W. B. (1902b) Remains of animals found in the Dictian Cave in 1901. *Man* 2: 162-165

Dawkins, W. B. (1902c) On Bigbury Camp and the Pilgrims Way. *Archaeological Journal* 59: 105-129

Dawkins, W. B. (1902d) The Red Sandstone rocks of Peel, Isle of Man. *Quarterly Journal of the Geological Society of London* 58: 633-646,

Dawkins, W. B. (1902d) The Carboniferous, Permian, and Triassic Rocks under the Glacial Drift in the north of the Isle of Man. *Quarterly Journal of the Geological Society of London* 58: 647-661.

Dawkins, W. B. (1903a) The buried coalfields of southern England. *Statement in Evidence before the Royal Commission on Coal Supply, Final Report, Part X* 26-35.

Dawkins, W. B. (1903b) Review of C.H. Read. (A Guide to the Antiquities of the Stone Age in the Department of British and Medieval Antiquities.) *Man* 3: 58-60.

Dawkins, W. B. (1903c) On the discovery of an ossiferous cavern of Pliocene age at Doveholes. Buxton (Derbyshire). *Quarterly Journal of the Geological Society of London* 59: 105-132.

Dawkins, W. B. (1904) On the pre-Roman roads of northern and eastern Yorkshire. *Archaeological Journal* 61: 309-318.

Dawkins, W. B. (1906) The origin of the Welsh People. *Welsh Review* 1: 1-3

Dawkins, W. B. (1907) The discovery of the south-eastern Coalfield. *Journal of the Society Arts 55*: 450-8

Dawkins, W. B. (1910) The Huxley Lecture: The arrival of man in Britain in the Pleistocene Age. *Journal of the Royal Anthropological Institute of Great Britain and Ireland* 40: 233-263

Dawkins, W. B. (1912) Certain fixed points in the history of the Welsh. *Archaeologia Cambrensis* 12: 61-108

Dawkins, W. B. (1913a) The south eastern coal-field, the associated rocks and the buried plateau. *Transactions of the Manchester Geological Society* 33: 49-77.

Dawkins, W. B. (1913b) Coal and salt in the Isle of Man. *Mannin 1:* 28-32

Dawkins, W. B. (1914) The retreat of the Welsh from Wiltshire. *Archaeologia Cambrensis* 14: 28pp.

Dawkins, W. B. (1915). The Geological evidence in Britain as to the Antiquity of Man. *The Geological Magazine Decade VI Vol 2*: 470-472.

Dawkins, W. B. (1916). The antiquity of Man and the dawn of art in Europe. *The Edinburgh Review, or Critical Journal* 226: 80-98.

Dawkins, W. B. (1918) The Maltese cart ruts. *Man* 18: 87.

Dawkins W. B. (1921) The dwellers in Wiltshire in prehistoric times. *Archaeological Journal* 78: 309-312.

Dawkins, W. B. (1923). Obituary of Sir Henry Hoyle Howorth, K.C.I.E, D.C.L. F.R.S. *Man* 23: 138-139.

Dawkins, W. B. (1925a) Late Palaeolithic art in the Creswell Caves. *Nature*: 115: 336.

Dawkins, W. B (1925b) Late Palaeolithic art in the Creswell Caves: *Man* 25: 48.

Dawkins, W. B. and Sanford, W. A. (1866-72) *A Monograph of the British Pleistocene Mammals: Vol 1. British Pleistocene Felidae*. London: The Palaeontographical Society.

Dawkins, W. B., and Mello, J. M. (1879) Further discoveries in the Cresswell Caves. *Quarterly Journal of the Geological Society of London* 35: 724-735.

Dawkins, W. B. and Tiddeman, R. H. (1873) Report on the Victoria Cave, explored by the Settle Cave Exploration Committee. *Report of the Forty-Second Meeting of the British Association for the Advancement of Science, Brighton, 1872*: 178-180.

BIBLIOGRAPHY

Dawson, C. and Woodward, A.S. (1913) On the discovery of a Palaeolithic human skull and mandible in a flint-bearing gravel overlying the Wealden (Hastings Beds) at Piltdown, Fletching (Sussex). *Quarterly Journal of the Geological Society of London* 69: 117-151.

Dawson, C. and Woodward, A.S. (1914) Supplementary note on the discovery of a Palaeolithic human skull and mandible at Piltdown (Sussex). *Quarterly Journal of the Geological Society of London* 70: 82-99.

Dearne, M. and Lord, T. (1998) *The Romano-British Archaeology of Victoria Cave, Settle: Researches into the Site and its Artefacts*. Oxford: British Archaeological Reports British Series 273.

D'Errico, F., Williams, C.T., and Stringer, C.B. (1998). AMS dating and microscopic analysis of the Sherborne bone. *Journal of Archaeological Science* 25: 777-787.

Duckworth, W.L.H. (1913) Description of a human jaw of Palaeolithic antiquity from Kent's Cavern, Torquay. *Report of the Eighty-Second Meeting of the British Association for the Advancement of Science, Dundee, 1912: 602-603*

Eagar, M. and Preece, R. (1977) Collections and Collectors of Note 14: The Manchester Museum. *GCG: Newsletter of the Geological Curators Group* 11(2): 12-40.

Eskrigge, R.A. 1880. Notes on human skeletons and traces of human workmanship found in a cave at Llandudno. *Proceedings of the Liverpool Geological Society* 4: 153-155.

Evans, J. (1862) Account of some further discoveries of flint implements in the drift on the Continent and in England. *Archaeologia* 39: 57-84.

Evans, J. (1872) *Ancient Stone Implements, Weapons and Ornaments of Great Britain*. London: Longmans & Co.

Evans, J. (1878) On the present state of the question of the Antiquity of Man. *Journal of the Anthropological Institute of Great Britain and Ireland* 7: 149-151.

Evans, J. (1897) *Ancient Stone Implements, Weapons and Ornaments of Great Britain (2nd Edition)*. London: Longmans & Co.

Fisher, O. (1872) On a worked flint from the brick-earth of Crayford, Kent. *The Geological Magazine* 9: 268-9.

Flanagan, C.E. (1982) Isle Of Man Natural History And Antiquarian Society 1879-1979. *Proceedings of the IoM Natural History and Antiquarian Society* 9: 169-181.

Foster, J. (1888) *Alumni Oxonienses : the members of the University of Oxford, 1715-1886*. Oxford: Oxford University Press.

Gardner, W. (1929) Obituary: William Boyd Dawkins. *Archaeological Journal* 86: 232-234.

Gamble, L. & Kruszynski, R. 2009. John Evans, Joseph Prestwich and the stone that shattered the time barrier. *Antiquity* 83: 461-75.

Garrod, D. A. E. (1926) *The Upper Palaeolithic Age in Britain*. Oxford: Clarendon.

Geikie, J. (1872a) On changes of climate during the glacial epoch - fifth paper. *The Geological Magazine* 9: 164-170.

Geikie, J. (1872b) On changes of climate during the glacial epoch - sixth paper. *The Geological Magazine* 9: 215-222.

Geikie, J. (1873) On the theory of seasonal migrations during the Pleistocene period. *The Geological Magazine* 10: 49-54.

Geikie, J. (1874) *The Great Ice Age, and its Relation to the Antiquity of Man*. London:

W. Isbister & Co.

Geikie, J. (1877a) *The Great Ice Age, and its Relation to the Antiquity of Man*. 2nd Edition. London: Daldy, Ibister and Company.

Geikie, J. (1877b) The Antiquity of Man. *Nature* 16: 141-142.

Geikie, J. (1881a) *Prehistoric Europe: A Geological Sketch*. London: Edward Stanford.

Geikie, J. (1881b) Prehistoric Europe. *Nature* 23: 336

Geikie, J. (1881c) Prehistoric Europe. *Nature* 23: 433-434

Gordon, E. O. (1894) *The Life and Correspondence of William Buckland, D.D., F.R.S, Sometime Dean of Westminster, Twice President of the Geological Society and First President of the British Association*. London: John Murray.

Grayson, D.K. (1983) *The Establishment of Human Antiquity*. New York: Academic Press

Green, S. (1984) *Pontnewydd Cave; A Lower Palaeolithic Hominid Site in Wales*. Cardiff: National Museum of Wales.

Hall, N.J. (Ed). (1983) *The Letters of Anthony Trollope. Volume Two 1871-1882*. Stanford: Stanford University Press.

Hamlin, C. (1982) James Geikie, James Croll, and the eventful Ice Age. *Annals of Science*, 39: 565-583.

Hancock, E. G., A. Howell and H. S. Torrens. (1976) Geological Collections and Collectors of Note 11: Bolton Museum. *GCG: Newsletter of the Geological Curators Group* 7: 323-335.

Harrison, E. (1928) *Harrison of Ightham: A Book about Benjamin Harrison of Ightham, Kent Made up Principally of Extracts from His Notebooks and Correspondence*. London: Oxford University Press.

Haward, F. (1912) The chipping of flints by natural agencies. *Proceedings of the Prehistoric Society of East Anglia* 1: 347-360

Herndon, R. (1898) *Men of Progress: Biographical Sketches and Portraits of Leaders in Business and Professional Life in and of the State of New Hampshire*. Boston: New England Magazine.

Heath, T. (1879) *An Abstract Description and History of the Bone Caves of Creswell Crags*. Derby: Wilkins and Ellis.

Heath, T. (1880) *Creswell Crags v. Professor Boyd Dawkins*. Derby: Edward Clulow (jun)

Heath, T. (1882) Pleistocene deposits of Derbyshire and its immediate vicinity *Journal of the Derbyshire Archaeological and Natural History Society* 4: 161-178.

Hedges, R. E. M., Housley, R. A., Bronk, C. R. , and Van Klinken, G. J.. (1992) Radiocarbon dates from the Oxford AMS System. Archaeometry Datelist 14. *Archaeometry* 34: 141-142.

Hicks, H. (1885) On the Fynnon Bueno and Cae Gwyn Bone-Caves, North Wales. *Report of the Fifty-Fifth Meeting of the British Association for the Advancement of Science, Aberdeen, 1885*: 1021-1023.

Hicks, H. (1886) Report of the Committee, consisting of Professor T. Mck Hughes, Dr. H. Hicks, and Messrs. H. Woodwood, E.B. Luxmore, P.P. Pennant and Edwin Morgan. Drawn up by Dr. H. Hicks, secretary. *Fifty-Sixth Meeting of the British Association for the Advancement of Science, Birmingham, 1886*: 219-223

Hicks, H. (1887) The faunas of the Ffynnon Beuno Cave and the Norfolk Forest Bed.

BIBLIOGRAPHY

The Geological Magazine 24: 105-107

Hobson, W. (1875) *Report of the Free Library and Museum Committee for the Year ending 29th September 1875*. Derby: Borough of Derby.

Hobson, W. (1876) *Report of the Free Library and Museum Committee for the Year ending 29th September 1876*. Derby: Borough of Derby.

Hobson, W. (1879) *Report of the Free Library and Museum Committee for the Year ending 29th September 1879*. Derby: Borough of Derby.

Hughes, T. M., (1878) On the evidence afforded by the gravels and brickearth. *Journal of the Anthropological Institute of Great Britain and Ireland* 7: 162-165.

Hughes, T.M. (1886) On the Pleistocene deposits of the Vale of Clwyd. *Fifty-Sixth Meeting of the British Association for the Advancement of Science, Birmingham, 1886*: 632

Hughes, T. M. and Thomas, D.R. (1874) On the occurrence of felstone implements of the Le Moustier type in Pontnewydd Cave, near Cefn, St. Asaph. *The Journal of the Anthropological Institute of Great Britain and Ireland* 3: 387-392.

Hunt, D. (1994) *The Tunnel: The Story of the Channel Tunnel 1802-1994*. Imaging Publishing: London

Jacobi, R. M. (2007) A collection of Early Upper Palaeolithic artefacts from Beedings, near Pulborough, West Sussex and the context of similar finds from the British Isles. *Proceedings of the Prehistoric Society* 73: 229-325.

Jacobi, R. M. and T. F. G. Higham. (2008) The 'Red Lady' ages gracefully: new ultrafiltration AMS determinations from Paviland. *Journal of Human Evolution* 55: 898-907.

Jackson, J. W. (1966) Sir William Boyd Dawkins (1837-1929): A Biographical Sketch. *Cave Science* 5: 398-412.

Jenkinson, R. D. S. (1984) *Creswell Crags. Late Pleistocene Sites in the East Midlands*. Oxford: British Archaeological Reports British Series 122.

Jones, I. G. (ed.) (1981) *The Religious census of 1851: A Calendar of the returns relating to Wales, Vol 11, North Wales*. Cardiff: University of Wales Press.

Jukes-Brown, A.J. (1887) Interglacial land surfaces in England and Wales. *The Geological Magazine* 24: 147-150

J.W.G. (1891) Obituary: Peter Martin Duncan, M.B. (Lond), F.R.S., F.G.S., F.L.S., Etc. *The Geological Magazine* Decade III. Vol. 8: 332-226.

Keith, A. (1913) . Modern problems relating to the antiquity of Man. *Report of the Eighty-Second Meeting of the British Association for the Advancement of Science, Dundee, 1912:* 753-759

Keith, A. (1914) Wookey Hole. *Nature* 94: 395-397

Kelly, R. E. (1876) *The Post Office Directory of Derbyshire*. London: Kelly & Co.

Kelly, R. E. (1895) *Kelly's Directory of Nottinghamshire*. London: Kelly and Co.

Kelly, R. E. (1899) *Kelly's Directory of Derbyshire, Nottinghamshire, Leicestershire & Rutland*. London: Kelly & Co

Kennard, A.S. (1947) Fifty and one years of the Geologists' Association. *Proceedings of the Geologists' Association* 58: 271-283

Kenyon, J. (1983) *The History Men: The Historical Profession in England since the Renaissance*. London: Weidenfeld and Nicholon

King, W. (1864) On the Neanderthal Skull, or reasons for believing it to belong to the Clydian period and to a species different from that represented by man. *Report of the Thirty-Third Meeting of the British Association for the Advancement of Science, Newcastle-Upon-Tyne, August and September 1863*: 81-82.

Knowles, J. (1883) *The Channel Tunnel and Public Opinion.* London: Kegan Paul, Trench & Co.

Kirkaldy, J. F. (1975) William Topley and 'The Geology of the Weald'. *Proceedings of the Geologists' Association* 86: 373-388.

Lankester, E.R. (1869) On the occurrence of *Machairodus* in the Forest-Bed of Norfolk. *The Geological Magazine* 6: 440-441

Lartet, E. (1861) Nouvelles recherches sur la coexistence de l'homme et des grands mammifères fossils reputes characteristic de la dernière période géologique. *Annales des sciences naturelles, quatrième série, zoologie* 15: 177-253.

Lartet, E. and Christy, H. (1875). *Reliquiae Aquitanicae; Being Contributions to the Archaeology and Palaeontology of Perigord and Adjoining Provinces of Southern France.* London: William & Norgate.

Leech, B. (1907) *A History of the Manchester Ship Canal, from its inception to its completion, with personal reminiscences.* Sherratt and Hughes: Manchester and London.

Lewis, S. (1833) *A Topographical Dictionary of Wales.* London: Samuel Lewis & Co.

Lewis, S. (1849) *A Topographical Dictionary of Wales (2nd Edition)* London: Samuel Lewis & Co.

Lord, T., Lundberg, J. and Murphy, P. (2012) A guide to the work at Victoria Cave - from the 19th to 21st Centuries. In: H. J. O'Regan, T. Faulkner and I. R. Smith (eds), *Cave Archaeology and Karst Geomorphology of North West England: Field Guide*, pp 84-97. London: Quaternary Research Association.

Lubbock, J. (1865) *Pre-Historic Times as illustrated by Ancient Remains and the Manners and Customs of Modern Savages.* London: Williams & Norgate.

Lucas, P. 2007. Charles Darwin, 'Little Dawkins' and the platycnemic Yale men: introducing a bioarchaeological tale of the descent of man. *Archives of Natural History* 34: 318-345

Lyell, C. (1863) *The Geological Evidence of the Antiquity of Man.* London: John Murray

McFarlane, D. A. and Lundberg, J. (2005) The 19th Century Excavation of Kent's Cavern, England. *Journal of Cave and Karst Studies* 67: 39-47.

McNabb, J. (2012) *Dissent with Modification: Human Origins, Palaeolithic Archaeology and Evolutionary Anthropology in Britain 1859-1901.* Oxford: Archaeopress.

Mello, J. M. (1875) On some bone-caves in Creswell Crags. *Quarterly Journal of the Geological Society of London 31*: 679-691.

Mello, J. M. (1876) The bone-caves of Creswell Crags - 2nd paper. *Quarterly Journal of the Geological Society of London 32*: 240-244.

Mello, J. M. (1877) The bone-caves of Creswell Crags - 3rd Paper. *Quarterly Journal of the Geological Society of London 33*: 579-588.

Mello, J. M. (1880) Notes on the more recent discoveries in the Cresswell Caves. *Transactions of the Manchester Geological Society 15*: 290-304.

BIBLIOGRAPHY

Mello, J. M. (1881) A short history of the Creswell Caves. *Proceedings of the Yorkshire Geological and Polytechnic Society* 7: 252-265.

Mello, J. M., and Heath, T. (1876) On the Exploration of the Creswell Crags Caves. *Transactions of the Manchester Geological Society* 14: 103-111.

Merk, K. (1876) *Excavations at the Kesslerloch near Thayngen Switzerland: A Cave of the Reindeer Period. Translated into English by John Lee.* London: Longmans, Green and Co.

Merriman, N. (2012) The Manchester Museum. In: H. Williams (ed.) *Liverpool and South Lancashire. Supplement to the Archaeological Journal Volume 169*, pp38-43. London: The Royal Archaeological Institute.

Moir, J.R. (1911) The flint implements of the sub-crag man. *Proceedings of the Prehistoric Society of East Anglia* 1: 17-24

Moir, J. R. (1912) The occurrence of a human skeleton in a glacial deposit at Ipswich. *Proceedings of the Prehistoric Society of East Anglia* 1: 194-202.

Moir, J.R. (1916) Pre-boulder clay man. Nature 98: 109

Moir, J.R. (1927) *The Antiquity of Man in East Anglia.* London: Cambridge University Press

Montagu, M. F. A. and Oakley, K.P. (1949) The antiquity of Galley Hill Man. *American Journal of Physical Anthropology* 7: 363-384.

Morrell, J. (2005) *John Phillips and the Business of Victorian Science.* Farnham, Surrey: Ashgate

Murchison, C. (ed.) (1868) *Palaeontological Memoirs and Notes of the Late Hugh Falconer, A.M. M.D.* London: Robert Hardwick

Murphy, P. J. and Lord, T. (2003) Victoria Cave, Yorkshire, UK: new thoughts on an old site. *Cave and Karst Science* 30: 83-88.

Newton, E.T. (1882) The vertebrata of the Forest Bed Series of Norfolk and Suffolk. *Memoir of the Geological Survey of Great Britain.* London: Her Majesty's Stationary Office

Newton, E. T. (1895) On a human-skull and limb-bones found in the Palaeolithic terrace gravel at Galley Hill, Kent. *Quarterly Journal of the Geological Society of London* 51: 505-527.

O'Connor, A. (2005) The competition for the Woodwardian Chair in Geology, Cambridge, 1873. *British Journal for the History of Science* 38: 437-461.

O'Connor, A. (2007) *Finding Time for the Old Stone Age.* Oxford: Oxford University Press

O'Connor, A. and White, M.J. 2004. Palaeolithic archaeology in 1902: Foxhall Road in Context. In: M. J. White and S. J. Plunkett, *Miss Layard Excavates: A Lower Palaeolithic site at Foxhall Road Ipswich 1902-1905.* Liverpool: WASP. pp: 27-38

Oakley, K. P. and Hoskins, C. R. (1950) New evidence on the antiquity of Piltdown man. *Nature* 165: 372-382.

Oakley, K. P. (1963) Analytical Methods of Dating Bones. In: D. Brothwell and E. Higgs (ed), *Science in Archaeology: A Survey of Progress and Research.* pp24–34. London: Thames and Hudson.

Oakley, K.P. (1979). Note on the Antiquity of the Sherborne bone. *Antiquity* 53: 215-216.

Oakley, K. P. (1980) Relative dating of the fossil hominids of Europe. *Bulletin of the British Museum (Natural History) Geology* 34: 1-63.

Owen, D. (1983) *The Manchester Ship Canal*. Manchester: Manchester University Press.

Owen, J. (2012) *Darwin's Apprentice: An Archaeological Biography of John Lubbock*. Barnsley: Pen and Sword.

Owen, R. (1846) *A History of British Fossil Mammals, and Birds*. London: John Van Voorst.

Oxford University. (1888) *The Historical Register of the University of Oxford*. Oxford: Clarendon Press.

Pearman, H. (1973) *Caves and Tunnels in Kent* . London: Chelsea Speleological Society

Pengelly, H. (1897) *A Memoir of William Pengelly, of Torquay, F.R.S., Geologist, with a selection from His Correspondence*. London: John Murray.

Pengelly, W. (1868). The literature of Kent's Cavern, Part I. *Transactions of the Devonshire Association for the Advancement of Science, Literature and Art* 1: 469-522.

Pengelly, W. (1869). The Literature of Kent's Cavern, Part II, including the whole of the Rev. J MacEnery's Manuscrpt. *Transactions of the Devonshire Association for the Advancement of Science, Literature and Art* 3: 191-482.

Pengelly, W. (1870) Fifth Report of the Committee for Exploring Kent's Cavern, Devonshire. The Committee consisting of Sir Charles Lyell, Bart., F.R.S., Professor Phillips, F.R.S., Sir John Lubbock, Bart., F.R.S., John Evans, F.R.S., E. Vivian, George Busk, F.R.S., William Boyd Dawkins, F.R.S., and William Pengelly, F.R.S. *Report of the Thirty-Ninth Meeting of the British Association for the Advancement of Science, Exeter, August 1869*: 189-208.

Pengelly, W. (1971) Sixth Report of the Committee for exploring Kent's Cavern, Devonshire. The Committee consisting of Sir Charles Lyell, Bart., F.R.S., Professor Phillips, F.R.S., Sir John Lubbock, Bart., F.R.S., John Evans, F.R.S., E. Vivian, George Busk, F.R.S., William Boyd Dawkins, F.R.S., William Ayshford Sandford F.G.S. and William Pengelly, F.R.S. *Report of the Fortieth Meeting of the British Association for the Advancement of Science, Liverpool 1870*: 16-29.

Pengelly, W. (1873). The cavern discovered in 1858 at Windmill Hill, Brixham, South Deven. *Transactions of the Devonshire Association for the Advancement of Science, Literature and Art* 6: 775-856.

Pengelly, W. (1884) The literature of Kent's Cavern, Part V. *Transactions of the Devonshire Association for the Advancement of Science, Literature and Art* 14: 189-334.

Penck, A. and Bruckner, E. (1909) *Die Alpen im Eiszeitalter*. Leipzig:Tachnitz.

Pennington, R. (1875a) On the ossiferous deposits at Windy Knoll, near Castleton. *Proceedings of the Literary and Philosophical Society of Manchester* 14: 1-5.

Pennington, R. (1875b) On the bone-caves in the neighbourhood of Castleton, Derbyshire. *Quarterly Journal of the Geological Society of London* 31: 238-245.

Pennington, R. (1877) *Notes on the Barrows and Bone-Caves of Derbyshire, with an account of a descent into Elden Hole*. London:MacMillan and Co.

Pennington, R. and Dawkins, W. B. (1877) The Exploration of the ossiferous deposit at Windy Knoll, Castleton, Derbyshire. *Quarterly Journal of the Geological Society of London* 33: 724-729.

BIBLIOGRAPHY

Pettitt, P. B., Bahn, P., and Ripoll, S. (2007) *Palaeolithic Cave Art at Creswell Crags in European Context.* Oxford: Oxford University Press.

Phillips, J. (1853) *The River, Mountains and Sea Coast of Yorkshire. With Essays on the Climate, Scenery and Ancient Inhabitants of the County.* London: John Murray.

Plant, J. (1874) On Pleistocene mammalia, found near Castleton, Derbyshire. *Transactions of the Manchester Geological Society* 13: 117-130.

Plant, J. (1876a) Evidence to prove that a bone from the Windy Knoll Castleton, named by Professor W. Boyd Dawkins F.R.S, 'Sacrum of young Bison', is a sacral bone of the cave bear *Ursus spelaeus. Proceedings of the Literary and Philosophical Society of Manchester* 15: 108-113.

Plant, J. (1876b) Discoveries at Creswell Crags. *Transactions of the Manchester Geological Society:* 14: 84-87.

Plarr, V., Power, D., Spencer, W. G., and Gask, G. E. (1930) *Plarr's Lives of the Fellows of the Royal College of Surgeons.* Bristol: John Wright.

Powell, W. R. (1978) *A History of the County of Essex: Volume 7.* Oxford: Oxford Univeristy Press.

Prestwich, G. A. (1899) *Life and Letters of Sir Joseph Prestwich.* London: William Blackwood & Sons.

Prestwich, J. (1873) Report on the exploration of Brixham Cave, conducted by a committee of the Geological Society, and under the superintendence of Wm. Pengelly, Esq., F.R.S., aided by a local committee; with descriptions of the animal remains by George Busk, Esq., F.R.S, and of the flint implements by John Evans, Esq., F.R.S. By Joseph Prestwich, F.R.S, F.G.S. &c., Reporter. *Philosophical Transactions of the Royal Society* 163: *471-572.*

Prestwich, J. (1889) On the occurrence of Palaeolithic flint implements in the neighbourhood of Ightham, their distribution and probable age. *Quarterly Journal of the Geological Society of London* 45: 270-297.

Prestwich, J. (1891) On the age, formation and successive drift-stages of the Valley of the Darent; with remarks on the Palaeolithic implements of the district and on the origin of its Chalk escarpment. *Quarterly Journal of the Geological Society of London* 47: 126-163.

Prestwich, J. (1892) On the primitive characters of the flint implements of the Chalk plateau of Kent, with reference to the question of their glacial or pre-glacial age, with notes by Mesrs B Harrison and de Barri Crawshaw. *Journal of the Royal Anthropological Institute of Great Britain and Ireland* 21: 246-276

Ramsey, A. C. (1855) On the occurrence of angular, subangular, polished and striated fragments and boulders in the Permian breccia of Shropshire, Worcestershire, &c, and on the probable existence of glaciers and ice-bergs in the Permian period. *Quarterly Journal of the Geological Society of London* 11: 185-205.

Ransom, W. H. (1867) On the Occurrence of *Felis lynx* as a British fossil. *Report of the Thirty-Sixth Meeting of the British Association for the Advancement of Science, Nottingham 1866.* p66.

Read, H (1902) *A Guide to the Antiquities of the Stone Age in the Department of British and Mediaeval Antiquities.* London: William Clowes and Sons Limited.

Reumer, J. W. F., Rook, L., van der Borg, K., Post, K., Mol, D., and de Vos, J. (2003).

Late Pleistocene survival of the saber-toothed cat *Homotherium* in northwestern Europe. *Journal of Vertebrate Palaeontology* 23: 260-262.

Reynolds, S. (1902-1912) *A Monograph of the British Pleistocene Mammalia. Vol. II. British Pleistocene Hyaenidae, Ursidae, Canidae and Mustelidae.* London: The Palaeontological Society.

Reynolds, S. (1922) *A Monograph of the British Pleistocene Mammalia. Vol. III. Part I. Hippopotamus* London: The Palaeontological Society.

Reynolds, S. (1929) *A Monograph of the British Pleistocene Mammalia. Vol. III. Part III. The Giant Deer* London: The Palaeontological Society.

Reynolds, S. (1933) *A Monograph of the British Pleistocene Mammalia. Vol. III. Part IV. The Cervidae* London: The Palaeontological Society.

Reynolds, S. (1939) *A Monograph of the British Pleistocene Mammalia. Vol. III. Part VI. The Bovidae* London: The Palaeontological Society.

Roach, C.S. and Jackson, J. 1848. Caves in which Romano-British remains have been discovered near Settle, in Yorkshire. *Collectanea Antiqua* I: 69-72

Rowbotham, J.R. (1901) *The History of Rossall School, Second Enlarged Edition.* London: John Heywood.

Rudwick, M. (1969) The glacial theory. *History of Science* 8: 136-157.

Russell, M. (2012) *The Piltdown Man Hoax: Case Closed.* Stroud: The History Press

Sainty, J. C. (1975) *Office-Holders in Modern Britain: Volume 4: Admiralty Officials 1660-1870.* London:University of London, Institute of Historical Research.

Skertchly, S.B.J. (1877) *The Geology of the Fenland.* Memoir of the Geological Survey of Great Britain. London. Her Majesty's Stationary Office.

Smith, G.E. (1913) Appendix – Preliminary Report on the cranial cast. *Quarterly Journal of the Geological Society of London* 69: 145-151

Sollas, W. J. (1924) *Ancient Hunters and their Modern Representative*s 3rd edn. Revised. New York: Macmillan.

Sollas, W. J. (1925) Late Palaeolithic art in the Cresswell caves. *Nature* 115: 420-421.

Sommers, M. (2003) The Romantic Cave? The scientific and poetic quests for subterranenan spaces in Britain. *Earth Science History* 22: 172-208

Spencer, F. (1990a) *Piltdown: A Scientific Forgery.* Oxford: Oxford University Press.

Spencer, F. (1990b) *The Piltdown Papers.* Oxford: Oxford University Press.

Spooner, S. (n.d) *A History of Brampton Church.*

Spurrell, F. C. J. (1880a) On the discovery of the place where Palaeolithic Implements were made at Crayford. *Quarterly Journal of the Geological Society of London* 36: 544-548.

Spurrell, F. C. J. (1880b) On implements and chips from the floor of a Palaeolithic Workshop. *Archaeological Journal* 38: 294-299.

Stanley, E. (1833) Memoir on a cave at Cefn in Denbigshire visited by the Reverend Edward Stanley, F.G.S., F.L.S etc. *Edinburgh New Philosophical Journal* 14: 40-53.

Stanley, M. (1976) Geological collections and collectors of note 13: Derby Museums & Art Gallery. *GCG: Newsletter of the Geological Curators Group* 8: 392-409.

Stephen, L. (ed.) (1901) Letters of John Richard Green. London: MacMillan & Co.

Stephens, W.R.W (ed.) (1895) The Life and Letters of Edward A. Freeman, in Two Volumes. London: MacMillan and Co.

BIBLIOGRAPHY

Stringer, C. B., D'Errico, F., Williams, C. T, Housley, R and Hedges, R. (1995) The solution to the Sherborne problem. *Nature* 378: 452.

Thompson, J. (1886) *The Owens College: Its Foundation and Growth and its Connection with the Victoria University Manchester*. Manchester: Cornhill.

Tiddeman, R. H. (1872) Discovery of extinct mammals in the Victoria Caves, Settle. *Nature* 6: 127-8.

Tiddeman, R. H. (1873a) The older deposits in the Victoria Cave, Settle, Yorkshire. *Geological Magazine* 10: 11-16.

Tiddeman, R. H. (1873b) The relation of man to the ice sheet in the north of England. *Nature* 9: 14-15.

Tiddeman, R. H. (1875a) The work and problems of the Victoria Cave exploration. *Proceedings of the Geological and Polytechnic Society of the West Riding of Yorkshire* 6: 77-92.

Tiddeman, R. H. (1875b) Second Report of the Committee, consisting of Sir John Lubbock, Bart., Prof. Hughes, Prof. W. Boyd Dawkins, Messrs. L. C. Miall and R. H. Tiddeman, appointed for the purpose of assisting in the Exploration of the Settle Caves (Victoria Cave) *Report of the Forty-Fourth Meeting of the British Association for the Advancement of Science, Belfast 1874*: 133-138.

Tiddeman, R. H. (1876) Third Report of the Committee, consisting of Sir John Lubbock, Bart., Professor Prestwich, Professor T. M'K. Hughes, Professor W. Boyd Dawkins, Rev. H.W. Crosskey, Messrs. L. C. Miall and R. H. Tiddeman, appointed for the purpose of assisting in the Exploration of the Settle Caves (Victoria Cave) Drawn up by R. H. Tiddeman. Reporter. *Report of the Forty-Fifth Meeting of the British Association for the Advancement of Science, Bristol 1875*: 166-175.

Tiddeman, R. H. (1877) Fourth Report of the Committee, consisting of Sir John Lubbock, Bart., Professor Prestwich, Professor Busk, Professor T. M'K. Hughes, Professor W. Boyd Dawkins, Prof. Miall, Rev. H.W. Crosskey, and Mr R. H. Tiddeman, appointed for the purpose of assisting in the Exploration of the Settle Caves (Victoria Cave) Drawn up by R. H. Tiddeman. Reporter. *Report of the Forty-Sixth Meeting of the British Association for the Advancement of Science, Glasgow 1876*: 115-118.

Tiddeman, R. H. (1878a) Fifth Report of the Committee, consisting of Sir John Lubbock, Bart., Professor Prestwich, Professor Busk, Professor T. M'K. Hughes, Professor W. Boyd Dawkins, Prof. Miall, Rev. H.W. Crosskey, and Mr R. H. Tiddeman, appointed for the purpose of assisting in the Exploration of the Settle Caves (Victoria Cave) Drawn up by R. H. Tiddeman. Reporter. *Report of the Forty-Seventh Meeting of the British Association for the Advancement of Science, Plymouth 1877*: 115-120.

Tiddeman, R. H. (1878b) On the age of the hyaena-bed at the Victoria Cave, Settle, and its bearing on the antiquity of man. *Journal of the Anthropological Institute of Great Britain and Ireland* 7: 165-185.

Tiddeman, R. H. (1879) Sixth Report of the Committee, consisting of Sir John Lubbock, Bart., Professor Prestwich, Professor Busk, Professor T. M'K. Hughes, Professor W. Boyd Dawkins, Prof. Miall, Rev. H.W. Crosskey, Mr. H.C. Sorby and Mr R. H. Tiddeman, appointed for the purpose of assisting in the Exploration of the

Settle Caves (Victoria Cave) Drawn up by R. H. Tiddeman. Reporter. *Report of the Forty-Eighth Meeting of the British Association for the Advancement of Science, Dublin 1878*: 337-379.

Tiddeman, R. H. (1881a) Prehistoric Europe. *Nature* 23: 434.

Tiddeman, R. H. (1881b) Prehistoric Europe. *Nature* 23: 528.

Topley, W. (1875) *The Geology of the Weald*. Memoir of the Geological Survey of Great Britain. London: Her Majesty's Stationary Office.

Tweedale, G. (1991) Geology and industrial consultancy: Sir William Boyd Dawkins (1837-1929) and the Kent Coalfield. *The British Journal of the History of Science* 24: 435-451

Underwood, W., Sturge, W.A, Clarke, W.G., Layard, N.F and Corner, W. (1911) Report of the Special Committee on Moir's 'The Flint Implements of Sub-Crag Man', pp. 17-24. *Proceedings of the Prehistoric Society of East Anglia* 1: 24-41.

Varley, P. (1992) *From Charing Cross to Baghdad: A history of the Whitaker tunnel boring machine and the Channel Tunnel 1880-1930.* Channel Tunnel Group Ltd: Dover.

Van Riper, A. B. 1993. *Men Among the Mammoths. Victorian Science and the Discovery of Human Prehistory.* Chicago: Chicago University Press.

Walford, E. (1884) *Greater London: A Narrative of its History, Its Peoples, and Its Places*. London: Cassell & Co.

Walker, E. A., and Hulse, T. G. (2012) The History of the Caves. S. Aldhouse Green, R. Peterson, and E. A. Walker. (eds) *Neanderthals in Wales: Pontnewydd and the Elwy Valley,* pp7-22. *Caves*. Oxford: Oxbow.

Warren, C. N. and Rose, S. (1994) *William Pengelly's Techniques of Archaeological Excavation*. Torquay Natural History Society: Torquay.

Warren, S. H. (1914) The experimental investigation of flint fracture and its application to problems of human implements. *Journal of the Royal Anthropological Institute of Great Britain and Ireland* 44: 412-450.

Watkin, E. W. (1882) *Channel Tunnel. Report of a Meeting of the members of the Submarine Continental Railway Company Limited held at the Charing Cross Hotel on Friday the 20th January 1882*. London: C.F. Rowarth.

Weiner, J. S, Oakley, K.P & Le Gros Clark, W. 1953. The Solution of the Piltdown Problem. *Bulletin of the British Museum (Natural History) Geology Series* 2: 141-146.

Whitaker, W. (1889) *The Geology of London and of part of the Thames Valley.* Memoirs of the Geological Survey of Great Britain. London: Her Majesty's Stationary Office

White, M. J. (2004) Moir, (James) Reid (1879–1944). *Oxford Dictionary of National Biography*. Oxford: Oxford University Press.

Wilson, D. 1851. *Archaeology and the Prehistoric Annals of Scotland*. Edinburgh: Sutherland and Knox.

Wilson, R. B. (1977) *A History of the Geological Survey in Scotland*. London:NERC.

Wood, K. (1987) *Rich Seams: Manchester Geological and Mining Society 1838-1988*. Warrington: Institution of Mining Engineers.

Wood, S. V. (1867) On the structure of the postglacial deposits of the south-east of England. *Quarterly Journal of Science* 23: 394-417.

Wood, S. V. (1868a) Reply to Mr. W. Boyd Dawkins, on the Thames Valley deposits,

BIBLIOGRAPHY

&c.; and to Mr. A. H. Green, on the Ouse Valley at Buckingham. *The Geological Magazine* 5: 42-46.

Wood, S. V. (1868b) Synchronous age of the Grays and Erith Brickearths. *The Geological Magazine* 5: 534-534.

Woodward, B. B., and rev. Foote, Y. (2004) Busk, George (1807–1886). *Oxford Dictionary of National Biography*. Oxford: Oxford University Press.

Woodward, A. S. (1914) On an apparently Palaeolithic engraving on a bone from Sherborne (Dorset). *Quarterly Journal of the Geological Society of London* 70: 100-103.

Woodward, H. B. (1897) Eminent Living Geologists: The Rev. P.B. Brodie, M.A. F.G.S. *The Geological Magazine.* Decade IV, Vol IV 480-485.

Wright, F. (1898) Agassiz and the Ice Age. *The American Naturalist* 32: 165-171.

Index

INDEX